D1563128

PATRICIANS, PROFESSORS,
AND PUBLIC SCHOOLS

BRILL'S STUDIES IN INTELLECTUAL HISTORY

VOLUME 53

PATRICIANS, PROFESSORS, AND PUBLIC SCHOOLS

The Origins of Modern Educational Thought in America

BY

ALLAN S. HORLICK

E.J. BRILL

LEIDEN · NEW YORK · KÖLN

1994

The paper in this book meets the guidelines for permanence and durability of the Committee on Production Guidelines for Book Longevity of the Council on Library Resources.

Library of Congress Cataloging-in-Publication Data

Horlick, Allan Stanley, 1941-
    Patricians, professors, and public schools : the origins of modern educational thought in America / by Allan S. Horlick.
      p.   cm. — (Brill's studies in intellectual history, ISSN 0920-8607 ; v. 53)
    Includes bibliographical references (p.   ) and index.
    ISBN 9004100547 (alk. paper)
    1. Education—United States—Philosophy—History. 2. Educational sociology—United States—History. 3. Public schools—United States—History. 4. Educational change—United States—History.
5. Social institutions—United States—History.   I. Title.
II. Series.
LA205.H57   1994
370'.1'0973034—dc20
                                      94-14314
                                          CIP

Die Deutsche Bibliothek - CIP-Einheitsaufnahme

Horlick, Allan S.:
Patricians, professors and public schools : the origins of
modern educational thought in America / by Allan S. Horlick.
– Leiden ; New York ; Köln : Brill, 1994
  (Brill's studies in intellectual history ; Vol. 53)
  ISBN 90–04–10054–7
NE: GT

ISSN 0920-8607
ISBN 90 04 10054 7

PRINTED IN THE NETHERLANDS

To Margaret and Peter

CONTENTS

ACKNOWLEDGMENTS

Over the years that I have been working on this book, I have received help and encouragement from many friends and colleagues. It is a pleasure to acknowledge their support here. Steve Diamond, Tessa De Carlo, B. Edward McClellan, and Paul H. Mattingly each did me a great service by thoughtfully reading an early version of the manuscript. In addition to making specific recommendations to improve it, they convinced me that my argument made sense, and was worth pursuing. Paul's help was especially valuable. Drawing on his great knowledge of the subject, he offered comments that combined attention to points small and large, to individual phrases and overall design. He made me think twice about almost every sentence in the book, and the manuscript is immeasurably stronger as a result. Although I doubt he will agree with everything I say here, I hope he will recognize how important his criticism has been.

William R. Taylor read the manuscript twice at different stages of its development. As he did on a past project of mine, he read with care and attention, and gave me characteristically incisive suggestions for improvement. His belief in the contribution the study makes to the debate about school reform returned to me often as I worked to complete it.

At the most recent stage in the life of the manuscript, I received generous advice from Robert McClintock. He read a late draft with uncommon closeness, and raised questions about style and substance that were both profound and provoking. He was critical and supportive at the same time; as a result, his suggestions were hard to ignore. That I sometimes managed to do so reflects on my stubbornness, not on his judgment.

Some of the most important, and certainly the most ongoing, assistance I received came from my colleagues in the history department at Trinity School. Members of the department, through their inescapable proximity to the author, could hardly avoid hearing about the subject I was working on. They were always interested in discussing my ideas, and in offering suggestions about sources and other references, even when—as was usually the case—they had more pressing demands on their time. The patient hearing that I received from Bill Major and Max McClintock were notable in this regard. I am especially grateful to

Steve Cohen for the many ways that he has encouraged me over the past several years. Deeply involved in research and writing about the period covered in this study himself, he has been a source of ideas, advice, and stimulation that have had a continuing influence on my thinking about the issues discussed here.

Outside of the history department, I wish to thank Suzie Reardon for the many kindnesses she has extended to me over the years. She seemed never too busy to take a few minutes to help me resolve the problems that invariably arose whenever my fingers made contact with the computer keyboard. I am also happy to have the opportunity to thank a former Trinity headmaster, Robin Lester. In a way rare among school leaders, he understood how scholarship is related to good teaching, and how it enhances the intellectual life of the institutions where it is nurtured. I am deeply grateful for the support he gave me.

I am also grateful to Ida and Heiko Oberman for leading me to my publisher. Professor Oberman's response to the manuscript was particularly gratifying.

Finally, a few non-historians bear some responsibility for the completion of this project. Over the course of a long friendship, Rudy and Lulu Leibel have been good listeners, and have helped sustain my sense of the importance of this work. My wife, Mary, has also supported this project in ways too numerous to mention, or even remember. Her confidence in what I have had to say has meant a great deal to me as I worked to turn my initial ideas into a finished book.

INTRODUCTION

I

Public education across the nation, we are being told with increasing insistence, is in serious trouble. From presidential commissions and national magazines to regional educational journals and local newspapers, the story of empty coffers, dropping standards, teacher "burn-out," failing and apathetic students, and deteriorating facilities is heard again and again. In one of the most publicized reports of the early eighties, we read that mediocrity is now the norm in our schools, and that it is a condition we have brought on ourselves. We have wasted past gains in achievement, said the National Commission on Excellence in Education in 1983, "we have dismantled essential support systems which helped make those gains possible." In general, the Commission reported, we are a nation that has been pursuing a path of one-sided "educational disarmament"; we "have lost sight of the basic purposes of schooling."[1]

The recognition is long overdue. During the decade and a half preceding the report, for example, it was more common to read that our schools were not very important at all. To a considerable number of writers, the history of the schools was misread, at least if it had been claimed that training in them made a direct contribution to the intellectual progress of our people or, through the application of that progress to scientific and technological innovation, to the economic development of our nation. The schools, some of these critics said, either never made that kind of contribution or, if they once did, the unsettled economic conditions of the decade made the contribution an unaffordable luxury. To some this was regrettable but unavoidable. To others, who saw the schools as the agents for reproducing the inequalities of status and position that characterized the wider society, not much had been lost.[2]

---

[1] National Commission on Excellence in Education, *A Nation at Risk: The Imperative for Educational Reform* (Washington, D.C., 1983), p.5.

[2] For the most popular piece of anti-establishment educational criticism of the period, see Ivan Illich, *Deschooling Society* (New York, paperback edition, 1970). Other important statements of the point of view are Samuel Bowles and Herbert Gintis, *Schooling in Capitalist America* (New York, 1976); and the less well-known but significant contribution to the Phi Delta Kappa Educational Foundation "Fastback" series, "Alternatives to Growth: Education for a Stable Society" (Bloomington, Indiana, 1976), by Robert M. Bjork and Stewart E. Fraser.

This emphasis has changed today. Especially in light of current discussions about restoring American competitiveness, the consequences of the views of the late sixties, seventies, and early eighties have become too glaring to ignore.[3] But the "deschooling" rhetoric of those years did not come to prominence in debate about the schools only recently; it has been integral to discussions that have shaped the schools for over one hundred years. It is, in fact, no small measure of the continuing strength of this rhetoric that its echo still can be heard in recommendations being put forward today.[4]

In the 1880s, a reform movement appeared that first accustomed the nation to the "dismantling" and "disarmament" of its educational apparatus decried by many observers in recent years. This reform movement was based on assumptions that inevitable economic slowdown meant that the amount spent on education had to decline, and that the kind of programs funded had to shift.

It may be true, as one historian argues, that turn of the century reform can only be defined by clusters of ideas and not a single ideology.[5] But one of the clusters—in addition to those he notes—is surely an opposition to a program of economic growth based on diversified and expanding industrial development.[6] And this opposition first came from an identifiable group. Men and women best called patricians—because of the sense they had of themselves as an elite capable of determining the fundamental commitments of their society—believed that accelerating, decentralized economic growth could only diminish their power and influence in American life. Soon applied to education, the premise became central to a critique of the schools that, with little reference to its origins, spread to a large portion of the nation.[7] Developing arguments that ran counter to the buoyant optimism of

[3] See, for example, Richard M. Cyert and David C. Mowery, "Technology, Employment, and U. S. Competitiveness," *Scientific American* 260, number 5 (May, 1989): 54-62; the series of articles in the *New York Times*, September 25-27, 1989; and the letter from physicist C. J. Martoff in the *Times*, November 25, 1990, sec. 4, p. 10.

[4] The problems of the calls to arms that Andrew Hacker noted in "The Schools Flunk Out," *New York Review of Books* XXXI, no. 6 (April 12, 1984): 35-40, apply with equal force to much current writing on the plight of the schools. See also, from a different perspective, John E. Chubb and Terry M. Moe, *Politics, Markets, and America's Schools* (Washington, D.C., 1990), chapter 1, "The Root of the Problem."

[5] Daniel T. Rodgers, "In Search of Progressivism," in Stanley I. Kutler and Stanley N. Katz, eds., *The Promise of American History: Progress and Prospects* (Baltimore, Md., 1982), pp. 113-132.

[6] Clearly, not all industrial development is meant to have either characteristic. For example, as Robert F. Dalzell, Jr. has shown, the early nineteenth century Boston Associates invested heavily in the then new textile industry. But they did so to hold back expanding economic growth—connected in their minds to the destabilizing forces they feared might lead to a loss of their security and power—not to advance it. (Robert F. Dalzell, Jr., *Enterprising Elite: The Boston Associates and the World They Made* [Cambridge, Mass., 1989], pp. 66-67, 71, 97, 110-112, 187-190.)

[7] The importance of stressing the regional sources of the cultural (and related educational) critique offered by late nineteenth century patricians is suggested by Peter Dobkin Hall, *The*

the founders of public schooling in the 1830s and 1840s, this movement knew a large measure of success by the early years of the twentieth century.

To a large extent, the change occurred with remarkable swiftness; its early outline can be discerned within a single decade, the 1880s. As late as the depression of the mid-1870s, most Americans signaled their approval of the schools by continuing to fund them at high levels, and by ensuring that the number of teachers kept pace with increases in the number of students.[8] Despite economic reversal and hardship, Americans believed that their setbacks were temporary. Rather than accommodate themselves to contraction, they prepared for the upturn they took to be close at hand. Americans would maintain their investment in education, understanding that the institutions responsible for improving the intelligence of the next generation had to be well-maintained if they were to continue functioning smoothly.[9]

By the end of the 1880s, much of this faith in the value of education had been cast aside, and the schools were set on a new course that has compromised their effectiveness ever since. Earlier the schools' program stressed a commonality of skills and values for students and a commitment to subject mastery by teachers. By the end of the 1880s, it was well on the path to stressing local variety, ability grouping, and a vague "child-centered" instructional method, devised to control teachers as much as to educate students. Americans who had once taken the coupling of education, intellectual development, and economic expansion to be axiomatic, now responded to a new logic. They came to believe that education had to be made appropriate to life chances that, because of the impossibility of sustaining past rates of industrial growth, would have to be restricted within boundaries more narrow than anyone had previously imagined.

Exploring the reasoning that led to this change forms the subject of this book. Neither consensus historians of the post-World War II period nor revisionist historians of the post-Vietnam period have given us the accounts we need to understand this momentous transition. Consensus historians, generally interested in viewing the school as part of the success story of American democracy, have not noticed any fundamental problem in think-

Organization of American Culture, 1700-1900: Private Institutions, Elites, and the Origins of American Nationality (New York, 1982); T. J. Jackson Lears, *No Place of Grace: Antimodernism and the Transformation of American Culture, 1880-1920* (New York, 1981), biographical appendix, pp. 313-323; Thomas L. Haskell, *The Emergence of American Social Science: The American Social Science Association and the Nineteenth Century Crisis of Authority* (Urbana, Ill., 1977); and, though it is not his intention, David P. Thelen, "Social Tensions and the Origins of Progressivism," *Journal of American History* 56 (September, 1969): 323-341. See also G. Edward White, *The Eastern Establishment and the Western Experience: The West of Frederic Remington, Theodore Roosevelt, and Owen Wister* (New Haven, Conn., 1968), pp. 19-20.

[8] David B. Tyack, "Education and Social Unrest, 1873-1878," *Harvard Educational Review* 31 (1961): 198.

[9] See Daniel Calhoun, *The Intelligence of a People* (Princeton University Press, 1973).

ing about the schools.[10] Revisionists have noticed a problem, but it has not always been the one that needs examination. To them, American educational history is the obverse of the story told by consensus historians. If consensus historians see our educational history as a reflection of the expansion of democracy (and of the pluralism that is its characteristic form of expression),[11] then revisionists see it as a reflection of democracy's eclipse. If consensus historians see education as a tool of integration and promise, revisionists see it as a tool of exploitation and oppression.

To revisionists, the education required by the young to gain control of their future and the education required by the beneficiaries of the status quo are always in opposition. As one revisionist writer has put it, American educational history represents a conflict between "the self-perceived needs of students" and the "preservation of social peace and prosperity." A rising middle class or an established upper class, it is argued, used the schools to impose curricular and social goals on a population (often poor, newly arrived, and potentially refractory) that did not share them.[12]

This way of putting things seems to me to mislocate the conflict of the period. The important fight in the educational history of the late nineteenth and early twentieth centuries was not between ruling or middle class manipulators and lower class manipulated, but (cutting across class lines) between those who have supported the connection between public schooling and economic growth and those who have tried to sever it. It was the latter group far more consistently than the school promoters who are criticized in revisionist accounts, that pursued an antidemocratic program. This is especially true in the decades surrounding the turn of the century on which I focus here.

Writing that adopts the manipulator-manipulated division makes the mistake of employing as a framework of analysis the reform polemic that should be the object of investigation. Like the charges of reformers, this

---

[10] The inadequacies of these accounts were noted three decades ago by Bernard Bailyn, *Education in the Forming of American Society: Needs and Opportunities for Study* (Chapel Hill, 1960). See also my "Comprehensiveness Versus Comprehension in American Educational History," a review of Lawrence A. Cremin, *American Education: The National Experience* (New York, 1980), in *The Review of Education* 7 (Summer, 1981): 305-317.

[11] On the connection between democratic theory and pluralism in the decades after the Second World War, see Michael Paul Rogin, *The Intellectuals and McCarthy: The Radical Specter* (Cambridge, Mass., 1967), chapter one.

[12] David Nasaw, *Schooled to Order: A Social History of Public Schooling in the United States* (New York, 1979), p. 242. Other influential variations of this point of view are Michael B. Katz, *The Irony of Early School Reform: Educational Innovation in Mid-Nineteenth Century Massachusetts* (Cambridge, Mass., 1968); Joel H. Spring, *Education and the Rise of the Corporate State* (Boston, 1972); Colin Greer, *The Great School Legend: A Revisionist Interpretation of American Public Education* (New York, 1972); and Clarence J. Karier, Paul C. Violas, and Joel H. Spring, *Roots of Crisis: American Education in the Twentieth Century* (Chicago, 1973).

writing assumes that the "self-perceived needs" of the child were ranged against "peace and prosperity," in a natural opposition of good and evil. Unfortunately, this is only another kind of the presentism that is found in consensus writing. It also reads a real or imagined present back into the past, and gives us as little sense as consensus writing of the differences between the two.

Many expressions of concern for "the needs of children" represented neither an educational advance nor opposition to the "peace and prosperity" favored by threatened elements of the status quo. Calls to reorient the curriculum to children's needs have as often served a constraining purpose as a liberating one. They have justified calls for cutting educational budgets, attacking attempts by teachers to unionize, and denying the highest aspirations of large numbers of the population as much as they have justified improved instruction or learning.[13] The work of late nineteenth century reformers, in other words, was surely innovative, but it did little to benefit a growing society that required increasing infusions of technologically sophisticated labor and the talents of a professional class. This is as true of John Dewey as of the other figures discussed below with whom he might be considered to differ. As I will try to show, Dewey's thinking is rightly seen not as an alternative to the elitism of E. L. Godkin, Charles Francis Adams, Jr., Felix Adler, and Nicholas Murray Butler, but as its necessary culmination.

Dewey may have placed his hopes for democracy at the center of his work, as Robert B. Westbrook notes in an important new book.[14] Unfortunately, at decisive moments in his life he expressed these hopes with an abstraction and detachment from his society's most vibrant political currents that only provided ammunition for the forces of elite control that he (guardedly) claimed to oppose. This was especially true during the decades between the late 1880s and the outbreak of World War I, when, as Westbrook notes, Dewey's increasing caution led him to confine his reflections on these issues to his educational work.[15] Far from being immune to the historical environment he inhabited (either by defining a place to the left of mainstream liberalism, as Westbrook asserts, or above the battle of contending forces, as others have argued),[16] he, like his contemporaries,

---

[13] In the fiscal context of the early 1990s, this possibility was raised by President Bush's announcement of the New American Schools Development Corporation, a foundation dedicated to create an "educational revolution." Using the Rand Corporation's Institute on Education and Training as its research arm and with a board dominated by leading business executives, it hoped to initiate, according to the president, "nothing less than a new generation of schools." (*The New York Times*, July 9, 1991, p. A13.)

[14] Robert B. Westbrook, *John Dewey and American Democracy* (Ithaca, N. Y., 1991), p. xi.

[15] See Westbrook, pp. 92, 119-120, 151.

[16] Westbrook, pp. xiv-xv; and Herbert M. Kliebard, *The Struggle for the American Curriculum, 1893-1958* (London, 1986), pp. xi-xii. On considering where to place Dewey in

oriented to it by accepting the political requirements for making one's way professionally.[17] Starting with the same pessimistic assumptions about the possibilities for continued economic growth, and determined to build a career in an institutional setting that placed clear limits on reform thinking and activity, he could do little but come to conclusions that posed little challenge to conventional views. Although he was able to make these conclusions more palatable to a newly assertive middle and working class for whom education had growing importance, his guidance would ultimately be as barren of long-term benefits[18] as that of those against whom he is often pitted in historical accounts.

"the interplay among the predominant interest groups" that he holds to account for the "several reform movements in education during the twentieth century," Kliebard concludes: "I decided in the end that [Dewey] did not belong in any of them and that he should appear in the book as somehow hovering over the struggle rather than as belonging to any particular side."

[17] Considering his prominence, the demands being made on the public schools at the turn of the century, and the historic link in American life between education and democracy, Dewey's preoccupation with the latter concerns was unlikely to have had other than a guiding influence on the schools. In education, at any rate, this accounts for much of Dewey's importance. I therefore could not agree more with Westbrook that Dewey's thought deserves careful study; I differ only about why. Where Westbrook argues that Dewey's democratic thinking was more radical than usually thought (and hence can serve to give direction to current debates about the meaning of democracy), I argue that it was less (and that we need to look elsewhere for help in formulating a meaningful democratic program).

It seems to me that Westbrook's evidence and judgments about the specific episodes of Dewey's career often support my conclusion better than his own, and that at crucial points in his account he suspends criticism—relying instead on summary and reiteration of his thesis—rather than confront the questions his own investigation raises. For examples (taken from the period central to my own account) of Westbrook's reluctance to explore the relationship between his evidence and his general assessment of Dewey's significance, see pp. 48-49, on Dewey's "vagueness" about "the conditions of liberty" and how they were "to be provided" amidst the stormy political events of the early 1890s; pp. 49-50, on the influence that H. C. Adams's "forced" recantation of his defense of the Knights of Labor had on Dewey (whom Westbrook more than once—without elaboration—calls a friend of the labor movement); pp. 57-58, on Dewey's attraction to the "Thought News" project; pp. 90-92, on what Dewey learned from the Pullman strike and the dismissal of Edward Bemis from the University of Chicago in 1895; pp. 101-109 and 167-179, on the interpretation of *The Child and the Curriculum*, *The School and Society*, *Schools of Tomorrow*, and *Democracy and Education*; pp. 179-182, on the difference between Dewey's and the "administrative progressives'" concepton of the Gary system, especially in light of Dewey's remarks on it and a related educational "experiment," in *Schools of Tomorrow*, chapters 7, 8, and 10; pp. 202-204, on Westbrook's explanation of the problems of Dewey's thought that Randolph Bourne raised in the wake of American entry into World War I; pp. 211-212, on Dewey's explanation of domestic repression during the war and his role in Bourne's dismissal from the *Dial*; and pp. 219-220, on Dewey's willingness to employ the manipulation his radicalism would have had him eschew in the "Polish question." Westbrook's assessment should also be compared with Dorothy Ross's account of "Dewey's pragmatism" in *The Origins of American Social Science* (Cambridge, Eng., 1991), pp. 162-171.

[18] The legacy of the educational arguments that I attribute to Dewey has been explored by a number of recent economists. See, for example, Stephen S. Cohen and John Zysman, *Manufacturing Matters: The Myth of the Post-Industrial Economy* (New York, 1987); Robert Reich, *The Next American Frontier* (New York, 1983); and Lester Thurow, *The Zero-Sum Solution: Building a World-Class American Economy* (New York, 1985).

Historians who stress the use of the schools to serve the manpower needs of an industrial economy may therefore have missed what is of most long-range significance about the reform efforts that are central to this account. If reformers were interested in adjusting workers to industrialism or corporate capitalism, it was not primarily to provide employers with arguments for wringing more profit out of labor. Instead, reformers first of all looked to education to shore up the position that they occupied in American life. The notion of limits that they disseminated became the starting point not only for programs of adjustment but for programs of liberal studies as well. Because this notion of limits—expressed as a refurbished Malthusianism that connected assumptions of reduced resources and educational policy— has not been adequately discussed, the hold of late nineteenth century reform analysis has been difficult to confront.

For reformers who talked about a slowing economy were offering ideology, not observation. They were not describing an economic landscape clear to everyone who stood before it; they were arguing a policy about which there was heated disagreement. Industrial change has never been inevitable, and certainly not in the United States of the late nineteenth century, as writers from a number of disciplines have recently emphasized.[19] Political force has always decided the issue, and in this period of American history political force (though generally not expressed in electoral terms) was on the side of a new way of looking at education. Except for brief moments, when a burst of short-lived popular energy (as in the early twentieth century fight to stop the Gary Plan in New York City) or a sense of national crisis (as after the launching of Sputnik) led to a reassertion of older traditions,[20] the new ideas of reformers would more and more serve as the starting point for thinking about the schools.

At their most basic level, the underlying political issues of this period still involved the struggle to determine the way and pace that changes in

---

[19] Martin J. Sklar, *The Corporate Reconstruction of American Capitalism, 1890-1916: The Market, the Law, and Politics* (New York, 1988), "Introduction: Corporate Capitalism and Corporate Liberalism"; James Livingston, "The Social Analysis of Economic History and Theory: Conjectures on Late Nineteenth-Century American Development," *American Historical Review* 92, no. 1 (February, 1987): 69-95; Richard Edwards, *Contested Terrain: The Transformation of the Workplace in the Twentieth Century* (New York, 1979); and Robert Kuttner, *The Economic Illusion: False Choices Between Prosperity and Social Justice* (Boston, 1984).

[20] On the Gary Plan, see Ronald D. Cohen and Raymond A. Mohl, *The Paradox of Progressive Education: The Gary Plan and Urban Schooling* (Port Washington, N.Y., 1979); and Diane Ravitch, *The Great School Wars: New York City, 1805-1973* (New York, 1974), pp. 189-233. On the response to Sputnik, see Joel Spring, *The Sorting Machine: National Education Policy Since 1945* (New York, 1976), chapter 3, "The Development of a National Curriculum"; and Diane Ravitch, *The Troubled Crusade: American Education, 1945-1980* (New York, 1983), pp. 228-233.

standards of living would occur.[21] So central have our schools been to these changes—through their role in guaranteeing the flow of innovation on which they are ultimately based—that their control has always been the object of intense political combat. James B. Gilbert, in his excellent *Work Without Salvation* (1977), is right when he says that education "was the principal arena in which the issues of modern industrial capitalism were joined," and wrong only in believing that this arena was divorced from politics instead of being its direct reflection. Education "was the terrain upon which paraded competing theories of personality, industrial alienation, and labor,"[22] but these theories were not, as Gilbert implies, abstract cultural questions for the intellectuals who formulated and debated them. Rather, conclusions about personality, causes of alienation, and the will to work (as they applied to curricular and psychological questions in education) quickly became part of a more wide-ranging political battle to determine the nation's path in the years ahead.

                                        II

That this political battle of national reorientation was seen by patrician reformers through a lens colored by feelings about the importance of esteem and social position has long been noted by historians.[23] Social position and the identity based on it often supplied both the motivation to enter reform work and the outlook to turn reform work in a specific policy direction. Questions of "status" were not settled by joining clubs and neighborhood associations or by setting up vacation enclaves and educational preserves. Social position was established not by a withdrawal from a threatening population but by the attempt to engage and master it.[24] In a traditional

---

[21] Samuel Bowles and Herbert Gintis, in their recent work of political theory, seem to agree that while the goals of political struggle have changed today, in earlier periods—though they refer only to "the last great crisis"—they were framed in terms of a more long-standing fight to control material wealth. (*Democracy and Capitalism: Property, Community, and the Contradictions of Modern Social Thought* [New York, 1987], p. 7.)

[22] James B. Gilbert, *Work Without Salvation: America's Intellectuals and Industrial Alienation, 1880-1910* (Baltimore, 1977), p. 110.

[23] For example, Richard Hofstadter, *The Age of Reform: From Bryan to F. D. R.* (New York, paperback ed., 1955), part IV; and Christopher Lasch, *The New Radicalism in America, 1889-1963: The Intellectual as Social Type* (New York, 1965).

[24] A well-documented account affirming this view for New York City is David C. Hammack, *Power and Society: Greater New York at the Turn of the Century* (New York, 1982). Other important accounts emphasizing elite activism include Hall, *The Organization of American Culture*; Geoffrey Blodgett, *The Gentle Reformers: Massachusetts Democrats in the Cleveland Era* (Cambridge, Mass., 1966); and John G. Sproat, *"The Best Men": Liberal Reformers in the Gilded Age* (New York, 1968). See also Richard Hofstadter's account in the *Age of Reform*. Hofstadter tries to explain the entry of the patricians into a wide range of political ventures by reference to some of the preoccupations noted here, and he correctly describes the well-known expressions they led to (associating them, as I have also, with the

society where the pace of change was still relatively slow, where the need for new ideas was not pressing and their quality hard to evaluate, much of this mastery came through the advice and opinion that position allowed local patricians to dispense with assurance and confidence. They had the ability and resources to command attention and the stature to determine who else should command it.

At least they did as long as a population unsure of its abilities and the productive possibilities of its society believed that it needed the guidance and direction of its "betters." But by the last decades of the nineteenth century this was no longer the case. A large part of the American people

---

views of E. L. Godkin's laissez faire economics and elitist politics). But although Hofstadter talks about the motivation to enter reform work, he has nothing to say about why these reformers pursued the specific policies they did. For they did not engage in politics for politics sake; it was not the *act* of exercising power that would reduce their "status anxieties." To serve as a meaningful solution to the problems of authority and position from which they suffered, political involvement had to make a contribution to creating a world in which their claims to privilege would be safe. Political activity exercised on behalf of democratic programs (such as have been identified with some of the reformers, especially those of a later generation) could only hasten the patricians' demise as men of repute, and would hardly recommend itself on that account.

Hofstadter is not much interested in this aspect of the problem, but because he is not he cannot explain the changes in reform posture that, in the form of the Progressive movement of the turn of the century, he does want to talk about. Hofstadter believes that the same social preoccupations were somehow at the heart of both earlier Mugwump and later Progressive efforts. Status worries were involved in both, and he maintains that "the Mugwump type"—identifed with the "aristocratic local gentry" that had particular affection for the "cultural ideals and traditions of New England, and beyond these of Old England" (pp. 137-139)—had to be "somewhat transformed" before it could gain a following. But he is not sure how this occurred: "The sons and successors of the Mugwumps [he writes] had to challenge their fathers' ideas, modify their doctrinaire commitments to *laissez faire*, replace their aristocratic preferences with a startling revival of enthusiasm for popular government, and develop greater flexibility in dealing with the demands of the discontented before they could launch the movement that came to dominate the political life of the Progressive era. If the philosophy and spirit were new the social type and the social grievance were much the same." (p. 143)

To Hofstadter, the revival of enthusiasm for democracy seems "startling" because, given the explanatory method he chooses, it seems so unexpected. The motivational stimulus he concentrates on is too unchanging to account for such significant shifts in political and social sympathy. The development of a popular following, electoral victory, and legislative success seems to matter to the Progressive reformers where it did not seem to matter much to their Mugwump predecessors. Why should the change in outlook have occurred?

A large part of the difficulty is that Hofstadter assumes that while the "social type and the social grievance" of both groups "were much the same" the politics of the two were really different. In fact they were not—except superficially. At the level of its deepest objectives, a significant part of the Progressive movement was as continuous with its Mugwump origins as its heredity and social pedigree. These objectives can be made clear by identifying the common assumptions and policy orientation—as opposed to the different rhetoric used to express them—that ran through the thinking of both groups. This is particularly true in education. The rhetoric shifted (as from that of Butler and Adler to that of Dewey) but the policies and assumptions, representing as they did a sharp departure from older common school ideals, remained largely the same in both cases. In the areas of industrial training and curriculum planning, for example, Progressives took over, with little alteration, a way of thinking about economic growth first introduced by Mugwumps.

was feeling its strength. This was especially true of the growing urban middle class and the part of the working class influenced by the trade union movement.[25] These groups were more and more convinced by past achievement and present opportunity that they could chart the future for themselves and the nation as well as, or better than, those to whom they had looked for wisdom in the past. Improving the schools naturally played a large part in plans to make more of the decisions of life themselves.

By the 1880s, patricians, who had used their service as arbiters of belief to shore up their status as social leaders, recognized the danger to their position. Their claim to the deference, elite privilege, and the prerogatives out of which their identity had been fashioned, would be unenforceable if popular ambition went too far. But it was just this ambition that late nineteenth century industrial growth nurtured. Industrial growth generated a need for higher levels of skill, intellectual competence, and improved living standards. To supply these needs more and more of the population were being introduced to methods of inquiry, scientific investigation, and independent thinking that increased their intolerance of patrician pretensions to wisdom and authority.

To rebuff the challenge from upstarts they feared would discredit the body of doctrine that enforced their social claims, reformers committed to strengthening elite privilege had to attack, in one way or another, industrial development itself. Popular aspiration went to the very heart of the identity problems of the new reformers because the objects to which this aspiration was attached—the rising skill and intellectual requirements encouraged by a modern, industrial economy—would, if not rechanneled, undermine the traditional role patricians had become accustomed to playing. New skills and education were establishing new tests of truth according to which patrician claims to authority were being found empty. With so large a part of their identity located in the work of dispensing advice and passing judgment on the advice of others, the patricians found the threat, represented by the confluence of industrial need and popular ambition, particularly disturbing. And just as antebellum southern planters understood that such threats had to be confronted head-on, so did the patricians.[26] Both groups, to preserve the

---

[25] See Burton J. Bledstein, *The Culture of Professionalism: The Middle Class and the Development of Higher Education in America* (New York, 1976); Nick Salvatore, *Eugene V. Debs: Citizen and Socialist* (Urbana, Ill., 1982); Richard Edwards, *Contested Terrain*, chapter 4; and David Montgomery, *The Fall of the House of Labor: The Workplace, the State, and American Labor Activism, 1865-1925* (New York, 1987).

[26] Not surprisingly, planters and their apologists also made good use of Malthusian arguments. An excellent example is George Fitzhugh, "Slavery Justified," reprinted in R. N. Current, J. A. Garraty, and J. Weinberg, *Words that Made American History: Colonial Times to the 1870s* (third ed., Boston, 1978), pp. 415-428. For a discussion of the planters' cast of mind that suggests something of the situation patricians found themselves in, see Eugene

innermost core of their being, decided to fight—though only the latter, in its Progressive incarnation, proved successful.

When the patrician elite began to realize that it would be facing a force of unprecedented numbers, a force so potentially disruptive that discipline would become an ongoing preoccupation, it began to take the steps to situate control of belief and opinion more firmly in its own hands. The most congenial and, as it turned out, the most tractable institutions to mold to its purposes were those of education.[27] For even if the direct administration of these institutions was not possible (as a number of inconclusive political battles throughout the early reform years demonstrated), the teaching that took place in them might be. If the ideology of the schools could be changed, and if the changes could be passed on through schools of education that asserted values closely mirroring patricians' own, then hands-on control would either be superfluous or, as would occur in the following century, fall to them and their allies with much less effort. Through discussions of the curriculum, reformers responsive to patrician concerns could talk about what was best for the child and proper for the teacher with few people recognizing that questions concerning the nation's industrial future were being debated at the same time.

Especially significant in the success of the patricians' effort was the new institution they created to assist them, the modern university. Building on the very career aspirations that they wanted to control, and incorporating the teachers colleges and other specialized schools that would appear to satisfy these aspirations, the modern university would allow, even encourage, the entry of middle class men and women ambitious to acquire a wide range of professional and scientific expertise. This expertise, required by an advanced, interdependent society, would be provided by a new class of academics. But the language these academics used to supply the expertise carried more than technical knowledge. For embedded within the scientific discourse academics developed was the full range of social assumptions that would reestablish the patricians' position on new and more secure ground.[28]

Academics had the credentials and communally-derived critical standards that pronounced them fit to certify opinion as orthodox; they were

---

Genovese, *The Political Economy of Slavery: Studies in the Economy and Society of the Slave South* (New York, 1965), passim.

[27] Other institutions that educated the public, like museums, libraries, zoological and botanical gardens, also got increased attention. See Helen L. Horowitz, *Culture and the City: Cultural Philanthropy in Chicago from the 1880s to 1917* (Lexington, Ky., 1976); and Alan Trachtenberg, *The Incorporation of America: Culture and Society in the Gilded Age* (New York, 1982), pp. 154 and 164.

[28] See the discussion at the beginning of chapter six for an elaboration of this argument. The best examples are in Mary O. Furner's account of the growth of academic economics in her *Advocacy and Objectivity: A Crisis in the Professionalization of American Social Science, 1865-1905* (Lexington, Ky., 1975). See also Ross, *The Origins of American Social Science.*

encouraged to do so as long as they understood the socially preservationist function such opinion was, in important part, to serve. If the patricians and their spokesmen (who directed the early fortunes of many of the new universities) could use their faculties to show why resources were dwindling, why industrial growth could not be sustained, and why living standards could not be improved, they were on the way to survival with their identity intact.

But mere survival was not the healthiest state that they could imagine. Real security and longevity suggested that academically sanctified opinion reach the masses—the part of the population not expected to go to college but not entirely without ambitions either. To convince them that their sights were set too high would be the job of public schools now outfitted with a new curriculum and ideology, and staffed by college graduates dedicated to introducing both. Because of the way that the schools touched the lives of the mass of the population, and because of the cultural guidance reformers felt comfortable exerting, educational reform became the primary ingredient of a political strategy to turn the clock of American society back to an age when respect and deference had a more unambiguous role in the social order. As the history of the American economy in much of the twentieth century shows, reformers were not as successful as they always hoped; traditions of growth were too well-established to be easily replaced. But significant changes in thought nevertheless occurred. As part of an educational reform program that seemed merely to recognize new realities of industrial life, patricians and their spokesmen introduced a set of ideas that helped preserve aspects of a world where their special contributions were still valued.

III

The best way to get at these issues is to look at the most well-known texts of the educators involved. The position that I argue is one that many readers familiar with the subject and current accounts of it are little disposed to accept. I have therefore felt it important to work closely with the texts usually offered as the most influential reflection of their authors' views. What authors "really meant" must be here—in what was commonly read and searched through for practical advice—or it is irrelevant in understanding the impact reform ideas had. If there is a smoking gun in the writings of the new educators, it is in what they said when they thought people were listening to them, not in what they said when they thought they were not.

One problem with current accounts is that they too often rely on premises that became popular during the 1960s when many educational historians came of age (politically and academically). Disillusioned by the emptiness of American capitalism and its consumer culture, they also attacked the economic growth that capitalists claimed to be the system's most characteristic product. In fact, American consumerism in part began as a substitute for the transforming economic development that American capitalism found it more and more difficult to supply. For historians and other educational writers who confused the two, the notion of a capitalist society that used programs of industrial expansion to build a more egalitarian society had to be self-contradictory and—when found in the mouths of nineteenth century educators—hypocritical.

This conclusion (or rather assumption, so reflexive has it become) makes little sense historically. To nineteenth century Americans, the promise of an egalitarian society was intelligible *only* in the context of a vigorous, expansive capitalism whose growth was assisted by the state. That nineteenth century Americans like Abraham Lincoln downplayed the incipient conflict between worker and employer and the extremes of wealth and poverty already visible in their society does not make them dishonest; it only points up how different their society was from ours. For them and later writers, there was no natural obstacle to the application of their ideas. The problem was political will.[29]

Far from examining this tradition and the efforts made to discredit it as an exercise in nostalgia for, or rehabilitation of, the common school and the teaching methods of the late nineteenth century, I have hoped that a discussion of the tradition's brush with late nineteenth industrialism and the new reformers that industrialism set into motion will help us to recover a truth about education we seem largely to have forgotten. This truth—relating to the connection between educational policy and economic well-being in a democratic society—is much discussed today among liberal economists, but neglected by those who would call themselves liberal educators. Taking their cue from the outlook and strength of the New Deal, writers like Robert Kuttner have stressed that, contrary to claims of laissez faire adherents, economic growth can accompany social equity. Indeed, they argue, one requires the other—as almost all other industrialized democracies that provide more of both to their people have recognized.[30]

An essential part of this effort to provide both equity and growth has been the recognition that educational investment, committed to realizing the intellectual potential of each individual, is at the heart of the process. To examine the fights of turn of the century America is to be reminded that this

---

[29] An excellent example of how Americans of this period conceived their society is in Lincoln's speech at the Wisconsin state fair in 1859. The speech is reprinted in the Library of America edition of Lincoln's *Speeches and Writings, 1859-1865* (New York, 1989), pp. 90-101.

[30] Kuttner, *Economic Illusion*; and *The Life of the Party: Democratic Prospects in 1988 and Beyond* (New York, 1987).

was once as well understood in the United States as it now is in the rest of the industrialized world. Far from the views of directed educational investment being foreign to American thinking, they were once taken for granted by most Americans. The recovery of the story that follows might be a first step in once again making this commitment central to American life.

CHAPTER ONE

THE LATE NINETEENTH CENTURY CONFRONTS THE COMMON SCHOOL TRADITION

I

In order to gauge the magnitude of late nineteenth century educational redirection, it is useful to place it against the work of those reformers who, two generations earlier, established the institutional patterns and arguments that patricians and their followers were led to discredit. For over forty years, an inclusive vision first developed before the Civil War stimulated the proliferation of the largest network of public schools in the world. To the common school reformers of the 1830s and 1840s, virtually all children— deviants and incorrigibles might be excepted—deserved the same education. Since there was no telling where each child might finally settle in life, education had to be as open-ended as life chances. Personal achievement through a system of schools would be powerfully connected to national destiny; for both individuals and the nation, the benefits would be incalculable. Although the rapid expansion of the network based on this vision sometimes included rote teaching and unimaginative lessons, students sensed that they were being prepared to enter a world full of possibility, even urgency. In such an atmosphere, schoolmen were certain that motivation would not be difficult to generate.

By the end of the 1880s much of this sense of open-endedness had disappeared. Earlier in the decade, most schoolmen still scorned views suggesting that their students' abilities or opportunities were limited; the idea might be entertained for those on society's margin but not for the vast majority in the mainstream. But now schoolmen listened with a new attentiveness to views that questioned the social and economic distance the masses might be capable of traveling. Perhaps it was not just the delinquent, racially inferior, or incompetent child who had to be approached with lowered expectations; as the nineteenth century ended, many were concluding that every child had to be approached this way.

Common school reformers had started from very different premises. For them, national economic and social development required improving the educational level of the whole population. This objective, they believed, could best be accomplished in a system of public schools. To be sure, the concern about worker docility is an important part of the story of common school reform, as revisionist historians have pointed out. To too great an extent, common school thinking incorporated elements that contradicted one another, and the contradictions created tensions that often threatened to divert the common school movement from its primary goal. Desires for worker tractability and economic development coexisted uneasily, and compromises, often viewed as necessary to generate essential support, added considerable ambiguity to reform arguments.

But the main thrust of these arguments is clear nevertheless. Many revisionist historians, starting from premises that commonly confused disaffection with capitalist society and disaffection with economic growth itself, have failed to appreciate the way that the "boundless" conditions of antebellum America, and the faith in the future that they encouraged in most Americans, led to the projection of an educational system that reflected a fundamental optimism. At some level many Americans may have feared that boundlessness was an illusion.[1] Ultimately, however, they were successful in putting fear behind them. The promise of achievement more than outweighed worries about prideful overreaching. This was certainly true among common school reformers. Often coming from Whig political backgrounds, they combined in their outlook confidence in the individual's ability to control his own fate and a belief that institutional help to foster control was necessary. For them, threats to the future came less from refractory workers, other members of the lower orders, or aggressive nouveaux riches—all of whom received attention in reform writing—as from the Jacksonians who provided many of these groups with political leadership after the late 1820s.[2]

To antebellum reformers, American society seemed to be facing its most serious crisis since the wars with Great Britain ended in 1815. The Jacksonians seemed determined to reverse the achievements of the nation's founders. They had destroyed the Second Bank of the United States, sacrificed internal improvements to solidify political ties with southern planters, and had allowed speculation and rotten currency to threaten the nation's growing manufacturing potential.

---

[1] See the discussion in George B. Forgie, *Patricide in the House Divided: A Psychological Interpretation of Lincoln and His Age* (New York, 1979), pp. 96, 121.

[2] On the Whigs' outlook and their connection to educational reform, see Lawrence Kohl, *The Politics of Individualism: Parties and the American Character in the Jacksonian Era* (New York, 1989); Daniel Walker Howe, *The Political Culture of the American Whigs* (Chicago, 1979); Carl F. Kaestle and Maris A. Vinovskis, *Education and Social Change in Nineteenth Century Massachusetts* (New York, 1980), chapter 8, "The Politics of Educational Reform in Mid-Nineteenth Century Massachusetts," pp. 208-233; Carl F. Kaestle, *Pillars of the Republic: Common Schools and American Society, 1780-1860* (New York, 1983), pp. 77, 100, 153-154, 156; and Robert Church and Michael W. Sedlak, *Education in the United States: An Interpretive History* (New York, 1976), pp. 61-65.

Jacksonian political methods also disturbed common school reformers. To these critics, Jacksonian tactics amounted to little more than the encouragement of mob violence, the coordinated sabotage of the electoral process, and an open contempt for Congress and the Constitution. To those convinced of the tie between economic well-being and a stable political and social order, Jacksonian antics posed unimaginable dangers, especially among a people that seemed to possess insufficient intellectual or moral equipment to withstand the excitement associated with them. Reason, by all evidence, was hardly flourishing among them. On the one hand, the large rural population seemed to have accepted the notions of Jacksonian publicists that their brutish and isolated condition was virtuous and worthy of emulation. Cut off from one another and from the urban culture and sense of purpose of the Revolutionary period, and scratching out a hard living with limited tools and capital, they seemed to lack the ability to resist Jacksonian appeals. On the other hand, the urban poor, pauperized through a fluctuating national commitment to real production, victimized by real estate speculation, and clinging to a clannish parochialism, seemed too willing to soak its brains in liquor and to riot senselessly for redress of its grievances.

Approaching Jackson and his cohorts with ideas like these led only to the conclusion that they were determined to play on the population's most primitive beliefs instead of helping it rise above them. Jackson's 1832 Bank Veto message was to his opponents a perfect example of Old Hickory's appeal to ignorance and cultural narrowness. In the message, Jackson turned a number of deep-seated fears against what the "forward-looking" considered one of the government's most beneficial ventures. Jackson seemed to be suggesting that large-scale business operation reduced opportunity, that foreigners were gaining a stranglehold on American affairs, and that available wealth would either give out or be monopolized at the expense of the "humble" and powerless. These ideas were all groundless, critics charged. In resorting to them the president fully justified the opprobrium heaped upon him.[3]

To combat the thinking that characterized Jackson's appeal, men and women committed to development attached themselves to the Whig party,

---

[3] On these themes, see Marvin Meyers, *The Jacksonian Persuasion: Politics and Belief* (Stanford, Cal., 1957); Rush Welter, *The Mind of America, 1820-1860* (New York, 1975), p. 117; John William Ward, *Andrew Jackson: Symbol for an Age* (New York, 1955); and Howe, pp. 9, 13-14, 21, 30, 35, 88, 127-129, 265. On rioting during the period, see David Grimsted, "Rioting in its Jacksonian Setting," *American Historical Review* 77 (April, 1972): 361-398. Relevant portions of Jackson's "Bank Veto Message" and Whig leader Daniel Webster's reply are reprinted in Richard Hofstadter, ed., *Great Issues in American History*, 2 vols. (New York, 1958), 2: 291-301.

and looked to the schools.[4] The schools, they hoped, would provide the skills that would transform the social base on which Jacksonianism fed.

Because of the mediating work of an earlier generation (many members of which had their opinions forged during the Revolution), antebellum common school reformers were well aware of the preoccupation of Americans with these institutions. Reformers were familiar with the words of Benjamin Franklin that youth should leave school "fitted for learning any business, calling, or profession."[5] They agreed with the physician and historian David Ramsay that the struggle with England would cause the arts and sciences to "bloom and flourish," and that education could remake "the face of our interior country...from a barren wilderness into the hospitable abodes of peace and plenty."[6] They also supported the view of New England Federalist and lexicographer Noah Webster that schools, in promoting uniformity of language, promoted "political harmony," and the elimination of "a dissocial spirit between the inhabitants of the different states, which is often discoverable in private business and public deliberations."[7]

These and similar sentiments had been kept alive for Americans of the mid-nineteenth century by local teachers who had themselves experienced the sense of revolutionary excitement about the nation's future, and strove to pass it on to their students.[8] Noah Webster's hope for human betterment, hardly confined to the areas of pronunciation and orthography, set the tone for much of the enthusiasm a younger generation would convey about the new nation's possibilities:

---

[4] Although Whigs varied greatly in their conception of economic development, in the first decade of their existence as a coherent opposition to the Jacksonians, there was little need for these differences to become explicit. Given the views of their political enemies and the undeveloped economic conditions of the 1830s, most Whigs at this time had little to fear from seeming to encourage accelerating rates of expansion, especially through the application of new technology. The 1836 speech by Daniel Webster (in part reprinted in Edwin C. Rozwenc, ed., *Ideology and Power in the Age of Jackson* [Garden City, N. Y., 1964], pp. 32-44), is a good example of the approach many of them took. It would be later, in the context of the fight over slavery in the 1840s, that serious divisions about the meaning of development would appear among them. For the story in Massachusetts, the state that witnessed some of the earliest and most important school reform battles, see Robert F. Dalzell, Jr., *Enterprising Elite: The Boston Associates and the World They Made* (Cambridge, Mass., 1989), pp. 188-222.

[5] For a discussion of the significance of Franklin's words, see Bernard Bailyn, *Education in the Forming of American Society: Needs and Opportunities for Study* (paperback ed., New York, [n. d.]; orig., Chapel Hill, N.C., 1960), pp. 33-36.

[6] "David Ramsay on the Arts and Sciences in a New Republic (1778)," in Wilson Smith, ed., *Theories of Education in Early America, 1655-1819* (Indianapolis, Ind., 1973), pp. 225-228.

[7] "Noah Webster's Plea for an American Language (1789)," in ibid., p. 269.

[8] One example is the influence of Horace Mann's teacher, Nathaniel Emmons. See Jonathan Messerli, *Horace Mann: A Biography* (New York, 1972), pp. 9-11.

America [Webster wrote in 1789] is in a situation the most favorable for great reformations; and the present time is, in a singular degree, auspicious. The minds of the men in this century have been awakened. New scenes have been, for many years presenting new occasions for exertion; unexpected distresses have called forth the powers of invention; and the application of new expedients has demanded every possible exercise of wisdom and talents. Attention is roused; the mind expanded; and the intellectual faculties invigorated. Here men are prepared to receive improvements, which would be rejected by nations, whose habits have not been shaken by similar events.[9]

Half a century later these messages of harmony and improvement seemed as important as they had earlier—all the more so because new dangers threatened. Rising Whigs like Horace Mann (in Massachusetts) and Henry Barnard (in Connecticut and Rhode Island) gave up promising careers in state politics to assume what seemed to others to be powerless and insignificant positions as the secretaries of the newly formed, poorly funded, and purely advisory state boards of education. But Mann, for example, did not see himself leaving politics to become a simple school reformer. To him, school reform was the way to wage the political battle against Jacksonianism more effectively. A lawyer just elected to the presidency of the state senate, a railroad promoter and a persistent advocate of sustained, industrial growth,[10] he believed that a population whose educational and, for him, economic level was rising could be weaned away from the policies of the Jacksonians. His own experience in the early 1840s had made clear to him how urgent a task this was.

Between 1840 and 1842 Mann had been engaged in a running battle to stop Jacksonian Governor Marcus Morton's attempt to abolish the newly created (1837) Board of Education. Morton had little use either for the board or for Mann, who had been chosen by Whig governor Edward Everett to head it.[11] A Democratic Party faithful, Morton finally had been elected after twelve unsuccessful tries, by promoting repeal of the state's temper-

---

[9] Wilson Smith, ed., *Theories of Education in Early America, 1655-1819*, p. 289.

[10] For an expression of Mann's attitude toward industrial growth before he became education secretary, see his 1833 speech supporting railroad expansion westward to link the state with the Hudson River. In a striking anticipation of his education reports, Mann went far beyond the immediate situation in Massachusetts to make a general argument for economic progress based on technological innovation and the qualities of mind that generated it. The speech, entitled "Argument for a Western Rail Road," can be found in the Horace Mann papers of the Massachusetts Historical Society. The backward-looking elements of the Jacksonian appeal are central to the accounts of Kohl, *The Politics of Individualism*; Meyers, *The Jacksonian Persuasion*; and Michael A. Lebowitz, "The Jacksonians: Paradox Lost?" in Barton J. Bernstein, ed., *Towards a New Past: Dissenting Essays in American History* (New York, 1968), pp. 65-90.

[11] Everett was himself an important publicist of educational improvement going back to the 1820s. See his *Importance of Practical Education and Useful Knowledge: Being a Selection from his Orations and Other Discourses* (New York, 1854). His views are best expressed in "On the Importance of Scientific Knowledge, to Practical Men, and On the Encouragements to its Pursuit" (1840).

ance law. To his detractors, he seemed to assume that a population too drunk for anything but herding to the polls at election time would not have much use for schools or the education they would provide.

Temperance, of course, was no more a silly fad of the 1840s than was school reform. Both were part of the Whig political thrust, and it is not surprising that the men who advocated the latter believed the former to be equally necessary. Mann, for example, was a long-time temperance advocate and strongly backed the state's fifteen gallon law, so-called because it outlawed liquor purchases in quantities of less than fifteen gallons. This, it was hoped, would end the days of local grog shops and taverns, the organizing centers of the Jackson machine's electoral manipulations. Democrats at the time, and more recently as well,[12] argued that the law was another example of inequality and class legislation. In general, the crusades of the period, whether they related to schools, prisons, hospitals, or taverns, were motivated by the most serious worries about stabilizing a society constantly threatening to go out of control.[13] In a period of rapid industrial and urban growth, one in which the ordering features of an older society had broken down, these concerns, if sometimes foolishly expressed, came naturally to those who advocated economic expansion and the tranquil social life that they felt undergirded it.[14] Jacksonians, insufficiently sensitive to very real dangers around them, seemed only to be encouraging behavior that would make the situation worse.

To Whigs who advocated industrial development and the uniform skill levels to make growth rates predictable, the localism of the schools made them ideal candidates for reform. Morton, however, saw little that needed change. In his 1840 inaugural address he declared that the common schools were already in a "high degree of perfection," and argued that the best guarantee of their future success was to make sure they were managed exclusively by the towns, those "little pure democracies," without any supervision by the state. Responding to the austerity drive caused by the Panic of 1837, and with the Jacksonian passion for budget balancing, Morton

---

[12] See Arthur Schlesinger, Jr.'s account in *The Age of Jackson* (Boston, 1945), p. 256.

[13] See my *Country Boys and Merchant Princes: The Social Control of Young Men in New York* (Lewisburg, Pa., 1975); and David J. Rothman, *The Discovery of the Asylum: Social Order and Disorder in the New Republic* (Boston, 1971).

[14] This was as true for Whigs like Mann, genuinely committed to innovation and opportunity, as it was for Whigs like the Boston Associates, whose interest in industrial development remained almost solely focused on textile manufacture. For the Associates, textile manufacture was the route to their prized goals of security and control. But the pursuit of these goals put them in opposition to the kind of industrial growth—where innovation and opportunity played central roles—sought by Whigs like Mann. As mentioned above (note 4), differences on the slavery question closely paralleled these economic differences, and in time the latter would become the subject of public discussion also. In addition to the pages in Dalzell, *Enterprising Elite*, referred to in note 4, see also pp. 69-72, 111-112, 187-188; and Messerli, *Horace Mann*, chapters XIX-XXI.

demanded that funds for school books and district libraries be cut drastically, and that the Board of Education and the normal school that trained many of the state's teachers be abolished.

Two arguments used by his supporters on the House Education Committee against the new normal school, one of Mann's first achievements, confirmed for Whigs the parochialism that they hoped to eradicate. Since district schools were operated only three or four months each year, asserted the committee the same year Morton took office, "it is obviously impossible, and perhaps, it is not desirable, that the business of keeping these schools should become a distinct and separate profession, which the establishment of Normal Schools seems to anticipate." And even if normal schools were valuable, there was "no adequate security that the teachers, thus taught at the public expense" would remain in the state. "It seems hardly just," they therefore concluded, "that Massachusetts, in the present state of her finances, should be called upon to educate, at her own cost, teachers for the rest of the Union."[15] To Whigs, the committee seemed incapable of imagining change, or the possibility that the state—wealthier than its neighbors—had responsibilities beyond its borders.

Mann knew, as he confided in his correspondence to Henry Barnard,[16] that the two year debate over funding and the political fight to prevent the Jacksonian interment of progress were identical. In an 1842 July 4 Oration he made the connections plain by detailing the consequences that "an ignorant and corrupt people" would have for a developing republic. Such a population permitted the social wealth, the mainstay of industrial growth, to be "squandered," business activity to collapse, and unemployment to rise. It allowed "capital which has been honestly and laboriously accumulated [to be] turned into dross."[17] Bad as the situation was, schools and dedicated teachers to staff them, agencies like lyceums, libraries, and mechanics' institutes could arrest the slide into anarchy that such ignorance presaged. It could also, Mann continued, moving to the politics of the day, end electoral contests marked by "turbulence and riot." Mann was passionately committed to popular government; one look at a literally burnt out England and its aristocracy, a country and class he constantly held up for ridicule, made the advantages of universal suffrage plain. Yet the dangers, where people remained "uneducated" and "ignorant" were real. Manipulation of the

---

[15] "Two Criticisms of Educational Reform in Massachusetts," in Rush Welter, ed., *American Writings on Popular Education* (Indianapolis, Ind., 1971), pp. 83, 94. See also the account of this dispute in Kaestle, *Pillars of the Republic*, pp. 152-153.

[16] See Vincent P. Lannie, ed., *Henry Barnard: American Educator* (New York, 1974), pp. 51-83; and Kaestle and Vinovskis, *Education and Social Change*, p. 216.

[17] Mary P. Mann, *Life and Works of Horace Mann*, 5 vols. (Boston, 1891), 4: 360.

population would make a shambles of the finest example of representative government in the world.[18]

Unfortunately, the degeneration of an orderly to chaotic electoral process was already far advanced. At election time, Mann said, the "rival parties begin to play their game for the ignorant, and to purchase the salable." Mass meetings were held, hired speakers criss-crossed the country, and campaign literature blanketed the cities and towns. Then "as the contest approaches, fraud, intimidation, bribes are rife. Immense sums are spent to carry the lame, to hunt up the skulking, to force the indifferent to the polls. Taxes are contributed to qualify voters, and men are transported, at party expense, from one State to another" (386).

After describing the way this absence of principle resulted in political chaos and an endless recombination of worthless political groupings,[19] Mann tied the process directly to the deterioration of the nation's economic health. Focusing on the worst aspect of Jacksonian policies, Mann discussed the way Democratic monetary schemes destroyed real productive values. In the period since Jackson's veto of the bill to recharter the Second Bank of the United States, Mann said that national and state policy on currency questions had been fluctuating so wildly "that all of the prodigality of nature, pouring her hundreds of millions of products, annually into our hands, has not been able to save thousands and thousands of our people from poverty." Ultimately, the ignorance of the population itself was responsible for this economic dislocation. Again and again, the question had been decided by illiterate voters "to whom the simplest proposition in political economy, or in national finance, is as unintelligible as a book of Hebrew or Greek" (386-87).[20]

Mann then offered a full catalogue of the social disruption that he associated with the Jacksonians. He stopped short of sectional examples like South Carolina nullification only because, he said tongue in cheek, "they are implicated with strong party feelings," and on July 4 he intended "to touch no party chord." Even so, he warned, a full-scale social conflagration, engulfing the North and South in war and bringing commerce, manu-

---

[18] Ibid., 4: 361, 379, 380-383.

[19] Ibid., 4: 274-275, 383, 396.

[20] Mann was not very careful about distinguishing clearly between the illiterate electorate, "voters who could not read or write" (p. 387), and the "uneducated" electorate, "voters who have never possessed either the intellectual or the moral advantages of a school" (p. 382). Although the two notions are very different from one another, Mann probably took little notice of the difference because to him neither true education, which included large doses of moral instruction, nor literacy could be guaranteed outside of the common school setting. The hope of reformers was to get students to attend common schools more regularly and for longer periods each year. Recent scholarship has concluded that literacy was in fact widespread before the common school movement began. See Kaestle and Vinovskis, *Education and Social Change*, pp. 34-35, 40, 45.

facturing, and agriculture to a stand-still, awaited the nation unless the level of popular intelligence was immediately raised (398-399).[21]

To Mann and his associates, these were the stakes that the battle for school reform would decide. Only an educated people could return the United States to the principles of its founders, and prevent the breakup of organized social and political life. Only an educated people, through its own creative intervention, could alter and improve the conditions of its own existence. By increasing the intellectual power of all of its members, human society moved closer to achieving its own perfection. Economic advancement was linked to intellectual advancement in this vision; for Whigs committed to it, the need to build a strong common school system was an early article of faith. The production of intellectual talent had to be as reliable as that of raw materials in order for the processes of intellectual and economic advancement to work. Systematic school organization was the surest way of guaranteeing that the connection of the two would be certain.

One of the best places to see how the elements of this point of view came together is in the section entitled "Intellectual Education as a Means of Removing Poverty, and Securing Abundance" in Mann's final annual report as Board of Education secretary (1848). Mann began with a characteristic attack on a debased class- and poverty-ridden Europe whose members, especially the British, were bent on returning to a feudal era more unrelenting than the Middle Ages. He then turned to the backward reform schemes that Jacksonian leveling had spawned. Of these, he said, the worst was "Agrarianism," nothing but "the revenge of poverty against wealth." In its most extreme form it led to the "demolition of machinery because it supersedes hand labor."[22]

The thinking behind educational reform was the opposite of this "madness." Education did not just "disarm the poor of their hostility toward the rich," said Mann disputing the argument used to characterize his efforts, "it prevents being poor." The Jacksonian notion "that some people are poor because others are rich" was absurd. Getting to the heart of the thinking that separated him from his opponents, Mann presented an argument that bears examination at length. In attacking the Jacksonians as he did, he defined the issues that have dominated educational debate ever since.[23] The idea, Mann said, that some people are poor because others are rich

---

[21] Mann also touched the same themes in his annual reports. See in particular (Mary P. Mann edition), his second, pp. 556-557 (vol. 2); eighth, pp. 440, 466 (vol. 3); and ninth, pp. 15-18 (vol. 4).

[22] Mary P. Mann, 4: 251.

[23] Mann's argument is especially important to review because of the criticism he has received from revisionist historians. They have argued that the evils of capitalism were defined by its oppressive hierarchical and class relationships and not by the "Agrarian" mentality or

supposes a fixed amount of property in the community, which by fraud or force, or arbitrary law, is unequally divided among men; and the problem presented for solution is, how to transfer a portion of this property from those who are supposed to have too much to those who feel and know that they have too little. (p. 252)

But the argument was false, insisted Mann. There were no limits to wealth. Man's reason, developed through education, "creates or develops new treasures—treasures not before possessed or dreamed of by anyone" (252). Human history confirmed this. Instead of falling prey to other "irrational tribes" to which he would have been inferior, and of which he would have been the prey, had he been "endowed with only the instincts of the brute creation," man continued to advance and to make the powers of Nature serve him. In this way he was able to "add to the wealth of the world—unlike robbery, or slavery, or agrarianism, which aim only at appropriation, by one man or one class, of the wealth belonging to another man or class." Mann offered specific examples to make his meaning clear. Technology, the product of human intelligence alone, had revolutionized human existence. "One man with a power press," he noted, "will print books faster than a million of scribes could copy them before the invention of printing. One man, with an iron-foundery [sic], will make more utensils or machinery than Tubal-Cain could have made had he worked diligently till this time." This ability of man to alter his environment, he said, provided everyone, not only with the bare necessities of survival but with "all the means of refinement, embellishment, and mental improvement" (pp. 254-255).

This was the meaning of human progress for Mann; at bottom it depended on what he called "intelligent labor" freely applied in its own behalf. The ignorant savage or the slave—Mann chose specific problems in naval architecture and freight transport to make his point—could never compete with the intelligent man who "makes his wits save his bones." Extinguish human intelligence and the race would plunge at once "into the weakness and helplessness of barbarism" (p. 258).

But intelligence did not grow magically. It had to be institutionalized and thereby made capable of wide dissemination. This was the role of education:

[When] intelligence was confined to a very small number...improvements were few; and they followed each other only after long intervals....But just in proportion as intelligence—that is, education—has quickened and stimulated a

---

speculatively created scarcity that may have caused them. Two examples in educational writing are Colin Greer, *The Great School Legend* (New York, 1972); and Samuel Bowles and Herbert Gintis, *Schooling in Capitalist America* (New York, 1976). See my review of the first in *History of Education Quarterly* 14 (Summer, 1974): 251-259; and of the second in *The Review of Education* 3 (May-June, 1977): 168-182.

greater and greater number of minds, just in the same proportion have invention and discoveries increased in their wonderfullness, and in the rapidity of their succession. The progression has been rather geometrical than arithmetical. (p. 259)[24]

The political economy which took no account of this process, said Mann, was folly. "The greatest of all the arts in political economy is to change a consumer into a producer; and the next greatest is to increase the producer's producing power—an end to be directly attained by increasing his intelligence" (p. 260). Mann was far from accepting the anti-growth views spread so widely by interests in trade, commerce, and, by this time, textile manufacture who feared displacement by rising industrial forces.[25] These views asserted that knowledge and the expansion of human intelligence were less pressing priorities "because mechanical ingenuity and scientific discovery must have nearly reached the outermost limit of possible advancement; that either the powers of Nature are exhausted, or human genius is in its decrepitude." In contrast, Mann maintained that "all past achievements of the human mind [are] rather in the nature of prophecy than of fulfillment....Ever-expanding powers are within us; eternity lies before us" (pp. 260-61). The underdeveloped resources of the earth, he continued, would be discovered by the

> exercise of the human faculties, in the same way that all scientific and mechanical improvements of past times have been brought to light—that is, by education. And the greater the proportion of minds in any community which are educated, and the more thorough and complete the education which is given them, the more rapidly...will that community advance in all the means of enjoyment and elevation. (p. 263)

Mere copying of the advances of others could never substitute for this activity. The imitator would always remain inferior. In the first place, Mann pointed out, "all copying is in the nature of empiricism." The copyist knew nothing of principle and therefore acted like a blind man. When confronted with an unfamiliar problem he was incapable of acting because "the light of example shines only in one direction." Principle, on the other hand, "circumfuse[s] its beams, and...leave[s] no darkness in any direction" (p. 264). In the second place, even if the imitator became as proficient in the use of any one process or technique as the man who devised it, the latter will have spent time creating something new thereby continuing to maintain his advantage.

---

[24] On this point, see also Horace Mann, *Lectures on Education* (Boston, 1855), pp. 19, 20, 55.

[25] See Horlick, *Country Boys and Merchant Princes*; and Dalzell, *Enterprising Elite,* pp. 69-72.

Mann was explicitly thinking of the differences between northern and southern economies in saying this; the argument that followed was soon to become an integral part of the free labor ideology of the Republican Party. The slave states, Mann wrote, might buy textile machinery made "by the intelligent mechanics of the free states," and planters might train slaves to operate these machines with a fair degree of skill. But no matter how well they succeeded, even to the extent of satisfying their entire home market, it would still be the case "that in the meantime, the new wants and refinements generated by the progress of the age will demand some new fabric requiring for its manufacture either more ingeniously-wrought machinery or greater skill in the operator." Under these conditions, "the more educated community," a community Mann obviously felt could only be found in the free states, would "forever keep ahead of the less educated one" (p. 265).[26]

This was Mann at his best. It was a standard that even he could not live up to all the time. Impressed with the immediate dangers of the late 1840s, Mann felt under intense pressure to act and often did so without carefully thinking through the consequences. In his denunciation of greed and selfish ambition, in his approval of the passive and impotent youth admired by reactionary mercantile interests, in his concern with social stability, and in his calls for worker docility,[27] he often came close to echoing the backward-looking views of his friends Emerson and Channing. In his eagerness to stop the rote teaching then current, and with his fears about the aimlessness of a younger generation, he embraced phrenology and Pestalozzian pedagogy. Both embodied a kind of empiricism that would have serious repercussions during the fights, some decades later, against Sheldon's object method and Dewey's instrumentalism.[28]

Yet his achievements were substantial nevertheless. For twelve years Mann had organized to put his views into practice. Through the dissemination of his annual reports; through the influential *Common School Journal* which he founded and edited; through his travels and correspondence; through the legislation he authored to require local school committees to

---

[26] For another perspective on the problems slavery created for education in the antebellum South, see William R. Taylor, "Toward a Definition of Orthodoxy: The Patrician South and the Common Schools," *Harvard Educational Review* 36 (Fall, 1966): 412-426.

[27]27. For a good example of the confusions that entered his thinking on this question, see his *Fifth Annual Report* in *Life and Works of Horace Mann*, volume 3. The most damaging parts of the report have been excerpted in Michael Katz, ed., *School Reform: Past and Present* (Boston, 1971), pp. 140-149.

[28] For these problems in Mann's thinking, see *Lectures*, pp. 40-42, 44, 99; Seventh Annual Report (1844); and Ninth Annual Report (1846), pp. 97-99, in Mary P. Mann, *Life and Works of Horace Mann*; and his lecture to the Boston Mercantile Library Association, "A Few Thoughts for a Young Man," (Boston, 1850). See also the discussions of phrenology in Allan S. Horlick, "Phrenology and the Social Education of Young Men," *History of Education Quarterly* XI (Spring, 1971): 23-38; and of Pestalozzianism and of the object method in Church and Sedlak, pp. 95-99, 104-111.

keep records and make annual reports, to pay committee members a salary out of the state education fund, to enable the board to draw up lists of recommended titles for district libraries, and to create state-controlled teacher training institutions; and through his work for higher teacher salaries and school district consolidation, he worked tirelessly to improve education across the nation. He quit as Secretary of the Board of Education only when, as his biographer has paraphrased his words, "the real possibility of slavery in the new territories forced him to alter his own more immediate priorities," and assume the congressional seat vacated by John Quincy Adams's death.[29]

The efforts of Mann and those of others who shared his views, began to change the face of education in the United States. Their work went far toward breaking up the insular and divisive district system by introducing paid local superintendents, graded instruction, certified teachers, a longer school year, and better attendance. Their work established uniform texts and classroom programs, libraries, high schools, normal schools and compulsory education laws. As a result, expenditures and attendance after 1840 expanded rapidly, significantly reversing the downward trend of the previous, Jacksonian directed, decade.[30] In Massachusetts, for example, between 1840 and 1865, student enrollment increased 53.8 percent, the number of teachers 74.4 percent. The investment was such, in other words, that even as the number of students increased the number of students per teacher decreased. Teacher salaries also went up. The salary of male teachers increased 65.5 percent, that of female teachers 71.1 percent. And since inflation was minimal before the Civil War, these increases meant real gains. Taking the decreasing pupil-teacher ratio and rising teacher salaries together, the result was a per pupil expenditure increase of two and a half times.[31]

By the 1870s, this pattern of unified city systems and graded classrooms, carefully planned curriculums and uniform examinations, welltrained and certified teachers, consolidated districts with centralized authority in the person of the superintendent had brought the United States (which by 1850 was already spending a percentage of national income on education far exceeding England and France) close to becoming the most literate and productive nation in the world. Graded schools encouraged systematic work and regular advancement, and enabled criteria of progress to be established in the schools for the first time. Administrative changes freed teachers from

---

[29] Messerli, *Horace Mann*, p. 456.

[30] Kaestle, *Pillars of the Republic*, chapter 6, "The Common School Reform Program," pp. 104-136; Church and Sedlak, p. 68, reporting the findings of Albert Fishlow, "The American Common School Revival: Fact or Fancy?" in Henry Rosovsky, ed., *Industrialization in Two Systems* (New York, 1966), pp. 40-67.

[31] Michael Katz, *The Irony of Early School Reform* (Cambridge, Mass., 1968), pp. 11-12.

wasteful tasks, allowing them to concentrate on their subject matter and begin to take satisfaction in the results. Students began to work harder, requiring less purely disciplinary supervision. This, in time, attracted more and better trained teachers to the schools. Bent on professionalizing, they made themselves increasingly valuable to their society.

II

To the heirs of Horace Mann, the system and uniformity characterizing the network of schools created after the Civil War were well matched to prepare the inhabitants of an industrialized urban society for the new tasks they would be facing.[32] Drawn to the cities by economic opportunities available nowhere else, immigrants from southern and eastern Europe and Americans from local farms and villages would be taking on responsibilities defined by the expanded variety of human contacts, the enlarged scale of business enterprise, the complexities of specialization and coordination required by urban life. The schools' emphasis on regularity and order, embodied in new training in both moral and scientific education, corresponded to the regularity and order that dominated life in these modern cities. Educators who developed this argument understood, as had Horace Mann before them, that improved productiveness and the rapid development of new technology depended as much on moral discipline as on intellectual training. One could not be meaningfully divorced from the other; a modern educational system would have to provide both.

The most forceful spokesman for this point of view in the last decades of the nineteenth century was William Torrey Harris. Born to a well-off Connecticut farm family, Harris had spent some time at Phillips Academy in Andover and at Yale before moving west to seek his fortune. He settled in St. Louis in 1857 and established close ties with the German Republican community. Along with the latter, he became a strong supporter of Lincoln's efforts during the Civil War. He also became the central figure in the American Hegelian movement and the founder of the anti-Spencerian *Journal of Speculative Philosophy*. At the same time, capitalizing on his past education, he had entered the school system, moving up through its ranks to the superintendency in 1868. Working at this post until 1880, a period coinciding with the growth of St. Louis into one of the nation's greatest cities, he turned the schools into a model of organization and innovation. He was so admired for his administrative ability that he was offered such positions as head of the Boston schools, the presidencies of Johns

---

[32] See William Torrey Harris's annual reports to the St. Louis Public School Board. One representative example is in the *Fourteenth Annual Report of 1868*, pp. 88-97. See also the conclusions of Kaestle, *Pillars of the Republic*, p. 135.

Hopkins University and the University of California, and of the largest lead-mining company in the country. In 1880 he gave up his position in St. Louis for one at the Concord School of Philosophy and remained there until 1889. In that year, seeking a wider forum for his views, he began a seventeen year tenure as the U.S. Commissioner of Education.[33] Although his active organizing of school systems diminished during these years, Harris's writings on education became voluminous. In one article after another in the 1880s and 1890s, he defended a point of view coming under increasing attack. There is little in these articles that had not been prefigured by the annual reports he wrote as St. Louis superintendent, but the arguments he presented in national journals during this period were more coherent and fully developed, no doubt as a result of an increasing familiarity with the objections of his antagonists.

Throughout his career Harris supported the reforms that would give the United States the strongest integrated network of educational institutions. He backed legislation to establish a system of land grant colleges and universities, a national university, and federal funding for nation-wide elementary and secondary schools (as provided by the Blair bills of the 1880s).[34] At the same time, he denounced proposals like the elective system, vocational education, the child-study movement, and the theories of cultural relativism that he believed were being used to justify contraction of the "common curriculum," the basis of traditional school systems. Unfortunately, denunciation, especially in the polite tones that Harris rarely departed from, unconnected to any mobilization of political forces, would be far too little to stop the efforts of the new patrician reformers who opposed him. So gentle was Harris in his "attacks" on his critics that John Dewey, in time to put forward the best arguments for the positions they first championed, was at one point openly uncomprehending of his attitude.[35]

Unlike the new reformers, Harris viewed urban industrial civilization as the high point of human existence. With the rise of manufacturing and the growth of cities, rural squalor and abject poverty could finally be eradicated. A higher standard of living could be provided for the entire popula-

---

[33] Kurt Leidecker, *Yankee Teacher: The Life of William Torrey Harris* (New York, 1946). On the St. Louis school system, especially in the nineteenth century, see Selwyn Troen, *The Public and the Schools: Shaping the St. Louis System, 1838-1920* (Columbia, Mo., 1975).

[34] On the significance of the Blair bills, see chapter 2 below, and Gordon C. Lee, *The Struggle for Federal Aid, First Phase: A History of the Attempts to Obtain Federal Aid for the Common Schools, 1870-1890* (New York, 1949).

[35] See, for example, W. T. Harris, "Professor John Dewey's Doctrine of Interest as Related to Will," in *Educational Review* (May, 1896); Dewey's review of Harris's *Psychologic Foundations of Education*, reprinted in *John Dewey: The Early Works, Volume 5, 1895-1898* (Carbondale, Ill., 1972), p. 272ff.; and especially, Dewey's, "The Psychological Aspects of the School Curriculum," in ibid., pp. 165-167. On the gentility of this generation of schoolmen, see Paul H. Mattingly, *The Classless Profession: American Schoolmen in the Nineteenth Century* (New York, 1975), especially chapters 3 and 7.

tion. "Whereas formerly," he noted, "the whole population had to struggle in a hand-to-hand fight with nature for a meagre subsistence, it is now aided by machinery, and the few can supply the many with raw materials and leave two-thirds of the population to engage in manufacturing and the collection and distribution of goods."[36] The moving force behind this process was invention, especially, he said, "mechanic invention" or technology. This, in turn, was the product of human intelligence. "Mind,—not the body,—is the inventive power," he said, making a distinction he would insist on throughout his writings. "The directive power that can manage and use machines to advantage is mental and not physical skill."[37]

The educational problems of the day stemmed from these new facts of life. An industrial economy placed new responsibilities on the human mind; a vast upgrading of the intelligence of the workforce was required to deal with them. The worker was no longer a mere drudge. He now had to be in a position to "direct and manage machinery"; he was now "primarily a directing brain, and only secondarily a laboring hand."[38] As new technology was developed, greater demands on the versatility and nimbleness of mind would be made. "Not a special apprenticeship to some particular machine is required," he said, taking aim at the narrowness of vocational education proposals, "but a general insight into the conditions and laws of mechanism in general." Vocations, in today's industrial society, were shifting so rapidly, with innovations constantly producing new job categories and new professions, that manual labor would soon almost completely disappear. The most "practical" education under these conditions "is not an education of the hand to skill, but the brain to directive intelligence."[39]

The issue was of more than local importance. If education did not develop the necessary qualities of versatile intelligence in all children, America's new claims to industrial and world leadership would dissolve. Harris put the choice facing the nation's leaders bluntly:

> Either educate your people in common schools or your labor will not compete with other nations whose people are educated up to the capacity of inventing and directing machinery. If you cannot compete with other peoples in the matter of the use of machinery, you must recede from the front rank of nations in every respect.[40]

Harris tied the second range of educational problems to the new duties of citizenship. In addition to conceptual skills, city dwellers also had to

---

[36] "Educational Needs of Urban Civilization," *Education* (May, 1885): 446.
[37] "Does the Common School Educate Children Above the Station They are Expected to Occupy in Life?" *Education* (May, 1883): 461.
[38] "Educational Needs of Urban Civilization": 447.
[39] "Does the Common School Educate Children Above the Station They Are Expected to Occupy in Life?": 462.
[40] "Educational Needs of Urban Civilization": 448.

assimilate a new moral culture. They had to learn habits like punctuality and regularity, qualities of disciplined industry and common civility, and the political responsibilities of a democratic people. But the essence of the "spiritual phases of this new order of civilization" went beyond absorbing these habits and duties. The morality imparted to students would equip them not merely for day-to-day urban life, but for an understanding of the ethical qualities that urged humanity forward. Each student had to understand that the qualities of directive intelligence and common morality were not just valuable to the individual trying to survive in an unfamiliar environment. In addition, they were also meant to lead the individual to "become a rational self, a spiritual self, governed by moral and universal ideas." Each person had to understand "that the welfare of the highest is connected, indissolubly, with the lowest, so that each and all must, in the main, see clearly that he is his brother's keeper." Human beings, in Harris's view, were not atomistic, unconnected individuals wandering blindly, alone, and isolated through the nation's cities. Many popular writers of the day may have seen them this way, but to Harris individuals were tied to one another by a common purpose. Proper moral training would allow each to recognize the responsibilities he now had to assume, and the "inborn divinity" that would help to discharge them.[41]

These requirements for directive and moral power translated into a two-part curriculum. Scientific and mathematical training was necessary to provide the knowledge that would advance the "conquest of nature"; literature, including history and the study of grammar, was necessary to give each student a sense of the possibilities toward which his mind could aspire. To dilute or narrow this curriculum would make it impossible to achieve its objective, the expansion of that human knowledge which partakes of both "enlightening power" and "general applicability." The study of science and literature would begin to prepare students for their larger responsibilities because they initiated students into thought processes that went beyond the assimilation of mere sense data, the only contribution of the reigning object method.[42] The qualities of moral discipline and scientific innovation could

---

[41] See "Industrial Education in the Common Schools," *Education* VI (June, 1886): 608; and "Does the Common School Educate...?": 466. See also his sixteenth annual report (1870), pp. 22-24; and seventeenth annual report (1871), pp. 30-34 to the St. Louis Board of Education.

[42] The term refers to the popular method developed at the Oswego Normal School after 1859. As Church and Sedlak (p. 104) describe it, the school "concentrated on teaching young people how to perceive rather than what to think. Teachers were to appeal to the children's senses by bringing into the classroom objects, or pictures of objects...that the students could see and touch....In all cases the point of the lesson was to have the children describe the objects as fully as possible—thus improving their power of observation." While to some this method encouraged students to see their world afresh, to others, like Harris, the result was an emphasis on rote memorization instead of the development of more conceptual skills. For a valuable portrait of the educator who devised the method, and an explanation of its attractiveness to other educators, see Church and Sedlak, pp. 105-111. For other examples of Harris's criticism

be developed only by minds capable of generalization and abstraction about the needs of all humanity.[43]

The setting uniquely appropriate to locate these demands was the classroom. Here, established texts and the recitation method would result in both freedom and self-determination, and obedience and responsibility. Recitations would protect the student against the dependence on oral instruction and, at the same time, maintain a central role for the instructor. In the classroom the focus of activity had to be on those qualities of concept formation that distinguished human beings from lower forms of animal life. Human thinking was very different from the sense perception by which many normal school textbooks characterized it. The formation of the concept of causality, for example, could only be described as "an original acquisition" and not, as Hume or Pestalozzi had it, as a habit built out of recurring sense data. In this connection, Harris emphasized, current attention to manual training was nothing but an absorption with the activities of infants.[44]

Manual training was the reform that acted as the stalking horse for Progressivism's pedagogical centerpiece, vocational education. Its leading advocate nationally was Calvin Woodward, the man who, from his base at Washington University, led the effort to overturn Harris's work in St. Louis on behalf of a common curriculum.[45] Woodward developed his case for manual training by quoting Emerson's 1844 attack on formal schooling. Like Emerson, Woodward also was convinced apparently that "we are shut up in schools and college recitation rooms for ten or fifteen years and come out at last with a belly full of words and do not know a thing. We cannot use our hands, or our legs, or our eyes, or our arms."[46] The importance of manual training for Woodward was that it ensured that society did not deny "to those who must labor with their hands that sort of mental cultivation which can lift the humblest occupation to a higher level, and invest them [sic] with a new dignity...." Woodward, unlike Harris, accepted the Progressive idea that a permanent labor-intensive work force was inevitable,

---

of the Oswego method, see his fifteenth annual report (1869), pp. 113-114; and his eighteenth (1872), p. 149.

[43] See "Industrial Education in the Common Schools": 608-610.

[44] "The Psychology of Manual Training," *Education* IX (May, 1889): 579-581. See also the discussion in Marvin Lazerson and W. Norton Grubb, eds., *American Education and Vocationalism: A Documentary History, 1870-1970* (New York, 1974), p. 13.

[45] The story of this drive is told by Troen, *The Public and the Schools*, pp. 167, 171, 181 and, especially, chapter 9, pp. 183-207.

[46] The full Emerson passage can be found in Rozwenc, ed., *Ideology and Power in the Age of Jackson*, p. 173.

and focused on investing the available jobs (which presumably would not be changing much) "with a new dignity."[47]

Harris attacked these ideas head-on. Manual training, he said, was nothing but a throwback to Rousseau, a writer who made no distinction between the higher and lower faculties of man. For Harris, man steps above the brute when he

> looks beyond things as he sees them existing before him and commences to consider their possibilities....What we call directive power on the part of man, his combining and organizing power, all rests on this power to see beyond the real things before the senses to the ideal possibilities invisible to the brute. The more clearly man sees these ideals, the more perfectly he can construct for himself another set of conditions than those in which he finds himself.

The ability to do this was fostered by science and the humanities, not by the hand-work that characterized manual training. In itself, hand-work was no different, Harris said, from the skills learned by a child in his pre-school years.[48] Answering Woodward at the 1889 National Education Association meetings, Harris identified the thinking behind manual training with the mentality of the budget cutter. "We must never," he said, "yield to the economic spirit that proposes to curtail the humanizing studies in our schools." On the contrary, the period of study in pure science and the humanities had to be extended. This, said Harris, was because "all which goes to develop the ability of the youth to see possibilities and ideals goes to make him a more productive laborer in the fields of industry."[49]

Instead of approaching children as the new reformers were coming to, from the standpoint of their supposed immediate wishes and needs,[50] Harris approached them from the standpoint of an adult understanding of social goals. "Man," he wrote, "reveals his true nature not as a child but as mature men and women, in the process of making world history." Man reveals what he is "not in the cradle, but in the great world of human history and literature and science."

These subjects alone would give each student, regardless of background, a sense of the unique capabilities of his own mind, and of the goals

---

[47] See Woodward's address, "Manual Training," in *Proceedings* of the National Education Association (1889): 90-91; and "The Function of an American Manual Training School," *Education* (May, 1883): 517. See also Charles M. Dye, *Calvin Milton Woodward and American Urban Education* (Ann Arbor, Mich., 1976); and Troen, *The Public and the Schools*, pp. 168-174. The national movement that Woodward led is discussed in Troen, pp. 174-180.

[48] "Vocation Versus Culture; Or the Two Aspects of Education," *Education* XII (December, 1891): 204-206.

[49] *Proceedings* of the National Education Association (1889): 98.

[50] John Dewey, for example, argued, as late as 1901, that manual training had a valuable role in every elementary school because children, according to the popular psychology of the day, were incapable of responding to more abstract intellectual demands. (John Dewey, "The Place of Manual Training in the Elementary Course of Study" [1901], in *John Dewey: The Middle Works, Volume 1, 1899-1901* [Carbondale, Ill., 1976], p. 235.)

toward which he had the responsibility to contribute as a representative of humanity. Unlike manual training, the study of any branch of mathematics (Harris took geometry as an example) resulted in an

> immeasurably higher feeling of self in the perception of the power of the intellect not merely to know passively, but to know actively, not merely to know the small portion of the universe presented to its immediate senses, but to know the conditions of all matter, near and remote, now, in the past and in all future time. What a glimpse of the dignity and commanding eminence of mind arises through the study of geometry!...Compare the feelings of selfhood that is gained by the soul in the use of the tools of thought with that gained by any form of manual labor.

It would be in providing this sense of selfhood that a traditional curriculum was invaluable. To Harris, selfhood was transmitted not through special methodology, employed to convince students they should learn, but through subject matter. Students who had gone through a program of rigorous intellectual training would be equipped to pursue valuable careers after formal schooling ended.[51] The industrial system was constantly pushing outward; if its growth was accompanied by a complementary network of schools, Harris believed, advanced opportunities would always exist.

That there was a self-defeating blindness in this view is perhaps unnecessary to point out. Harris had an ability to remain remarkably sanguine in the face of disasters that might be expected to raise troubling doubts in others. His annual reports barely took notice of the 1873 Depression and its effects. The faith in the nation's "boundless possibilities" noted in his 1873 report was unmuted in his report for 1874, the first he wrote after the depression began.[52] It seemed easy for him to neglect problems t hat would complicate the realization of the positive vision he projected. Class conflict, unemployment, strikes, the inequalities of wealth, ghettos and slums made no appearance in his writings.

The inability to take the dislocations of the new industrial world into account was especially serious when widespread economic distress generated new ways of responding to the schools. Harris had to incorporate the

---

[51] "The Psychology of Manual Training," *Education* IX (May, 1889): 571-582. Other important statements of Harris's ideas during this period are "What Shall the Public Schools Teach?" *Forum* IV (February, 1888): 573-581; "Excessive Helps in Education," *Education* IX (December, 1888): 215-221; "The Study of Arrested Development in Children as Produced by Injudicious School Methods," *Education* XX (April, 1900): 453-466. See also Harris's seventeenth annual report (1871), pp. 93-94.

[52] In the 1874 report Harris could note, with no reference to the recent economic dislocation, that "during the past twenty years, there had been an unparalleled growth in wealth and population, and still greater possibilities of commanding the services of nature." ("Annual Report of the Superintendent" in *Twentieth Annual Report of the Board of Directors of the St. Louis Public Schools for the Year Ending August 1, 1874* [St. Louis, 1875], p. 77. See also the *Nineteenth Annual Report of the Board of Directors of the St. Louis Public Schools for the Year Ending August 1, 1873* [St. Louis, 1874], p.56.)

new atmosphere into his thinking or find himself unable to maintain the credibility of his educational program. His arguments would be pushed aside, dismissed as irrelevant. Calls for a stepped up building program, a rejection of vocationalism, and a reaffirmation of the classical curriculum, critics could charge, might have made sense in the hopeful period after the Civil War. But to offer the same analysis and prescription at the end of the century only served to advertise how out of touch one was with the nation's real needs. New conditions called for a new response.

Yet it should also be noted that Harris was hardly alone. Few of the men entering educational work when he did believed that the problems spawned by industrialism could not easily be solved. A later generation, educated in the nation's new universities, might see the future more darkly. But for men who had reached maturity in the Civil War era, anything seemed possible, especially for a population blessed by universal schooling.

It was true that many of the champions of public education had risen without the benefit of regular schooling themselves. But they came to view the halting, start-over again quality of their progress, though personally rewarding as a mark of their ability to overcome adversity, as wasteful and inefficient. Somehow they and the rapidly growing communities they lived in had uncovered the skills and talents needed to move ahead. But who could say that others would always be as fortunate, especially when the pace of change had quickened so dramatically? Good fortune had to become routine, and the schools seemed the perfect agency for the task. If they played the role charted for them—in extensive, centralized, and systematized units modeled on the industrial machine they served—the future would be secure.

III

The connection between systematized schooling and ongoing progress dominated the views of school-builders throughout the 1870s, a decade that, marred as it was by depression and the century's most serious strike wave to that time, continued to maintain, and even increase, its investment in public education. During the period, the length of the school term and the number of teachers both kept pace with an increase in the number of pupils. Even during the middle, and most depressed, part of the decade expenditures remained high—compared to the drop that would begin to take place by 1880.[53] As the school promoter A. D. Mayo recognized in 1877, "With due allowance for the popular panic that always accompanies a season of 'hard

---

[53] See David B. Tyack, "Educational and Social Unrest, 1873-1878," *Harvard Educational Review* 31 (1961): 195-212.

times' in the country, the appropriations, State and local, for popular education have been remarkably liberal."[54]

Educators during the 1870s retained the confidence and hopefulness that motivated these expenditures. Only with the opposition that began to grow in the next decade would their tone acquire a new defensiveness. Before that, however, they remained optimistic, committed to earlier republican traditions of growth and increased public school investment. Even when they explored the ideas that new reformers advanced, most continued to affirm the need to provide all classes with the same education, one that would increase the productivity, inventiveness, and political understanding of the whole society.

Most schoolmen approached education as Harris and Mann did, by starting with the requirements of an expanding industrial order, and the responsibilities of the state to teach "knowledge of general application...for all classes of the young." Trade training, unlike the consideration it would receive in the 1880s and the 1890s, was still discussed with barely concealed scorn. E. E. White, the former Ohio school commissioner and current president of Purdue University, revealed the dominant predisposition of his fellow schoolmen. "Why," he asked in 1881, "should the value of the public schools to the great majority of its pupils be lowered to teach trades to a small number of young?" With opportunity so great, White could not understand why anyone but a minority—the service of whom, he believed, meant lowering the value of education—would be attracted to such studies.

For White, the young men streaming to the cities were not thinking in terms of the fixed jobs such training would prepare for, but of a desire to give up menial rural employment for new challenges. The prospect was very different from the feeling such a movement of population would later generate. White's remarks, filled as they were with a welcome of diversity and the chance to start over, made this plain. "How many different employments," he asked, reflecting on the growth of the nation's urban areas in much the same way Harris had, "have thus been created and what a multitude of desirable positions have thus been opened to American youth! Is it any wonder that the intelligent and ambitious have been attracted to them? Doubtless many a good farmer or mechanic has been spoiled to make a poor lawyer or an unsuccessful merchant; but, on the contrary, all the professions and all departments of trade have been enriched and vitalized by contributions of brain power and character from the farm and shop."

In this positive atmosphere it was only the "aristocracy" that opposed the expansion of the public schools. This group, made up, according to White, of men like Harvard's Charles William Eliot—a group that held

---

[54] A. D. Mayo, "The Assault on the Normal Schools," American Institute of Instruction, *Lectures* (1877): 29-44.

views directly contrary to those of William T. Harris on virtually every educational issue of the day—were convinced "that the masses are born dullards,...that all attempts to educate them are futile," and that "the few on whom God has bestowed the gift of brains are commissioned to do the world's thinking, and they thus monopolize the right to education." Such men, White said, "opposed the education of the people," whenever they could. As an example, he pointed to the recent depression that offered the members of this aristocracy "a coveted opportunity to renew their assault on popular education." Unemployment and business contraction "made the idleness of youth painfully evident and gave increased plausibility to the oft asserted opinion that popular intelligence is resulting in a growing disinclination among our youth to earn a living by hard work. The schools were assailed as the enemy of industry and labor, and even the ridiculous complaint of Bacon against the schools of the seventeenth century, that they 'filled the realm of indigent, idle, and wanton people,' has been made against the public schools of the United States."[55]

Contrary to the disgruntled few that White identified, most Americans of this period, especially those working in education, had a more genial sense of the future, a sense that it would unfold in a grand and dynamic way, challenging the creative energies of the whole society to keep the pace from slackening. Education had to act, not as a weight slowing this momentum, but as its stimulus. Expenditures had to be increased;[56] those who proposed cutbacks were dismissed without serious debate. Federal and state agencies, contrary to the advice of Eliot and his circle, had to take a larger hand in the work. If they did, said one schoolman who characteristically linked the future to the traditions of the nation's past, "the coming century will complete that system of beneficent oversight of the school which was contemplated by Washington."[57]

It was "an age of enthusiasm in education,"[58] one in which few questioned that "we must either move forward in this path which Providence has opened before us, or relapse into the condition of former and less-favored generations." To the man who wrote these words, and hundreds like him in school systems across the country, neither Malthusianism nor Socialism— both of which were recently being offered as solutions for the increase in unemployment and poverty—were possible to contemplate. Both would

---

[55] E. E. White, "The Relation of Education to Industry and Technical Training in American Schools," *Circulars of Information, No. 2*, U.S. Bureau of Education (Washington, D.C., 1881), pp. 7-21.

[56] W. F. Phelps, "Inaugural Address," *Proceedings* of the National Education Association (1876): 12-15.

[57] A. D. Mayo, "Demands of the Coming Century on the American Common School," ibid.: 28.

[58] Barnas Sears, "Fifty Years of Educational Progress," American Institute of Instruction, *Lectures* (1880): 110.

result in a scarcity and contraction that they were unwilling to consider. "Our humanity revolts," wrote an elderly Barnas Sears in 1880, "against the inhuman theory of Malthus,—death and starvation,—and our sense of justice, no less than of expedience, makes us averse to Socialism. The instincts of human nature are opposed to taking their earnings from the industrious and giving them to the idle." The way to alleviate poverty and unemployment was not reallocation, but economic and intellectual development. We should, Sears wrote, be "multiplying and expanding the branches of industry, and educating a larger class to practice arts hardly known to us now."[59]

At times other sentiments did appear. Some noticed the "lowering skies" that portended "evil times" for the schools. Some feared the influence of a narrow-minded minority of the wealthy who did not believe working class children "should receive much education, because they cannot see how such an investment can return a semi-annual dividend of 5%."[60] Others associated material well-being with mental sloth and attacked them both.[61] But these were asides, footnotes to arguments that moved in a very different direction.

It was a direction in which they continued to travel well into the 1880s. By then, however, a competing set of beliefs focusing on fears of disorder and the irrationality of human behavior, took on a new forcefulness. A sense of "crisis in our national existence" seemed more insistently to fill the air. An earlier, easier ability to believe in the harmony of classes had evaporated. Ominously, educators now were referring "to the prevalent contest between labor and capital," and the need for an education of "obedience, respect, and order." Such teaching would enable students, once they reached adulthood, to "stand as a wall against anarchy, Communism, and riot on the one hand, and the unjust aggressions of money on the other."[62] Apparently, teachers had to put their charges on guard against both workers armed with foreign ideas and a money power that readily neglected the niceties of capital accumulation and distribution. Both seemed ready, in their own way, to agitate and disrupt a society better left undisturbed.

In this atmosphere, discussions of social discipline were the order of the day, with National Education Association forums like the 1888, "How Can Our Schools Best Prepare Law-Abiding Citizens?" stirring up new interest. The phenomenon of children questioning received wisdom was

---

[59] Sears, pp. 80-112. See p. 111, in particular.
[60] A. P. Stone, "The Educational Outlook, and its Lessons," American Institute of Instruction, *Lectures* (1877): 52-56.
[61] H. P. Warren, "The Spiritual Side of the High School Question," ibid.: 35.
[62] See the speech of Topeka, Kansas Mayor W. H. Rossington, welcoming educators to the 1886 National Education Association meetings. (*Proceedings* of the National Education Association [1886]: 59-60.)

now not taken as a sign of inquisitiveness or curiosity, nor even of simple disobedience and recalcitrance but, as a number of writers variously suggested, of the future anarchist, murderer, horse thief, saloon-keeper, or machine politician. The latter two, along with the constituency of foreigners they fed on, were waiting to assume the management of public affairs unless an educated, disciplined citizenry was readied to stop them.[63] National prosperity, once seen as a laggard that could not come quickly enough, now appeared to have arrived too quickly; to many it was a curse as much as a blessing. The wealth of others prompted not only thoughts of new opportunities to be searched out but also thoughts of demoralization, corruption, and a spirituality abandoned.[64]

Manual and trade training also received more serious discussion. They were still far from encountering the welcome they would soon receive, but more and more educators agreed that many youngsters could benefit from their offerings. This was especially true, it was felt, of those prey to overwork, a result of efforts in the classroom futilely made to alter one's chance of rising in the social order.

Some, while admitting the enticements of the new programs, and also the changed conditions of American society that appeared to recommend them, still struggled to reaffirm an earlier faith. One schoolman expressed the assumptions competing for recognition in himself and others. "Have we ever had in America," he asked, "that spirit of oriental caste which would keep a rail-splitter a rail-splitter still? No, no; let every avenue of education be as open as the blue sky, and let every aspiring child determine by his own energy whether he will be merely the creature of circumstances, or whether he will exclaim, with the great Napoleon, 'Circumstances! I make circumstances.'" The fear that the avenues that led from almost mythological, backwoods starting points on the way to the apex of American life no longer existed had to be willfully and vociferously exorcised by pronouncing Napoleon's aphorism. Conscious articulation of the opposing tendencies of will and circumstances would make the young aware of the stakes. It would also strengthen the resolve to avoid becoming "the creature" of the latter.[65]

---

[63] See the contributions to the forum by Duncan Brown ("The Discipline Most Valuable to the End"), p. 104; and Joseph Baldwin ("The Culture Most Valuable for Educating Law-Abiding and Law Respecting Citizens"), p. 111. (*Proceedings* of the National Education Association [1888].)

[64] See John W. Cook, "The Schools Fail to Teach Morality or to Cultivate the Religious Sentiment," *Proceedings* of the National Education Association (1888): 128-130.

[65] George A. Littlefield, "Chief Needs of the Schools," American Institute of Instruction, *Lectures, Discussions, Proceedings* (1886): 53-54. Any annual meeting of educators in these years produced many contributions to the subject. See, for example, in the 1888 *Proceedings* of the National Education Association, articles by R. K. Buehrle, William E. Sheldon, J. M. Greenwood, J. Allen, and J. P. Irish.

By the mid-1880s the effort to rouse and stiffen the moral fiber of the young would hardly seem worth it. Instead, educators were admitting that the problems they faced might be too intractable to solve by moral calls to arms. Samuel T. Dutton, then superintendent of schools in New Haven (and later to move to Brookline, Massachusetts and Teachers College in New York), expressed the helplessness and foreboding to which many schoolmen were succumbing. There was virtually no place or no group to which one could turn with the assurance of finding stable, teachable populations. "Dangerous forces" and poisonous impulses, Dutton was convinced, "lie pent up" in almost every person's heart. "Look at our prisons," he said, "crowded not merely with the rank and file of the degraded, but with a large and apparently growing contingent of men and women decently born and bred!" Wasn't it clear that teachers had to "keep in mind the possibilities for evil that are inherent in every child, as well as the possibilities for good?"[66] The dimensions of the problem seemed to overwhelm him. "Whole families," he said, referring to the cumulative effects of crime and pauperism, "are so degraded that mental and moral recovery seems impossible....The turbid stream of poverty and ignorance, of intemperance and immorality, has persistently coursed its way down through the generations of the past, and today often threatens to overflow and carry ruin to the existing order of things."[67]

With the propensity for crime and evil so near the surface, with the area of criminality enlarged so as to now encompass (at least potentially) every member of society, educational measures once reserved for criminals could be given wider currency. Dutton argued that the old curriculum, "almost exclusively directed to the culture of the intellect," had to be replaced by a curriculum that placed greater weight on the manual arts, the studies proving to be the best "moral corrective" in reformatories, prisons, and schools for blacks and Indians (the "savage races").[68] Given what he took to be the

---

[66] Samuel T. Dutton, "Education as a Preventive and Cure for Crime," American Institute of Instruction, *Lectures, Discussions, Proceedings* (1886): 17-18.

[67] Samuel T. Dutton, *Social Phases of Education in the School and the Home* (New York, 1903; orig. 1899), p. 202.

[68] Ibid., pp. 116, 155, 160, 161. Some major change was clearly necessary for Dutton. The problems that youth faced were too serious; the opportunities of old seemed gone. Talking about the attempts of a young man to find work, Dutton noted how "comparatively helpless" he seemed. "There is no open door to the position he desires to obtain. The temptations to become a clerk or a salesman to an ambitious American youth are very strong. This leads me perhaps to the most serious count of all against our educational system, that it does not provide such trade instruction as enables the grammar school graduate to enter at once upon the pursuit of a handicraft. I need not enlarge upon the great and pressing need of trade schools. Social changes have brought the bulk of our population into cities, where every idle and shiftless member of the community is a menace to the public peace and welfare. It is indeed pitiful to see our young American men pleading for the opportunity to work, and yet failing to find employment because their hands are untrained." (Dutton, p. 161.)

barely controlled, beast-like nature of human beings, moral behavior was not likely to be affected by intellectual training. The "mere culture of intellect is hardly at all operative upon conduct," he wrote. "Education should be the development of habit; not moral conscience."

An education in habit for a life of habit. This was what Dutton expected many of the young to be facing, and the vocationally-oriented schooling that fit them for it would produce a remarkable change of social prospect. "When the youth is bred to honest industry," he wrote, "there is no congestion, no bilious insurrection, but rather free circulation to every member of blood purified in God's air and sunshine."[69]

IV

Within just a few years a new way of talking about the schools and education had appeared. Not that older emphases were completely overshadowed; they remained to compete for the attentions of the public and fellow schoolmen. Even so, they never carried the same weight of assent that they had earlier. Preoccupations had clearly changed, and not merely in response to immediate economic or social events. True, in the 1880s and 1890s, these events had been traumatic enough. But the older ways of talking did not reappear after the reaction to the disruptions of those decades had run their course. Instead, they became a side channel in educational thought, ready to enter the mainstream only under unusual circumstances.

Although Harris, in his 1898 report as Commissioner of Education, could look back upon the period since 1870 as one of great accomplishment—the number of children in public schools, he noted, had more than doubled and school expenditures had more than tripled[70]—the achievement had been compromised by the growth of serious opposition. The system of belief that, in part, had made the gains possible was becoming less and less able to defend itself against attack. The ground won earlier—on behalf of, at least, a potentially more democratic social and political environment—was being eroded. Patrician reformers, and then Progressives who gave the initial reform thrust a popular sound and mass appeal, were developing a new set of ideas.

Yet traditionalists who sensed the change were strangely inarticulate in formulating a response. Although they recognized that new opportunities somehow were disappearing and that traditional schools were woefully inefficient in preparing children for the ones that remained, they had little to say about the cause of the problem or how to solve it. The best of them, like

---

[69] Dutton, pp. 203 and 218.

[70] [United States Bureau of Education], *Report of the Commissioner of Education, for the Year 1897-98*, volume 1 (Washington, D.C., 1899), p. xii.

Harris, understood that something was very wrong, that the pace of the economic expansion they had taken for granted was slowing down. Unfortunately, they were able to do little more than wonder what had happened. Writing for a national magazine at the same time that he catalogued the end of century progress in education, Harris sought to sound a similarly reassuring note about industrial civilization's prospects in general. Workers (who had just gone through the harrowing Depression of 1893) need not fear their displacement by modern machinery. As human wants expanded, labor that had been well-schooled would easily be "readjusted"; it would "ascend from mere handwork to the supervision and direction of machinery, and to those employments requiring greater skill." In field after field, Harris showed how more and better jobs were being created. But a troubling note appeared at the very end of his piece. Everything, it seemed, was not as well as he had been suggesting. "Discontent" did exist "at the present time," and it "originates largely in the feeling that there is too much drudgery and too little time for science, art, literature, and the contemplation of ideals." Earlier in the article, discussing the appearance of vocations that "furnish amusement and recreation," he had also noted "a constant tendency to such diseases as result in melancholia." "The friction of life," he acknowledged, "is augmented; and life is shortened[;]...diversion to preserve the sanity of the individual" was a necessity.

These isolated statements were, however, as far as Harris could proceed. Beyond an insightful closing remark that "instead of coming too fast, useful inventions are not coming fast enough," he had literally nothing more to say.[71] He was troubled by the stagnation around him, worried about the swing to a labor-intensive, job specific vocational education that was well underway by the turn of the century. He understood that the battles of the 1890s, centering around the introduction of vocational education, had been lost, and that therefore the question of automation, the starting point for his remarks, would hardly be the problem. But with the statement that inventions were not coming fast enough, that progress, in effect, had slowed to a dangerous crawl, he was finished. He offered no speculation about why the situation existed (even though it would be one that would have a direct effect on the process of readjustment—always left vague in the article—in which he put such faith), or how it could be corrected. But without clarifying these questions he would be unable to defend a curriculum rooted in a belief in the universal value of the mind and its role as the driving force of improvement. He would be unable to convince others that the general skills that prepare the mind for creative activity were worth taking the time to acquire. Given the obstacles to survival facing a demoralized, disconnected

---

[71] William Torrey Harris, "Is There Work Enough for All?" *Forum* XXV (April, 1898): 224-236.

population, such an education only wasted time. Effort would be more profitably spent acquiring skills that helped one to find a secure, if less meaningful, slot in the contracting economy of the day.

This problem confronted all traditionalists who hoped to defend the growth of the schools, and their inability or unwillingness to deal with it was a large part of their undoing. As they soon recognized, without any ideas about how to restore the economic development they prized, they began to sound irrelevant. Reformers argued that a new, although slow-growing, industrial world, with extremes of inequality and a permanent working class, created new needs and interests in children. The situation, they said, required a new education to prepare each child for a "realistic" future. Traditionalists had little answer to these claims unless they could subject the underlying views that reformers held about the future to searching criticism. Were reform assumptions about economic growth justified? What educational and political implications did the assumptions have? Who stood to lose or gain if reform views took hold? But instead of asking the necessary questions, traditionalists sat helplessly as they watched what they considered to be the unchallengeable forces confronting them.

The way Charles A. McMurry discussed the growth of vocational studies at the turn of the century, provides a clue to their state of mind.[72] In a study of curriculum for the first eight grades, McMurry at one point let his deepest anxieties, expressed with a telltale passivity, come to the surface. In the midst of a discussion of the new subjects such as geography and natural science that had been entering the curriculum, he suddenly broke off as he recognized the dominating position that vocationalism (or manual training as he here referred to it) was coming to have:

> Out of all this [he said] is emerging the vague but gigantic form of a new study sometimes called manual training. It is now spreading its clumsy limbs somewhat promiscuously through the whole school course. No one seems to know as yet how large a place this intruder is to occupy, but a fear falls upon many that some of the old studies and teachers may have to move out of the way or shrink back into a corner to make room for this giant upstart.[73]

Thinking like this, marked by twin measures of awe and apprehension that completely dwarfed the intended note of superiority, would pose little

---

[72] McMurry was a leading member of the Herbartians, a group distantly descended from the German philosopher and educator Johann Herbart. Herbartians often criticized the methods of traditionalists, but always shared with them the belief that society's future needs were the starting point of the curriculum. Methods needed to change—to emphasize the growth of ideas in the child's mind—but Herbartians, like traditionalists, asserted that the teacher still had to concentrate on transmitting the humanistic core of modern culture, especially its central moral ideas. See Harold B. Dunkel, *Herbart and Herbartianism* (Chicago, 1970), especially chapter 8, "Psychology" and 9, "Instruction"; Dunkel, *Herbart and Education* (New York, 1969); and the early works of McMurry and Charles De Garmo.

[73] Charles A. McMurry, *Course of Study in the Eight Grades* (New York, 1906), p. 2.

problem for educators and their patrician sponsors who advocated the new doctrines.

Patricians had been spurred to action by the accelerating changes of the century's last decades. A maturing, indeed what now appeared to be an often overpowering, industrial system had created new centers of strength. Industrial magnates, willing to use their money to get favors from governments large and small, contended against workers, suddenly organized and assertive. Recurrent economic fluctuation led to new uneasiness about the possibility of avoiding debilitating instability and the dissolution of democracy itself. The surge of immigrants, more alien in custom and aspiration than earlier groups, led to other worries. Like industrialists and skilled workers, immigrants partook of an independent cultural life that gave them the strength to resist patrician appeals. It also helped them to develop their own approaches to power. In addition, the Republican Party, the traditional home of the patrician reformers, was becoming dismayingly receptive to policies that appeared likely only to push the nation further along the path they abhorred. Especially by turning, in 1884, to James G. Blaine, one of the most determined advocates of American economic expansion, the party seemed intent on ignoring patrician interests and preoccupations.

In the face of these provocations, it became clear that the moment for action could not be long delayed. Nor was it. Soon, in areas as wide-ranging as immigration restriction, civil service and taxation reform, commercial regulation, social work, conservation, and electoral politics, patricians began to assert themselves. Perhaps no area received more attention than education. Here, concentrated effort promised to produce the most long-standing results. To a greater extent than elsewhere, patricians believed they had found the way to regain the influence and attention that they had begun to fear could never be situated in their hands again.

They would gain control of the schools directly or, failing that, gain control of what the schools taught. They would use the schools to assert values that reaffirmed their own position and importance. This would mean discrediting an earlier set of assumptions connecting systematic education, intellectual development, and economic advancement. It would also mean discrediting the arrangements built on these assumptions. Over-built and over-organized, reformers would charge that the schools led to routine drill, uninspired teaching, waste and corruption.[74] New approaches, starting from new assumptions that dealt in the hard reality of funding and a reassessment

---

[74] A characteristic statement of this indictment is J. M. Rice, *The Public School System of the United States* (New York, 1893). See also the discussion of Rice's book in Lawrence Cremin, *The Transformation of the School: Progressivism in American Education, 1876-1957* (New York, 1961).

of actual need too often neglected by out-of-touch schoolmen, would be necessary. Traditional ways and traditional educators would have to be put aside.

CHAPTER TWO

E. L. GODKIN, PATRICIAN TUTOR: LIMITED GROWTH,
EDUCATION, AND THE DEFENSE OF CASTE

I

The defeat of a little remembered piece of federal legislation helps us to understand the new climate that traditionalists confronted. During the 1880s,
New Hampshire Republican Henry W. Blair introduced a bill in the United
States Senate that would have appropriated more than $77 million to
improve the nation's public schools. For the first time in the nation's history, federal aid would flow directly to the states, in amounts based on the
proportion of illiterates to the states' total population.[1] The formula was
intended to direct the largest portion of the aid to the South, where supporters believed it was needed most, but the overall intention was to benefit the
nation as a whole. In essence, Republican political leaders were attempting
to generate the human performance required to build a modern nation—the
goal first put forward during Reconstruction, twenty years earlier.[2]

Accomplishing this meant facing the question of how to prepare the
people of the South—whose poor education was yet another legacy of
slavery—so that it could profit from the industrial expansion that many
Republican leaders wished to make the center of policy. Industrialization,
these leaders believed, was the only way to eliminate the South's former
backwardness and the constraints backwardness imposed on the development of the nation as a whole.[3] A well-structured system of schools was
clearly part of any plan that might succeed, and Blair still hoped one could
be created. "Of all the old Reconstruction programs," Blair said in 1884,

---

[1] Robert L. Church and Michael W. Sedlak, *Education in the United States: An Interpretive
History* (New York, 1976), pp. 127-128; Daniel W. Crofts, "The Black Response to the Blair
Education Bill," *Journal of Southern History* 37 (February, 1971): 43-44, 55; Gordon C. Lee,
*The Struggle for Federal Aid, First Phase: A History of the Attempts to Obtain Federal Aid for
the Common Schools, 1870-1890* (New York, 1949), p. 158; and Allen J. Going, "The South
and the Blair Educational Bill," *Mississippi Valley Historical Review* 44 (September, 1957):
275, 289.
[2] Crofts, "Black Response to the Blair Education Bill": 43-44.
[3] See Blair's 1884 speech and the ensuing debate in the Senate in *Congressional Record*, 48
Cong., 1 sess., pp. 1999-2070 passim; and two other important speeches by Blair: "The
Common School Bill," in the American Institute of Instruction's *Lectures, Discussions, and
Proceedings* (Boston, 1889): 228-229, and *Address Delivered at the American Federation of
Labor Convention at Philadelphia, Pa., 1892* (New York, 1892).

educational legislation "alone commanded enough support, North and South, to stand a chance of passage."[4]

Far from being a partisan expedient as some have suggested,[5] the bill expressed much that was of continuing importance to Blair and his northern supporters. It was true that by the 1880s sentiment for reconstructing the South along industrial lines was waning. The rest of the nation, increasingly beset with its own industrial and labor problems, had both less willingness to expend its energies correcting the waywardness of the South and less desire to alter its agrarian orientation. The section, argued many who continued to think in adversarial terms, could be more useful as a raw materials supplier than as an industrial competitor.[6]

But some Republicans, still committed to prewar ideals and the central role of education in realizing them, were determined to promote a more inclusive vision of national growth, perhaps, they realized, for the last time. Too large a part of their careers had revolved around this vision to give it up easily, and even as they expressed frustration at being abandoned by former allies, they continued the fight to give it some tangible form.[7] And given the educational climate of the 1880s, the plan promised other benefits apart from its connection to Reconstruction motives. Blair may have sensed how his legislation might help schoolmen go beyond the constraining alterna-tives that were being presented to them in numerous local struggles to main-tain the funding and building levels of the past decades. Federal aid that made it possible to expand the nation's overall productive capabilities

---

[4] Henry W. Blair, "Conditions and Prospects of Temporary National Aid to Common Schools," in J. C. Hartzell, ed., *Christian Educators in Council. Sixty Addresses by American Educators with Historical Notes Upon the National Education Assembly...1883* (New York, 1884), pp. 42-43.

[5] C. Vann Woodward, *Origins of the New South, 1877-1913* (Baton Rouge, La., 1951), p. 64; and Going, "The South and the Blair Education Bill": 272.

[6] See Eric Foner, *Reconstruction: America's Unfinished Revolution, 1863-1877* (New York, 1988), esp. pp. 524-601; Going, "The South and the Blair Education Bill": 289; Woodward, *Origins of the New South*, p. 219, and his *Reunion and Reaction* (Boston, 1951); William Gillette, *Retreat from Reconstruction, 1869-1879* (Baton Rouge, 1979), xi; and H. Wayne Morgan, *From Hayes to McKinley: National Party Politics, 1877-1896* (Syracuse, N.Y., 1969), pp. 269-270. Some northerners who seemed to accept the South's transformation did so only on the condition that the black population have no part in it—it was to remain in the fields— thereby virtually guaranteeing the failure of any serious effort at development of this kind. (See the speech during the 1884 debate on the Blair bill by Democratic senator Daniel W. Vorhees of Indiana, in *Congressional Record*, 48 Cong., 1 sess., p. 2688.) And many in the South were less committed to the program than Blair and his northern supporters may have believed. Labor-intensive, extractive industry was the only kind introduced in the South to any substantial degree. See Jonathan Wiener, *Social Origins of the New South: Alabama, 1860-1885* (Baton Rouge, La., 1978); and C. Vann Woodward, *Origins of the New South*, pp. 140-141.

[7] See the portrait of the Republican leadership drawn by William R. Brock, *An American Crisis: Congress and Reconstruction, 1865-1867* (New York, 1963), pp. 93-94; and Church and Sedlak, pp. 125, 126, 143, 149-150. The frustration of abandonment can be seen in Blair's defense of his bill in *Congressional Record*, 48 Cong., 1 sess., p. 2100.

would also free those who shared the outlook of Mann and Harris from resistance they faced more and more often.

That the bill could pass the Senate three times in the 1880s was a sign that many agreed. Unfortunately it would get no farther. By 1890—as old southern agrarians, mainstream Republican leaders after 1888, and Mugwump-allied Republicans and Democrats in the North came together in opposition—it became a dead letter.[8]

To many observers the efforts of one leading Mugwump were particularly crucial in defeating the bill. The proposed legislation was the expression of everything that E. L. Godkin, the editor and virtual one-man voice of *The Nation* and the *New York Evening Post*, had spent his journalistic career fighting. Education and modern industrial growth were to be joined in a mixture that threatened to disrupt the decision-making prerogatives of the patrician elite he represented. To Godkin, a long-time foe if not of all industrial development then certainly of the part dependent on modern technology and the widespread social mobility it fostered, the bill threatened too directly to revive the leveling aspect of Republican free labor theory. If successfully implemented, it would help advance an integrated plan of national development that was certain to be no respecter of existing opinion or position. Godkin had long been pledged to defend both.

By 1886—with Grover Cleveland, Godkin's choice for president, well established in the White House, and with E. P. Clark, an aggressive new editorial writer on staff to run the campaign—his journals energetically attacked the bill in article after article. Collected under the title *A Bill to Promote Mendicancy*, they were sent, with an effect Blair admitted had great force, to all congressmen, major newspaper owners, and educators.

---

[8] Strictly speaking, the Mugwumps were Independent Republicans who broke with their party in 1884 to support Democrat Grover Cleveland for the presidency. Throughout this book, I have used the term somewhat more broadly—to stand for a group sharing a general outlook about society, politics, and culture. This is the group Hofstadter calls "men of the Mugwump type" (*The Age of Reform: From Bryan to F. D. R.* (New York, 1955), p. 139. See also John G. Sproat, *"The Best Men": Liberal Reformers in the Gilded Age* (New York, 1968), chapter 5, "The Myopic Mugwumps." For the story of the defeat of Blair's bill, see Lee, *Struggle for Federal Aid*, p. 158; Crofts, "The Black Response to the Blair Education Bill": 55; Going, "The South and the Blair Educational Bill,": 275, 289-290; and Stanley P. Hirshson, *Farewell to the Bloody Shirt: Northern Republicans and the Southern Negro, 1877-1893* (Bloomington, Ind., 1962), pp. 193-200. A few powerful free traders in the House—fearing that the measure would deplete the treasury surplus and fuel arguments for a higher tariff—apparently kept the bill from coming out of committee against the wishes of what Blair judged to be two-thirds of the House membership. The bill was also strongly opposed by the Catholic Church. The Church feared that the amounts funneled to northern public schools under the bill's provisions would strengthen them in a way that would soon undermine the entire role of the Church in the United States. This opposition was important (and Blair made a great deal of it at times), but it does not seem to have been decisive. See John Whitney Evans, "Catholics and the Blair Educational Bill," *Catholic Historical Review* 46 (October, 1960): 294-298; and Lee, *Struggle for Federal Aid*, pp. 122, 159.

Although Blair could maintain, in an 1892 speech to a sympathetic American Federation of Labor audience, "that the day is now at hand when those who have opposed the common school system will see a more excellent way," he also admitted, perhaps revealing how forced his optimism was, that the "mighty influences which combat and seek destruction of the common school system in this country" had been successful.[9] Educational debate had once revolved around questions of national development and popular aspiration. Now it had shifted to questions with a parochial focus dictated by the reduced expectations and retrenchment of the decades to come.

The latter were the themes that Godkin's journals made central to its case against the Blair bill. For *The Nation* and the *Evening Post* American strength and power relied not on investment and growth but on saving and sacrifice; not on the production of wealth but on the husbanding of scarcity; not on government assistance but on marshaling local and personal resources. Republican institutions and the well-educated electorate they were based on could come at too high a price. If purchased with the outside aid sure to foster dependence, neither was worth having. A "debilitating number of illiterates" might threaten "the very theory upon which our whole system of government is based," said one of the articles reprinted in the *Mendicancy* pamphlet, but the "demoralization" caused by watching others do work more properly one's own was worse. "Undoubtedly more Southern voters will be able to read eight years hence if the Federal Government extends $77,000,000 upon Southern schools, but the South can much better afford to have fewer intelligent voters eight years hence than to have purchased their education at the expense of its own self-reliance and self-respect."[10]

In fact, the article continued, introducing an argument that would become a favorite with southerners themselves, the southern states were

---

[9] *Address Delivered at the American Federation of Labor Convention*, p. 8. On introducing Blair and congratulating him on his recent reelection to Congress, Samuel Gompers said, "Your triumph is a compliment of the highest order, a vindication and an answer to the tirade of abuse heaped upon you by a malicious and ignorant press." For Blair's opinion of the importance of Godkin's *Evening Post* in particular, see Stanley P. Hirshson, *Farewell to the Bloody Shirt*, pp. 196, 200. Gordon Lee has offered this assessment of Godkin's role: "Undoubtedly the very severity and concentration of editorial attack upon the Blair Bill under Godkin's influence outweighed the less persuasive voices of the supporting journals. One cannot avoid the conclusion that with a Godkin favoring the bill the results might have been quite different." (*Struggle for Federal Aid*, p. 139.) Good examples of the uses to which Godkin's materials were put are the speech of Kansas Republican Preston Plumb in the 1886 debate on Blair's bill, in *Congressional Record*, 49 Cong., 1 sess., pp. 1699, 1725-1726, 2104, and the letter by Columbia College president F. A. P. Barnard, published in the literary review *The Critic* on May 29, 1886, pp. 265-266.

[10] *A Bill to Promote Mendicancy: Facts and Figures Showing that the South Does Not Need Federal Aid for Her Schools* (New York, 1888), p. 4.

taking up the burden. The number of children in school was steadily
increasing. Even though the South had a long way to go to reach the educational levels of the North (defined by attendance rates), it was already close
in some cases and ahead in others.[11] True, the South's educational system
had many defects. But an improving economy would soon eliminate them.
Then, with words intended to express its own position also, the pamphlet
quoted an ex-slaveholder and ex-Confederate soldier who explained what
improvement meant. Though deeply interested in public schools, the
southerner opposed national aid:

> You cannot *plaster* the South [he was quoted in the pamphlet] with this sys-
> tem. It is a growth, and its certain and healthy growth can only be secured by
> *each community providing for its own schools*. The Blair bill is simply, in
> another form, the old hallucination, "forty acres and a mule," which has
> caused more briers and sassafras bushes to grow in Southern fields than all
> else. (His italics.)[12]

Here was the epigraph for Godkin's entire campaign. For in a single
quotation, the pamphlet's source tied the legislation to one section of the
country exclusively; associated it with punitive, and widely resented,
federal measures felt to have been designed to maintain the area's inferior-
ity, and overturn its class structure by unfairly elevating former slaves; and

---

[11] As the *Mendicancy* writer's opponents would point out, this was not the point. For supporters of Blair's plan, the goal of the legislation was not to help the South approach or even
exceed the educational level of any northern state but to approach or exceed the level of the
most prosperous and, as one article in *Mendicancy* admitted unintentionally, that meant the
most industrial. See the speeches of A. D. Mayo and Senator Blair, *Congressional Record*, 48
Cong., 1 sess., pp. 2006 and 2147, respectively; and articles from the *Evening Post* reprinted in
Mendicancy, pp. 19 and 26. The articles in the pamphlet argued that the South was making
significant improvement if North and South were compared fairly. "The proper comparison,"
one article maintained, "is with thinly settled agricultural states, like Maine, New Hampshire,
and Vermont....Illiteracy has been avoided in these New England states by a school system no
better than that which many Southern States already have and which others will soon have at
their present rate of progress." But elsewhere, in discussing the kind of comparison that would
not be fair, another *Evening Post* article made a telling admission. It was obvious why a built-
up area like Massachusetts would have more wealth and more money to spend on its schools
than an area like Vermont—or the South: "The reason is of course because Vermont is almost
exclusively an agricultural community, while Massachusetts has diversified industries, a host
of cities and towns, and all of the aggregations of capital natural to a thickly settled state. The
South is almost entirely composed of rural communities like Vermont, and the argument for
the Blair bill from the South's valuation being smaller than the North's is as ridiculous as it
would be to say that Vermont cannot properly educate her children, as she has always done,
because she is not nearly so rich as Massachusetts."

What the article was saying, perhaps without realizing how it undermined the general case
that Godkin's journals sought to make, was that a state like Massachusetts had more money to
spend on its schools because it had more money to spend on everything. And it had this
money, as the article put it almost too positively, because it had "diversified industries, a host
of cities and towns," and large amounts of capital for investment. Massachusetts' schools were
better than Vermont's, and if not the *Evening Post*, many others, especially businessmen in the
South, may have been asking at this point, "How can all this be ours too?"

[12] *Mendicancy*, p. 4.

reinforced the provincialism that men like Blair were trying to overcome. In addition, the passage arrayed the idea of "growth," which it associated with the indigenous and normal, against development force-fed from outside.

The outlook could not have been more different from that of Blair and his supporters. Blair advocates still believed that the intellectual and moral level of all Americans could be raised significantly. Without such improvement a truly republican society could never be achieved. Steady, even spectacular, improvement was palpable to this generation of post-war leaders; fueled by the tie between increased intelligence and economic progress, experience had confirmed it for them again and again. Even as late nineteenth century Republicans tempered their optimism after the 1873 Depression with a new fear of uncertainty and instability,[13] they still retained their early sense that the process of growth had boundaries that could be pushed ever-outward. Until the accumulated shocks of the late 1880s and 1890s finally and reluctantly forced even the most committed to give up the idea, they continued to believe as they had before the war, that progress had limits only in the unrealized potential of the human mind, not in inherent obstacles posed by the environment.

But for men like Godkin (and the people who hung on his every word) this sense of limits was pervasive and inescapable. It was a corollary of their belief that a social and cultural elite was necessary to give tone and direction to society and receive deference and obedience from it. The two notions—of limits and of the need for a guiding elite—had always gone together. The association was especially obvious to those who relied on it to justify their claims to high position within the upper reaches of privilege in American life. Like the British aristocratic circles on which they liked to model themselves, they opposed the modernizing trends of the age—especially in politics and government promotion of an industrial economy.[14] Largely connected to what historians like Henry Steele Commager and William R. Brock have described as a tightly knit club of genteel patricians they were the men who

---

[13] Edward C. Kirkland, *Industry Comes of Age: Business, Labor, and Public Policy, 1860-1897* (New York, 1961), chapter 1, "Business Vicissitudes."

[14] Given their aspirations, it is perhaps not surprising that American patrician thinking about modernization—in which industrialism and technological innovation played central roles—bore many similarities to that of the British aristocracy during the same period. See Martin J. Wiener, *English Culture and the Decline of the Industrial Spirit, 1850-1980* (Cambridge, Eng., 1981); and Walter L. Arnstein, "The Survival of the Victorian Aristocracy," in Frederic Cople Jaher, ed., *The Rich, the Wellborn, and the Powerful: Elites and Upper Classes in History* (Champaign, Ill., 1973), pp. 203-258. On the British orientation of the elite, see Barbara Solomon, *Ancestors and Immigrants: A Changing New England Tradition* (Cambridge, Mass., 1956), pp. 16 and 57; Ronald Story, *The Forging of an Aristocracy: Harvard and the Boston Upper Class, 1800-1870* (Middletown, Conn., 1980), pp. 124-134; and Richard Hofstadter, *The Age of Reform: From Bryan to F.D.R.* (New York, 1955), pp. 139-140.

had gone to the best schools..., associated with the best people, belonged to the Century or Harvard Club, read the *Nation* or the *Independent*, and knew politics, for the most part, at second hand....They had the same abiding faith in the efficacy of moral sentiments that H.G. Wells ascribes to English liberals of the period in his *New Machiavelli*, and the English example was constantly in their minds. Good government, they believed, would follow axiomatically from the merit system and the participation of gentlemen in politics, and when they thought of gentlemen they thought of each other....They had no real faith in democracy, quoted Tocqueville on the tyranny of the majority, and distrusted the political party.[15]

By the early 1880s they had good cause to worry. The Republican party, under James G. Blaine's leadership, was more committed to doctrines of economic expansion pursued with government help than at any time since the Lincoln administration. In addition, the American people, shaking off the unsettling experience of the 1873 Depression, was throwing its support to such policies in growing numbers.[16] Patricians, feeling that the developing momentum might forever preclude an attempt to reverse the tide of national sentiment, threw their weight in the opposite direction. "Holding government to the noninterventionist line meant resisting popular pressure from many quarters," writes Brock of this group, "and there was thus a fundamental contradiction between the social philosophy of an elite and the demands of a democratic electorate."[17]

Economic change, especially if it occurred too quickly, disrupted established patterns of authority, released unmanageable expectations, and raised the potential for social dislocation to dangerous levels. At one time, writes Geoffrey Blodgett, the gentry elite may not have been alarmed by "the country's porous social arrangements." They believed that while "mobility at the bottom created problems...it oriented people at the bottom toward the top and kept them accessible to instruction from above."[18] Lately, however, these patricians were becoming prey to unsettling doubts. In an industrial economy characterized by both a tremendous capacity for productive output and frightening confrontations between capital and labor, mobility and high hopes in any form might be too dangerous to contemplate.

---

[15] Henry Steele Commager, *The American Mind: An Interpretation of American Thought and Character Since the 1880s* (New Haven, 1950), pp. 318-319. See also William R. Brock, *Conflict and Transformation: The United States, 1844-1877* (Baltimore, 1973), p. 445.

[16] See H. Wayne Morgan, *From Hayes to McKinley*, pp. 169, 223, 225, 232; Morton Keller, *Affairs of State: Public Life in Late Nineteenth Century America* (Cambridge, Mass., 1977), pp. 371-397; and Kirkland, *Industry Comes of Age*, chapters VIII, XI, XII.

[17] Brock, *Conflict and Transformation*, p. 445. See also Robert Kelley, *The Transatlantic Persuasion: The Liberal-Democratic Mind in the Age of Gladstone* (New York, 1969), pp. 300-301.

[18] Geoffrey Blodgett, "Reform Thought and the Genteel Tradition," in H. Wayne Morgan, ed., *The Gilded Age: Revised and Enlarged Edition* (Syracuse, N.Y., 1970), p. 60.

Politically, the sense of beleaguerment led these forces into an intensified defense of their position through a devotion to policies that strengthened the virtues of restricted development and, by extension, the value of minority stewardship. Development necessarily required the skill and educational levels that gave a population confidence in its own judgment and authority, in its own capability to make decisions about its best interests. Under such circumstances, the claims of the few to superior wisdom and morality would be more carefully scrutinized, more critically evaluated, and more effectively challenged. Development would breed conditions of intellectual awakening and power that would be an increasingly fragile base upon which to build claims to special leadership and elect status. According to the patrician spokesmen who addressed the problem, economic growth may have been an important element in the nation's past, but the faith that growth could continue at the same pace or with the same democratizing tendencies had no justification.

Contrary to the beliefs of perennially optimistic Americans, sharp limits to the extension of economic growth existed. No matter that this truth was not obvious yet. It soon would be, and much would be gained by facing the reality it portended early, however unpleasant it might be. Dwindling resources meant that the rising intellectual levels and deepening political involvement of the masses would not soon, if ever, come to pass; neither were likely in a society growing too slowly to call them into being. And without them, arguments put forward to justify the need for ongoing elite guidance might carry new force. The conservation of dwindling resources and the conservation of the dwindling esteem of an elite—a group with leadership abilities that now appeared to be in shorter, and hence more valuable, supply—were tied. The latter was as necessary as the former.

To help make these connections clear to Americans, especially to those who already shared the point of view and could be expected to support it, a publicity campaign would be of immense importance. Journals of opinion, the surer their grasp of the ground of values and assumptions to be secured the better, would play an indispensable role. Godkin sensed early what was required. Better and sooner than others, he understood the educational and moralizing function that such magazines could exercise; he supplied his with a consistency of focus, unwavering purpose, and acerbic prose that his competitors could only envy. Because he did, Godkin had a unique influence among readers seeking a guide to the political issues of the day. Over the course of his tenure at *The Nation* and the *Evening Post* (1865-1900), he helped shape an approach to reform that few Americans—including a remarkable number active in school reform—could fully escape.

II

Godkin was well-prepared for his journalistic and publicist labors. Born in Moyne, County Wicklow, Ireland in 1831, he was the son of a Presbyterian clergyman turned newspaperman. The father had lost his pulpit as a result of championing the cause of Irish home rule, and had become active operating newspapers in Londonderry and Dublin and serving as Irish correspondent for the *London Times*. Godkin also went into journalism after his graduation from Queen's College, Belfast. He first served as a war correspondent in the Crimea for the *London Daily News* and then on the editorial staff of Belfast's *Northern Whig*. Although a promising career appeared to lay before him—he was offered the editorship of the *Northern Whig* at age twenty-five—he decided to emigrate to the United States instead. He seemed to hope that he could achieve in America the social status and appreciation he doubted could be his in England.[19] He had already acquired the beliefs, attitudes, and tastes congenial to the English aristocratic circles in which he longed to travel. Perhaps in the United States he would be better rewarded for serving an American elite eager to exhibit similar attitudes and beliefs.[20] For close to ten years, Godkin bided his time writing articles on American life for the *London Daily News*, studying law, and making valuable contacts among important eastern Republicans. When these people, including, in particular, Boston Brahmin Charles Eliot Norton, founded *The Nation* in 1865 to put forward their ideas on politics and economics, they chose Godkin to be editor.

In *The Nation* and the daily *New York Evening Post*, linked to it in 1881, Godkin and the men he served had ideal vehicles. Both were virtual extensions of Godkin's thought, and as such became the indispensable guides to politics for a generation of disaffected Mugwump intellectuals and reformers. "Among many men who were young when the nation was young," wrote publisher Henry Holt, "Godkin was little less than the object of a cult." Norton wrote Godkin that he told his English friends, "Don't expect any more letters about public affairs from me,—I send you the *Nation* instead." Woodrow Wilson took detailed notes on Godkin's editorials while a student at Princeton, and William James wrote that, to his generation, Godkin "was certainly the towering influence in all thought

---

[19] See William M. Armstrong, *E. L. Godkin: A Biography* (Albany, N.Y., 1978), p. 187; Armstrong, *The Gilded Age Letters of E. L. Godkin* (Albany, N.Y., 1974), p. 384; Armstrong, *E. L. Godkin and American Foreign Policy* (New York, 1957), p. 15; *Dictionary of American Biography*, vol. 7, Allen Johnson and Dumas Malone, eds., (New York, 1931), pp. 347-350; and Robert L. Beisner, *Twelve Against Empire: The Anti-Imperialists, 1898-1900* (New York, 1968), pp. 54-55.

[20] Armstrong, *E. L. Godkin*, pp. 9-10, 12-13, 50, 64; and Armstrong, *Gilded Age Letters*, passim. See also James G. Murray, "Edwin Lawrence Godkin in the *Nation*: A Study in Political, Economic and Social Morality" (Ph.D. dissertation, New York University, 1954).

concerning public affairs, and indirectly his influence has certainly been more pervasive than that of any other writer of the generation, for he influenced other writers who never quoted him and determined the whole current of discussion."[21] British ambassador Lord Bryce's *American Commonwealth* was so greatly indebted to *The Nation* that he purposely refrained from publicly acknowledging Godkin's influence on him. He wrote Godkin that he wanted to dedicate his book to him but was afraid that "if I had said what I owed you in the Preface, you being the head and front of the Mugwumps and Reformers, those who are attacked in the book...would at once have said, 'this is an utterance of the Mugwumps; the Mugwumps have put up an Englishman to say this and that'...."[22]

Godkin's cultural, economic, and political outlook remained remarkably, and perhaps for his audience comfortingly, consistent throughout his editorial life. His laissez faire doctrines, his fear of, and disdain for, popular government, his belief in immigration restriction and Anglo-Saxonist imperialism,[23] his leadership of Republican mavericks, and his disgust with ward politics (expressed in particular by his fight to elect an anti-Tammany candidate in New York's 1895 mayoral race) were not lightly held. If anything, his positions grew more rigid and pessimistic as he grew older. There was little that Godkin witnessed as the late nineteenth century drew to a close to make him more sanguine than he had been earlier in his journalistic career. Given his starting point it could hardly have been otherwise. Like the group he spoke for, his fidelity to the twin notions that economic growth had sharp limits and that the nation's fortunes would be lost without an elite to guide it kept any hope he may have entertained of an improving humanity firmly in check.

Godkin's convictions about the finite possibilities for economic improvement stemmed from a deep-seated Malthusianism, a cast of mind he brought most sharply to bear when he considered the problems of poor and working people. Notwithstanding the years that separated them and the remarkable advances those years had brought, Godkin, like Malthus, believed that population would always outstrip the ability to provide for it adequately. As a consequence, the quality of life for most human beings

---

[21] Diana Klebanow, "Edwin L. Godkin and the American City" (Ph.D. dissertation, New York University, 1965), p. 2; Ralph Barton Perry, *Character and Thought of William James*, 2 vols. (Boston, 1935), 2: 291. In 1889 James had written to Godkin: "In the earlier years I may say that my whole political education was due to the *Nation*; later came a time when I thought you looked on the doings of Terence Powderly and Co. too much from without and too little from within; now I turn to you again as my only solace in a world where nothing stands straight. You have the most curious way of always being *right* [his italics], so I never dare to trust myself when you're agin me." (Perry, *Character and Thought of William James*, 2: 291.)

[22] Armstrong, *E. L. Godkin*, p. 95.

[23] Armstrong, *E. L. Godkin*, p. 172; and Armstrong, *E. L. Godkin and American Foreign Policy*, pp. 185, 190-194. For another view, see Beisner, *Twelve Against Empire*, chapter four.

was more bound to decline than rise. The gentry would do much better. Unlike the central tenets of mainstream Republican party doctrine, Godkin declared, for example, that the "labor problem" was insoluble. Defining the problem as that "of making the manual laborers of the world content with their lot," he concluded that "no discoveries nor [sic] inventions will ever solve it, as long as population continues to press close on the available products of human industry."[24]

His opposition to socialism, based on similar reasoning, provides another good example of his approach. Looking at the world as he did, he could not imagine how the increased costs of the programs socialists advocated would be met. His economic philosophy gave him no understanding of how production could be expanded to meet the new human needs that would arise. "It is quite evident," he wrote in 1894, "that when the change [to socialism] comes about, it will make a great increase in the mere living expenses of every civilized population, without any increase of income that I can see or hear of." Although he did agree that all previous social evolution had been accompanied by great productive and industrial advances, for unexplained reasons the process had suddenly ended.

One result of the halt was "the working-class trouble" that so agitated the public mind and made so many consider socialism as an alternative to current arrangements. This was easy to understand. "It is the workingman's want of money," Godkin wrote, "which makes him the object of so much pity, and dread, and speculation." But why did the worker "want money"? Godkin's reply was characteristic: "The answer is that he gets now all there is for him, and that, if he is to have more, it must come from some great and sudden increase of production unattended with any great increase of population." Godkin gave no details about why the shift, as he put it, from "a money-making to a spending evolution," was occurring. But in the next sentence, explaining his view that working class living standards might not easily be raised, he revealed his operating assumptions:

> The income of this and every other country in the world, since the plunder of foreign nations has ceased, is the product of its land and labor. Some of this income goes to pay wages, some goes to repair machinery and buildings, and some goes to pay profits to capital, or in other words, to reward men for saving or for supplying long-felt wants. Consequently, to do justice to the laborer and greatly increase his comforts, so that he shall be as well off as anybody else,

---

[24] E. L. Godkin, *Problems of Modern Democracy: Political and Economic Essays*, edited by Morton Keller (Cambridge, Mass., 1966; orig. 1896), p. 193. Godkin was not alone in being attracted to Malthusian thinking. As Lee Benson has noted, many people were interested in Malthus's ideas at this time. Most of this interest focused, however, on the implications for food production, not on the implications for controlling the demands of labor as Godkin did. See Lee Benson, *Turner and Beard: American Historical Writing Reconsidered* (Glencoe, Ill., 1960), pp. 59-60.

we must cut down the profits or interest on capital, or seize the capital, unless
hitherto unknown source of supply has been discovered.[25]

For Godkin, economic growth was explained without any consideration
of the role of new technology and scientific discovery in raising mankind's
productive output. His reliance on "land and labor" to account for economic
growth took little notice of the economic thinking prominent in nineteenth
century America. Especially interesting is Godkin's suggestion that past
development depended on the margin made available from despoiling other
nations. With the notion of capitalist production he held there was very little
else that could account for it. And he drew the right conclusion once he
established the premise: when the plunder ended, development would too.
The pessimism he drew around him was inevitable. Discounting the
possibility that mankind, by its application of new technology, determined
what counted as riches, he had to conclude that there simply was no hidden
"reservoir of wealth somewhere." So dismal were the prospects that not
even those who saw some grand leveling scheme as beneficial, based on the
discovery of "a new law of distribution," could come up with a believable
way to implement it. Even those so disposed had to make the discovery
"unnecessary by predicting a change in human nature which will make us
all wise, just, industrious, and self-denying."[26]

Artificial tampering with the actualities of human nature, however,
could never better the poor; attempts "to enable simple majorities to get at
people's property"—through organized political or trade union movements—would fail as surely as any action stemming from such low motivation must.[27] History proceeded according to natural laws; human intervention to alter their course would avail nothing. It says much about Godkin's
deepest preoccupations that he had a persistent knack for seeing interventionist attempts only as petitions for entry into social circles where their
promoters did not belong. No talk of political or economic dislocation dis-
tracted him at times like these. Time and again, he seemed most bothered by
the chance that those who championed some sort of government interference would delight in "bringing people together socially who do *not* live in
exactly the same way, do not belong to the same caste or circle or class"
[his italics]. With noticeable relief, he pointed out that not even in the most
democratic countries "has the workingman made his way as yet into any-

---

[25] *Problems of Modern Democracy*, pp. 230-234.

[26] Ibid., pp. 240-241. See also pp. 247-248.

[27] Of the efforts of the trade unions Godkin wrote: "The workingman may rest assured that
as long as the methods of Trade Unions are criminal and anti-social they will not permanently
or considerably improve their condition. These methods may now and then extend a temporary
and small rise in wages, but more than this they cannot do. They cannot raise the laborer in the
social scale. There is, in this world, no future for fraud or force." (*The Nation*, November 22,
1883, p. 448, quoted in Murray, p. 114.)

thing that can be called 'society,' that is, into any circle which gives 'social position.'" Legislation or force of arms were powerless to alter these realities—a good thing too, as the best expressions of social refinement, unsullied by foreign petitioners, represented for him the ultimate measure of social progress. "The difference between a lady's drawing-room full of guests," he said, "and a wigwam packed with squaws and warriors, tells better than even science, or art, or laws, or government, the distance the community has travelled in its upward course."[28]

Schemes like profit-sharing suffered from the same deficiencies. They too could do little, except for an "aristocracy of [labor,] talent and character," to raise the status of the worker. They would have such limited effect not because of the specific details of the plans but, again, because of inexorable natural laws. "We can no more by profit sharing," he wrote in 1889, "escape the working of the law of population on subsistence than we can by taking thought add one cubit to our stature."[29]

This outlook defined the boundaries of politics for Godkin. Politics became not the struggle to expand the opportunity of wider layers of the population, but the process of holding the wolf from the door. Anything less would not allow men to call themselves civilized; anything more would be a fruitless waste of energy. Appealing to the ethic of struggle, he wrote, "There is no doctrine with which the race is more familiar in practice than the doctrine that the strongest must have the best of it, which is really Darwinian doctrine expressed in terms of politics. The progress of civilization under all forms of government has consisted simply in making such changes in the environment of the multitude as will increase the number of the fittest." Given the assumptions that he brought to bear in such calculations, this number would always be limited—there would never be plenty enough to make competitive skirmishing unnecessary. The unfit could find no escape from doing battle with the fittest. But, Godkin noted, "any abandonment of the effort to protract their existence and make it more tolerable would mean the stoppage of civilization itself."[30]

Godkin took the opportunity of an attack on redistributionists to further elaborate his Malthusian vision. Unlike Horace Mann, who nearly a half century earlier had taken the same opportunity to advance a vision of perpetual growth and expansion, Godkin used it to make explicit his pessimism. The working of natural laws made it clear to him that the "dividends" that redistributionists proposed could not "make any material change in the condition of the great bulk of the population." With this Mann

---

[28] *Problems of Modern Democracy*, p. 248.
[29] *The Nation*, May 2, 1889, p. 370, quoted in Murray, p. 79.
[30] *Problems of Modern Democracy*, pp. 85-86.

would not have disagreed. But as Godkin continued, he revealed the gulf
that lay between them:

> There is no deduction from the operation of nature more certain [he wrote]
> than that the earth is not meant to afford much more than a fair subsistence to
> the dwellers on it. The mass of mankind have been poor from the earliest ages,
> simply because they multiply close up to the provision which the earth
> normally makes for them. They have always done, and probably will always
> do so, in every country.

The only answer to the dilemma, Godkin continued, seeming to move
toward the old Republican position, was to increase the productivity of the
planet. But the concession was more apparent than real for he maintained
that increased production had to occur "without any corresponding increase
in population, and without any abatement in the industry, enterprise, and
energy of the existing workers." Any other approach to the problem, such as
an approach that did not rely on an intensified physical output of the
workforce, would bring Malthusian law into play again:

> When we think of the enormous resources of the globe which are still
> untouched [he concluded], we are apt to forget that, in order to get at them, we
> have to go on breeding an increased number of men and women, who will
> keep alive, generation after generation, the old story of unequal and unjust dis-
> tribution.[31]

Godkin saw increased population as the source only of additional
mouths to feed. He also assumed that only existing, and according to him,
basically labor intensive, forms of technology were available to provide the
food that the masses would consume. Even more significant was his inability to imagine that this limiting condition could ever change. "Generation
after generation," he said, the old problem would continue. Not surprisingly,
he identified "resources" with simple extractions from nature, instead of
with the operations of man's intelligence and its transforming influence on
the world around him. For Godkin, resources were fixed and finite, like
hidden treasure that, once recovered by man, could never be replenished.

The problem was further complicated by the sense of expectation that
past changes had wrought. Americans had come to believe that boundless
opportunity was still within the reach of each of them. For Godkin this
meant that, contrary to the understanding of "educated men," "hope of
better things...has largely, among the working classes, taken the place of
religious belief. They have brought their heaven down to earth; and are
literally looking forward to a sort of New Jerusalem, in which all comforts
and many of the luxuries of life, will be within easy reach of all." Godkin
did not completely reject the value of this. On the one hand, he recognized,

---

[31] Ibid., pp. 204-205.

as did other "educated men," the world's need for a religion of some kind and, looked at this way, the religion of hope had its advantages—it made the working class "peaceful, industrious, and resigned under present suffering." On the other hand, such a religion also had its drawbacks. If the expectations religion released were not fulfilled, it could exacerbate the very problem it was intended to solve. In the end, he concluded, it was probably best to tell the truth and prepare the population for the worst.[32]

III

It was because of the population's unrealistic expectations that Godkin saw both the need to justify the existence of, and to project a special role for, an elite. Such a group, by virtue of its position and culture, was best able to provide the guidance and education that the people, especially the working classes, needed to face reality. Though they might find the role unpopular, here was a responsibility these "men of cultivation" were uniquely capable of discharging. To call them to their duty would be Godkin's special task.

Although Godkin often talked about the widespread preoccupation with material prosperity as the cause of American collapse,[33] it was the pursuit of wealth rather than its actual accumulation that he most often deplored. In addition to the belief that everyone had ability and could succeed, this single-minded fixation was a serious cause for dismay. Heedless of the laws of nature, most Americans ignored limiting conditions that were powerfully operational. With little justification, they believed that they actually could solve any difficulty they encountered. Such unwarranted overconfidence was the breeding ground of riot and confusion. "A society of ignoramuses who know they are ignoramuses leads a tolerably happy and useful existence," he wrote, "but a society of ignoramuses each of whom thinks he is a Solon would be an approach to Bedlam let loose, and something analogous to this may really be seen to-day in some parts of this country." Godkin then attacked those agencies of public education that nineteenth century school promoters, for example, thought so valuable. In contrast to someone like William T. Harris, he lamented the appearance of people who "under the influence of the common schools, magazines, newspapers and the rapid acquisition of wealth" felt they had attained all that any one could hope to in the areas of "social, mental, and moral culture." Without reason, they now felt competent to

---

[32] *Problems of Modern Democracy*, p. 206.

[33] The preoccupation was, he wrote, "now associated in people's minds with so much moral corruption that the mention of it produces in some of the best of us a feeling not far removed from nausea." (E. L. Godkin, *Reflections and Comments, 1865-1895* [New York, 1895], p. 279.)

tackle all the problems of the day...with supreme indifference to what anybody else thinks or has ever thought, and have their own trumpery prophets...whom they worship with a kind of barbaric fervor. The result is a kind of mental and moral chaos, in which many of the fundamental rules of living, which have been worked out painfully by thousands of years of bitter human experience, seem in imminent risk of disappearing totally.[34]

Godkin took it upon himself to speak for the guardians of this experience, and to tutor them in their responsibilities. The masses, heady with the supposed opportunities of a democracy, needed to be shown how to conduct themselves properly. Without this teaching, the traditions of order and stability, "the rules of living" of which the elite had special knowledge, would never be acquired. For Godkin, there was little time to lose. The destructive force of the masses had to be reigned in before the markers of gentility and position were obliterated. The way the masses "rush into the forum and into the temples and palaces and libraries," he noted, "is not an agreeable sight to witness, and it would be foolish to expect that under their ruthless touch many gifts and graces will not be obscured, many arts will not be lost, many a great ideal, at whose shrine the best men and women of three generation have found courage and inspiration, will not vanish from the earth to be seen no more."[35]

The "best men and women" possessed advantages that a society bent on avoiding extinction could scarcely neglect. Yet the advantages seemed forgotten by the post-Civil War generation of Americans. For them democracy still meant equality, Godkin wrote in 1869, but an equality that included little respect for the special minority he represented. "Privileges and privileged classes are gone," he wrote, and "society is hereafter to exist for the benefit of the many, and not of the few. But it sometimes looks as if in warring against them a spirit of disbelief in the value of things old, and of belief in the capacity of each generation to work out for itself all problems that may be presented to it, of whatever nature, had been developed, which if not resisted now at the outset, would assuredly carry us into some strange regions." But so important was the work of the privileged classes in resisting this flight that he would not accept their passing. If they no longer existed, it would be necessary to conjure them up. As early as 1867 Godkin was calling for "the creation, by some means or other, of an educated class amongst us, to be the guardian of the high traditions and feelings and aspirations of high culture and the diffuser of an atmosphere of thought."[36]

Godkin had not fully accepted the conclusion that the former keepers of the traditions he valued had become extinct. But he did view them as an

---

[34]*Reflections and Comments*, pp. 203-204.

[35] Godkin quoted in Beisner, *Twelve Against Empire*, p. 62.

[36] *The Nation*, May 13,1869, quoted in Armstrong, *E.L. Godkin*, p.98; and *The Nation*, February 21, 1867, pp. 151-152, quoted in Murray, p.84.

endangered species. At one point, defining them as the graduates of the "principal colleges," he noted the effect their disappearance would have on national life. "In no other way," he said, "could we make so great a drain on the reserved force of character, ambition, and mental culture which constitutes so large a portion of the national vitality." Godkin acknowledged that their numbers would hardly be missed at the polls, and that politicians would view their attempt to run a candidate for president as a huge joke. But if they ceased to exist for forty or fifty years, wide-reaching changes would appear. "The politicians," he wrote, "would somehow find that they themselves had less public money to vote or steal, less national aspiration to trade upon, less national forces to direct, less national dignity to maintain or lose, and that, in fact, by some mysterious process, they were getting to be of no more account in the world than their fellows in Guatemala or Costa Rica."[37]

Considering the invaluable role this "class of men" was called upon to play, considering the "common stock of traditions, tastes, and associations" it would be called upon to uphold, it was essential that, especially during the college years, it should "be educated together." For this reason, Godkin hoped to see a concentration of university training. Despite the claims of hometown boosters, smaller, locally-based colleges were inadequate to the task of preparing this group. The arbiters of America's tastes and values would come from among the graduates of higher education institutions that had a properly national orientation. These schools, not provincial colleges little better than high schools, had to receive them.

But this hardly meant that Godkin supported the idea of a national university or large, regional land-grant schools as they were being conceived in this period.[38] Ultimately, the determining factor in his support was not resources but values. Godkin wanted to be sure that the few institutions operating as national training centers could be certified orthodox on the basis of past performance. In essence, as he suggested in an article on "The Hopkins University," he wanted those who qualified to have a Harvard caliber education not because such schools had the best "professors, books, apparatus," but because their cultural orthodoxy and allegiance were assured. Money for education was too easily squandered if placed in the wrong hands. "To make the most of the resources of the country for educational purposes," he wrote, "it is necessary above all things that they should be placed at the disposal of those who have made education a special study,

---

[37] *Reflections and Comments*, pp. 157-158.
[38] See letters to Charles William Eliot in *Gilded Age Letters of E. L. Godkin*, pp. 200 and 202; and David Madsen, *The National University: Enduring Dream of the USA*, (Detroit, 1966).

and who are free...from any special bias or bond, and are ready or willing to look at the subject from every side."[39]

This was the kind of exposure required to produce the men of culture that would ensure the continuation of civilization. Of course, "in the nature of things," such an education could be accorded to only a select few. Denying the traditions on which the land-grant colleges were being built, Godkin argued that no one believed that these institutions "be allowed to exist only on condition that they will give a degree, or at least offer an education, to every male citizen of sound mind." Those who did have the opportunity for the kind of education he valued however (Godkin never discussed how this would be determined), "and can afford to take it, should get it, and should get it of the best quality."

Only a few could benefit from such teaching, and Godkin was frank in urging that those who could not be purged from institutions of higher learning. In support of his view, he cited John Stuart Mill's attack on the English universities. The latter, Mill had said, should be engaged in the work of "keeping philosophy alive," and should leave "'the education of common minds for the common business of life' for the most part to private enterprise." For Godkin, here was posed what he considered the most intractable problem faced by university reformers at elite schools like Harvard and Yale. These reformers had to decide "how to rid the universities, properly so called, of the care of the feeble, inefficient, and poorly prepared students, and reserve their teaching for the better-fitted, older and more matured; or in other words, how in the interest of both economy and culture, to reserve the highest teaching power of the community for the most promising material."

As usual in remarks like these, Godkin's fundamental assumptions came to the surface. Doubting that the resources existed to educate everyone who wanted to learn, he maintained that the resources that did exist be "reserved" for those who had already demonstrated, by prior commitment and intention, their "fitness" for the special kind of learning that should be found there. Lesser institutions existed in large numbers to provide the masses with the modest learning he suspected they would be content with. Any youth, Godkin noted, "who desires to learn a little mathematics, get a smattering of classics, and some faint notions of natural science or even to support himself by manual labor while doing this" could easily satisfy his meager ambition and exercise his limited talent at an ample number of local schools.[40]

A two-tier system like this also had another advantage. It minimized the otherwise risky possibility that the masses might be exposed to, and

---

[39] *Reflections and Comments*, pp. 160, 166-167.
[40] Ibid., pp. 168, 169-170, 171-172.

"dangerously stimulated" by, knowledge with which they were as yet ill-equipped to deal. This was especially true of the findings of science, an area Godkin saw ranged against "literature" and its aristocratic caretakers. Even though Godkin could dismiss most of those seeking scientific knowledge as "dabblers," he was not happy that their numbers—because of "the arrangements of one sort or another made by colleges and schools for scientific education"—would continue to increase. Granting that scientific training might improve abstract thinking, he also thought there was "reason to fear a considerable increase of dogmatic temper, of eagerness for experimentation in all fields, and of scorn for the experience of persons who have never worked in the laboratory or done any deep-sea dredging."

Science, Godkin did not doubt, had great value for humanity, especially "for purposes of legislation and social economy," but he could not help worrying about the "mischievous" effects of widening its audience too haphazardly, through popular lectures, for example. The "promiscuous crowds" of "small knowledge and limited capacity" that flocked to lectures had, after all, little reason to be concerned with such matters, Godkin concluded only partly in jest. "For what does it matter," he asked, "or rather ought it to matter, for social purposes, in what part of a man's system his conscience lies, or whether pressure on a particular part of the brain may convert him to a thief, when we know, as of experience, that the establishment of good courts and police turns a robbers' den into a hive of peaceful industry, and when we see the wonders which discipline works in an ignorant crowd?"[41] For Godkin, scientific knowledge unrelated to "social purposes," held little interest.

One might be tempted to think Godkin was speaking tongue-in-cheek if he did not make so many similar and non-ironic utterances to the same effect. The outlook was too consistent with the rest of his thinking to be unreliable. Here, as elsewhere, was the comfortable reliance on experience and the disdain for the theoretical (as in his association of laboratory work and deep-sea dredging). Here was the emphasis on application (especially in questions bearing, as above, on social order). And here was his contempt for the public's need to understand how scientific knowledge might contribute to solving more than immediate social problems.

This was especially true in relation to pure science, another area, like education, slated, as far as Godkin was concerned, to become the domain of the expert. It was either too abstruse an area to orient laymen to, or too unrelated to the historical and literary interests of a cultured elite. It was admittedly useful "as a field for mechanical discovery," but even this was no unalloyed blessing, resulting as it did in the "worship of material

---

[41] Ibid., pp. 136-137.

things."[42] Godkin cared little that this restrictive and narrow attitude had retarded development in the past. The latter might be just the chastening the population needed to return its sights to more appropriate goals and leaders.

Once again, Godkin's conclusion stemmed directly from the anti-growth premises that underlay his other opinions—on elitist higher education, on his doubts about true democracy, or on an educational system committed to raising the intellectual level of the whole society. It is perhaps the surest indication of his overall orientation. He saw science as an interloper, as an antagonist to established ways of communication and conceptualization,[43] and as a force disruptive of social order and social relationships, in particular those defined by the deference of one class to another. Science was too unsettling to be welcome for Godkin, unless it was kept under the watchful control of the responsible few. It was too much of an egalitarian force—private canons of literary taste did not enter into its judgments and private standards of evaluation were not useful in testing its findings. If too many wanted access to its method and a share in its expansion, the prerogatives and fortunes of an elite would quickly evaporate. The door to the future would be unlocked and every man would have the key.

IV

It was in controlling aspirations like those unleashed by science that education and the specialists to whose care its direction was entrusted had their role. Godkin subscribed to the doctrine he again may first have encountered in Mill. "It is not necessary," the British philosopher had written, "that many should be perfectly wise, that is, practically concerned with their own governments; it is sufficient that they be duly sensible of the value of superior wisdom."[44] The masses, not capable of wisdom themselves, must be trained to recognize wisdom and the fitness to dispense it in others. An education that improved this capability could only help, since some of the "wisdom" offered might not be what the population hoped to hear. Still, it was the special duty of the "educated man," the "critic...not open to the suspicion of particular interest," to pronounce it, no matter how unpopular it might be.

---

[42] Godkin, quoted in Beisner, p. 61.

[43] Godkin summed up the latter by the term "Literature," "the recorded experience of the human race and the recorded expression of human feelings." (*Reflections and Comments*, p. 136.)

[44] Murray, p. 87. The sentiment was common among the Mid-Victorian British. See Geoffrey Best, *Mid-Victorian Britain, 1851-1875* (New York, 1972), pp. 232-237. For a later period, see Barbara W. Tuchman, *The Proud Tower: A Portrait of the World Before the War, 1890-1914* (New York, 1966), chapter one, "The Patricians, England: 1895-1902."

An example of the required offering, said Godkin, was the idea that progress was the result of superior personal attributes and nothing else. Only a few could hope to develop those attributes, and those who could not had little choice but to accept an unfortunate but inevitable fate. Qualities like intellectual ability, thrift, and industry were the substance of Hope; "miracle or accident" figured only in a religion of ignorance. "The great law which Nature seems to have prescribed for the government of the world, and the only law of human society which we are able to extract from history," he wrote without noticing how the idea conflicted with his view of the qualifications necessary for entrance to the nation's elite educational institutions, "is that the more intelligent and thoughtful of the race shall inherit the earth and have the best time, and that all others shall find life on the whole dull and unprofitable." This was why the socialist movement, a favorite target of Godkin's, could not succeed. It attempted to contravene this law and guarantee a good time for everyone regardless of talent or character. But, Nature would not be frustrated, warned Godkin. The role of educated men—and the educational system that they dominated—was constantly to "call attention to this fact, that is, [n]ever cease to preach hopefulness, not to everybody, but to good people."[45]

For most of the population, it would be better to keep expectations and aspirations low. This was the perspective more in keeping with the day's realities, and Godkin became a booster of the educational program he felt could do most to advance it. This program was industrial education, a reform that, as we will see in the chapters below, became central to the efforts of the specialists soon to become prominent in educational work.

For Godkin, industrial education was the most important approach to the "labor problem." This issue continually troubled him and others who had come to maturity during the mass strike ferment of the 1870s and 1880s.[46] Given the importance of industrial education, funds for its development could be justified in a way he generally found inapplicable to expenditures for other municipal services. In Godkin's eyes, many municipal expenditures were grudging accommodations to necessity only. They had little value in advancing the social conditioning and disciplinary training he would rather have seen them used for, unless those purposes could be advanced by the threat of their withdrawal. This drawback did not attach to industrial education, and it therefore became an appealing object of reform. In a December, 1886 article on its benefits for young women in New York City (by the end of it he was also urging the virtues of industrial education

---

[45] *Problems of Modern Democracy*, pp. 207-212.

[46] See, in particular, the discussions of Felix Adler and Nicholas Murray Butler below, chapters four and five. On the events of the 1870s and 1880s so troubling to men like Godkin, see Nell Irvin Painter, *Standing at Armageddon: The United States, 1877-1919* (New York, 1987), chapters one and two.

for young men as well), Godkin showed how it could be used to carry indispensable social values.[47]

"There is something almost hideous," Godkin began, "in the mischief and waste of much of the education which is given at public expense to the children of the poor." He could not see how the daughters of common laborers and mechanics, who one day would have to make their own living, were taken "by the hundred every year" and carefully tutored in belles-lettres, music, and languages in preparation for entrance to a teacher training program. So excessive were the graduates of these programs that applicants for public school jobs outnumbered vacancies twenty-five to one. Godkin was sickened by the disappointment and bitterness this caused, and held the administrators of the public schools "directly responsible." Any young woman so deceived faced a grim future:

> There can hardly be a more miserable and helpless being than a female teacher, fond of city life, who can find no place in a common school. There is nothing else she can turn her hand to. She is a surplus member of one of the most overstocked professions, and she only knows enough to enable her to instruct those who hardly know anything at all.

These problems of superfluity and poor preparation were bad enough, but there was worse to come. Sounding like the antebellum novelists who saw the causes of social cataclysm in the most innocent moral transgressions,[48] Godkin continued to discuss the ripple effect that one child's misfortune had on everyone around her. Her falsely raised expectations had a variety of unanticipated effects. The family's standard "of food and dress and furniture is raised." They buy a piano. The parents, proud of their daughter's prospect of becoming a "lady," begin to spend more. The sons, if there are any, react to the new airs being put on by their sister by developing a disgust for any kind of manual labor; now they only "aspire to some kind of 'clerking,' or speculation...and it is well if they do not decline work altogether, and try to live in idleness 'off the old man.'" More and more, in the evenings, they talk about Gould and Vanderbilt and soon the "old man" has run into debt, thinking his daughters will help pay it off when they get places in the public schools. The end of the tale outdid even Timothy Shay Arthur or Catherine Maria Sedgwick for completeness and effect. For Arthur and Sedgwick, living in a society still unsettled enough to be without

---

[47] Eighteen eighty-six was a particularly disturbing year for Godkin's audience. During the spring, culminating in the "Haymarket Affair" in May, the United States experienced the most well-organized and widespread wave of strikes to that time. See Jeremy Brecher, *Strike!* (New York, 1972), chapter two, pp. 48-81; and Philip S. Foner, *History of the Labor Movement in the United States, Volume II: From the Founding of the American Federation of Labor to the Emergence of American Imperialism* (New York, 1955), pp. 93-132.

[48] See my *Country Boys and Merchant Princes: The Social Control of Young Men in New York* (Lewisburg, Pa., 1975), chapters six and seven, for a discussion of this literature.

the necessary restraining institutions, the first taste of sin, in whatever form, especially for those congenitally weak in character, inevitably led to full-scale disaster. And for Godkin also, the result was familiar. "Very likely, too," Godkin proceeded, speaking of the father, "he, in his extremity makes free with his employer's property, and gets turned adrift when the appetites of the young people for genteel life are fully formed."

Admittedly, the picture was not a pretty one. But Godkin, perhaps suspecting that its novelistic parallels were showing, vouched for its accuracy. "Such cases by the dozens," he assured his audience, "are within the knowledge of large numbers of our readers in this city." So numerous were the examples and so great the dislocation they represented that Godkin barely hesitated in asserting "that the education we give the daughters of the poor is one of the curses of our society." Instead of an education that could be useful to them, they were filled only with "delusion and prejudice." The education they currently received made sure that "few or none of these women learn, in their learning years, to do anything for the promotion either of their own material comfort or that of anybody else, or to follow any calling for which there is a real and growing demand." They could not cook, sew, wash and iron, or clean. Worst of all they could not "even think of learning" these skills. Their fate, as a result, was pitiful.

But Godkin was not writing to encourage sympathy for them; he was thinking of something else. If the plight of women like this was pitiful, he went on, "every taxpayer here helps bring it upon them." There was no reason for such expenditures to continue:

> It is true, and high time, that this most ridiculous and most un-American waste of money came to an end. Belles-lettres scholars ought not to be turned out at the expense of poor people who pay the bulk of the taxes. But even if they ought, the opportunity of industrial training—that is, of learning the arts which make life comfortable and convenient, for which the demand increases with the growth of wealth and civilization—should also be put within the reach of the children of the people. The clerical force, both male and female, of the United States is too large already. We have a super-abundance of teachers, and writers, and thinkers of moderate or no capacity. "Sales-ladies" are also deplorably abundant. But good seamstresses, housekeepers, cooks, laundresses, bakers, and good artisans of every description, both male and female, are scarce, and seem to grow scarcer in proportion to population. Oral laborers, in short, multiply apace; but the honest and excellent manual laborers, who can stand on their own feet and be the self-respecting and independent members of a free commonwealth, like the old New England mechanics, do not.[49]

Godkin had more than the specific problems of the economy, the workforce, or the curriculum on his mind. Certainly these problems troubled

---

[49] *The Nation*, December 23, 1886, pp. 517-518.

him. But they all pointed to a deeper set of issues. Once again, behind these specific concerns was the more familiar one of the social instabilities brought on by expanding expectations during periods of doubtful economic growth. Under conditions that Godkin and his friends judged increasingly to be the norm rather than the exception, existing institutions were too weak to help. In Godkin's tale, the authority of the family (personified by the father) completely crumbled under the pressure of dealing with needs totally foreign to it.

Furthermore, new institutions like the public schools, were not turning out to be fruitful substitutes. The schools were expanding but were misguided. With revenues and profits declining or unreliable, the impracticalities of belles-lettres could no longer be justified. An education of this kind benefited neither the people who paid for it nor the people who received it, as he had been at pains to show. And even if such an education had value, with the reduced funding available, a choice now had to be made. If life for all Americans could not easily be made better it could at least be "comfortable and convenient." Given present circumstances, such a life could be provided only by substituting industrial education for belles-lettres, a euphemism for the traditional common schooling that many mainstream Republicans still wished to expand.

The society of "old New England" was worth taking a lesson from. Its population had a self-respect and an independence rooted in a competence in traditional artisan skills. In the society of the 1880s such values and the old ways that bred them might perhaps have more relevance than they at first glance appeared to. In the old days workers seemed to know what they were capable of, and also what their limits were. They would not have thought of entering careers, those of "writers and thinkers," that were already the preserve of people with the proper cultural and social pedigree. These careers hardly needed new infusions in a period when the "oral labor" in which they specialized was not likely to reach expanded numbers capable of appreciating or assimilating it.

V

Dealing with problems of disciplining the goals of a growing, heterogeneous, and possibly refractory population led to a variety of approaches. Many of them depended on the proliferation of educational institutions of one sort or another, as recent scholars have noted. Yet there were other methods of compelling social assent at the disposal of men of influence. One of the most useful had traditionally been the power over finance, and Godkin urged its exercise for this purpose also. The extension or withdrawal of funding had always been a way for ruling circles to remind

the masses of their claims to, and hold on, power. Curtailing public spending was not just a way of promoting the self-interest of those who provided
the funds—in the form of loans to, for example, municipal governments—
and who, in times of instability, feared that a hoped-for increase of city
revenues to pay them back might not be forthcoming.

More important was the potential for social education that control of
municipal funding presented. Demands for austerity and retrenchment, far
from being "scientific" or "impartial" assessments of financial reality, were
a way of enforcing cultural and political commands, a way of promoting the
social policies that reinforced existing social relationships and routing. In
this case, education funds, in effect spent on raising the expectations of
working class children who had no reason to entertain them, were a waste of
taxpayer earnings. But funds spent on fixing these children in occupations
that did not challenge existing social roles, funds spent on fixing them in
occupations that took the pressure off a strained economic mechanism, were
wisely advanced. This is the context for understanding Godkin's interest in
municipal finance.

It was no accident that expressions of worry about New York's changing political and social conditions and expressions of worry about its financial condition surfaced together during the late 1870s and 1880s. By that
time the city was well used, in the words of a recent historian, to "serving
for its own as well as many other citizens as the epitomy [sic] of prodigal
misgovernment."[50] So it seemed to one concerned citizen, who in 1884
"pointed with alarm" at a New York City debt level that by the beginning of
the decade was larger than the combined debt of all major southern cities,
larger than that of all New England cities, and almost as large as the debts
of all western cities. The writer, like other long-established residents fearful
of the rising influence of immigrants and the unwashed in the city's
political life, attributed the problem to the fraud, graft, and patronage needs
of debased party machines, not the needs of a city that had grown phenome-
nally in the preceding fifty years. "How [the city] came to be what it is, is a
matter of history," he wrote in *Harper's*, "the story of official frauds, and of
the decline of public spirit, and of increased neglect on the part of the citizens, far more than of the increased needs of municipal expenditure."
Reform, undertaken by businessmen and others who could act responsibly,
was necessary in order to place "some check upon municipal expenditures,
of devising some fraud proof system in our municipal bureaus."[51]

Godkin, of course, had early felt the same way. "The purses of the rich
cities," he had written in 1866, "are everywhere passing into the hands of

---

[50] C. K. Yearley, *The Money Machines: The Breakdown and Reform of Governmental and Party Finance in the North, 1860-1920* (Albany, N. Y., 1970), p. 7.
[51] William Ivins, "Municipal Finance," *Harper's* 69 (1884): 779-784.

the ignorant, the vicious, and the depraved, and are being used by them for the spread of political corruption, for the destruction of the popular faith in political purity, for the promotion of debauchery and idleness among young men of the poorer classes, for the destruction of our system of education."[52]

The immediate target in these years was the political control, in the person of Boss William Marcy Tweed, that Tammany Hall had established. Through its neighborhood political apparatus and its attention to the needs of a swelling immigrant population—achieved in part by an impressive expansion of city services—it had built a powerful machine. But increased services meant an increased debt (from $67 million in 1870 to $87 million in 1871 alone)[53], and cries of debt and tax reform became a potent way to attack the power these elements had built up. Led by *The New York Times* and its editor, George Jones, worried locals soon began a campaign to tie the need for retrenchment and the corruption of the Tweed machine. Although Godkin played no role in bringing Tweed down, at Governor Samuel J. Tilden's request he did participate in a state commission inquiry into the "decay of municipal government," prompted in large part by the noise surrounding his fall. In 1877 the commission presented its report, the most significant part of which included a proposal for a constitutional amendment that would have prevented citizens without property from voting on municipal money questions.[54]

Both Tweed's downfall and the commission recommendation gave Godkin the opportunity to lay out editorially what was at stake. Tweed's nefarious career in government, Godkin wrote late in 1877, "should at least open the eyes of all loose talkers about natural rights and human brotherhood to the only possible practical effect of their *a priori* theories in a great commercial city." New Yorkers for too long had allowed the city's "paupers and criminals" (those whose interest in municipal government extended no further than fear of the police, a desire for free soup, or a city job) to have as much say in financial decisions as those who supplied the money. But this made no sense to Godkin. Clearly, only the latter were "likely to desire...economical administration." To give the responsibility for city spending to people who had nothing to do with acquiring the money and every reason to squander it would soon, he felt, "be looked upon in

---

[52] *The Nation*, October 18, 1866, p. 312, quoted in Armstrong, *E. L. Godkin*, p. 122.

[53] Critics, quick to point this out, neglected to point out, as has a historian sympathetic to Tweed, "that after Tweed the debt continued to rise. In 1874 it was $118 million, in 1880, $123 million, in 1890, $142 million, in 1896, $186 million. Population was then about 2 million [up from 1 million in 1870]. No one person or 'ring' was responsible. It was New York, a quality of life, population growth, industrialism, inflation, a host of factors." (Leo Hershkowitz, *Tweed's New York: Another Look* [Garden City, N. Y., 1977], pp. 170-171.)

[54] For background on Jones's role in the attack on Tweed, see Hershkowitz, passim; on the commission, see Armstrong, *E.L. Godkin*, p. 123; and Klebanow, pp. 122-134.

municipal affairs as the method of madmen, and any attempt to defend it as too irrational to call for serious discussion."[55]

A few months later, Godkin wrote in disbelief that the legislature had refused to vote even to submit the commission's proposal to the electorate. The commission simply proposed to do openly what many had already tried to do secretly. Its goals, in fact, were modest. The plan only sought to create a "better body" than currently existed to oversee city spending. "It would in other words...put the city treasury in the keeping of a board of citizens of character and repute, place it out of reach of the General Committee of Tammany Hall which is probably the most discreditable organization which has ever controlled the government of a civilized community, and is about as much influenced by universal suffrage or public opinion as King Koffee Kalkalli." It was true, Godkin went on, that even without passage of the amendment section restricting suffrage, the city would be prevented from running into debt for current expenses. "But," he emphasized, "the fundamental evil of municipal affairs would still be untouched—viz., the levying of enormous taxes, to be expended by a low class of officials in a wasteful and corrupt manner." The Tweed Ring did not create these evils but it rapidly aggravated them. Without the suffrage section, the Board of Finance would remain in an inferior position to the present Board of Supervisors or Board of Alderman. The likelihood was good that the Finance Board would end up being controlled by a "ring of jobbers...probably most of them without property, and animated by the contempt for property-holders which seems to be the latest fashion among American demagogues." The educational principle was perhaps the most important. The bulk of the voters had to understand that "municipal affairs are business affairs, to be managed on business principles." Only the restriction of suffrage to property holders and taxpayers could make this clear. Otherwise, the "resident" working class member will never understand why he should take more of an interest "in the proper conduct of municipal business than any tramp who begs by day and sleeps in the station house at night."[56]

A week after Tweed's death two months later, Godkin looked at the "great city problem" again. The problem was political in nature, and it attended the growth of all American cities. The influx of population that was responsible for urban growth "has had many of the characteristics of a plebs, and rapidly began to ask for leaders which should put it in the way of living off the rich without violating the law." The problem, of which Tweed's success was only the best example (of a leader who perceived "the work which this class wished to have done, and the first to discover the way

---

[55] *The Nation*, October 18, 1877, pp. 237-238; and see Armstrong, *E.L. Godkin, p.* 124.
[56] *The Nation*, February 14, 1878, pp. 108-109.

of doing it"), was that "by which the seeds of the communistic spirit which is now assailing the nation's finances was sown and is being steadily fostered."[57]

Godkin fused a number of important ideas here. Urban financial difficulties were a problem attending the growth of cities. More specifically, however, they were the problem of the political determination of a new class, one with an outlook conceived by Godkin, significantly, in a way that complemented his fixed resources and limited development assumptions. The new class, as he pointed out earlier in the article, was different from the traditional American working class that saw itself as the guardian of the public interest. Unlike this older group, the new class sought only to bolster its narrow, partisan interests; it hoped only for the chance to live off the wealthy, propertied members of society. Cities had not grown because of any productive contribution of these new members, but in spite of their depredations. Honest, industrious workingmen, he implied, would do well to ally with the groups committed to preventing the further excesses of these interlopers. If honest workers hesitated, the alien "communistic" notions of the new group would reduce not just the city's, but the nation's, credit to rubble. Perhaps because he had the national struggle over Resumption and the remonetization of silver on his mind, or because he viewed the cities' struggle as having national repercussions, Godkin extended his focus well beyond the local context that had first occasioned it.

Godkin understood that the power of the purse had important social uses. Credit institutions could be used to create or dissipate social and economic energy that determined the pace and nature of the nation's development. Questions of fiscal management and credit allocation were, therefore, always tied to issues of social policy. Godkin did not want the power tampered with, especially by a population with very different ideas about how financial institutions should be used.[58]

In this sense, the preoccupation with questions of finance and curriculum, often commingled in Godkin's thinking, flowed from identical sources. At bottom, Godkin was intensely worried about the forces he viewed to be remaking his world with terrifying swiftness. Through the extension and direction of credit, through the management of debt and the determination of the terms guaranteeing its repayment, control could be extended into even the private recesses of ambition and aspiration of those

---

[57] *The Nation*, April 18, 1878, p. 257.

[58] For competing conceptions of credit and finance, see the writings of political leaders and economists like William D. Kelley, William C. Elder, Stephen Colwell, Willard Phillips, Henry Carey, and John Rae. See also, Joseph Dorfman, *The Economic Mind in American Civilization, 1606-1933*, five vols. (New York, 1946-1959), 2: 566-574, 585-593, 771-826; and Sidney Fine, *Laissez Faire and the General Welfare State: A Study of Conflict in American Thought, 1865-1901* (Ann Arbor, Mich., 1956), pp. 14-18.

he held responsible. An individual's or a society's sense of possibility could be strongly influenced by a careful manipulation of the levers of finance, whether exercised on a national or local level. Opportunities once widespread could be extinguished; expectations once encouraged could be squelched. Through decisions seemingly scientifically and impartially arrived at, cycles of hope and despair, certainty and doubt could be set into motion. Amidst such fluctuating conditions, the hold that native-born and immigrant Americans had on the belief that their intelligence and skill made them indispensable to advancing their prospects and the nation's might be dislodged.

This belief, and not the background of the worker, was ultimately what separated Godkin's "traditional" working class from the "new" class he identified in his articles marking Tweed's death. The new class no longer seemed able or willing to accept a limited share of goods and services that, it had been told, were in short supply. It wanted more. But Godkin could not admit the possibility that the pie to be divided by all members of society could be significantly enlarged. Such an admission could only unleash the democratizing aspirations he feared, and he instead saw the demands of the new class as an attack designed to reduce the accumulations of its host. Although Godkin's charge that the working class was out to plunder the rich had little literal accuracy, it did embody a large measure of psychological and political truth. And in these areas, any reduction of power could not be easily ignored. A loss of control might never be regained; the habit of authority might never be recovered.

CHAPTER THREE

PATRICIAN REFORM AND TRADITIONALIST
REACTION IN BOSTON:
CHARLES FRANCIS ADAMS, JR. AND JOHN PHILBRICK

I

Among those who looked to Godkin, there was wide recognition of the connection between educational reform and the achievement of broader political objectives. This recognition was especially evident in Boston where school reform engaged the energies of one of the nation's most prominent Mugwumps, Charles Francis Adams, Jr. For him and his fellow Brahmins, education was part of a wide-ranging campaign to retain the influence they thought properly belonged to them and their class. The pervasive reach of the schools—through control of curriculum, large budgets, and the authority that school administration conferred to speak out on other monetary matters, like taxation reform—might allow gentleman reformers like Adams to press a collection of social claims that otherwise seemed to be going into eclipse. Facing an opposition that, while politically sensitive, too often had only an indistinct sense of how best to repel patrician reform thrusts, Adams's group had a forum to demonstrate how much influence they might yet secure.

Adams had eminent Mugwump credentials. He had attacked railroad speculators like Jay Gould and politicos like the Tweed Ring; he had acted to curb the excesses of railroad development by serving on Massachusetts' Board of Railroad Commissioners and as chairman (through the influence of fellow Mugwump Carl Schurz) of the government directors of the Union Pacific Railroad; he had written widely on electoral and civil service reform, free trade, taxation questions, and immigration restriction; and he had left his early political home in the Republican Party to vote for Tilden in 1876 and Cleveland in 1884.[1]

Like his other political allies, Adams had good reason to focus reform attention on the schools. School reform was both a way of regaining the

---

[1] "Charles Francis Adams, Jr.," *Dictionary of American Biography*, volume 1, edited by Allen Johnson (New York, 1928): 48-52.

political influence that the men of his circle sought,[2] and of reintroducing the values and ideals they felt a rapidly industrializing America was otherwise relegating to oblivion. Adams understood not only the role of the schools in reorienting opinion but also the value of the attention that was paid to them. "The common schools," he said in 1880, "are the one thing in regard to which there is no division of opinion in America. The people...cling to them and lavish appropriations upon them in the firm belief that they are the ark of the national salvation."

That fact had far-reaching implications. For, it was clear to Adams, whoever was in a position to determine what these schools taught, would determine "the destinies of the continent."[3] As a result, he and others like him became involved in a two-pronged effort to reorganize the administration of the schools and to provide them with a new curriculum. Boston was the city into which his efforts spilled from their point of origin in his hometown of nearby Quincy. Along perhaps with New York, Boston was the place where Mugwumps were best organized, and the reform activity and debate there provide a good example of the strategy and outlook that would characterize patrician-led reform work elsewhere.[4]

In Boston, reformers mounted criticism both inside and outside the common school system. Accompanying their moves to reduce the number of school board members and to introduce a new level of administrative personnel, reformers used the magazines of middle class gentility, local newspapers, and school reports to saturate the area population with their point of view. At the same time, they were also moving to revise the city charter, a change that would reduce the patronage and partisan activities of the entrenched Democratic machine.

In 1879 and 1880, Adams set the tone and style of the educational campaign in a series of articles he had gathered into a pamphlet extolling the innovations wrought in Quincy, and in an address to the National Education Association calling for professional university training in peda-

---

[2] Although it was his brother Henry who, as early as the Civil War, said, "We want a national set of young men like ourselves or better to start new influences not only in politics, but in literature, in law, in society, and throughout the whole social organism of the country—a national school of our own generation," the sentiment could have been attributed to Charles as well. See Geoffrey Blodgett, "Reform Thought and the Genteel Tradition," in H. Wayne Morgan, ed., *The Gilded Age: Revised and Enlarged Edition* (Syracuse, N.Y., 1970), p. 57.

[3] Charles Francis Adams, Jr., "The Development of the Superintendency," *Proceedings* of the National Education Association (1880): 72.

[4] For details of the campaigns that they undertook in both cities, see Michael B. Katz, "The Emergence of Bureaucracy in Urban Education: The Boston Case, 1850-1884," Parts I and II, *History of Education Quarterly* 8 (Summer and Fall, 1968); Diane Ravitch, *The Great School Wars: New York City, 1805-1973* (New York, 1974); and Sol Cohen, *Progressives and Urban School Reform: The Public Education Association of New York City, 1895-1954* (New York, 1964).

gogy and administration. Perhaps these efforts could help hold the line against the changes in power and influence he abhorred.

For Adams, these changes were many, and they had early made him feel that he would never find a comfortable place in American life. Though his dread of failure never became quite the reality he imagined it would, especially as he cast around for a career after an uncommitted performance in the Civil War, he never felt easy about the renown he achieved. The well-paying work he took as Union Pacific president, as head of the Kansas City stockyards, or as an adviser to the state and federal government gave him little satisfaction. He always hated the materialism of the "coarse, realistic, bargaining crowd" around him, and looking back on his years in corporate life, he is said to have "resented every minute he had dutifully spent as a man of action in industrialized America."[5] Out of step with the present, he seemed much happier spending time exploring the past and writing historical accounts of his family and its early pre-industrial locale. Especially later in his life, as a member and then as president of the Massachusetts Historical Society, he was able to devote more and more of his time to these pursuits.

Men who presently acted with the push and drive of his forebears elicited no respect from Adams. He could never believe that he shared any common ground with them, even as he too often made his money in the same kind of speculation he denounced when they did it from Wall Street.[6] If the mobility and egalitarianism of the late nineteenth century brought these men to prominence, then mobility, egalitarianism, and the society that valued both could hold little attraction for him. Writing in 1869 from the Anglo-Saxonist perspective that pervaded the thinking of many New England patricians,[7] he gave early voice to what would become a recurring disappointment with the "philosophers of the school of material progress," this time for welcoming another group he disdained—the cheap immigrant labor that was building American cities, railroads, and factories. For Adams, those who promoted the immigration of cheap workers seemed to pay no attention to the requirements of morality or the "emphatic lesson" of social science, "that the accumulation of wealth is not the loftiest end of human effort."

Welcoming the immigrants (including, apparently, blacks also) by giving them the vote was the particular worry he addressed in his essay. Discussing it, he moved from social to political analysis, from the dangers

---

[5] Barbara M. Solomon, *Ancestors and Immigrants: A Changing New England Tradition* (Cambridge, Mass., 1976), pp. 27 and 30.

[6] Edward Chase Kirkland, *Charles Francis Adams, Jr., 1835-1915: The Patrician at Bay* (Cambridge, Mass., 1965), p. 77.

[7] See Solomon; and John Higham, *Strangers in the Land: Patterns of American Nativism, 1860-1925* (New Brunswick, N.J., 1955).

of moral corruption to fears of the loss of power and a sense of being hemmed in on virtually all sides by alien forces. The result of giving the vote to what amounted to unprepared outsiders would mean "the governance of ignorance and vice:—it means a European, and especially Celtic, proletariat on the Atlantic coast; an African proletariat on the shores of the Gulf, and a Chinese proletariat on the Pacific." Adams feared that unless access of the proletariat to the ballot were restricted "the purity and significance" of the elective system would be destroyed. Viewing the proletariat as "the organization of ignorance and vice to obtain political control," he argued that an educational test of some kind was the best means to contain its influence. "If universal suffrage," he concluded, "inevitably tends with an advancing civilization to bring about such a vicious combination [political control by ignorance and vice and the destruction of the ballot's integrity] then no one who believes in a Social Science as applied to the study of permanence in free institutions, can place any faith in that form of suffrage. The tendency of the day is clearly, in a wrong direction."[8]

These attitudes explain in part Adams's continuing involvement in public life in the family home in Quincy. In the late 1870s and 1880s, Adams served on a number of town committees, concerning himself, in particular, with the schools, taxes, and the reform of the town meeting. In the mid-1880s, just before he would describe the innovations he and his brother John had introduced (such as those relating to town finance) as having broken down "under the pressure of the labor and communistic elements"; just before he would describe the immigrant newcomers who forced through new wage and hour regulations as "young, vulgar, badly dressed, of the hoodlum type" (they also forced Adams to stand in line to vote in town elections), and as "apt to be round-shouldered and hollow-chested, thin and long-limbed"; and just before he would note that Irish Catholics "instinctively sided against all settled political traditions," he would talk about Quincy in tones less of anachronism than of fantasy. "There is," he said, "stability and permanence in the town which in America is not always seen."

> It adheres to the ancient ways. The inhabitants yet meet in their own hall and manage their own affairs as their fathers for generations before. And just as, a century and a half ago, John Quincy by common consent presided over each town meeting that was held, so now does a descendant [John Quincy Adams II, Charles's brother] five generations removed but still bearing his name. Never in the history of the town were those meetings more orderly, more intelligent, or more prone to do right.[9]

---

[8] "Protection of the Ballot in National Elections," *Journal of Social Science* I (June, 1869): 108-109.

[9] Kirkland, *Charles Francis Adams, Jr.*, pp. 153-154.

It is difficult to call this picture anachronistic because the town it described never existed in a country changing as fast as the United States; the static relationships he spoke of bore little resemblance to late nineteenth century American towns. Still, these were the qualities he hoped to bring to life, at the very least, in the backyard of his ancestors. Control of the schools was one part of the effort he undertook.

In 1872 Adams became a member of Quincy's school committee, and took up the duties of school visits, selection of teachers, and annual evaluation of the schools' work that by 1875 convinced him that far-reaching changes, centering in the office of superintendent, were necessary. In the articles and addresses that he wrote and made in the next five years, he described the benefits that the innovations had produced. A new superintendent, Francis W. Parker, had been hired and given new powers. Adams, identifying the themes that would be embellished by others who took up the battle for school reform in the decades to come, discussed the problems that could now be remedied. Adams focused on the "mechanical" nature of the schools, so systematized that they had "fallen into a rut" providing only "smatter, veneering and cram." In addition, and a matter of decisive importance for him, was the problem of cost. The schools, as presently run, were wasting a tremendous amount of money. Adams, like other gentleman reformers he knew, was determined to put a stop to it.[10]

As we have seen in the case of Godkin, raising questions of education and financial circumspection together often had a common political root. The men and women of Adams's circle were bothered not so much by the fact that they were paying, in the form of increased property taxes, for services that they and their families were not likely to use.[11] Instead, they were more concerned that rising service expenditures indicated a radical shift in the realities of, and hold on, power. Certain that the money appropriated could not be used to raise the cultural and material levels of a population inflated by recent immigrant infusions, they feared that it was funding the political machines that upstart groups, relying heavily on immigrant support, were putting together. With the base these machines were establishing, the deference and leadership patricians usually took for granted was

---

[10] "The New Departure in the Common Schools of Quincy," appears in a pamphlet (Boston, 1879), p. 33, of the same name.

[11] Education in the common schools, for example, would only put Adams's circle in contact with the working class that they did their best to keep distant from. Adams probably reflected the attitude of others he knew when he wrote in his autobiography: "The common schools my father did not care to send his children to; and I have always been glad of it. I don't associate with the laborers on my place, nor would the association be agreeable to either of us. Their customs, language, habits and conventionalities differ from mine; as do those of their children. I believe in school life; and I believe in the equality of men before the law; but social equality, whether for man or child, is altogether another thing." (Charles Francis Adams, Jr., *An Autobiography, 1835-1915* [Boston, 1916], pp. 15-16.)

being openly challenged. It was no accident that Adams, and his younger brother Brooks in particular, looked to the reform movement as a way to hold back a tide they viewed with growing alarm. Though education occupied them most, for related political reasons they were also interested in other parts of the reform movement as well.

One of these was library reform, an address on which seemed relevant and important enough to include in the pamphlet collecting Adams's educational utterances. Though perhaps less emotional and weighty an issue, with far less money and far fewer voluntary patrons at stake, library reform related directly to work with the schools. Library reform reinforced Adams's other arguments about the feasibility—indeed the advantages—of cutting costs in education. The savings were not only of monetary, but of ethical, currency.

In discussing the reading habits of the young—"I care nothing about the adults," he asserted, apparently having given up on them—Adams struck a characteristic moral pose. "Since the days of long-continued famine suddenly came to a close, some fifteen years ago," he said, referring to the end of the Civil War, we "have been passing through a period of indiscriminate indulgence. We have been abusing our plenty. We are now just beginning to doubt whether this excess of liberty does not verge on license. Presently we will conclude that it does, and then a reaction will set in. The world always moves in this way." What he proposed, in an effort to make the public library "an active influence in our educational system," was the preparation of annotated catalogues of popular non-fiction reading that would make holdings in the areas of biography, history, travel, and science more accessible to the town's children. Adams foresaw possibilities for great savings, "both of labor and money." In the first place, it would be possible for other towns to use the same catalogues. Since only standard works would be included, the titles could be "kept permanently set up" in print, and it "would merely be necessary to reset the shelf numbers to adapt the pages to any library." In the second place, it would demonstrate how much "more important and valuable [a] factor in popular education [it was] than the whole high-school system, which now costs us so much and in my opinion, accomplishes so little."[12]

This kind of sensitivity to cost naturally spilled over into the movement for tax reform (or rather tax reduction) that had its beginning in this period also.[13] Brooks Adams was only the most vocal of patricians who, in the late 1870s and early 1880s, tried to direct the middle class forces that began

---

[12] "Fiction in Public Libraries, and Educational Catalogues," (1879) in *The New Departure in the Common Schools of Quincy*, pp. 29-30.

[13] See C. K. Yearley, *The Money Machines: The Breakdown and Reform of Governmental and Party Finance in the North, 1860-1920* (Albany, N.Y., 1970), chapter one; and Charles Phillips Huse, *The Financial History of Boston, 1822-1909* (Cambridge, Mass., 1916).

calling loudly for cutbacks in municipal services. In a series of articles for the *Atlantic Monthly*, he pointed out how every state, city, and town he could think of was living beyond its income and falling deeply into debt. A system of excessive taxation (for municipal services) was simply not suited to the hard times that the nation had just come through. No doubt, he granted, "unavoidable misfortunes have caused much of the discontent which is daily breaking out in riots, in socialism, and in efforts for repudiation [of existing debt, especially in the South]; but much is certainly due to the suffering caused by unwise, excessive and unnecessary taxation." The answer was simple, and Adams stated it bluntly: Boston, and other cities like it, should stop borrowing and pay cash.[14]

Then, in an implicit attack on the new political alliances that Adams held responsible for increased municipal spending, he developed an analogy that revealed how out of touch he was with the problems faced by the rapidly growing cities of late nineteenth century America. "Nothing can be plainer," he exclaimed, "than that Boston has no more right to lay out parks, to build expensive school-houses and to broaden streets than a man with a declining income and a heavy debt has to buy a yacht, fast horses, and a house at Newport, because all these things would certainly give him pleasure and might benefit his health." The services necessary to maintain the very existence of a city like Boston as a viable, habitable entity Adams compared with the symbols of a hedonist who refused to give up "pleasurable" but superfluous luxuries. The only way to save the situation was the "scientific" management of the debt, akin to the "splendid success of the system of common sense" then in use in England. He was not at all surprised that America had riots, socialists, and repudiationists. "The wonder is not that people have been restless under this terrible and needless strain, but that the country has not been plunged into a convulsion that would have shaken it to its center" (p.457). Budget cuts, it seemed, would both reduce the debt and help restore the discipline, by encouraging the building of character, on which survival depended. In the process, it would help keep intact the social fabric that then seemed so close to tearing.

II

The object of the educational "experiments" at Quincy dovetailed closely with these tax efforts. They were meant, above all, "to secure, if possible, a thoroughly good common-school education at a not unreasonable cost."[15] For Charles Francis Adams, Jr. achieving good education centered on the

---

[14] "Abuse of Taxation," *Atlantic Monthly* 42 (October, 1878): 453, 456.
[15] "New Departure in the Common Schools of Quincy," p. 31.

school superintendent. It was from him that he hoped would emanate "the spirit necessary to any permanent improvement" in a teaching force that had grown tired and stale. In this one reform, which Adams would make the centerpiece of his soon-to-be nationwide campaign for university-based superintendency training, could be fused both aspects of his hopes for economy and quality. The hiring of one inspired administrator could make up for the inability or unwillingness to hire a well-trained, well-paid, or inspired teaching force.[16] The argument he developed had more than local significance. The promotion of the superintendent was a way to reduce costs generally, and to undermine the existing, even if weak, independence of teachers and the political machines that often stood behind them.

The superintendent was to play a role very different from that envisioned by an earlier generation.[17] Noting that the annual cost of educating each child in the town had, in the ten years before 1873, increased from six to fifteen dollars, Adams pointed out that

> to secure the services of a better grade of teachers, those qualified to give a direction of their own to their instruction,—men and women of ideas, of individuality, as it is termed,—would have necessitated a general rise of salaries which would have increased the annual cost from fifteen dollars to at least thirty. *This was out of the question* [my italics]. The burden on the tax payer was already heavy enough. Even education can be paid for at too high a price, and it is useless to have model schools if no one but the tax gatherer can afford to live in the town which supports them. The only other way to improve the system was to concentrate the directing individuality in one man, and trust to him to infuse his spirit into others. One man the town could afford to pay; twenty men it could not afford to pay.[18]

With this innovation the schools for the first time in a long while could be transformed into institutions that would nurture, not stifle, "individuality." System would be dispensed with; "machine-process" and arbitrary time-tables would disappear. Instead, classrooms would begin to follow the urgings of "natural processes, which have forever been going on before our eyes and our families," and the curriculum, formerly characterized as "tedious," would become "full of life and interest." Adams, it seemed, was no longer speaking about "secur[ing]...a thoroughly good common school education at a not unreasonable cost," as he was earlier in the article. The changes he envisioned, he now wrote, amounted to "a complete

---

[16] For an account of how Adams's plan was put into practice, see Michael B. Katz, "The 'New Departure' in Quincy, 1873-1881: The Nature of Nineteenth Century Educational Reform," *New England Quarterly* 40 (1967): 3-31.

[17] The discussions in Stanley Schultz, *The Culture Factory: Boston Public Schools, 1789-1860* (New York, 1973), pp. 145-53; and David Tyack, *The One Best System: A History of American Urban Education* (Cambridge, Mass., 1974), pp. 40-45, 76-77, help clarify the contrasting conceptions.

[18] "New Departure in the Common Schools of Quincy," p. 35.

negation of the whole present common school system." Whereas traditionalist support for the old system was "founded on faith in the infinite capacity of children to know at an early age a little of everything," Adams's
Quincy committee proceeded from very different assumptions. For the
latter, "utility was the one and only end which should always be kept in
view." The committee felt that the curriculum "should be so pursued that it
may result in something of direct use in the ordinary lives of New England
men and women." The success or failure of the new departure he outlined
was "to be measured by what it actually accomplished in that way, and by
nothing else."[19]

In the first essay of his pamphlet Adams had made clear that only a few
students would require anything more. Speaking to the Norfolk County
school committees association, he compared the schools to a mixed area of
vegetables and woodland, hoping that the former would be "not mere fields
in which you turn out regular crops of human cabbages and potatoes, but
they should be plantations also in which you raise a few trees, at least, in the
individual growth of which you take a master's interest." There was always
the chance that others might follow the lead of the few ("human beings are
always and everywhere like sheep, in that they will go where the bell-
wether leads"), but the feeling that made a teacher's life "ennobling" could
only be "the finding out among his pupils those who have in them the
material of superior men and women."[20]

At the end of his talk to the association, Adams returned to his worry
about costs. Even if improvement was apparent, the all-important question
was after all, "At what money cost was it bought?" As far as Adams was
concerned, "If it involved a heavy addition to taxes, no matter how great the
improvement" it was none the less a failure. The common school system of
Massachusetts was "in very great danger of crushing the community it was
meant to protect....It has already been suggested that there is such a thing as
taxing a community to death, and it is quite apparent that the recent ratio of
increase in taxation for school purposes, will, if it goes on, soon afford in
the case of Massachusetts a practical illustration of the process" (p.11).

Like Godkin's approach to fiscal questions, Adams's was also dominated by social goals. Rising taxes, a process which the patricians often
found themselves unable to control as tightly as in the past, was a phenomenon that brought home sharply how far their power and influence had
eroded. Control of the purse strings was a long-standing means of chan-
nelling the political aspirations of groups that might otherwise forget to

---

[19] Ibid., p. 43. The policies that these ideals led to in Massachusetts are described in Marvin
Lazerson, *Origins of the Urban School: Public Education in Massachusetts, 1870-1915*
(Cambridge, Mass., 1971).
[20] "The Public Library and the Public Schools," (1876) in *The New Departure in the
Common Schools of Quincy*, pp. 9-11.

show respect for their "betters." Calls for belt-tightening, or reminders that flush times had a way of coming to an abrupt end were, therefore, warnings for a community to adopt a recommended social, as well as financial, posture before it was too late.

It was from this standpoint that Adams advanced his administrative changes. It was clear that in larger cities like Boston the patronage dominated "committee system...is wholly outgrown." It should long ago have given way to nonpolitical commissions made up of professionals who understood the scientific basis of education. School committees were the focus of intrigues, slow-working, and costly. Although Adams admitted that "our people have a democratic, and perhaps, healthy prejudice against commissions," the fact was, he noted, that "they come to them at last." "Though no one has yet uttered the word, it is probably not unsafe to predict that the next interest to be entrusted to them for development will be the common schools of our larger cities."[21] Adams no doubt wished that the battle to follow—to dismantle constituency-based school committees— would be as easy and proceed as logically as he hoped he made it appear. Instead, it would turn into a protracted conflict between forces fearful of losing their old prerogatives and those fearful of losing the new found power with which their constituency and ethnic-based politicking had endowed them.

The commissions Adams proposed would become the stronghold of the educational specialists well-trained in the methods of efficient and economical management. Unfortunately, these supervisory personnel did not yet exist; the professional schools needed to train them had never been established. Normal schools, coming as they did from a different educational tradition, could not be expected to do the job that Adams had in mind. Their function was far more simple. "They supply teachers, and they have their hands full doing that," he said. Teachers had a modest role to play anyway. Unlike the future superintendent, they did "not need to have the enlarging influence of an entire liberal education....The professional teacher of the common school...must be a person contented with the smaller prizes of life."[22] For the superintendent, the situation was different, however. Given the influence he would exert, a special course in educational institutions was essential. Without it, attempts at an "organized superintendency" would certainly fail. Yet it was on the success of this new position that Adams and other reformers pinned their hopes to enlist the schools in the political counterattack they were planning.

In July, 1880 Adams took his case to a wider forum, the National Education Association's annual meeting in Chautauqua, New York.

---

[21] "New Departure in the Common Schools of Quincy," p. 49.
[22] Ibid., p. 50.

Although he added little of substance in this speech, he sharpened his indictment of the "old system" and the educators that perpetuated it. The schools led to pedagogical incapacity and purged children of originality. They saw children as sub-humans kept in line, despite a sickening dislike of school, by semi-military methods, more appropriate to the regimentation endured by factory workers, inmates of the state's model prison, and monkeys in the zoo. Teachers and old-line supervisors were self-satisfied, plying students with the "useless cramming" that was the only method they knew. Again asserting education's claims to scientific status, he urged the new generation of superintendents, and by implication the teachers they would soon influence, to enter into the modern spirit he advocated by becoming followers of Francis Bacon. Presumably, he hoped they would adopt a more narrow empiricism consistent with the posture being struck by New England Brahmins active, like Adams himself, in both the American Social Science Association and in proposing a more practical course of study.[23] The child's mind was a living, growing organism not a plastic mass; the best education followed the child's process of assimilation. Once again he argued that a corps of scientifically trained superintendents was necessary to introduce these ideas, and maintained more strongly that university level training was necessary to turn them out. Only with such training would the superintendent's office gain the professional status—and the authority that went with it—to get the job of reform done.[24]

The issue for him went beyond matters of science and educational method, however. "The question I am discussing," he said, "is politically of the most far reaching consequence....The question is how to impart to the average human mind in the mas [Adams apparently wanted to extend his concern with economy to orthography also] the greatest possible amount of training, at once elementary and useful, in the least possible time and at the minimum of cost" (p. 73). Placing limits on time and cost changed the issue from education or pedagogy to politics, and Adams knew he had to defend his plan on these grounds. Professional training for supervisory personnel

---

[23] The American Social Science Association, according to Thomas Haskell, was an organization to provide gentry like Adams and their spokesmen in intellectual and university circles with a forum for "accumulating and systematizing" the knowledge by which "the alarming new social tendencies of the age [after the Civil War could] be confronted and made humanly tolerable." The organization was not very scrupulous about hiding the class bias of the opinions it offered, however. The organization's charter (as quoted by Blodgett, "Reform Thought," p. 73) for example, "stressed the 'responsibilities of the gifted and educated classes toward the weak, the witless, and the ignorant.'" By the last quarter of the century, it began to lose credibility as a source of authoritative information. As it did, a younger generation of members abandoned it, turning to the new universities as an alternative. (Thomas Haskell, *The Emergence of Professional Social Science: The American Social Science Association and the Nineteenth Century Crisis of Authority* [Urbana, Ill., 1977], p. 86. See also Haskell, pp. 65, 120-121; and chapter 6 below.)

[24] "The Development of the Superintendency," pp. 67-71.

was one answer reformers were urging. To extend the existing system—by organizing it into a county system, with a central administration—"means simply more mechanical organization,—a further infusion into our schools of the spirit of the factory, the rail-road and the state prison" (p. 76).

Unfortunately, feared Adams, the universities were not listening; without them, places like Quincy would remain isolated and the victory it represented would remain unconsolidated, easy to ignore. "The tendency is always backward, into the surrounding ruts,—old, worn, and hard." Reform had to be institutionalized or its force would be dissipated, its influence diffuse. "There being as yet no provision for the constant supply of men trained to carry on this work," he said, "the movement such as it is, is, for the present local, spasmodic, and unreliable." Speaking like a strategist mapping out a long campaign for his lieutenants, he pointed out that "it is an advance by points, not along the line; and the ground gaind [*sic*] is never secure" (p. 73).

III

The keepers of common school traditions in Boston did not let Adams's criticism pass unnoticed. They recognized that his attack would compromise their organizations, their resolve to resist subordination, and their understanding of the inheritance of republican education. By virtue of his long service as Boston superintendent (1856-1878) and of his national reputation (he would write a major study on the nation's school systems for the Bureau of Education in 1885), John D. Philbrick was considered the leader of these forces. It fell to him to answer Adams's charges.

This answer is important not so much because of its specific denials—its dispute of Quincy's uniqueness, its denunciation of the method Adams advocated as a throwback to more primitive educational times, or its refutation of the findings of the Walton report, upon which Adams had based his indictment. Instead, Philbrick's answer is important because, ultimately, it also posed the issue—though in a veiled and incomplete way—as a political one. Philbrick too understood that issues of power and influence lay behind discussions of schools and curriculum.

Philbrick was probably very little surprised by Adams's foray, having locked horns with Boston reformist circles a year earlier. By the time Philbrick answered Adams, that battle had been won by the traditionalists—though only for the time being. They had succeeded in installing their own candidate as superintendent after years of wrangling with a reform-minded school committee led by Adams's younger brother, Brooks. Philbrick, who had written a series of articles in the traditionalist *Journal of Education*, had been instrumental in the victory, and had no intention of watching its significance diluted by allowing the credibility of one of the reformers' most well-known voices to remain unchallenged. Philbrick correctly saw Adams and his Boston coterie as allies in a fight that extended beyond the boundaries of the city and its suburbs.

During the Boston fight Philbrick had denounced the reformers' innovations for what he took them to be—school dismantling in the service of political retrenchment and alliance with the city's most backward ele-ments—the Irish.[25] Schoolmen like himself had worked too hard to stand by idly as the system they had built over the past twenty five years was, as they saw it, razed virtually overnight. Yet contraction of the system was what reformers, led by Brooks Adams, in control of the school committee, had proposed in a series of reports released in 1879. Among the proposals offered were recommendations to abolish the kindergarten and the interme-diate schools, reorganize and centralize the high school system, eliminate special instructors, and prune the curriculum of unwanted subjects. "By the end of the year," notes one historian, "the board reported with pleasure that it had already reduced per-pupil spending in Boston, the highest in the nation, and expected the decrease to continue."[26] Most significant were the recommendations calling for ending the supervision of the primary schools by the grammar school masters, and for replacing them with a newly elected group of supervisors. Samuel Eliot, member of the old Brahmin family and the new superintendent who had defeated Philbrick for reelection in 1878, welcomed the changes and predicted their success. As Michael Katz notes, "Reform required not only new curricula and more charismatic personnel but also a massive redistribution of power and influence. To effect such redistribution was the purpose of the removal of the grammar masters from the primary schools."[27]

Philbrick entered the Boston fight with a response to an article by Francis W. Parker, the Quincy superintendent hired by Adams in 1875. Parker, in calling for an invigoration of teaching as the next stage of educa-tional progress, denigrated the more institutionally-focused achievements of the "conservative" schoolman. "He graded, organized, ventilated, pro-grammed, found comfortable desks, got apparatus,—in fact, against great opposition *organized the machine* [his italics]," said Parker. Then, referring

---

[25] On this alliance, see Geoffrey Blodgett, *The Gentle Reformers: Massachusetts Democrats in the Cleveland Era* (Cambridge, Mass., 1966), chapters three and six in particular.

[26] Michael B. Katz, *Class, Bureaucracy, and the Schools* (New York, 1971), p. 86.

[27] Ibid., p. 88. To Philbrick, writing in the late 1870s, the scheme to replace the masters by new supervisors was a plan only to "take charge" of the schools not to upgrade them; it was a plan to usurp the authority of the superintendent and to interpose a new and confusing level of administration between him and the teachers. "The New Departure," *New England Journal of Education* V (January, 1877): 9-10. A more temperate indictment of "The New Departure" appears in Philbrick's *Thirtieth Semi-Annual Report of the Superintendent of the Public Schools* (Boston, 1876), pp. 104-111.

to Philbrick, he went on, "Whatever we may say of Boston's old and faithful leader, however much he seems swallowed up in the self-satisfaction of the past and its glories, we gladly bear witness that he did a work which has made an advance all along the line possible."[28]

Doubting that Parker's reference to him was "altogether in the very best taste," Philbrick disputed his implied charge that "the perfecting of the organization of school systems is a line of activity inferior in importance to that in which he is himself so prominently engaged,—that of teaching and directing instruction in the classroom." There was no point in establishing a hierarchy of educational work. Honoring the classroom teacher did not make it necessary "to disparage the importance of a good *system* [his italics] of schools." While there was no question that improved teaching was important, it was not the "only thing to be done." In addition to having good teachers, he noted, "very important work is to be done in 'organizing the machine,' before the educational millenium will come in this Commonwealth, and by this I mean something more important than the furnishing of school houses, or the making of programs,—I mean the creating and perfecting of instrumentalities of progress."

Horace Mann had not become a renowned educator because of his attempts to clarify teaching method or publicize his achievements in his annual reports. Instead, said Philbrick, Mann was remembered for his institution-building, for "what he did in creating and improving parts of the system." And to guarantee that institution-building, better teacher training, more competent inspection, and state-wide superintendence continued, sufficient funding, provided by a new state tax, was required. Instead of spending less money as the reformers were urging, it was necessary to spend more.[29] Here was a way not only to reverse the dismantling of the school system, or the other retrenchment drives (most of which came together in the tax relief movement) that reformers were pursuing. It was also a way to counter the assumptions on which they were based. High living did not demand the corrective of austerity.

As if to reinforce the anti-tax reform thrust of Philbrick, the next issue of the *Journal* (edited, with A. D. Mayo, by another tireless school promoter, Thomas Bicknell) published a short but strategic article by William T. Harris. In philosophical garb, it provided a strong argument for increased school taxes and appropriations. People like Bicknell and Harris recognized that underlying the reformers' coupling of budget cutting and the need for improved teaching (at the expense of the schools' institutional fabric) was the desire to undermine the existing control of the schools. Cuts in spending easily could be translated into larger classes, reduced space and materials,

---

[28] "The Situation," *New England Journal of Education* XI (January 22, 1880): 52.
[29] "Organize the Machine," *New England Journal of Education* XI (January 29, 1880): 73.

layoffs of staff, and the introduction of new programs designed for efficiency and economy. In this form, the cuts could be used to increase the insecurity, uncertainty, and vulnerability of teachers, making them more amenable to manipulation and control by supervisory personnel with commitments very different from those of the traditionalists formerly in command.[30]

Harris's article was an important piece of ammunition for the latter to use against the reformers.[31] Wealth, or property, Harris argued, could be truly secure only in a nation whose members understood that its origin was "not of individual industry alone but [due to] the recognition of society as a whole." An awareness of this ultimately depended on the society's cultural level, a level that the educational system had the job to improve. This was the reason schooling was paid for by the public. "Whatever taxation of property is necessary to support a free system of education," Harris noted, "is a requisition made upon an element or source (property) created by the recognition of the community." He continued:

> All property is a reflected existence,—an existence resting for its validity upon the recognition which the community, as a whole, extends to the individual. But the recognition of the community at large is conditioned through the intelligence of its members....Taxation for school purposes is directly applied for the culture of the individual, or in other words, for his initiation into this very "reflected being" which creates property. It is, therefore, the application of property for its own production and security. Without any of this recognition which education produces, there could be no security of property, and hence no security of life.

A democratic republic, founded on a belief that individuals had a right to advance as far as their abilities allowed, was the best way to secure these goals. It was commended by the simple self-interest of its members, the same self-interest that required the government of that republic to provide all of its members with the most advanced education possible. In so doing it would guarantee the emergence of a true aristocracy—one based on achievement and wealth, not birth or rank. Harris's point was clear: the kind of aristocrat that would deny the taxes to support "a free system of education" was incompatible with the future of a democracy, either in the United States or elsewhere.[32]

---

[30] For an argument to which this formulation is indebted, see David W. Swift, *Ideology and Change in the Public Schools: Latent Functions of Progressive Education* (Columbus, Ohio, 1971).

[31] It also shows how far he was from being a simple apologist for the unfettered rights of capital, as Merle Curti argued in his influential *Social Ideas of American Educators* (New York, 1935), chapter nine, "William T. Harris, the Conservator, 1835-1908."

[32] William T. Harris, "The Mutual Relation of Property and Education," *New England Journal of Education* XI (February 5, 1880): 83-84. Harris's final words pointed up how encompassing was his vision of the possibilities for democratic education. For him, such edu-

Philbrick shared the page with Harris, and in the first of a series of articles began his dissection of the reports of the 1879 committee. Boston had for years been seen as the finest example of American schooling, and any innovation in its educational system would be carefully reviewed by cities all over the world. Given this position, it seemed remarkable to Philbrick that the revision committee was proceeding so summarily—holding no hearings, taking no expert testimony, and issuing six reports in rapid succession. The reports were written, said Philbrick speaking about Brooks Adams, by a self-confident youth wishing to play "the role of the reformer, without however, having taken the pains to study his part." Having no prior experience in the school system, having been on the school board scarcely a month, he somehow had a "bundle of theories on the subject of popular education, which he seems to be anxious to put into practice." Philbrick characterized the theories to clarify the social and political questions involved. One of them, he said, "is that the people are getting educated above their needs; another is, that the State has no right to provide free education except in its rudimentary steps; and another is, that if there is not a curtailment of the expenses of schooling, the tax-payer will rebel, and destroy our system of free schools from off the face of the earth."[33]

An editorial following Philbrick's March 4 installment made a further attempt to lay out what was at stake. The editors objected to the charges recently levied in a new book by the   popular writer Gail Hamilton. In *Our Common School System*, the editorial said, Hamilton charged that many of the proudest achievements of the traditionalists—the high schools, industrial schools, normal schools, office of superintendent, and new educational methods—only impeded the true work of education. To the editors, the book was a "miscellaneous attack on about everything new and systematic in the schools." For Hamilton, all was decline after the rural school house had been left behind. Her ideal of school life "is 'a little country village, a few miles from Boston, which has neither supervisor, nor superintendent.'" But if the old district system was so perfect, the editors asked, why did its own graduates turn so disrespectfully against it? "Why this defection from the good old way?" The answer was obvious. It was "because everybody competent to have an opinion, and not blinded by sentimental glamour, or a victim of her own smartness, found out, thirty years ago, that this arrange-

---

cation, if successful in one place, would soon spread throughout the world: "One generation of well-educated people in a State forces upon adjacent States the necessity of public education as a war measure,—as a means of preserving the State. So, also, will the existence of one successful democracy force upon the world the adoption of democratic forms of governments as the condition of self-preservation. An ignorant people can be governed, but only an educated people can govern itself."
[33] "The New Departure in Boston: The Annual Report of the School Board, 1879," *New England Journal of Education* XI (February 12, 1880): 101.

ment had utterly broken down....To seriously propose to educate the American people, today, in a school the enlargement of a red, Yankee, district schoolhouse...is like proposing to set back the American people, all round, into the chairs of their grandfathers."[34]

The editors then drew a potentially revealing parallel. Hamilton, they said, reminded them of nothing so much as the "old-fashioned Coos county Democrat of the era before our national flood" who could talk of nothing but the degenerate quality of public life and the way the abolition of all government except the town meeting would provide the needed remedy. A Blaine Republican who most resembled an old, out of touch Jacksonian! What were the editors suggesting? For Gail Hamilton, as the editors surely knew, was the pen name of Mary Abigail Dodge, a well-known writer on domestic and religious subjects, a participant in Washington, D.C. social life as a winter member of the Maine senator's household, and his biographer, likely speechwriter, and memoir collaborator.[35] Blaine had generally been a supporter of the positions favored by the editors, but with the 1880 presidential nomination up for grabs in the months ahead, they may have feared that the Senator could not be counted on to hold his position. Blaine's ambition and willingness to compromise were sufficiently acknowledged even by his admirers, and the most staunch of them may have become nervous. Questions of school building and funding could easily become enmeshed, as we have seen above, in questions of Reconstruction politics, and when Reconstruction politics was the issue Blaine, it may have been suspected, was too willing to exchange principles for votes.[36]

Did the editors wish to send a message to Blaine and other mainstream Republicans by attacking someone so close to him? Did they believe that Republicans who thought about education as Mary Abigail Dodge did—by 1884 many of them would leave the party altogether and, as Mugwumps, throw their support to Cleveland—were no better than a metaphorical back-country New England Democrat? What political point were they arguing? Had they drawn out the comparison they were making, their understanding of the forces they were confronting in local school battles would have taken

---

[34] "The Gospel According to Gail," *New England Journal of Education* XI (March 4, 1880): 153.

[35] Margaret Wyman Langworthy, "Mary Abigail Dodge," in E. T. James, ed., *Notable American Women, 1607-1950: A Biographical Dictionary*, 3 vols. (Cambridge, Mass., 1971), 1: 493-495.

[36] This is exactly what happened in 1884 when Blaine did secure the Republican nomination. Early in the year he abandoned former pledges to fight for the rights of blacks, and embarked on an effort to draw a group of southern whites with industrial interests to the Republican party. When they failed to respond as he hoped, he returned to his old position. See Stanley P. Hirshson, *Farewell to the Bloody Shirt: Northern Republicans and the Southern Negro, 1877-1893* (Bloomington, Ind., 1962), pp. 124-126.

on new coherence—and the strategies to combat them might have too. Unfortunately, the insight was allowed to pass without expansion. The editors missed the opportunity to argue that the proper ancestor of the Republican, and later Mugwump, who opposed public school spending was the Jacksonian: for all their cultural differences, both had profound misgivings about the urban and industrial developments changing the nation.[37]

In one of his last articles responding to the Boston school commission reports, Philbrick contrasted the work of the reformers with that of the preceding twenty years, the years when Philbrick himself had charge of the system. His goal then had been to defend "the policy of progress" he inherited. He had sought to "expand, develop, elevate, and perfect the public school system," and during this period he "never once felt himself under the necessity of trying to show in his reports that the tuition per scholar in the Boston schools was as cheap as in other cities." The question of cost could not be divorced from quality, as the reformers kept insisting. For his own part, he said, "If it could fairly be shown that the excellence of the schools corresponded to their cost, he was already ready to face any charge of extravagance." But such charges were nonexistent. The quality of the public schools was such that even the well-to-do sent their children to them. The ones that did not still shared the benefits because private schools were forced to improve in order to stay in business. "Hence," he concluded, "school taxes were in the main as cheerfully paid as they were liberal in amount."

With the "new departure" things had changed radically, however. Its goals, in Philbrick's view, were frankly reactionary. How else was one to characterize the attempt "to reduce the scope and grade of instruction, and to bring down the expense per scholar to the level of that in cities where the children of the people have never enjoyed such advantages of free instruction as the Boston schools have afforded?" Almost every step the reformers took was "directly in opposition to the progressive movement in building up and expanding public instruction now witnessed in every civilized country on the globe."

The essence of the report, Philbrick said, could only be described as "one of demolition." It was obvious that "the commended 'industry' of the revisers has not been employed in building up, in repairing, in instituting new and beneficial instrumentalities,—a work requiring wisdom and skill. Their industry has been an industry in destroying and pulling down." Take, for example, the reasoning behind the "annihilation" of the kindergarten.

---

[37] On the Jacksonians, see Marvin Meyers, *The Jacksonian Persuasion: Politics and Belief* (Stanford, Cal., 1957); Michael Lebowitz, "The Jacksonians: Paradox Lost?" in Barton J. Bernstein, ed., *Toward a New Past: Dissenting Essays in American History* (New York, 1968), pp. 65-90; and Lawrence Kohl, *The Politics of Individualism: Parties and the American Character in the Jacksonian Era* (New York, 1989); and chapter 1 above.

Established for pre-school children in 1870, it had been called, even by the revision committee, "a decided success." Had the recommendation he made six years ago been acted upon, the number of schools would have been increased by three or four. This was never done, however, and now the reformers were calling for the abolition of the original.

But on what grounds? His indignation at high pitch, Philbrick para-phrased the committee's reasoning for his readers: "The kindergarten is a good thing; all the children of proper age should have its benefits; but it would cost too much to supply all at once; therefore we recommend that this one kindergarten be abolished." Or the intermediate schools; why abol-ish these? The reformers claimed that the schools were found in unsatisfac-tory condition. "But why were they allowed to get into an unsatisfactory condition?" Philbrick asked. There was a time when they were in good condition and doing excellent work; with proper determination to take on the problems of their management they could still be doing well. Difficulties of some kind were always present in work of this nature; generally they were dealt with as they arose. But in this case the board sim-ply decided "it was an easy thing with a word 'to abolish the vice and the establishment altogether.'" To send the pupils of the intermediate schools to the grammar schools meant going backward, not forward. Anticipating developments like the comprehensive high school and the drive to engraft vocational education onto existing high schools; Philbrick said that educa-tion did not advance "by consolidating schools having different functions but by creating new schools for special functions. The creation of these schools was a departure in the right direction; the discontinuance of them is a movement in the wrong direction."[38]

The elitist assumptions that so bothered Philbrick about the reformers could best be seen in the commission's recommendation to abolish the upper part of the evening high school, another institution introduced during his long tenure as school superintendent. Instead of viewing it as virtually "a college for working men and women," the reformers sought to reduce it to lower school status. The reformers planned to take a vital institution, one whose enrollments were growing rapidly, one that offered, especially in its upper grades, a wide range of literary and scientific courses, and gut it. "The

---

[38] "The New Departure in Boston: The Annual Report of the School Board, 1879," *New England Journal of Education* XI (February 19, 1880): 116. In arguing this way, Philbrick, to some extent, anticipated the arguments that would appear over thirty years later in the debate about the Cooley bill in Illinois. This episode of far-reaching consequences originated when industrialists, fearful of reform attacks on industrial and scientific programs, tried to set up a separate system of schools for these programs alone instead of arguing on general educational grounds for their strengthened inclusion in schools to be attended by all. See the discussion below, chapter 8; and the accounts in Mary J. Herrick, *The Chicago Schools: A Social and Political History* (Beverly Hills, Cal., 1971), pp. 117-120; and Julia Wrigley, *Class Politics and Public Schools: Chicago, 1900-1950* (New Brunswick, N.J., 1982).

revisers," Philbrick said, "laid their destroying hands on this noble institution, and without offering a reason, excuse, pretext, or apology for their act, demolished its upper stories, leaving nothing but its lower stage—reducing the school in fact to the elementary grade." The contempt the revision committee exhibited for working people—committed as it was to a push for industrial education just building among its members[39]—was apparent in their report. Philbrick quoted a passage that highlighted it. Speaking of the night school, the report noted that

> its proper work has been woefully obstructed by a ridiculously pretentious programme or course of study. The ancient languages, higher mathematics, elocution, and advanced French and German hardly seem to be proper educational pabulum for those whose opportunities for elementary instruction in youth were of the most limited character, and whose lot, now in maturer years, is grinding daily toil.

Trained in an era when all things seemed possible, Philbrick could barely contain his disgust. What the reformers seemed to be saying, he noted, was that day school students, who had easier schedules and fewer responsibilities, could be allowed to study the subjects under attack. But working class children, who had to earn their living by the most enervating daily labor, had no right to be interested in them. "They must not aspire to anything higher than bookkeeping and commercial arithmetic." Reviewing the general thrust of the committee's reforms, Philbrick concluded that while the policy in Boston had in the past been the expansion and enlargement of the public school system "in accordance with the universal movement in all civilized nations," suddenly a "new departure" with new goals had been adopted. Instead of an earlier emphasis on growth, now, said Philbrick, the "leading purpose is to limit, restrict, and curtail the system." Under such circumstances, he regretted, "it is very natural that the different parties to this movement should try to justify their action on different grounds." Here was an important insight, but unfortunately Philbrick went no further. Valuable as it was to identify and characterize the actions of the committee, it was more important to identify the reasons they believed such actions were necessary. But this he did not try to do.

Philbrick looked instead at the immediate political target of the reformers, the power of the grammar school masters. Since 1866 the masters, about fifty in number, raised to supervisory status and relieved from part of their classroom duties, had in effect become principals of the district grammar school and associated primary schools. Lately, however, the reformers had terminated this arrangement. They had set up a handful of middle level supervisors to oversee the work that had formerly been done

---

[39] The movement for industrial education in Massachusetts is described in Lazerson, *Origins of the Urban School.*

by the masters, now returned to full-time work in the classroom. The isolation and chaos that ensued were only secondarily on Philbrick's mind. He was far more concerned about the effect the move would have on the ability to attract superior talent to the emerging profession. Referring to the masters' change of status, he asked, "Is there a principal who did not feel degraded when he read that regulation? Is there one whose love for his profession was not chilled? What could be more humiliating to the masters than such a regulation?...Will the exercise of such petty tyranny over principals tend to attract first rate men to the service?"[40]

Politically, of course, the reformers could have hoped for nothing better. The masters, the mainstay of resistance to reform policies, had been dislodged from the supervisory positions they had held. The masters now were little different from the hundreds of teachers they had formerly directed. Administratively, their power had been stripped. But even more important, their psychological willingness to exercise the qualities of leadership they had developed must have received a sharp blow. It was especially necessary to undermine such leadership qualities if a political attack on the control of the schools hoped to succeed. Returning the masters to the classroom full-time would be just one in a series of moves that would have the effect of making teachers docile and submissive. When natural leadership qualities were ungratefully rewarded they were hardly worth exercising.

IV

In the short run (as noted above), the battle in Boston would be won by the traditionalists,[41] but not before a significant amount of discussion spilled over into national journals of opinion. Genteel magazines like *Harper's*, the *Atlantic Monthly*, and the *North American Review*, closely linked by personal and political ties, published articles during 1880 that focused attention

---

[40] "The New Departure in Boston: The Annual Report of the School Board, 1879," *New England Journal of Education* XI (February 19, 1880): 116. The editors of the *Journal* backed Philbrick up in strong editorials. See, "The People and the Schools," February 19, 1880, p. 121, and "The Duty of the Hour," February 26, 1880, p. 137.

[41] In mid-1880, buoyed by the support of professional journals and organizations and by the return of prosperity, they recaptured the superintendency (Eliot had resigned, supposedly for reasons of ill-health). By 1882, a newly elected school board—now minus Brooks Adams whose support within his own (Democratic) party had so withered that he decided not to run for reelection—voted to turn the primary school principalships back to the masters, and to subordinate the supervisors to the superintendents. See the account in Katz, *Class, Bureaucracy, and Schools*, pp. 95-102. For the story of the long-run, see Lazerson; and below, chapters 7 and 8.

on the Boston reforms.[42] *Harper's* published an abridgement of Charles
Francis Adams Jr.'s NEA address. The *Atlantic* and the *North American
Review* published variations on his themes, one by the New York literary
figure, Richard Grant White, and the other by Brooks Adams. Philbrick
answered the three of them in 1881, with articles in the *North American
Review* and *Education*.

White relied heavily on Charles Francis Adams, Jr.'s articles, and
argued that there was no necessary connection between ignorance and vice,
the relationship traditionalists since Mann had always considered so direct.
Challenging the traditionalists' views, White said that the population spending more time in the public schools caused more crime, not less. Again like
Adams, he went on to call for immediate cuts in spending. Not only did the
money, supposedly earmarked for books, teachers' salaries, and public
colleges, seem to have little effect on popular morality. It also, through a
taxing system he not surprisingly opposed, provided the grease that lubri-
cated political machines like Boss Tweed's in New York. Instead of lavish
expenditures on the schools, all frills should be eliminated. Only the poor
should receive publicly funded education, and only those with exceptional
ability should receive higher education. Since schools seemed only to
advance the "deterioration of morals," the government would be better off
providing public farms and workshops in their place. In such settings, future
citizens could be more effectively trained "to get their own living honestly
and respectably."[43]

Brooks Adams, soon to become the most intractably gloomy of all the
Adamses, echoed these and other sentiments earlier set out by his older
brother Charles. Shifting his focus from Quincy to Boston, he made essentially the same thrust as his brother (and used almost the same language)
against "the old system of routine and cram." Adams argued that "immense
buildings, costly apparatus, multitudes of studies, forms, parade, and show,
do not make good schools." Once again, he was especially bothered by the
question of cost. "The expense at which [the schools] are carried on," he
noted, "is crushing."[44] Like his brother, he too talked about "natural"
methods and "interested" students in an attempt to justify a conception of
elitist schooling that he hoped might replace older common school practices. Those practices were more deeply rooted in the population than
Adams may have thought and not as easily pulled up as he may have hoped.
But he was beginning to touch the chords—in his appeals to "nature" and

---

[42] On the nature of these magazines and the people who ran them, see John Tomsich, *A
Genteel Endeavor: American Culture and Politics in the Gilded Age* (Stanford, Cal., 1971).

[43] Richard Grant White, "The Public-School Failure," *North American Review* 131
(December, 1880): 537-550.

[44] Brooks Adams, "The New Departure in the Public Schools, "*Atlantic Monthly* 45 (March,
1880): 408-412.

"interest"—that would produce the response he desired. As we will see in later chapters, once these chords were tied by others to a populist rhetoric, and once majoritarian aspirations had been reduced by more persistent hardship, reform achievement would begin to measure up to reform expectation.

Philbrick understood much of what the ideas of White and the Adamses foreshadowed. Quincy, for Philbrick, far from representing an advance in educational method, was if anything, a throwback to primitive "mediaeval" ideals that had "been utterly abandoned and repudiated by all other free countries and civilized monarchies on the face of the globe." He called the notion first put forward by Charles Francis Adams Jr. the "three-R ideal" because it rejected the value of a varied, differentiated (and therefore costly) curriculum, and called for a return to the days when school districts had the limited facilities and funds to teach only the three R's.

In an analysis that portended the future too well, Philbrick then went on to identify the combination of forces bent on establishing this program:

> They are found [he wrote] in the two extremes of the social scale. Here the least liberal portion of the aristocracy and the illiterates join hands and fight under the same flag. The aristocracy furnish the officers of this army, while the mobocracy constitute the rank and file, using ballots for bullets. Mr. Adams seems to have assumed command of the American division of this army. His Chautauqua manifesto was a declaration of war. One of his lieutenants, a brother, who is a rising litterateur, has two years ago been elected a member of the Boston school committee, has already made some progress, aided by the late superintendent [referring to Samuel Eliot who, in response to the masters' counterattack, resigned in mid-1880], in carrying that city. He has begun there the reactionary movement.[45]

Philbrick was deadly serious in his charges. He was talking about a fight the importance and dimensions of which gave it the status of a "war," one that went beyond the boundaries of the United States. Philbrick saw Adams's role as only a part of a much larger effort. In fact, when he spoke of the "American division of [the] army," he appeared to suggest that Adams was part of a conspiracy whose leadership was headquartered outside the country. It was a conspiracy that had built its power out of an alliance between the aristocracy and the mob, two groups that had joined forces (as they had at other critical periods of history) to turn the clock backward.[46] Philbrick asserted that Adams and his allies were planning a major campaign which, with the aid of forces "marshalled under the flags of the

---

[45] John D. Philbrick, "Which is the True Ideal of the Public School?" *Education* I (January, 1881): 303. See Blodgett, *The Gentle Reformers*, for the political background behind Philbrick's charges.

[46] For a contrasting interpretation, see Edward Kirkland's biography of Adams, p. 149. Kirkland attributes only local meaning to the fight, and dismisses the significance of Philbrick's attack.

Richard Grant Whites and the Bishop McQuaids,"[47] planned to "discredit the American theory of education,...create a public opinion in favor of the ideal he represents, [and] secure the training of a class of specialists to administer it." In short, stated Philbrick, "the aim is to do for the whole country, beginning with Massachusetts, what he has attempted to do in Quincy."

The differences between himself and the reformers could not be more clear. He would take his stand under the banner "bearing no such miserable device as '*Three R's only for the children of the masses*,' but that other motto, dear to the hearts of the American people, '*The public free school, make good enough for the best and free to all.*'" (His italics.)[48] Given the ideal it stood for, the money spent on public education could hardly be wasted, and Philbrick had little difficulty in defending anyone responsible for increasing expenditures that would expand it. Even the New York City politicians that White charged with taking Boss Tweed as their model were owed "a heavy debt of gratitude" for adding a new city college and normal school to the existing public school system, already the city's "crowning glory."[49]

This way of approaching the problems of the schools created an unbridgeable gulf between Philbrick and the Adamses and White. Despite his own lapses of vision,[50] Philbrick was committed to extending the edu-

---

[47] Philbrick was referring to Bishop Bernard J. McQuaid of Rochester, N. Y., an outspoken critic of the public schools. A few years later, during the Blair bill debate, McQuaid would call the schools a wasteful, "communistic system" that had lapsed into paganism. See his articles in the January 18 and March 15, 1883 *Journal of Education*. See also John Whitney Evans, "Catholics and the Blair Education Bill," *The Catholic Historical Review* XLVI, no. 3 (October, 1960): 282.

[48] "Which Is the True Ideal of the Public School?": 303.

[49] John D. Philbrick, "The Success of the Free-School System," *North American Review* 132 (March, 1881): 257.

[50] Twenty years earlier, in 1861, Philbrick had not been as secure in his common school advocacy as he would later become. At that time he had proposed charity industrial schools for the "class of children...which is too low down in the depths of vice, crime, and poverty, to be reached by the benefits of a system of public education." Under the pressure of the great immigrant influx of the 1840s and 1850s, second thoughts about the desirability of mixing all social elements in the same schools had invaded Philbrick's thinking. Some children, those Philbrick, along with many other citizens of his day, placed in "the perishing and dangerous classes," would apparently so debase the educational process that its assimilating and community-building functions could not be discharged. For the minority involved, a minority that included many newly arrived Irish, special institutions for training "to habits of industry as well as of study" were needed. The majority, the working, industrious poor, he made clear, would be expected to attend the public schools. "Second Semi-Annual Report of the Superintendent of Public Schools, for the Year 1861," in *Annual Report of the School Committee of the City of Boston, 1861* (Boston, 1861), pp. 92-93. See also John Dudley Philbrick, "Course of Study for Grammar Schools; Special Report to the Committee on Textbooks by the Superintendent of Public Schools...," (Boston, 1868); Stanley K. Schultz, *The Culture Factory: Boston Public Schools, 1789-1860* (New York, 1973), p. 278; and Philbrick's 1876 argument against new proposals to add industrial education to the public

cational network that he felt would bring the common school curriculum within reach of every student. The reformers, assuming a shortage of resources and opportunity—or fearing the consequences of the depletion of one and the growth of the other—were committed to slowing that extension or eliminating it altogether.

In the years ahead, the slowdown that reformers sought would mean adopting a posture of opposition to rising costs and taxes, and forming political alliances with minority religious and ethnic groups who sought increased funds for control of their own schools and community institutions. It would also mean creating a body of specialists that patricians hoped would pursue their program with new efficiency. With limited ties to earlier political traditions and experience, with training in new techniques of cost analysis and scientific management, the educational experts would be more single-minded about their work and commitment.

Efforts in both of these directions were already well underway in Boston and elsewhere. Philbrick was hardly noting them for rhetorical or demagogic effect. He hoped to remind those willing to fight that education was only partly determined by abstract ideas of method and psychology. Far more fundamental was the political reality that conditioned their uses. To forget this reality was to imperil the gains that two generations of schoolmen had won.

Unfortunately, Philbrick himself forgot the message all too often. Like his friends at the *New England Journal of Education*, he too never pinned down for his audience what he sensed was responsible for reform efforts. Nor did he explore very deeply the meaning of the bedfellows he found co-habitating with one another. What overriding commitments brought "aristocrats" and the "mobocracy" together? What enabled them to overcome the prejudice that usually divided them? Posing the question as Philbrick did provided a rare opportunity that should not have been squandered as unreflectively as it was. Instead of searching for the answers he needed, he left his most powerful insights undeveloped, the connections between pedagogy and politics indistinct, and the motives of patrician preoccupation with each undefined. Developments in other cities would soon reveal how serious the omission would be.

---

schools in his *Thirtieth Semi-Annual Report of the Superintendent of Public Schools* (Boston, 1876), pp. 54-56.

CHAPTER FOUR

FELIX ADLER, ETHICAL CULTURE, AND EDUCATIONAL REFORM
IN NEW YORK: FROM THE WORKINGMAN'S SCHOOL TO "THE
ETHICS OF NEIGHBORHOOD," 1876-1900

I

At the same time that the Adams family was having it out with Philbrick in
Boston, another Mugwump in New York was making his first excursion
into the world of educational reform. In 1878, Felix Adler, the young
twenty-seven year old who had founded the Ethical Culture Society only
two years before, had initiated, along with other members of the
organization, a Workingman's School and Free Kindergarten. This effort
seemed to be best suited, and most natural, to the reform and philanthropic
sympathies of the Society; Adler, at the first meeting marking the school's
inauguration, reported that the school was doing well. Proud of what had
been accomplished, he wanted to explain how the work fit in with the
general purposes of the Society and the moral predisposition of its
members.

In the course of this explanation, Adler demonstrated why he was so
important to the reorientation of educational work then in progress: unlike
others of his outlook who had only a dim or narrowly self-interested understanding of the changes overtaking American society, Adler saw clearly that
arguments for school restructuring had to be tied to an appreciation of the
revolution in social and economic life then occurring across the nation. This
revolution was creating an America with permanent social classes, unavoidable business cycles, severe limits to mobility, and a potential for conflict
and confrontation unimaginable to an earlier generation of reformers. Adler,
more than perhaps any of his contemporaries, had a surer and earlier sense
of how unsettling the changes would be. Although, as we will see, he did
not come to the conclusion without a few false starts and considerable
uncertainty, he also understood the way that education—in a variety of
institutional forms—could help deal with them.

Education, as he saw it, was the most important work for the organization to be involved in. The particular focus of the Society, on schools for the
children of workers, was also the most urgent. All right-minded people, he
said to his audience, wanted to help the poor. The inclination, he noted, was

widespread, and for many well-to-do New Yorkers, almost certainly for members of the Society, he was no doubt right. The Society had been founded by Reform Jews who, because of their own experiences with prejudice and rejection, were probably more sensitive than others with their wealth to the concerns of the neglected. Prosperous and eager to assimilate, they had often been faced with the exclusion and hostility that were the common lot of those with none of their cultural or material qualifications for social standing. They had genuine sympathy for the socially outcast, consistent with the mandate of their religion to take prophetic injunctions to social justice seriously. They also desired to demonstrate their intention to play responsible public roles corresponding to the claims to social leadership and acceptance they were putting forward.

Unfortunately, Adler acknowledged that many got little satisfaction from the reform work in which they engaged. The task just seemed so hopeless, "so much like pouring water on a hot stone." The problem was that the "evil weed" of poverty could not easily be prevented from growing. "When lopped off at the surface," it continued to grow "with such unconquerable malignity from the roots." Not that his audience was willing to engage only in "surface" measures. A way of getting at the root of the evil and helping the poor to help themselves did exist. Education, everyone agreed, was the way to do this. The only question was, how to "give the poor the right education." Though the news was disheartening, Adler found the "opinion" of the "distinguished American writer," Charles Francis Adams, Jr. convincing. Adams—a man who, "at any rate will not be charged with importing foreign ideas into his criticism"—was saying that the public schools, which had responsibility for much of the work, were not acting very constructively. "The fact that our vaunted common school system is shown to be so egregiously deficient," he noted, reading to his audience parts of a recent magazine article that Adams had written, "must be depressing and saddening in the extreme."

Adler believed this situation could be changed, but neither political agitation nor university reform (the answer Adams had offered) seemed very promising. The latter, given the immediacy of the need, was sure to be too slow; the former, given the rough and tumble nature of politics, was too messy. A system of teaching so extreme and strongly entrenched, a system employing so many people, "cannot be assailed without exciting violent hostility." Perhaps not yet sure of his organization's strength, Adler wanted to avoid exciting such hostility (and the political organizing it might encourage) if he could. Instead, he suggested, it would be far better to demonstrate by example what the proper teaching and school design methods should be. For this purpose a model school would serve perfectly. "The right example," he said, "when it has once been set, will be followed;

and the persuasiveness of excellence will here, as in other instances, become apparent."[1]

Much of the plan for the school he projected, Adler admitted, was not new. The changes he was recommending in the teaching of history, geography, language, mathematics, and nature study were simply appropriations of what others, especially Europeans, had been doing for some time. But there was one area where Adler did claim originality. His model school would give "hand education" a major role to play in all grades. Hand education, another name for manual training, referred to work with hand tools and the qualities of skill and physical dexterity their use would encourage; in Adler's plan the entire curriculum was to be suffused with it. No matter what the subject, hand work would be made central to its instruction. Here was the key to the model's value. Adler assumed that free popular education had to be adapted to the special needs of its primary constituency, the poor. The children of working people today would be the working people of tomorrow, and the job of public education was to "fit this class for their future station in life" (p. 8).

This task was complicated, however, by the fact that while the future seemed clear and unalterable to Adler, it was not clear and unalterable to the workers. They could not seem to believe that the lowly work they were destined to perform was as valuable or "attractive" as that of others, more favorably situated. What Adler hoped to show them was that just as scientists were constantly involved in work that was personally discomforting and physically wretched; just as physicians had to constantly discharge "menial and repulsive" services without seeing them as degrading, so the laborer should also feel uplifted and ennobled by his exertions. True, unlike the others, his work lacked the prestige without which it would be hard to make attractive. But to see it as if it were was exactly what the "common welfare" demanded. "The tedious work of the working people could be rendered more easy to them, and even elevating, if greater dignity could be made to attach to it." It was to accomplish this noble purpose that manual training instruction was to be applied. By investing hand work with "intellect," "some of the coarsest and some of the most repugnant kinds of labor" could be made interesting. "Saturated with understanding," he said, "the labor of the hands becomes attractive, because it blooms with mind" (p. 9).

---

[1] Felix Adler, "The Workingman's School, A Discourse Delivered Before the Society for Ethical Culture....October 24, 1880," pp. 4-5. See also his remarks in an early lecture, "The Ethics of the Social Question" (January 13, 1878), p. 12, in O.B. Frothingham and Felix Adler, *The Radical Pulpit* (New York, [1878]): "I know very well that we cannot do a great deal with our limited number, and we cannot venture on great undertakings now. But we can do this, which is not a little: we can give the direction."

Adler knew, of course, that he was not the first to propose these ideas, although few had seen the necessity of presenting them as early in the life of the future worker as he did. For Adler, the most important part of the "new departure" he was proposing—his appropriation of Adams's term was no doubt meant to emphasize his agreement with the latter on, at least, the need, if not the purpose, of the changes they both recommended—was the use of industrial education with the "youngest children, in the lowest classes of the school." This was the reason he was so early a supporter of the kindergarten. As far as Adler knew, the use of early schooling for the purpose of introducing the youngest children to what he also called "work education" had never been tried before. It had never, said Adler, "been combined organically with the *whole scheme of education* [his italics], and been made to support and coalesce with all the other studies of the child." With so early a start, the "elevation" of the workman, an elevation that would be more aesthetic (the result of the "artist's pleasure" he would begin to take in his work), would be assured. In addition, and not unimportantly, it would also assure him greater skill and higher wages. But whether or not the latter benefits did materialize was almost secondary. His main concern was to foster "the dignity and independence of the workman." It was these qualities that would determine "whether the social inequalities that exist between the working people and other classes of society will be gradually ameliorated, or so long as they must exist, will be endured in the right spirit" (p. 10).

Adler had now reached the heart of the problem that appeared to motivate his interest in education. The United States was a nation where the political equality of the people was the very cornerstone of government. Unfortunately, history had made clear, "in lessons whose terrible significance ought not to remain unheeded," that the combination of political equality and extreme social inequality was "the greatest danger menac[ing] republican liberty." Where the rich and poor had equal rights before the law, said Adler, every man saw himself as a king. But these days "thousands on thousands of these kings are kings in rags." They were proud and felt independent, but they lived in abject poverty, in the most wretched sections of the nations's largest cities. They looked around, comparing their lot with the leisure and plenty of their neighbors and, Adler continued, as they did "they cannot help reflecting that those others are no more than their equals, and they are goaded even into mob fury by the thought that those who are more fortunate than themselves have no title to what they possess. It is in this way that anarchy arises, and freedom is entombed amid the ruins of civil order" (p. 11).

Like many other Americans, Adler was shaken by the turmoil of the mid-1870s. But unlike them he did not, as one historian has noted, put that turmoil "out of mind with surprising ease." The strikes and depression of the 1870s were classified as exceptions and became no more than a bad memory for most Americans. But for Adler, the strikes and depression continued to exert a powerful influence. Most Americans by the end of the decade may have been "preoccupied once again with building, growing, expanding,"[2] but Adler could not throw the experience of the early seventies off so easily.

Adler was unique in seeing that a social crisis of enduring proportions was brewing. Many gentleman reformers with the same political leanings would not become sensitive to the question of crisis for another decade at least.[3] Their early turn away from the common school tradition and toward vocational practicality was defined more by the way industrial progress had eroded the foundations of aristocratic pretension than by a perception of deep-seated economic malfunction or the potential for social eruption. Unlike them, Adler understood that reform was necessary not just to preserve special privilege but to preserve the entire social fabric.

Part of this understanding may have come from the insight gained through growing up within a Jewish community that had both strong assimilationist urges and a sense of mission to others. Rewards had been great for the members of this community, but so had been the sensitivity to rejection and offenses received. Jews cherished their success and applauded the nation that had offered the opportunities to achieve it. But they also knew that their position could not be fully satisfying as long as other, more recent immigrant groups, especially of their own religion, believed that they were being denied complete access to their society's rewards. They were too susceptible to feelings of guilt that stemmed from the charges of others and their own self-generated sense that they had ignored their religion's mission. These feelings reinforced the conviction that the most valuable kinds of reform work would center on education. Carried out in schools or

---

[2] Robert Wiebe, *The Search for Order, 1877-1920* (New York, 1967), p. 10. See also David B. Tyack, "Education and Social Unrest, 1873-1878," *Harvard Educational Review* 31 (1961): 195-207.

[3] A good example comes from Wiebe, pp. 88-89. Discussing the proposals for urban reform made by "gentlemanly reformers" in the 1890s, Wiebe notes how a "strain of fear that barbarism would never die ran through all of [them]." He then quotes a parable of slum life that Jacob Riis, "journalist and aspiring gentleman," included in his 1890 book "addressed to the upper-class conscience," *How the Other Half Lives*. The similarity between Riis's preoccupations and Adler's is noteworthy: "A man stood at the corner of Fifth Avenue and Fourteenth street the other day, looking gloomily at the carriages that rolled by, carrying the wealth and fashion of the avenue to and from the big stores down town. He was poor, and hungry, and ragged. This thought was in his mind: 'They behind their well-fed teams have no thought for the morrow; they know hunger only by name, and ride down to spend in an hour's shopping what would keep me and my little ones from want a whole year.' There rose up before him the picture of those little ones crying for bread around the cold and cheerless hearth—then he sprang into the throng and slashed around him with a knife, blindly seeking to kill, to revenge."

in the settlement houses that became another major focus of reform energy, educational work was directly related to the problems of social connection that many of those attracted to Adler found so preoccupying.

The preoccupation with problems of social connection and belonging had a number of causes. One may have been that the remedy of swift economic advancement, so much an ingredient of the drive for acceptance by earlier groups, no longer seemed so assured a possibility. Adler had recognized well before his 1880 address celebrating the success of the Workingman's School that "it is not true that everyone can rise; a few only can now and then. The avenues of opportunity are closed against them [*sic*]; the doors of circumstance are locked."[4] Educational institutions could bring this truth home to both poor and rich. The poor would learn how to be realistic about the future, and the rich would learn that the poor needed to be respected, not dismissed, for accepting its fate.[5] Misunderstanding, the "fruitful source of hatred and dissension" among social classes that were "so widely separated by differences of interest and pursuit," was not inevitable, despite the rigidities of class structure itself.[6] Another cause of the preoccupation with problems of social connection may have related to the apparent increase of attempts to exclude Reform Jews socially by the early 1880s.[7] Teaching others how to adapt to American ways may have been a way to press their own claims for acceptance.

Adler continued to develop a picture of the fears he wanted to harness to the purposes of reform. Conjuring up visions of the fall of Florence to the Medici, and of the perversion of the French Revolution, he noted that all was not well at home either. Though safeguards in the United States were still strong, though the idea of subversion of its institutions seemed improbable, there had been warnings—such as "the flames of the Pittsburgh riot....kindled during the last financial crisis"—too startling to ignore. Prosperity may have returned, and many may have forgotten the events of a

---

[4] "The Ethics of the Social Question," pp. 6-7.

[5] One of Adler's arguments on behalf of introducing manual training throughout the school system emphasized this point: "Let the son of the rich man learn, side by side with the son of the poor man, to labor with his hands; let him thus practically learn to respect labor; let him learn what the dignity of manual labor really means, and the two classes of society, united at the root, will never thereafter grow asunder." ("The Influence of Manual Training on Character" [1888], in Felix Adler, *The Moral Instruction of Children* [New York, 1895], pp. 269-270.)

[6] "The Influence of Manual Training on Character," p. 269.

[7] The son of the rabbi of New York's Temple Emanu-El in the 1880s, wrote that in that decade "private schools began to be closed to Jewish children....Advertisements of summer hotels, refusing admittance to Jewish guests, commenced to appear in the newspapers," and "in 1893, the Union League Club of New York had refused to admit Jews to membership." (Richard Gottheil, *The Life of Gustav Gottheil* [Williamsport, Pa., 1936], pp. 182, 232 quoted in Nathan Glazer, *American Judaism* [Chicago, 1972], p. 45.) See also Stephen Birmingham, *Our Crowd: The Great Jewish Families of New York* (New York, paperback edition, 1968), pp. 169-180.

few years ago. But, said Adler expressing recurring fears that were at the heart of his efforts,

> another panic will come after the prosperity; the experience of the past leads us to expect that with almost absolute certainty. And, when there are again want and starvation among the people, who will say why discontent should not again assume wild forms?[8]

The United States was becoming more, not less, like the rest of the world. In the process, the same kind of class divisions and inequalities were also appearing—highlighted, especially, by the rise of pauper classes. It was clear to Adler, in a way that certainly was not clear to an earlier generation of educational reformers, that such pauper classes were "incapable of permanently lifting themselves to better conditions, by their own exertions, incapable of obtaining the satisfaction of their most natural desires, and only rendered the more dangerous and furious by the sense of equality with all others, with which our political institutions have inspired them." Adler's picture of the problem, in terms of a near bestial mob angered by feelings of unjust victimization, was alarming. Fortunately, however, the situation was not as bad as it was likely to become. There was still time "to check the evil's growth."[9]

Education held the great promise of relieving the resentments the poor felt. It could do this not because, as Horace Mann or William Torrey Harris had thought, it could provide the worker with the intellectual advantages to help him rise with a growing economy. It was not because it could help alleviate, through widespread social mobility, the inequalities that created the social tensions men like Adler feared. And it was not because it could, through the advance of science and technology, expand opportunity and multiply new occupational and professional categories. If Adler entertained these possibilities, he never mentioned them. For him, the value of education at this time was its ability "to correct the false idea of equality which is everywhere current around us." It was not to raise expectations to keep pace with an expanding economy. Rather, its value was the ability to lower them, to make sure they would not run ahead of an economy that could no longer

---

[8] "Workingman's School," pp. 11-12. In a lecture he gave on January 25, 1880, Adler repeated the same sentiments virtually verbatim: "In this very season of prosperity [he said of his call for both rich and poor to conciliate their attacks on one another] is the time to provide for the rainy day that is surely coming. Because the history of modern industry, if it has demonstrated any one thing, has demonstrate this: that times of prosperity do not last, that as we have passed through a panic and are now again in a period of prosperity, so shall we surely pass through this period of prosperity and arrive once more at a period of panic." Then he added: "Now is the time to run up the danger signal for the mad engineers on both sides that seem bent on collision—to warn them of their danger and induce them perchance, to put the brakes upon their headlong course to destruction before it is too late." ("The Just Measures of Social Reform," pp. 8-9 in Felix Adler Papers, Columbia University, Manuscript Division.)
[9] "Workingman's School," p. 12.

be counted on to satisfy them. That period of American development was over; the crowding, the scarcity, the poverty that characterized the Old World would now become the American experience as well.

The meaning of equality—and the meaning of America, in effect—had changed under these conditions. The job of education was to prepare the children of the public schools, and through them their parents, to understand what had happened. This preparatory effort was what made Adler's work so important to him. It was the thread that tied together the wide variety of reform efforts he engaged in. It created the link between him and a younger group of reformers who would expand and popularize his point of view after the turn of the century. The most notable member of this younger group was John Dewey, whose first non-academic writings appeared in Ethical Culture Society journals. "Let us teach," said Adler

> the true meaning of the great principle of equality—namely, that all men are created equal in respect to certain fundamental *rights* [his italics]...but that there is by no means equality of natural fitness and endowment, and that the offices of life must always therefore be unequally divided. Let us impress upon the minds of the children that the business of life will always be carried on in a hierarchy of services, and that there is no shame in doing a lesser service in this hierarchy; that all honor accrues to us only in doing that function well to which we are committed, and taking pride and finding dignity in its performance. And to enable the working people of the future to take pride and find dignity in the work of their hands, is the object of the work education we are seeking to introduce in our school. (p. 12)

Adler made no pretense of claiming that the "present hierarchy" was just or fair. The opposite, he admitted, was as often true. But though he sympathized with those disadvantaged by current arrangements, he did not see altering the hierarchy as his concern. This kind of change was strictly a problem for working people to deal with themselves. Without noticing any difficulty in his formulation—how would an education meant to accustom the working class to their existing situation simultaneously encourage them to change it?—he concluded, "It is their sense of dignity as working people, which will alone enable them to accomplish the wished-for result."

But then, with these words, Adler's tone and emphasis changed. As if he recognized the direction and preoccupation his thoughts were taking, he turned abruptly to a discussion of the theme that with increasing regularity was soon to be invoked almost ritually among advocates of manual training. Hand work, he said, was actually a way to provide the students, "though they are only the children of the working people," with a truly *liberal* education. Independence of judgment was central to this purpose, and it was most important that it be exercised "in that which constitutes the daily practice of men's lives—in their vocations." For Adler, this independence would be best expressed by a determination "to ask the reasons why," and it was essential for men to ask for reasons about "those things which they practice daily." The habitual, automaton-like nature of their life on the job would be diminished; in its place a new sense of value and understanding would appear. These were the benefits of a thorough-going exposure to manual training. In tones that prefigured arguments to be made a generation later by people like John Dewey and Jane Addams, Adler concluded, "There can be nothing more salutary, nothing more wholesome, nothing more efficient for good, than a system of work education, which shall relieve industry of its deadness and its dullness, and give to the laborers the reasons why of those occupations with which they are daily concerned" (p. 14).

Hand education was essentially "object-creation," a general educational method that could be applied to any subject. Its effect would not be to shift emphasis away from mental and intellectual development, but to make that development more effective, "by giving it the salutary corrective of the demonstrations of the hand." In this sense, the training Adler had in mind was the furthest thing from the trade training offered by industrial schools. His purpose was not "to yoke" the souls of the young, "before they have had time to expand at all, into the harness of trade, merely for the sake of getting their bread better afterward." Not that he expected trade training to be neglected. But he hoped it would not be pursued without providing "many of the higher treasures of human existence...besides" (p. 14).[10]

Adler believed the goals of the school were worthy of the highest support, and urged his audience to contribute generously to it. They should follow, he said, the lead of people like the banker Joseph Seligman whose gift of $10,000 had helped get the school under way.

---

[10] Adler did at times argue that manual training had value for all members of society: it maintained the ties "to the primal sources of strength from which mankind has always drawn its vitality"; it preserved tool using capabilities in an increasingly machine dominated civilization; and it created widespread social sympathy. But it was the working classes that seemed able to derive the most benefits from manual training. In an 1888 address to the National Conference of Charities and Correction, Adler presented the formulation he perhaps wanted best remembered, judging by its inclusion as an appendix to his 1895 work of general pedagogy. Too many young people, he said, could not make the mental connections that were central to developing will power and the ability to hold off the adversity that more and more of them regularly faced. The traditional common school curriculum did help students make the intellectual connections required for strong character but, he told his audience of social workers, "history, geography, and arithmetic are not as a rule, interesting to young children of the class with which we are now dealing. These listless minds are not easily roused to an interest in abstractions." These children did find manual training interesting, however: "Precisely those pupils who take the least interest or show the least aptitude for literary study [sic] are often the most proficient in the workshop and the modeling-room. Nature has not left these neglected children without beautiful compensations. They may be deficient in intellectual power but are more capable of being developed on their active side." (*Proceedings* of the National Conference of Charities and Correction, "The Influence of Manual Training on Character," pp. 261-263, 268.)

Adler ended his speech with a story that was meant to epitomize the kind of achievement member contributions might further. The other day on a visit to the school, he asked Mr. Bamberger, the principal, to point out the best student. Bamberger did so with words Adler repeated to his audience:

> This little boy [the principal had said] came to us almost covered with filth. And for a time it was necessary to wash him every morning in the School itself before he could be admitted to his class, so neglected he was, and he appeared to be utterly dull and stupid. But after a time it seemed as though with the physical filth the mental filth also wore off, and he became bright and attentive, and he is now our best pupil. (p. 16)

Perhaps Adler was captivated by the ease of transformation, the way a hygenic and cosmetic reform became a psychic one. Or, more attractive still, perhaps he was captivated by the lack of transformation: the riches he sought had been there all along—they had just been covered and disguised beyond immediate recognition. Was it possible that workers and their children could as easily be made to exhibit the same qualities with a method as simple and direct? The naivete of the hope indicated not that he actually believed such a change was possible, but that he desperately wanted to believe that something was possible. His underlying doubts were perhaps greater than he was willing to admit.

The report of Principal Bamberger, delivered after Adler's, touched many of the same themes. Much of his discussion focused on the manual training program; he detailed the application of its principles to lessons in geometry, general mathematics, and natural history. But Bamberger's main emphasis, like Adler's, fell on the moral benefits of the program. The school's curriculum fostered the "habit of working together." Children learned to "live harmoniously in social groups," and became used to helping one another. "No individual," he wanted to point out, "can place himself above another; all have similar duties, equal rights, equivalent claims." At the same time however, "there is no false, artificial equality." Leveling was not to be taken too far. "The children are taught from the beginning the necessity of subordinating themselves to the more able and skillful, while, warned by their own failures, they learn to sympathize with the weaker and more helpless." Humility was the attitude that most needed cultivation by the "artisan" class.

Bamberger's goal, as it had been for Adler also, was to aid the organization of successful cooperative societies among workers. To date, far too many quickly failed, the victim of member selfishness and the refusal to submit to collective goals. One of the ways the school would aid in remedying these problems was by allowing each class to elect its own foreman. The foreman would be a child who in addition to continuing to work "like an ordinary laborer"—"his rank increases his duties instead of diminishing them"—acted as the "general adjuster of difficulties and helper of the others." Possibly thinking of similar applications in industry being pioneered at the same time,[11] he noted, "The influence of an elected foreman is much greater and more efficacious than that of a pupil who should be appointed to this office by the teacher; for the latter is always regarded with distrust and envy by his fellows."

Nearing the end of his report, Bamberger reviewed the school's purpose. "Our ultimate aim," he said,

> is to build up a self-reliant working class, really educated for its own sphere, so competent for its duties as to be able to work independently. An educated working class, occupying such a position, would constitute a beneficent force in the community, instead of being, as it so often is now, an unformed chaotic power, more or less menacing to the order or even to the existence of the state. (p. 30)

But again, like Adler in his remarks, this note was suppressed as quickly as it arose. For Bamberger, too much talk of social unrest, in this case of a dimension that threatened the very existence of the state, was followed by a recitation of the benefits of hand work as liberal education.

It was almost as if expression of the school's "hidden agenda" set off a switching mechanism that placed the derailed line of thought back on the approved track. Thoughts of social disruption were so distasteful, and the anxiety it bared so difficult to deal with, that both were banished by an almost reflexive invocation of liberal educational method and purpose. Both men had found themselves drawn into a discussion of the central motivating fears underlying their work in the school. But, as if openly expressing such fears invested them with a reality they could otherwise be denied, they were forcibly shut out of consciousness. The discussion was unceremoniously returned to more comfortable psychological territory.

Such territory was no doubt the vantage point from which the gentleman reformers preferred to see their educational intervention: as a reasoned approach to discrete, definable problems capable of solution through institutional manipulation and prestidigitation. Instead, they found themselves making exasperated responses to problems threatening to get completely out of control. They had become attracted to educational reform partly because it seemed to admit of a laboratory approach, an approach whose effectiveness, as decreed by the emerging social sciences, could provide a sense that the problems were manageable. Actual cases were another matter, and they were reluctant to admit how intense a reaction the sense of crisis they felt could trigger. But such a sense of crisis was too powerful to be sidestepped as easily as they may have wished. It had dominated the founding of the

---

[11] See, for example, Loren Baritz, *Servants of Power: A History of the Use of Social Science in American Industry* (Middletown, Conn., 1960).

Society for Ethical Culture itself a few years earlier, and would have a profound effect on the other reform efforts begun under the Society's aegis. Activities like visiting nursing, kindergarten promotion, model tenements, child labor legislation, good government club work, the Public Education Association, and the settlement house movement were prefigured in the pressures Adler first felt in defining the meaning of the religious responsibilities being thrust upon him.

II

Begun in 1876, the Society was a reform-oriented, secular version of its parent, Temple Emanu-El of New York City. In the 1870s, Adler's father was the rabbi of Temple Emanu-El, one of the wealthiest Jewish congregations in the United States, and Felix was expected to succeed him. But young Adler had different ideas. In May, 1876, at the age of twenty-five, he led a number of Temple Emanu-El congregants into a new religious movement that exchanged sectarian theological tenets for an allegiance to a broader doctrine of ethical humanism and good works, especially in connection with the Society's schools.[12]

Adler, it could be argued, had simply taken Reform Judaism to its obvious conclusion. Reform Jews identified the core of their religion with two ideas retained from Judaism's prophetic tradition. The first was that Jews had a special mission to spread their religious insights, in particular those related to "monotheistic and moral truth." The second was that the ideal of social justice imposed special responsibilities on Jews. One direction in which the idea of mission could lead was toward a serious proselytizing effort. This, however, was almost never considered in America where by 1885 Christianity and Islam were being called "daughter religions" committed to disseminating the same message.[13] Those Reform rabbis who desired to remain faithful to the idea without becoming Jewish missionaries to the Gentiles, found themselves arguing that the mission had been largely accomplished since, as Nathan Glazer has put it, "many non-Jews now accepted the true faith namely, a humanistic ethical religion."[14] This solved the problem of proselytization but left Judaism with no distinctive qualities apart from the humanistic emphasis common to other religions. At this point, those who had accepted this view had little reason to remain Jews.

---

[12] Biographical details of Adler's early life can be found in Howard B. Radest, *Toward Common Ground: The Story of the Ethical Culture Societies in the United States* (New York, 1969), chapters 2-5; and Benny Kraut, *From Reform Judaism to Ethical Culture: The Religious Evolution of Felix Adler* (Cincinnati, Ohio, 1979).

[13] Sidney E. Ahlstrom, *A Religious History of the American People* (New Haven, 1972), chapter 35, "The Early Growth of Judaism," p. 581.

[14] Glazer, *American Judaism*, p. 48.

"Rather," writes Glazer, they started to maintain that "the Jews should merge with all those trying to fulfill the mission. Thus, some Reform rabbis were forced by the logic of the Reform Jewish position to abandon Reform Judaism and become apostles of a religion of progress in which the distinction between religions and peoples was of no account."[15]

This was the solution reached by Adler in 1876,[16] and it virtually ensured that humanitarian concerns and activities would dominate the organization. The question, of course, was how that humanitarian impulse would be defined. The mass of middle class Reform Jews was generally conservative and often resisted the commitments of its rabbis. But humanitarianism was the very reason for the existence of Ethical Culture, and its members no doubt expected more activism from their leadership. Still this expectation, like those of their middle class friends and relations who remained within Reform congregations, ran far short of any radical alteration of the social order. Adler understood this very well; throughout the last quarter of the nineteenth century he struggled hard to define for the membership and himself an ideal of social activism that did not make any sharp break with their deep commitments to the existing society.

Adler laid the basis for the new movement in two speeches made to his early supporters. Like other Mugwumps, Adler was more disturbed than elated by the material progress being applauded in centennial celebrations throughout the nation. Instead of wealth and plenty, he saw the "great and unexpected evils" that a lack of moral leadership typified. "An anxious unrest," he said, "a fierce craving desire for gain has taken possession of the commercial world, and in instances no longer rare the most precious and permanent goods of human life have been madly sacrificed in the interests of momentary enrichment." Adler feared that "comfort and well being" had become the primary objects of life, and that "life's grander motives and meanings" had been shunted aside. The tendency to depart from the pursuit of such goals had already gone too far, "and the present disorders of our time are but precursors of other and imminent dangers."

Swept up by the tide of business success, Americans were laboring under a false sense of security. They had become unable to recognize the emptiness and hollowness of their lives because they were intoxicated with the excitement of public affairs. Not that Adler thought the drunken complacency of American life could last. A time of rude awakening was at hand:

---

[15] Ibid.

[16] The same decision was reached by two successive rabbis of the important Temple Israel of Boston. See Glazer, p. 49; and Arthur Mann, *Yankee Reformers in an Urban Age: Social Reform in Boston, 1880-1900* (Chicago, 1974; original ed., 1954). Adler's reasoning can be found in his lecture, "When Are We Justified in Leaving Our Religious Fellowship?" (March 28, 1886), pp. 10, 14.

A crisis [said Adler] sweeps over the land. The sinews of trade are relaxed, the springs of wealth are sealed. Old houses whose foundations seemed as lasting as the hills, give way before the storm. Reverse follows reverse. The man whose energies were hitherto expended in the accumulation of wealth finds himself ruined by the wayside. His business was proved a failure. Is his life too therefore a failure? Is there no other object for which he can still live and labor?[17]

Here, at the organizing meeting for his new Society, Adler spoke not about an inward religious crisis of the spirit, but of the trials the spirit was suffering in a real world of financial storms and catastrophe. The reference point for the exercise of morality was the world his young audience knew at first hand from its business and political dealings.

Adler then turned to the subject of political corruption, an evil he knew could not easily be eradicated. The drive for civil service reform (the pet project of Mugwumps who saw it as the most likely candidate to break the power of unruly political machines) was sure to fail unless "the root of the evil be attacked, unless the conscience of men be aroused, the confusion of right and wrong checked, and the loftier purposes of our being brought powerfully home to the hearts of the people." Adler hoped that the forces of morality would win out—although "the world is dark around us and the prospect seems deepening in the gloom...there is light ahead" (p. 91). Personal sacrifice, he noted a few months later, was the way to make the resurgent morality he urged effective. Venality was rampant, and if the evils of the day he considered so widespread continued to be faced with the "hard, grasping spirit of selfish greed," "anarchy and disruption" threatened.[18]

Adler suggested that his audience take up new vocations to find the satisfaction that business pursuits, so pervaded by "selfish greed," were unable to provide. Success in business was ephemeral, risky, and productive of character distortions of the most dangerous kind. Far more certain rewards accompanied a life of high and consistent moral purpose. "We are like chronic patients that change about from one physician to the other," he said at his inauguration as leader of the new organization. "The true prescription, a careful regimen, a stringent diet," he noted, "we are too weak or too self-indulgent to observe. We forget that all physicians are here powerless; that the evil is in us, and with us must lie the cure." Instead of the false and short-lived satisfactions of the business world—now so unstable as to

---

[17] Felix Adler, "Address of May 15, 1876," in *Ethical Addresses*, Series III, no. 5. The copy in the Archives of the New York Society for Ethical Culture has the words, "the earliest word," handwritten on the opening page of the address.

[18] Felix Adler, "Ethical Problems: Inaugural Discourse," October 15, 1876, especially pp. 5-6, 15.

offer no sure rewards for either rich or poor[19]—he held out a different promise. Members could work for the "simple justice" that, while inadequate "to relieve present distress," might forestall the "causes of ever recurring misery in the future." In the attempt to work for this kind of justice, a new life-sustaining purpose might be found. "If thus," he concluded, "we shall kindle a lamp of hope for some of our poor toiling brethren, whom the load of unequal conditions daily consigns to inexpressible suffering; if our own souls shall, in the aspect of these larger purposes, be clothed in a new vigor for the battle of existence, we shall surely not have striven idly, nor followed the phantom of a dream" (p.16).

Adler moved closer to defining the proper object of reform in an address he gave two years later, in 1878. Adler now focused specifically on the working classes, and tied the organization's purposes to somehow improving their condition. But judging by the gap between the size of the problem he identified and the cautious solution he offered to deal with it, he was still far from sure of the best ground to take. After insightfully considering the material and psychological plight of the unemployed and poverty-stricken, Adler recommended nothing more concrete than the establishment of "a few hundred reading-rooms...where light and warmth could be obtained by the poorer classes."[20]

Adler's understanding of the economy had not come very far from that of the business community his members knew well to venture much further into the area of reform. Opportunity no longer existed for most of the population; there was, he acknowledged, no point in trying "to lift the laborer above the point of being a laborer." The latter's condition could be fundamentally improved in only two ways: the rich could cut its own spending (especially on luxuries) and pay workers more, or the number of workers "who apply for a share of capital" could be reduced. To this end a colonization society, he said, should be seriously entertained. It could "relieve great cities of their evil of over-population and provide the means to emigrate for those who have none" (p. 9).

Social policy was clearly running far behind social desire at this point, but Adler's mind was probably not yet fully focused on substantive action. He wanted first to identify the Society's appropriate mission, and use the

---

[19] As Adler said, despite the cause for gladness (because of the Centennial celebrations), "reasons for shame, indignation, and alarm have become only too apparent. A network of venality and fraud has been laid bare whose poisonous meshes extend throughout the length and breath of the country; rash speculation and reckless expenditure have depreciated the standard of living among the more comfortable classes; while the poor are daily becoming poorer, and vast numbers of the laboring classes are pressed close upon the very verge of starvation." ("Ethical Problems: Inaugural Discourse," pp. 5-6.)

[20] "The Ethics of the Social Question," p. 11.

mission to distinguish the organization from other religious fellowships. At the end of his speech, he spoke of his broad intention:

> Help is our philosophy, and help is our religion. I know we can do something towards helping, and for that reason I have undertaken to bring up this theme for discussion, because I know we can do what is needful. I have not shunned it, although, alas that it is so! there is a great odium attached to this discussion, although there are those who hold up against our efforts of reform the red flag, as if society were a mad bull to be frenzied by their flaunting the red flag of communism; as if society were a mad bull to be frenzied by their hoarse acclamations. We can rise to stop the alarmists; we see the way clearly before us leading to progress and peace.
>
> The issue between ourselves and the churches is all one of economy; they lavish their means upon false luxuries. We want to be a life and purpose in the community, a genius of life and good upon earth. For this alone can we work. (pp. 12-13)

Adler had no more idea than his followers or reform-minded colleagues in other cities of how to carry out the mission to which they felt the need to commit themselves. In time it would become clear, especially as a wide variety of approaches was tried.[21] More important, it seemed, was to convince the group that its role was essential, indeed prophetic. It knew what had to be done, and would maintain its cohesiveness in the face of doubting, name-calling, and blind contemporaries. To foster this sense of purpose, Adler stressed the group's courage, virtue, and foresight. His last words made the point even more forcefully. The dedication of the group was noble; one day it would receive its true measure of recognition. The strong and complacent might still command fealty and obedience, he said, but it was only a matter of time before these obstacles to progress were swept away. A more life-giving force would appear, and Adler intended his group to be its vanguard.[22]

III

By 1880, the purpose that would motivate the most important Ethical Culture work had begun to emerge. The uncertainty that existed even as the Workingman's School was being started two years before had passed. Adler, speaking for the Society, was now confident that the organization's focus on educational work was best. He brought his reasons together in a lecture he gave early in the year that he celebrated the anniversary of the

---

[21] For a similar sense of uncertainty at the outset of a reform career, see Jane Addams, *Twenty Years at Hull-House* (New York 1910), chapter 5, "First Days at Hull-House." For a different account of Adler's entry into reform work, see his *An Ethical Philosophy of Life: Presented in its Main Outlines* (New York, 1918), "Autobiographical Introduction," pp. 3-70.

[22] "The Ethics of the Social Question," p. 13.

School. "The total purpose of the school," he offered forthrightly, "is given in these words—To make men in humble occupations, contented with their occupations: that is the sum total of it." Most human beings were rooted to an existence dominated by manual labor and limited comforts. The question for them was simply, "How can they make it human for themselves to be tied down to such occupations?" Then, shifting significantly the motive force from the worker to the reformer, he added, "How shall we make them content with their lot?"

The need was clear. In these "days of disturbance," older methods no longer applied. The church's message (do nothing and wait) simply would not do. Such an idea was more and more attractive only to the rich; they continued to hope that the poor could be convinced to dream of the pleasures of the other world while they enjoyed the pleasures of this world. As painful as it was to accept, the truth was that "this strategy is becoming impossible." The people had grown tired "of the 'goody-goody' songs." They would no longer continue to defer to priests or self-styled aristocrats. In England, for example, workers were deserting the churches by the thousands, asking as they did why they should continue to "bear the inequalities of Fortune." The standard retort was still commonly circulated. The poor, it was said, had no choice. Lighting "the torch of revolution," sounding the "tocsin of insurrection," flooding "the streets of our cities with blood and kindl[ing] New York and Chicago" would change nothing. The poor "must submit" and listen to reason. "And if you do not hear reason," Adler finished his paraphrase, "we will talk to you logic from the cannon's mouth."

The problem with this line of thinking, Adler warned, pointing again to the sense of crisis never far from his mind, was that America had changed. Turning to force to keep the working classes quiet, he said, "answers very well in times of quiet, in times when people are sober and can reflect upon the consequences; for it is true that mere revolution will do no good and that the inequalities which are wiped out today will return tomorrow. But this answer will not do in times when people are stricken with panic and alarm."[23] Under these conditions, a new response was required. When the poor were both pressed by want and forced to witness "the frivolous extravagance of those who name themselves their betters" (those perhaps, Adler was suggesting, who had come to their wealth and power too quickly to have learned how to exhibit it diplomatically, without offensive gaucherie), something more positive needed to be done.

Adler, we have seen, thought he knew what kind of action was called for. As he would later repeat at the anniversary of the Workingman's

---

[23] "Just Measures of Social Reform," pp. 17-22. Adler's next lecture in the series returned to the same theme.

School, industrial education had special value. It would give the worker the sense of dignity that would reconcile him to his position in life. Here suggesting that it should also be coupled with the trade training whose importance he generally soft-pedaled, he contemplated a series of associated schools that, starting in kindergarten, would culminate in "instruction workshops" for teenagers who would be taught "wood turning, metal turning, fitting and forging and the like, and those other branches that will fit [them] directly for [their] vocation in life." At the present time, public and private schools alike fit children only for jobs in business; they "are not designed for the children of the working people."

Adler's school would be different. In addition to its special vocational orientation, it would also teach traditional subjects with new purposes in mind. Adler's statement of his approach to two of these subjects (mathematics and science) is interesting not only for the way it clarifies his general orientation, but also for the way it indicates how decisively he was rejecting an earlier tradition:

> And now we proceed [he said] to teach the Mathematics—Geometry and Algebra—only for the purposes of technical education coming on in later years. And then we proceed to teach the elements of Science; and this is of great importance in modern times, because we want our children to know enough of physics and chemistry, not to be physicians [*sic*] and chemists themselves, but to take an intelligent interest in every new discovery...and in this way the young men and young women whom we educate will have a sympathy with the great march of intellect in our days, and will feel the uplifting and the power of scientific achievement and will take a pride and a glory in it. [Think of the school that offers this,] think of the bright lads and merry little maids who will come out of it, and who will be satisfied with their conditions as workingmen and workingwomen. (p. 49)

The shift from Horace Mann's or William T. Harris's sense that in a growing economy it would be the workers themselves who would be the scientists of the future, that it would be the workers themselves who would be the primary investigators and not be just distant, detached observers of the work of discovery undertaken by others, could not be more marked. In the benevolent but hierarchical world that Adler envisioned, the widespread participation anticipated by an earlier generation would be impossible. "Every man to his place and all for humanity is our motto," he said. "Every man to his place, but every man to his right place." Not that the sons of the poor who were gifted "above their station" would have to "sink into the mass"; their talent was valuable and, proposed Adler, examiners should go through the public schools to "winnow off the children of superior endowments." That the many left behind might want to have the same chance did not seem to give Adler much pause, provided the model he suggested was followed. "I claim," he said, "that the workingmen who are educated upon the plan of such a school will be content, that they will cultivate the great virtue of patience, that they will confine passion."

Adler would argue much of this again. But here he touched a note that did not often recur in his speeches and writing; many of his listeners may have found it surprising. Assuming workers could acquire the virtue of patience he counseled, Adler now argued that he was willing to invite them to participate in the effort to which the gentleman reformers were themselves committed. Workers would be welcome, he said, to labor for social renovation "in connection with us their brothers and no longer look upon us as their natural foes—no but as their natural friends." It was the poor, not the rich, who were the favored allies of the patrician reform groups that Adler sought to ally with. Convinced that the Society and its members too often stood "between two classes and are heard by neither," he hoped an alliance with the workers could be forged to stop the depredations of the rich (pp. 56, 61). Geoffrey Blodgett has noted that in the decades after the Civil War, before the great social cataclysms of the century's close, "the gentry disliked the rich more than they feared the poor." He attributes their dislike in part to "abrasive behavior [that] was especially unpleasant because [the rich] presumed so much on recent success, and often claimed an instant power in public affairs." They flaunted, he notes, "a bold authority in politics which was profoundly unsettling."[24]

Even after the mass strikes of 1877 and the mid-1880s, the people with Adler's outlook did not fully reorient their focus to concentrate on the working class. They still continued to give equal or greater weight to the threat posed by the "rich," the term gentleman reformers often gave to the new industrial magnates. At times, these men could terrify patricians even more than workers. They had an expansive and aggressive vision of change; they valued the participation of workers in generating innovations, and believed that improvements in general educational levels were essential to successful competition—at least before the wave of consolidation beginning in the 1890s.[25] They also seemed convinced that individual entrepreneurs had the power, by simple force of will, to change the world. In view of what patricians knew about the accomplishments of these men, such claims could not easily be disregarded as exaggerations. The picture of power and energy at the command of a single willful individual that Andrew Carnegie presented

---

[24] Geoffrey Blodgett, "Reform Thought and the Genteel Tradition," in H. Wayne Morgan, ed., *The Gilded Age: Revised and Enlarged Edition* (Syracuse, N.Y., 1970), pp. 60-61.

[25] See James Livingston, "The Social Analysis of Economic History and Theory: Conjectures on Late Nineteenth-Century American Development," *American Historical Review* 92, no. 1 (February, 1987): 69-95.

in his 1889 essay "Wealth" may have given less comfort to Adler's reform constituency than the industrialist intended.[26]

A year after he offered his school proposals to SEC members, Adler spoke to them about the danger represented by these barons of business. Like his brother-in-law Louis Brandeis (soon to make his own reputation as a reformer by attacking railroad expansion),[27] Adler saw America's large industrial combinations and the men who ran them as a curse, not a blessing.

One source of the problem they represented stemmed, not surprisingly, from the way these executives were tied to the development of modern technology. This process did not get much notice from Adler for the gains in productivity it generated. Instead, it seemed only a way to oppress labor and to concentrate power and wealth in the hands of the owners:

> It has been especially [he said] the introduction of machinery which has conduced to the accumulation of large wealth in the hands of a few. We hear on all sides of labor saving machinery, yet at the same time the labor of those who labor is just as hard if not harder than it was before. It is those who hire labor who have been benefited by the introduction of machinery. The supply of labor is so large that an abundance of laborers can always be found who will consent to work just enough to keep body and soul together....I have said that while it is in the nature of machinery to keep down the laborer it is the tendency of machinery to raise him who hires labor to greater and greater heights of affluence and power.[28]

So fearful had such men now become, that Adler at one point went so far as to attribute to them a willingness to unleash the kind of riotous violence in pursuit of repressive ends that he normally reserved for workers alone. Talking about the Haymarket Riot in 1886, he argued that the "anarchists and extremists were really the tools of the great monopolists of the land." The latter had calculated their potential gain carefully, and "already there were heard," he said vaguely, "demands for infringing upon the liberty of the press, demands for an increased police force and so forth. There would follow a general demand for a strong government and then— the Republic would be at an end."[29]

---

[26] Carnegie's essay is reprinted in Richard N. Current, John A. Garraty, and Julius Weinberg, eds., *Words that Made American History*, third ed., volume 2 (Boston, 1978). See especially pp. 124-125.

[27] See the discussion of his early career in Albro Martin, *Enterprise Denied: Origins of the Decline of American Railroads, 1897-1917* (New York, 1971).

[28] "Great Accumulations: The Present and Future Relations of Labor and Capital," unidentified newspaper clipping dated January 3, 1881, in New York Society for Ethical Culture Archives.

[29] Clipping from *The New York Times*, May 18, 1886, in New York Society for Ethical Culture Archives.

It was not, in other words, the danger of conflict with an enraged working class that was excited in him as he contemplated the events of the spring of 1886. Unlike the calls for repression of the working class being heard in the wake of the Haymarket bloodshed, Adler still emphasized that "no one believes" they posed "any immediate danger." The rich were the problem, and the need for collaboration with the workers took on increased importance. Mindful of the dangers he had formerly associated with the working class, Adler offered an argument to ease the lingering resistance his audience may have harbored about the needed cooperation. By and large, he began, the "essential demands" of the poor, now increasingly organized, were "perfectly just." In a context where the representative system had broken down—as elected officials only served "the favored and the strong"—it was "necessary and proper...for the people themselves to take the matter in hand and make their demands felt." Considering the "utter stagnation" that now existed in American political life, they would deserve the thanks of the entire nation. He then described how the work should proceed:

> I do not see a signal danger in the present aspect of the labor movement. Class politics should be introduced into politics, but those class interests should not recruit their strength from one class. I do not believe the best leaders of the movement feel they are influenced by class bias. They know if one class of the community is in discontent, the whole body must suffer. But there are in this host of labor[,] growls that are ominous of evil consequences. These are mixed up with that host of elements that have become enraged with all society, those who long to become oppressors of their class as they themselves have been oppressed. The laboring people can do little. The labor movement must not remain the movement of the laborers. It is our business to see that they are not left alone. If it is true that their first political platform is crude and impracticable [referring to the 1887 New York City mayoral campaign, in which labor-backed candidate Henry George came too close—in the view of patricians—to winning], we must help them to present better ones.[30]

Here, amid a new and uncertain set of social and political conditions, Adler was trying to establish a foothold for leadership forces in danger of being swept aside. To sanitize the new movement, to purify it of "crude and impracticable" ideas, a transfusion of outside blood was needed. This new blood would keep it focused on those class interests that were paradoxically not "influenced by class bias," that would protect it from elements within it that threatened, by becoming its new oppressors, to destroy its viability and usefulness.

This was the kind of thinking underlying the innovations that Adler and the reformers attracted to Ethical Culture were putting into motion. Many of

---

[30] "Is There Danger of Conflict Between Classes?" Clipping from *The New York Times*, November 1, 1887, in New York Society for Ethical Culture Archives.

the innovations had their roots in the fears of social disorder that patricians believed would result from the incautious optimism of a rising industrial class. To patricians, this class was blind to obvious signs that economic activity would be sharply curtailed or interrupted.[31] Soon the innovations would be advanced under a different, more professional, and more democratic, standard. Adler is important because he mediated, both intellectually and institutionally, the change of sponsorship and argument that would come to prevail by the turn of the century. At first his arguments for hand education and vocational tracking relied as much on appeals to apprehensions about social crisis and reminders of natural hierarchy in a contracting or stagnating economy as on appeals to a new kind of democratic practice. Later, by the late 1890s, much of this early rhetoric dropped away. By then his language had become almost indistinguishable from that used by someone like John Dewey, the man who was in effect his most influential follower.

IV

The religious ideas that Adler fashioned were well suited to justify the reform work that he wanted to undertake. Although perhaps not conceived with this intention, the ideas would provide a basis for a cultural relativism that reinforced his conviction that economic growth was not likely to serve as a basis for continued social optimism. In an 1883 speech that drew on an article he had written for the *North American Review*, he identified some of his most important conceptions. According to Adler, Ethical Culture broke from the old religion by rejecting its three main tenets—the notion that Scripture had an unassailable authority; that the soul of an individual was immortal; and that God had a personal, tangible existence.[32] The way he drew out the consequences of the last had the most significance for the work of reform.

Adler did not argue that there existed no higher law than human willfulness. Such a law did exist—it was its personalization to which he objected. For to "raise an enlarged image of ourselves to the throne of the universe, and worship that as though it were the Infinte" could only mean that men's gods, as a reflection of their own likeness, would also reflect

---

[31] Again, Carnegie is a good example of what patricians feared. Aware of class conflict potential in a divided society, he could confidently present private philanthropy in the sweeping terms of a panacea: in "Wealth" he could call philanthropy "the true antidote for the temporary unequal distribution of wealth, the reconciliation of the rich and the poor—a reign of harmony, another ideal, differing, indeed, from that of the Communist in requiring only the further evolution of existing conditions...." (*Words that Made American History*, vol. 2, pp. 128-129.)

[32] "The Need of a New Moral Movement in Religion," *North American Review* 134 (February 11, 1883): 4.

their vices as well as their virtues (p. 7). Natural science, emphasizing cause and effect and the inexorable operation of physical law, had also discredited "the conception of an interfering and personal World Ruler."

So far Adler was on ground familiar to many dissenters from orthodox religious belief. But in examining another argument offered by believers in a personal Deity, he got to the heart of his trouble with their position. He disputed the contention that the personification of the Deity was simply an instance of poetic representation whereby "an abstract universal is represented by a living individuality." For example, he went on, although the wind "may be personified as a God...because the motion of air reminds one of the breath that emanates from human lips," the same is not true for the Deity itself. For

> the highest generalization, which includes all classes, cannot be represented by the members of any one class. The supreme universal, which contains within itself the possibilities of all individuals, cannot be represented by an individual, any more than the whole can be represented in a part. And the attempt to so represent it is an attempt to narrow, to demean, to pauperize the lofty, unapproachable ideal. (p. 9)

The old Hebrew religion had the right idea. It understood that mankind was only justified in saying that something Adler called a "highest" existed, nothing more. "The human reason," Adler said, "is impotent before the great mystery of the universe; it seeks in vain to penetrate it....The idea of the highest is to us invaluable; but is *an idea to which we can assign no appropriate conception*" [his italics]. The idea of the "highest" was nothing more than a "formal idea of the mind," a metaphysical postulate the mind required in the search for truth.[33]

Defining the "highest" in this way, left religion, as Adler foresaw, with little but its ethical dimension intact. Unfortunately, in clearing away the inessentials that clouded what he considered the ethical core of religion, Adler had also cleared away the inessentials that could give the personal or social morality he focused on enduring meaning; it is not his philosophy but his institution-building and organizing that makes him important today.

---

[33] Ibid., pp. 10-11. This view may help explain why Adler reacted so sharply to the first codified statement of Reform Judaic principles in the United States, the 1885 Pittsburgh Platform. Its first article stipulated that every religion was an attempt to "grasp the Infinite One" and the "consciousness of the indwelling of God in man." Judaism presented the highest conception of this idea, the Platform announced, and was its most committed defender. Adler responded quickly; in a lecture to the New York Society he denounced the Platform and Reform Judaism. Reform was impotent, he said. It "has retained the idea, the abstract idea, the spirit, as they say of the Bible, *the ghost* [his italics], one might be tempted to say, of the old religion, but it has not been able to give a new embodiment to the Jewish idea, to clothe it anew in flesh and blood." (New York Society for Ethical Culture Archives, Scrapbook for 1884 to 1890, p. 30.) On the Pittsburgh Platform, see W. Gunther Plaut, *The Growth of Reform Judaism: American and European Sources Until 1948* (New York, 1965), pp. 33, 38-39.

Absent from all of Adler's writings was an unvarying standard by which to judge the morality of human actions. Adler's central philosophic notions of personal worth and individuality remained so vague that they easily led to the very relativism one would have supposed it was his object to avoid. For example, at one point in discussing underdeveloped nations in his *Ethical Philosophy of Life* (1918), Adler's theory led him to champion the "ethical principle of national independence," in opposition to the "White Man's Burden." But this, in connection with his deeply-engrained aversion to the "commercial point of view," soon led him to endorse a cultural relativism that could as easily lead to the backwardness that would retard true "national independence," instead of its opposite. The results of trade were desirable, he granted, but not unreservedly so. There were higher considerations to keep in mind. "The education of backward peoples in agriculture and in industry for their own good and along their own line is indispensable," he said. "The fallacy of the commercial mind consists in erecting the means into the paramount end, in brusquing [*sic*] the love of independence which is so strongly entrenched, even among many primitive peoples, and in preventing their development in the direction prescribed by their own natures."[34]

By denying that the "idea of the highest" could be penetrated by man's reason, Adler denied that man's quest for perfection—the eternal quest to take on the universal qualities of creative, unfolding intelligence that were at the center of the Christian godhead—was anything but a sham. Indeed, since man could not penetrate the "unapproachable" idea of the "highest," since the idea included no qualities that could be translated into human aspiration (what was the tendency of the "highest"—did it simply order existence or did it also embody a drive to improve it?), since the mind was "impotent" before the mystery of the universe, Adler denied that the actions of men on behalf of all humanity were required to complete it.

---

[34] Felix Adler, *An Ethical Philosophy of Life*, pp. 327, 337. See pp. 7 and 295 for examples of attempts to give meaning to the concepts of personal worth and individuality.

Adler was hardly alone among his contemporaries in holding views that sought to preserve native mores against the modernizing pressures of industrial civilization. See, for example, the remarks of psychologist and fellow educational reformer G. Stanley Hall, who at one point in his *Adolescence* (a few pages after voicing his opposition to national efforts to assist school system building), noted that "it will be a dreary and monotonous world if the dreams of the jingoes of modern culture and uniformity are realized. As we travel around the world, everywhere we shall have steam and electricity; modernized costume and custom; the schoolhouse and the three R's; the Sunday church bell; the individuality of races slowly fading; their ideas growing pale in a common menstruum; possibly war eliminated by the parliament of man in a world federation; the food supply and the population enormously increasing; no illiterates—this is the millenium which has little charm for the biologist. (*Adolescence: Its Psychology and Its Relations to Physiology, Anthropology, Sociology, Sex, Crime, Religion and Education*, 2 vols. [New York, 1904], II: 717-718.) On Hall's career in general, see Dorothy Ross, *G. Stanley Hall: The Psychologist as Prophet* (Chicago, 1972).

We might expect that such a view would lead to the rejection of any connection between morality and the drive, expressed by the encouragement of work in science and technology to improve, and so make more godlike, the world mankind inhabited. This is what Adler maintained, in common with many others who shared his political and social outlook. Without specifying what he meant, Adler said that morality had to be cultivated "for its own sake and by its own methods," *apart* from science and art.[35] Such a distinction made it all too easy for morality to exist only in an isolated sphere of personal behavior and day-to-day social intercourse. As such it could remain unconnected to a notion of human advancement that required the intensified evaluation and assimilation of science and art by all members of society. It was a mistake, said Adler, to assume, as too many seemed to, "that from the pursuit of science and art morality will incidentally follow." Neither science, art, nor theology for that matter, could be adequate "to build up character and to perfect conduct" (p. 13).

This was what morality reduced to for Adler—here recalling the language of character and conduct that so often punctuated the utterances of New York's patrician class forty years earlier—and it will be no surprise to find Adler among the Mugwumps bolting the Republican Party in the pivotal 1884 presidential election. The Republican candidate, James G. Blaine, one of the most determined pro-development leaders the United States produced in the late nineteenth century, had been charged with influence-peddling and moral indiscretion by his enemies. He became, to Mugwumps who used deficiencies of "character" and "conduct" to cover more fundamental disagreements, too unsavory to support. In an election where the opposition to the Republicans would crystallize primarily because of their stand on issues of national economy and foreign trade, Adler, for example, saw no questions of policy at stake at all.[36] His appeal was to ethics. A few years later, he argued that "social reforms are, at bottom, moral reforms," and that the Ethical Culture Society "cannot merge itself with any of the special movements for social reform...because it directs its efforts to the cultivation of personal as well as of social ethics....The efforts to regenerate society must spring out of the whole character. The new social ethics must rest on the foundations of private morality."[37]

But this did not mean that politics was cast aside as of small importance by Adler. Given the wide area of reform activity that Adler and the Ethical

---

[35] "The Need for a New Moral Movement in Religion": 11.

[36] See Adler's address to the New York Society for Ethical Culture, "The Ethics of the Political Situation," October 19, 1884. On the issues in the 1884 campaign see, John G. Sproat, *"The Best Men": Liberal Reformers in the Gilded Age* (New York, 1968), pp. 112-114; and H. Wayne Morgan, *From Hayes to McKinley: National Party Politics, 1877-1896* (Syracuse, N.Y., 1969), pp. 223-225.

[37] "The Aims of the Ethical Society," *The Ethical Record* (October, 1889): 154.

Culture movement had carved out, the denial of the importance of politics could hardly have been the case. Rather, ethics for Adler and the group he spoke for became the language of the particular kind of politics they favored.

A good example of this transmutation appears in the correspondence of James B. Reynolds, headworker of the University Settlement Society, a New York settlement house founded by Ethical Culture members. By the late 1880s, Adler had turned the Ethical Culture Society into one of the leading agencies of urban reform in the United States. Branches had been set up in Chicago, Philadelphia, and St. Louis. Successful lecture programs, schools and kindergartens, visiting nurse ventures, and tenement house reform committees were continuing to attract increasing numbers of supporters.[38] Its most important, if not most widely recognized effort, however, was in promoting and organizing the settlement movement, now in the 1890s, getting off the ground in the immigrant wards of the nation's largest cities.

Ethical Culture members, such as Stanton Coit, an early Adler protege, were instrumental in founding a number of settlements in New York City alone.[39] Coit, a midwestern Episcopalian who first heard of Adler's work in New York as an Amherst undergraduate in 1881, became determined to serve his movement thereafter. Adler had sent him to Europe for graduate study, and while in England he came under the spell of Samuel Barnett's Toynbee Hall, one of the first attempts to develop an approach to social philanthropy that eschewed the methods of selective almsgiving favored by the leaders in private relief, the Charity Organization Society. Soon after his return to the United States in 1886, he was promoting, with Adler's blessing, the settlement idea as the ideal form of urban regeneration. In 1888 he founded the nation's first, the Neighborhood Guild, later renamed the University Settlement.

The advantage of the settlement to Coit and others was that, unlike the Charity Organization Society, it could be a truly integrating force for the area it served. The problem with the COS was that it was dominated by an effort to distinguish the "honest poor" from the "dangerous classes." It reacted to social dislocation not by constituting neighborhood life for the benefit of all residents, but by perfecting methods for isolating and separating out those with the "personal morality" that qualified them for special favor. In effect, it thereby became a force more divisive than cohesive in the

---

[38] See Radest, pp. 61, 78.

[39] See Radest, p. 73; Allen Davis, *Spearheads for Reform: The Social Settlements and the Progressive Movement, 1890-1914* (New York, 1967); and H. Graham Lowry, "The Social Settlement and the Search for Community: The Neighborhood Guild in New York," (master's thesis, University of Wisconsin, 1968).

work of forging the community solidarity that settlement workers thought
so important.[40]

James B. Reynolds became headworker of the University Settlement in
the mid-1890s after an internal shake-up had sent Coit off to England again
and some of his more adventurous supporters packing. The latter thought
the institution might be used as a base for trade union organizing in ways
wealthy donors deemed too dangerous. Reynolds, a young Mugwump
active in the anti-Tammany Committee of Seventy, was brought in to steady
the settlement and turn it in the direction evolving in cities like Chicago, the
home of Jane Addams's Hull-House.[41] In places like Hull-House the settlement was seen less as an organizing center for the disadvantaged than as
a communications device. It could be used to translate the needs and aspirations of a disparate immigrant population into a language comprehensible to
urban leaders. It could also be used to bring the political and social concerns
of urban leaders home to neighborhood residents. The latter function was
certainly as important as the former, and settlement backers were not
unwilling to make clear their understanding of the *quid pro quo* involved
when a local resident took advantage of the settlement's services and facilities.

We have at least one piece of evidence of the way Reynolds brought
the message to the community he worked in. On October 23, 1895, just
before the municipal elections that would help determine the direction of
reform (especially educational reform) in New York,[42] Reynolds wrote A.
L. Kalman, a leader of one of the Settlement's clubs, regretting the decision
of Kalman and the other club members to endorse Tammany Hall's local
ticket. Reynolds, of course, was not merely sending regrets; he hoped to
change Kalman's mind. The argument he used shows how, for him and
others in his reform circle, political choice and simple morality were one
and the same. Personal character and conduct were defined by political
orthodoxy. He came quickly to the point:

> You probably have not forgotten that last year I secured work for a number of
> members of your club and that I accepted the endorsement of the officers of
> your club as a sufficient guarantee of their character and worthiness. You will
> also remember that I did this at the time when votes were not in question. I
> wish to say that I gave your members places for work because I thought from

---

[40] Lowry, p. 17. See also Davis, pp. 8-9.

[41] The best source on Jane Addams is her autobiography, *Twenty Years at Hull-House* (New
York, 1910). See also Allen Davis, *American Heroine: The Life and Legend of Jane Addams*
(New York, 1973); and Jill Conway, "Jane Addams: An American Heroine," *Daedalus* 93
(1964).

[42] See Diane Ravitch, *The Great School Wars: New York City, 1805-1973: A History of the
Public Schools as Battlefields of Social Change* (New York, 1974); and Sol Cohen,
*Progressives and Urban School Reform: The Public Education Association of New York City,
1895-1954* (New York, 1964), chapters one and two.

what your officers and other members of the club had said of your members that they were men of character and integrity, as indicated by the position which they took in the last campaign [when a reform candidate had defeated Tammany]. I wish to say to you frankly, that it will be impossible to endorse any members of your club in the future if you take the action contemplated.

Reynolds had no desire to force Kalman and his club members to choose between "republicans and democracy," but when it came to endorsing the corrupt Tammany machine, "I should feel that your men had disproved the good character that I gave them and showed that for mercenary reasons they could be induced to abandon moral principle." Reynolds wanted it clear that he was not saying all this as a threat, "but merely because I do not think that you can understand the moral consequences of the step which you seem to be considering."[43] Someone, he apparently felt, who considered voting for Tammany had the kind of serious moral failing that called into question his ability to be trusted at everyday undertakings.

V

By the mid-1890s, much of the sense of crisis that had earlier animated Adler's reform efforts had dissipated. Not that Adler ceased to be interested or involved in reform. He worked to extend the settlement movement and to support the anti-Tammany cause. But the feeling of urgency seemed to have passed. The potential for breakdown and chaos that he had earlier felt so sensibly had vanished; the prospects for the future, if not a cause for optimism, were not as darkly portentous of imminent collapse as they had once appeared. Evil had not spread as quickly as he had feared, and it seemed as if the efforts to hold it at bay permanently might even succeed. No doubt reformers could not hope to wipe evil out altogether; it would be enough to keep it within controllable limits. The complete elimination of vice was "utterly Utopian." Adler's complaint was not that "it exists, but that it overflows its borders: that it invades the houses of the decent poor; that it sweeps young children along with it in its noisome stream; that the public authorities who ought to repress (not suppress) it, who ought to keep it within bounds, are artificially contributing to its growth."[44] This was a different sense than the one he originally brought to the founding of the Workingman's School over twenty years earlier. The pessimism and darkness were still there, but less danger lurked in the shadows.

This change of emphasis is evident as early as 1895 in the alterations that began to appear in the Workingman's School itself. In its catalogue for

---

[43] University Settlement Society collection in manuscript division, State Historical Society of Wisconsin. See also the letter to Reynolds from Adolph M. Radin (September 14, 1895).

[44] "The Redemption of New York," *The Ethical Record* (December, 1900): 52.

that year, the School noted that its name was no longer appropriate; its purpose had changed too greatly. For the past few years the school had begun accepting paying students, "children of well-to-do parents," in addition to the poor who were felt to be in greatest need of its advantages. The change was made to "bring out more clearly the fact that the system here adopted is applicable alike to the rich and the poor, to those who, later on, will obtain a college education, and to those who will graduate directly from the School into the active pursuits of life." In addition, the catalogue informed its readers, the School now recognized how important it was to "mingle social classes," much as the public schools had always done. In fact, the School now saw itself as a "model public school," experimenting with new methods for the benefit of the whole system. The most valuable of these "new methods" was still considered to be manual training, though the catalogue pointed out that the School was "in no sense a Trade School for the education of artisans, nor merely a Manual Training School."[45]

By 1904, the renamed Ethical Culture School displayed its "democratic aims" even more prominently. The school, as its catalogue, very likely written by Adler, noted, would never become a "class school." Its teaching would counterbalance "the pleasure loving and self-indulgent tendencies which are fostered by the life of a great commercial city." It hoped to deepen the spirit of social service in its students, especially by enlisting the students in the work of local settlement houses "with which the School is in touch." Ethical instruction, provided by Adler himself, would be a special feature of the school. Its purpose would be to turn out young men and women of a definite character, one appropriate to the aspirations of American society. This society was progressive; it was in the process of "readjustment or re-formation," and the school planned "to be a nursery of re-formers, of persons who shall sanely and wisely contribute their mite to the task of social readjustment."[46]

To reassure those who feared the commitment to reform might be taken too far, the catalogue also noted that true progress was balanced by conservatism—"the more perfect society cannot be extemporized in a moment, nor created without due regard to existing conditions and to the historic forces which have produced those conditions." An example of the proper mix was perhaps indicated by the high school freshman course curriculum. A summary of the New York State penal code, "to enforce the idea of social stability, and to impress the student with the objective character of the fundamental moral requirements," was included, followed by work to

---

[45] Workingman's School, *Catalogue* (New York, 1895), pp. 5-6.
[46] Ethical Culture School, *General Outline of Course of Study, 1904*, p. 5. On this theme, see also Felix Adler, "The Distinctive Aims of the Ethical Culture Schools: Four Addresses Delivered Before the Teachers of the Schools" (New York, 1902), first address.

develop each individual's sense of worth. An attempt would be made to enlist "the student's sympathy and interest in those classes of human beings in whose care this fundamental moral dictum is still practically denied." As part of this effort, the student was introduced to such subjects as slavery during the Middle Ages and the period of colonial expansion, the plight of the "abject" poor in the cities, and the "negro problem." The history of Ireland would be studied, "exhibiting as it does, the combined effects of poverty, political oppression, and racial prejudice." Lectures would also be given on the ethics of wealth and charity, "in helping the poor to become self-helpful." By the senior year students were ready for "a kind of short catechism of political ethics." In part, this course dealt with "the ethics of loyalty and treason, the ethics of party, the ethics of taxation, etc." Finally, relegated to the back of the catalogue, with no special importance attached to it, was the announcement of manual training courses. Like the other work in the school—to which most of the foregoing fifty pages of the catalogue had been devoted—it was intended "to discover and develop individuality," and in addition, "impart to the student something of the spirit and method of true craftmanship."[47]

Adler had traversed a great deal of ground in his nearly three decades as head of the Ethical Culture movement. He had started with fear of a dangerous working class and its potential for upheaval. He had moved to concern about the activities of industrial magnates. Now he passed to a preoccupation with social service, focusing in particular on the humane young people, many from a rising middle class, who would become its agents in various charitable and professional roles. In preparation for these roles and the outlook they would require, students of the Ethical Culture School would be provided with a course of study that seemed to look back more to traditional curricula (except for the ethics course) than forward to "progressive" offerings. Instead of worrying about whether disgruntled workers would accept their places "cheerily," Adler had moved to a guarded optimism. Now he seemed to feel that with a proliferation of the proper social welfare and educational institutions and the people from upwardly mobile working class and middle class families to manage them, American society, purged of its grasping, ugly materialism, might survive.

Not that Adler was, as noted above, especially confident that the city's problems could be solved completely. But there were indications that he felt more breathing room now existed. He was beginning to locate alternatives to life in the decaying inner city, and consequently beginning to feel less pressure to find a purely urban solution. If it could not be called hope, at least a sense of relief began to appear in him. He was beginning to believe that the intractability of the city's malaise and unwholesomeness did not

---

[47] *General Outline of Course of Study, 1904*, pp. 45, 46, 49, 50, 52, 55.

have to be overcome—perhaps it might be bypassed. Developments like the growth of the suburb, offered new fields to extend the work and new possibilities for the release from the urgency and constriction of past years. In a speech he gave in 1906 on the future of the University Settlement, Adler reflected on the suburb's significance.

The original motivation of the settlement movement, Adler said, came from the desire to close the gap that was forming between social classes, from the desire "to relate together what was threatening to disintegrate in unrelated diversity." But now, in view of the physical expansion of urban areas, what role could the settlement play? He believed that the future of the cities would be far different from what anyone had imagined twenty years ago when the movement had begun. With the growth, especially, of rapid transit facilities, he foresaw "a fringe of wholesome suburbs surrounding the business section of the city." This would make possible a resolution, or easing, of much of the past potential for disorder that life in crowded cities had seemed to promise. The suburbs would make possible the kind of harmony that city dwellers had once despaired of finding. In the suburbs, he said, "there shall live and dwell together the professional class, the merchant class, the bankers, the manual workers." In the suburb, in other words, would be found almost everyone who now lived so often unharmoniously in the city. Adler did not deny that differences of wealth would continue to exist. But he was convinced that "they will not be as glaring as at the present time, and absolute poverty will be unknown." The social conflagration so many had anticipated had not materialized, and many, including Adler, now felt that it never would.

But Adler was not therefore ready to write the settlement off. Although the institution was born at a time when the kind of optimism he now professed was not believed possible, there was still a role for it to play. Even if, he said, a "better day comes when the slums shall be abolished and we shall live, each of us, in one of those fringing suburbs of the metropolis, there will still be neighborhood centres for the encouragement of neighborhood duty." Neighborhood life in any setting, urban or suburban, imposed special obligations; "spatial nearness," he said, "constitutes a claim....There is the duty that springs from the circumstances of a certain district." These circumstances determined what common action was needed on the part of neighborhood residents. As examples, Adler pointed to cleaning the streets, vigilance against crime and vice, preventing the liquor traffic, and improving schools, parks and playgrounds. The settlement, which, after all, should be "considered as a neighborhood movement," could always discharge its special function—"to rescue for us and to develop a department of ethics which has almost been lost to us, namely, the ethics of neighborhood."[48]

The suburb possessed many metaphorical possibilities as the ideal Progressive period success. It was a palpable embodiment of so much of the harmonious, spacious, sanitized, and cooperative ideal Progressives extolled. Even more important was the way it embodied the local relationships common to the inner city political maneuvering and daily life that reformers wished to keep neighborhood residents focused on. As in the "new" education, it had been considered essential to inculcate immigrants newly arriving in the city's ghettos with values that emphasized local concerns. It would be considered just as important to pass these values on to their children, the future residents of the suburbs and the future benevolent bureaucrats of a growing social welfare apparatus. Translated into political activity, a local focus would keep residents of both areas preoccupied with the setting of their immediate existence, with the activities defined by the "claim" of "spatial nearness," or the "duty" of a "certain district." National or international questions would come to be seen as an unwanted and irrelevant intrusion into the job of getting on with one's future. To men and women who saw the world as either unsusceptible of general improvement, or who feared the consequences that such improvement would lead to, plans for local survival and adjustment offered the best strategy for managing the chances that life presented.

VI

An example of how ideas of localism and pessimism about growth entered the educational debates of the period can be seen in the interchange between two women that occurred in closely spaced issues of the *North American Review* in 1899. The first, an attack on public school goals, was by Rebecca Harding Davis, a novelist and short story writer for the polite magazines. The second, a defense of public school goals, was by Mrs. Schuyler Van Rensselaer, a member of one of New York's most distinguished families and president of the Public Education Association, a New York school reform organization that was the offspring of the Ethical Culture Society and the University Settlement.

While many genteel Americans understood and supported the interventionist intentions of the PEA, others, worried about creating expectations about self-improvement that the Association would be unable to fulfill, stood back and denounced the effort. Perhaps there was no reason to accept

---

[48] "The Ethics of Neighborhood," University Settlement Society collection in manuscript division, State Historical Society of Wisconsin.

any version of the maxim, "Educate; send every boy and girl to school." This was exactly what Mrs. Davis suggested in her assault on America's increasingly secular faith in itself. The nation's progress had exalted its trust in man at the expense of its trust in God. "Educate a man," it was enshrined, "teach him mathematics, chemistry or what not, and he can take care of himself in the universe." This, said Davis, had become the "unspoken creed" of Americans, and it had "made the schoolhouse a fetish." Americans now believed that some kind of "life-giving ichor goes out of it [the schoolhouse] which will conquer not only ignorance, but poverty and crime.[49] Like Richard Grant White almost twenty years before,[50] Mrs. Davis argued that the reverse was more likely true.

This reaction was natural enough since the faith in human exertion, no matter how Davis caricatured it, was just the kind that patricians and their spokesmen almost instinctively opposed. It meant the end of the stability with which they ultimately felt most comfortable. This response deepened as the nation found itself "besieged by hordes of ignorant Irish, Germans, Russians, Huns and Italians" from outside, and by "hordes of ignorant negroes and Indians" from inside. The demands of both groups only intensified distaste for the democratic creed that encouraged the upward strivings that the formerly neglected and outcast exhibited. That creed held that ignorance would destroy the nation, and that the cure for ignorance was the public school.

It was clear to Davis, however, that the proposed cure had not worked. Crime was a good example; it seemed only to increase with improvements in educational levels. Davis was willing to be charitable, of course. It was possible that education did not actually breed crime in students the way some had charged; but there was no doubt that it heightened a preexisting disposition wherever it found it. "The three R's," she noted, "never begot a desire in the mind of a boy to work harm to his fellows; but finding the desire there already, they taught him to forge a note instead of picking a pocket." The figure was notable. It was the expansion of scale that seemed to bother her, and interestingly, she chose an example from finance and business dealings to talk about it. As business and the speculative operations attending it expanded, theft in one form or another was becoming harder to guard against. Progress seemed to bring not more comfort and security, but an increased apprehension of approaching disaster. Indeed, as she talked, again about the boy who turned from pocket picking to forgery, she expressed sentiments that might have been applied equally well by the patricians she spoke for to the nation itself: "Without education, he tramped

---

[49] Rebecca Harding Davis, "The Curse in Education," *North American Review* 168 (May, 1899): 609-610.
[50] See chapter 3.

barefoot in the mire of the broad road that leads downward; with it, he drove in a chariot, but on the self same road and to the same dark end" (p. 611).

Pessimism about the benefits of modernization was the stock in trade of people like Davis, and in small doses it had a certain reassuring effect on them. It reinforced the conviction that little more than studied aloofness or pointed example was required of them. But the dimensions of the problems they now imagined were becoming too unsettling to be approached so casually. The example she offered next, again with the intention of downplaying the value of public schooling, indicated how far the retreat from the real world of urbanism and industrialism could be pushed. She pictured a community of French Acadians "in a lonely corner of Louisiana," living on half-cultivated farms in the following way:

> An isolated, separate clan, they had retained the character, the handicrafts and the bits of homely, useful knowledge which they brought with them, and also the same utter ignorance of the outer world. Very few of them could read or write. The men tilled the fields on the shores of the black bayoux which crept lazily through the banks of purple and yellow fleurs-de-lis, and the women in their cabins wore the soft, gay cotton stuffs in which they were all clad. They had no railways, no school-houses, no bosses with schemes for making big fortunes, no politics and no newspapers. For years, there had not been a case from among them in the parish court of theft or adultery or murder. They worked enough to keep them from want; they went to mass in the morning, and to a dance at night. They were faithful husbands, loyal friends, tender mothers; a single-minded, honest, merryfolk, *what more would you have*? (Her italics.)

Surely, she answered, not what a Northern philanthropist proposed for these people. Surely not aid to "send the schoolmaster among them, to open the way for railways, business and civilization." Not, in other words, a contribution to the policy that had turned the nation—including, after the Civil War, many parts of the South as well—into a great industrial power. For Davis, a policy like the one that she put in the mouth of the Northern philanthropist could only lower, not elevate, the Acadians "in the actual scale of being." For the community, she felt, was not just "Acadie" but a true "Arcadia." The rural peace and simplicity she was attracted to allowed her to ignore the cost in inefficient agriculture, illiteracy, and low standard of living to the static backwater. At least there were no bosses, corrupt politics, or newspapers. At least these people were content with the lowly station in life they occupied. This, after all, was more important than the benefits of modern civilization. What was unfortunate was that the coming of modern civilization made the retention of such admirable traits impossible. That the public school system acted as the agent of discontent was probably for Mrs. Davis its most reprehensible feature.

This, unfortunately, was just what was happening in the North. *Its* "lonely corners" could not remain isolated from the maincurrent, and the results were a calamity for the social life and health of the region. This time Mrs. Davis used the example of an old whaling community in New England. Fifty years ago it "was a live, prosperous village." The whalers and their families were literate, vibrant, and healthy. But then the whaling industry died, and nothing else grew up to take its place. A pall fell over the town; the only thing now keeping the townspeople alive was the money from summer rentals. At least, it was thought with some relief, the young had a passion for education. This, the common wisdom of the day had told them, would give the young the mobility needed to survive. Visitors to the town remarked with awe at "the three huge school houses and the free library, which tower over the village houses." But then they noticed "that there is not a cobbler nor a tailor nor a druggist nor a skilled mechanic in the village," and began "to wonder whether book learning is the only wholesome and needful thing in the life of a community" (p. 612).

The problems confronting the young women and young men seemed to have grown worse, not better. The situation, in fact, seemed very much like the one E. L. Godkin was writing about at the same time. Both point up how stereotypical and reflexive accounts like this were. The young women who have gone "through the course, nibbling at a dozen sciences, and philosophies, and two or three languages long enough to learn the flavor of each, but not long enough to find any actual food for their brains," could not, in an overcrowded market, find vacant teaching positions. And without the hoped for teaching positions, the young women remained at home, feeling too superior to cook or wash (as their mothers had been content to do) or to marry the honest farm workers who courted them. "They mope and look at the world in false lights through their tears, and join the great army of half-starved, hysteric, morbid women in New England—the most useless figures, perhaps, in the world's swarming myriads."

The town's young men faced the identical problem. They too had acquired an education that made them look down on the trades or other labor "in which was their chance for useful, earnest lives." They had no capital for business, and the professions—as was usual in these accounts—were "enormously overcrowded." Once again, expectations had outrun opportunity, and would have to be revised downward to reestablish the proper balance between supply and demand. Now, when dire need forced them to take up whatever work they could find, their education guaranteed that they would "loathe and despise" it.

Of course, said the author, no one would seriously argue that these young people had received too much education. The problem was that they had not received the right kind, the kind that would develop their "individual capacity and fit [them] for [their] special place in life" (p. 613). In not providing this kind of education the public schools had failed. Each child, of whatever "capacities, tendencies and destinies," was "crammed with the same dose of unassimilated facts—the alphabets of a dozen sciences, which he never learns to put together in an intelligible work." The reason for this system was as clear as it was ridiculous. It was due to the belief that

> every child must be prepared for any possible position. The boy who will end his days behind the counter of a village store, and who has no ambition nor qualification for other work, must have his smattering of Greek and philosophy, because he may some day be Senator or President....Dull good women by the tens of thousands meant by nature to brood over homes and to mother children [instead] grapple with the Semitic tongue or biology, with the hope that they will be club women or scholars and train their sons for college.
> It is, as we all know, the Chance for every man that constitutes the true greatness of America. But it is this Chance also which is at the bottom of our discontent, of our vulgar pretension, of our intolerable rudeness, and of the false values which we are apt to place upon the things of life. (p. 614)

The old doctrine, a doctrine at the heart of the common school reforms of Horace Mann or the earlier republican faith of Benjamin Franklin, now seemed so divorced from reality that Davis could describe it with mock seriousness only. So convinced that the belief in progress and social mobility on which it was based was an outmoded delusion, she could see the aspirations of young men and women who still took it to heart only as objects of sarcasm. Now such aspirations led only to "discontent," "vulgar pretension," intolerable rudeness," and materialism. These were the qualities that outraged a class of patricians used to a world where subordinates knew their places and did not try to alter relations that, because of a fragility increasingly seen as settling into American society, were best left alone. Wasn't it clear how false such hopes and expectations were? Wasn't it clear that American society could not possibly deliver the kind of growth that made such expectations reasonable? Underlying Davis's pronouncement of the "curse" of useless common school education was the same repudiation of assumptions of the need for, and possibility of, economic development that colored so many of the educational diatribes appearing in Mugwump journals throughout the late nineteenth century.

It is not surprising that Mrs. Van Rensselaer did not propose to let the force of Mrs. Davis's argument stand; it challenged too directly—in questioning whether any reform work was of value—the efforts of the PEA. Yet her reply, for all that, was curiously weak if it intended to combat her arguments effectively. For far from refuting Davis's charges, it actually demonstrated how widespread the values underlying her views had become. Some patricians and their spokesmen, like Adler, engaged in reform not because they held different assumptions about the opportunities that education extended to Americans, but because they had become convinced that a new crisis with a depth and intensity they had not considered before required remedial action. Only then could they preserve a semblance of order, and establish places for themselves amid the new centers of leadership that they believed were forming.

In defending the work of the schools, Mrs. Van Rensselaer could not bring herself to reject Mrs. Davis's charges altogether. While she argued that both examples Davis used—the Acadian outpost and the New England whaling village—were "not normal communities" but "survivals" and "anachronisms," she did not offer any alternative to them. To her, educational reform was a holding action, and not part of a broad-based effort to raise standards of living and intellectual levels. Mrs. Van Rensselaer's argument was negative—it held not that education had something especially valuable to add to the lives of the young; it was more that worse dangers threatened if education was curtailed. The influence of modern business, industry, technology, and newspapers made it impossible for "pastoral ignorance and innocence" to be perpetuated in any locality, no matter how remote or how distasteful modern culture turned out to be. "Little as we may like the kind of civilization they sometimes bring with them," she noted, "it would hardly be improved by the elimination of the schoolmaster."[51]

Schooling had not created the problems of the whaling village (where, she said, both she and Mrs. Davis spent many summers as neighbors). But perhaps it could help solve some of them. In a way she never specified, education was necessary to reduce—she agreed it would never "conquer"— ignorance, poverty, and crime. Keeping her language consistently vague, she described how her association with the school and "those classes of the population that most deeply need its help" had led her to a new level of understanding. "The more I have studied [the public school and its relationship to the poor]

> the more distinctly I have come to understand the difficulties with which it has to cope and the way in which it is often isolated in its effort to cope with them, the more clearly I have realized the difference between the average child that it now turns out and the average parent of foreign or even American birth, the longer I have reflected upon the picture our crowded and polyglot poorer quarters would present if it did not exist—the more I have been impressed, not by its defects but by its merits. (p. 89)

That was all. In an effort to sum up the value of the school to her society, Mrs. Van Rensselaer could offer no more than generalities. The diffi-

---

[51] Mrs. Schuyler Van Rensselaer, "Our Public Schools: A Reply," *North American Review* 169 (July, 1899): 78.

culties the schools must cope with, the differences between the child and his parents, the results of the schools' non-existence in the city's immigrant districts all were unspecified and unamplified. The merits of the schools, not the defects she readily admitted, were what impressed her, but nowhere did she say what they were. Why was she so inarticulate on so important a point? Her article did catalogue the efforts being made to change the schools—the efforts to improve sanitation, collect truants, begin kindergartens, introduce physical and manual training, extend nature study and civics instruction. But nowhere did she present an argument that related these efforts—or the reasons justifying each one—to any larger purpose or context.

It could be argued that this was not her intention, that a rebuttal of Davis's charges need not include it. Perhaps this was so—it may not have been necessary to include it, but it certainly would have helped in establishing the credibility of her work. The point is put into perspective by recognizing that such an omission would never have occurred to an earlier generation of schoolmen. They assumed that education always had to be related to a discussion of broad social and political purpose, that its role was not simply to do better what "the home and the church, active ever since the birth of civilization, have failed to accomplish" (p. 89). Consistent with the needs of a growing industrial nation, the job of education was not primarily socialization or ethical training, except as this was seen as an adjunct to the job of advancing the level of cultural and technical development of the society as as whole. Explaining the ties between social advancement and the schools was the basis for generating support from all social classes, and few opportunities were missed to educate the population about its benefits.

But Van Rennselaer, like the other reformers with whom she associated, had little dispute with the localist and anti-growth assumptions that pervaded Davis's remarks. Because she never challenged these assumptions, a statement of the purposes that would sharply distinguish her position from that of her seaside neighbor became impossible to enunciate. Davis's discussion of the effects of schooling on the young New England villagers assumed a closed environment shut off from the rest of the world. There was no hint that the condition of the town she spoke of had been caused by its relation to a changing national economy, or that its problems could never be solved within its own borders alone. The town appeared to be frozen in time, plagued with a myopia that prevented it from seeing developments in the rest of society. The educational policies of Mann and other traditionalist reformers had been introduced to eradicate this thinking and initiate the national economic growth that would forever rob it of plausibility. Whatever their tactical differences, both Mrs. Davis and Mrs.

Van Rennselaer shared the hope of restoring the blinders an earlier generation had fought to remove.

This hope was related to the other purposes pursued by late nineteenth century reformers. Public education was to be used as as tool to shore up existing social relations through tracking, cost-cutting, and the displacement or disciplining of teachers striving to establish an alternate seat of power. A necessary precondition of the attempt to shore up existing social relations was the reintroduction of a sense of isolation, helplessness, and the disruptiveness—and hence painfulness—of economic development. This was the sense that a conception like Davis's carried, but it was not unique to her alone. Reformers like Van Rensselaer and Adler shared it also, no less because they recognized that the isolation, helplessness, and dislocation on which they premised their work were located in the nation's largest cities, not its most remote backwaters. Collapsed local conditions were an unalterable fact of life in both areas. Somehow it simply had to be accepted—by becoming reconciled to a world of work defined by the variety of manual trades and the lowered aspirations that they enforced. Mrs. Van Rensselaer doubted the necessity of this reconciliation as little as Mrs. Davis. Without questioning the assumptions that led the latter to her position, Mrs. Van Rensselaer had little choice but to avoid the subject at the heart of Davis's discussion altogether. Like Adler, to whom her organization was closely tied, she disagreed not with the values that informed Mrs. Davis's complaint, but only with the form of its expression. Both quarrelled not with Davis's point of view, but with her posture of withdrawal and passivity. The reorientation of American values they all sought would take work, not just plaintive expressions of bereavement and loss.

CHAPTER FIVE

NICHOLAS MURRAY BUTLER:
FROM THE LABOR QUESTION TO TEACHERS COLLEGE

I

Among educators involved in the work of reform in the 1880s and 1890s, none had a better grasp of the ties between educational leadership and political purpose than Nicholas Murray Butler. Like Adler, his thinking was also conditioned by social and industrial ferment. But unlike the Ethical Culture leader, he saw the need to be in the midst not on the periphery of events. To some extent, the visibility this gave him restricted the innovative role he was willing or able to play; people less encumbered by broad public responsibilities would have to introduce the ideas and reforms he supported. But his support was critical. Based at Columbia University, one of the nation's most prestigious institutions of higher education, and working closely with mainstream elements in the Republican Party, he had enormous influence in determining the impact of new ideas and programs.

Butler had learned early that educational work had wide-ranging political significance. In 1881, Columbia's president, F. A. P. Barnard, had singled him out as an undergraduate, and convinced him that it was not the law that was the way to prominence and political influence, as the young man then thought. Instead, Barnard argued, a career in education had far more promise as a route to power.[1] In this period, new pressures were being placed on schools at every level. On the one hand, they were being asked to provide the knowledge and skills needed by a modern, industrial nation. On the other, they were being asked to deal with an America newly fearful of huge numbers of immigrants, a suddenly visible flood of the unemployed, and an increasingly powerful organized labor movement. With such responsibilities, educators, especially those in leadership positions, were likely to receive a more respectful hearing than they ever had before. Traditional politics, considered by many like Barnard in the 1880s to stand only for corruption, mediocrity, and inaction, seemed pallid and ineffectual by comparison. Butler took Barnard's message to heart. For him, academic

---

[1] See the accounts in Richard Whittemore, *Nicholas Murray Butler and Public Education, 1862-1911* (New York, 1970), pp. 1-2; and Albert Marrin, *Nicholas Murray Butler* (Boston, 1976), p. 20.

position was never a retreat from the world outside the university but a way
to confront it more forcefully. In and out of the university, few were better
skilled in the arts of publicity, deal-making, and organization that would
help turn the confrontation to advantage.

Early on, Butler put his talents at the disposal of that part of his society's leadership elite that feared the social changes caused by industrialism
far more than it welcomed the opportunity for gain that such changes
offered. This group understood that the key to maintaining its power and
prerogatives lay in capturing the minds of America's working people, and
replacing their notions of opportunity and mobility with notions centering
on acceptance of and resignation to the hard times that were likely to lay
ahead. To the most farsighted, this effort of value reorientation meant both
determining and redirecting the education that future workers would
receive. It also meant controlling the training of the teachers who would be
responsible for providing it. Curriculum revision of the kind Adler sought
would hardly be successful without a corps of well-trained advocates to put
it into practice. And this legion was not likely to emerge unless hard organi-
zational and public relations work preceded it. These latter tasks were ones
at which Butler excelled.

Although he remained active in Republican Party affairs well into the
1930s—he had been introduced to them very early by his father, an
importer and small textile manufacturer in Paterson, New Jersey—[2] he
never saw education as any less a way to achieve political goals. In the
period we are interested in, at the outset of his career, he was involved in a
wide variety of efforts, in both New Jersey and New York, to use
educational reform to effect the redistribution of political power. The best
example of this was perhaps Butler's work on the reform Pavey bill in
1895. Working through New York's Public Education Association and the
anti-Tammany Committee of Seventy, he was instrumental in devising the
legislation that, according to one student of Butler's career, had the effect of
stripping local boards of public school trustees of their patronage, and of
concentrating all real power in the hands of a city board of education
answerable to the mayor. "Executive authority," says Richard Whittemore,
"would be vested in a city superintendent, thus fixing responsibility and
lessening, if not eliminating, the opportunities for spoilmanships."[3] By the
time he became Columbia's president in 1901, only the prestige of national
political office was great enough to lure him away from his post on
Morningside Heights. "He firmly believed," another student of Butler's

---

[2] Marrin, pp. 36-37.
[3] Whittemore, p. 65. For another account of Butler's role in reform in New York, see Diane
Ravitch, *The Great School Wars: New York City, 1805-1973* (New York, 1974), chapters 11-
14.

career has concluded, "that aside from the presidency of the United States no other office would give him as much influence over the country's political and social climate."[4] As early as his student days at Columbia, he was considered, even more than a brilliant student, a born executive and politician.[5] It is because of his success in both roles that it is important to discuss the ideas on behalf of which he acted. Because of the forum from which and the energy with which they were delivered, these ideas became invested with an authority and recognition that added significantly to the force they were acquiring in this critical period of educational redirection.

In the 1880s Butler was far from the reputation and power he would later acquire. But he very early had a sense of the arena in which to establish his credibility. Questions of work and learning were at the heart of the decade's preoccupations, and they became his also. When, during the portentous year of 1886, he began to appear in print with remarkable frequency, both concerns were constantly intermingled. On almost a weekly basis, Butler moved back and forth between discussions of labor unrest, convict labor, industrial education, pedagogy, and teacher training, discriminating little in the emphasis he gave to each. The issues all seemed to flow together, and all, therefore, required exploration, as if thoughtfully dealing with one might reveal valuable approaches to the others. Teacher training seemed to be central to solving the problems of the age, and Butler, in the decade when he was establishing his career, gave it much of his energy.

Fundamental change in the schools depended not only on providing special training for supervisory personnel as Charles Francis Adams, Jr. thought, but for teachers as well. Like other patricians and their spokesmen, Butler was deeply preoccupied with the selection of leadership for both local and national responsibilities.[6] Teachers could not be poorly prepared; especially in secondary schools, their work was too important. Of course, they had the job of directing potential leaders to the colleges and universities that would ready them for their future tasks. But they also had significant obligations to the population left behind. In the view of Butler and others, most Americans, despite the shocks of recent years, were still eager for improvement and restless for advancement. Having been dangerously stimulated by the industrial developments around them, they were pressing demands that would most likely be impossible to fulfill. Though

---

[4] Harold S. Wechsler, *The Qualified Student: A History of Selective College Admission in America* (New York, 1977), pp. 71-72. Though he repeatedly refused to run for statewide office, he allowed himself to be considered as William H. Taft's running mate in 1912 and for the presidency in 1920.

[5] The assessments are, respectively, those of his teacher, John W. Burgess, and Whittemore in his *Nicholas Murray Butler and Public Education, 1862-1912*, pp. 10-11.

[6] See Wechsler, part two, "Columbia and the Selective Function," on this aspect of Butler's activities.

not through direct counsel, teachers would have to be the bearers of this bad news and mediate the change in values from expectancy to resignation and acceptance. The new values, in the form of new curricula and methodology, would be directed to the young people passed over by the elite selection process.

Properly monitored teacher training was one of the ways to guarantee that the desired social message would be well-marketed and received. Teacher training, therefore, meant special schools and doctrine, special expertise and credentials. It meant professionalizing the teaching corps. The certification that went with professionalization would give teachers so trained a special claim on available school positions, and would thereby become an important adjunct to efforts to wrest control of the schools from neighborhood-based political groups. These groups, far from curtailing and discrediting popular hopes and aspirations as patricians wished, were, often as a condition of their own survival, doing just the opposite. Moves to professionalize the training of teachers would include efforts to standardize and impersonalize their selection, a process that, along with other aspects of municipal reorganization schemes, denied a significant source of patronage, free publicity, and political leverage to "corrupt" city bosses and their machines. For Butler, a man to become one of the great power brokers of his day, these considerations were never far from mind.

As Butler began to argue in the mid-1880s, the process of education had to be examined scientifically in institutions designed for that purpose. Teaching was not simply a trade, like clerking; it had a special history, literature, and philosophy that required careful study before mastery could be assured. The teacher, he said in an 1886 article in the *New Princeton Review*, was "not engaged in some haphazard calling," but was a member of a profession. This idea was not a new one. Henry Barnard, in his *American Journal of Education*, had argued it for years, and the best normal schools, particularly in the Midwest, had offered more than mere trade training for some time. But in the East, the development of such a notion languished. In New York, Columbia College president F. A. P. Barnard had led Butler, struggling to find a permanent niche in the Columbia hierarchy, to hope that a school devoted to educating professionals might be attached to it. If the trustees agreed, Butler was encouraged by Barnard to believe, he might be the school's leader. But the trustees had balked at the idea, and reluctantly Butler agreed with Barnard that the institution might be easier to start without Columbia's formal support. If the school became successful, the hoped-for affiliation could be effected at a later date.[7]

---

[7] "The Scientific Treatment of Education," *New Princeton Review* II (September, 1886): 304; Whittemore, pp. 30-32.

The opportunity to put this second plan into operation came when Butler was asked to head the Industrial Education Association in 1887. The IEA, begun some years before, was an organization dedicated to introducing industrial education into the public schools, and was giving courses to practicing teachers expected to carry the message to a wider audience. Under Butler's leadership, these purposes were broadened considerably. Before the year was out, the organization, with the help of patrons many of whom had long-standing ties to Columbia, had become the New York College for the Training of Teachers, and by 1893, with the name changed to Teachers College, the desired alliance with Columbia (made permanent in 1898) had taken place.

The trustees had waited for the new institution to prove its usefulness, but they had not waited long. Perhaps they were already coming to understand, as they would more clearly a decade or two later, how Teachers College could be used to siphon off "undesirable" applicants to the University itself. As Harold Wechsler has shown, Butler's interest in using Columbia as a training ground for the selection and preparation of an elite would be undermined if it could not discourage or turn away applicants with unappetizing social backgrounds. Faced with what Columbia's leaders considered an invasion of undesirable students, especially those of eastern European Jewish origin, they would finally establish a quota system to keep them out. Before this day came in the 1930s, they turned to other, less obviously discriminatory practices.[8] One of the early attractions of Teachers College was very likely the role its leaders imagined it could play as an agency to redirect the energies and ambitions of talented, upwardly mobile immigrant children who were deemed unsuitable candidates for the places an education at Columbia College was expected to prepare its graduates for.

The dominating figure among the trustees was their president, Morgan Dix, pastor of Trinity Church, the Episcopalian stronghold that had historically exerted a powerful influence over the College's direction. Dix was, in many ways, the man responsible for translating the concerns of the church and its wealthy parishioners into College policy.

One of the best places to see what these concerns were is in Dix's Baccalaureate Sermon at the Columbia 1888 commencement exercises. Not the least of the sermon's interest is in the way in which it presages some of the most important values and attitudes that Butler himself, just then newly installed at the IEA's helm, assumed. The way Dix outlined the role of the new graduates, the way he defined the dangers they and their society faced, would have their echo soon enough in Butler's speeches and writings. The address gives us an important clue to the direction he charted for Columbia and the divisions allied to it—such as Teachers College. Butler toned down

---

[8] See Wechsler, pp. 151-166.

the rush of words, hysteria, and paranoia Dix was prey to, but his themes
always remained close to those of his patron's. In the 1888 sermon, Dix
explored one obsessive patrician preoccupation after another. Like others of
his circle, he spoke of social dislocation, and characteristically pointed to a
minority of paid revolutionaries as the cause. He called for individual
morality, informed by pragmatic common sense and patriotic reverence, to
act as a counterweight to these revolutionaries and the other forces he saw
threatening the influence and authority that his own group had grown used
to wielding. In the process, he lumped political bosses, labor unions, and
corporations together, much as the early Felix Adler had also:

> Note what upheaval of foundations [Dix said], what drift from ancient land-
> marks. Listen to the railings, the invectives of discontent, the protest of the
> demagogue, the pessimist, the professional agitator. What stirring up of strife;
> what inciting to riot and revolt in the name of human progress....Here, of a
> surety is need of sober men. Here do we need a rising generation, imbued with
> intelligent love of country, patriotic, loyal to the constitution, the laws, and the
> nation's flag, reverent as to the past, hopeful as to the future....Never was
> ebriety more apparent than that which is produced by imbibing in the saloons
> of those agitators of the day, whose trade it is to stir up the world, inflame the
> populace, and set classes by the ears. The Socialist, the Communist, the
> Agrarian, are among the tempters whom we must resist, steadfast in the faith
> in principles on which our political system rests, in an intelligent mistrust of
> centralization and paternal state government, and of everything that militates
> against the rights of men, the right to labor, and to enjoy the results thereof, the
> right to property, the right to security in house and land, in goods, in life, in
> limb. It appertains to sobriety of mind, to stem destructive currents and
> streams of evil tendency; to refuse support to theorists and fanatics; to watch
> the lights upon the coast, the signals from the outer main; and in an earnest
> spirit to gird oneself for the work of a man; to defend the social order; to
> purify society; to assert the principles of liberty received from our fathers; to
> oppose despotism, in what shape soever it may threaten, the despotism of
> political rings and parties, the despotism of class-organizations, the despotism
> represented by labor-unions, walking delegates and boycotters, the despotism
> of monopolists and corporations, the despotism of fashion.

Society, Dix concluded, would be looking to Columbia graduates, to
those "who have received a liberal education to that very end that you
should put your hand to the work." The University had therefore an important role in the years of growth ahead.[9] It would become "a dominant

---

[9] From the evidence of his diary, Dix hardly looked upon the growth he expected for an
improvement in the quality of human life. Writing in the diary after a walk home from a
trustees' meeting in 1906, he sounded much like merchant Philip Hone who, three generations
before, had contemplated New York's changing scene (farther downtown) in much the same
terms: "I never heard or saw such a turbulent, noisy, roaring, furious condition as the streets
presented, especially about the Columbus Circle; elevated trains thundering, surface cars
squealing in a curious jangling way, automobiles by scores teaming [sic] around, people running for their lives; an awful state of things, boding ill for the future." ("The Relation of Dr.
Morgan Dix to Columbia University: Data taken from the Diary of Dr. Dix, 1878-1907," type-

influence for wisdom, common sense and virtue...and the most attractive of the seats of sound learning in our western world."[10]

II

In retrospect—in view of Butler's educational preoccupations and allegiances—it is clear that the IEA was not simply a fortuitous and expedient springboard from which to launch an organization with the very different purposes of teacher training. From the first the objectives of the IEA and the teachers college complemented each other perfectly. Butler, earlier in the 1880s, was just as ardent an advocate of industrial training as he was of professional teacher training. The purpose and function of each conveniently overlapped.

Butler often wrote about teacher training in the pages of *Science*, the journal of the American Association for the Advancement of Science, edited by Johns Hopkins president, Daniel Coit Gilman. Indeed, one estimate is that hardly an issue between December, 1885 and November, 1887 lacked a contribution from him on this subject.[11] At the same time, however, he was also writing, with important consequences for the industrial education campaign he was shortly to join, about the convict labor problem then agitating many reformers.

Interest in the convict labor problem was no doubt heightened because of its tie to the larger social issue of unemployment. In the unstable economic atmosphere of the late 1870s and 1880s, unemployment received increased attention, especially from those worried about the potential for discontent that men without work represented. Particular focus centered on vagrancy and tramping. Certainly the increased numbers of unemployed gave vagrants a visibility they had earlier lacked.[12] But commentators were

---

script manuscript, Columbiana Collection, Low Library, Columbia University.) See also Allan Nevins, ed., *The Diary of Philip Hone, 1828-1851* (New York, 1936).

[10] Morgan Dix, Columbia College Commencement, 1888 Baccalaureate Sermon, pp. 11-12, 15, in Columbiana Collection, Low Library, Columbia University.

[11] Whittemore, p. 29.

[12] Paul T. Ringenbach, *Tramps and Reformers, 1873-1916: The Discovery of Unemployment in New York* (Westport, Ct., 1973). Sarah Sands Paddock, the president of the IEA in 1884, gave some idea of the fears that had been generated. The problem of unemployment was becoming so serious that it was "extremely difficult to know what to do with that improvident section of our community, the drift of idlers[,]...the great number of unemployed in our midst." More and more young people seemed never to acquire the skills and "industrial capacities" that would make them "marketable through life." Though, predictably, she attributed this deficiency to the "imperfect state of industrial education of the masses," she admitted that the "emergencies of the market" created the unavoidable "state of fluctuation in labor." Still, she believed that a child, if properly prepared, could by the age of fourteen, be sufficiently competent in a trade to get work that would enable him or her to be "thoroughly

worried about more than numbers. Vagrancy also pointed to a rootlessness, an unregulated and purposeless movement of men that raised frightening questions about the holding power of stabilizing social patterns and values. For in addition to the appreciation of external factors that was beginning to enter the consciousness of reformers, was an older understanding of the causes of unemployment. Until very recently the problem had always been considered a fundamentally moral one, dependent only on the strength of character of the individual worker for solution. Widespread unemployment more than anything else, therefore, raised the question of widespread immorality. But how was *this* to be explained? Why should so many have lost the drive to work hard or, worse, to work at all? Might moral deficiency, expressed in idleness and vagabondage, indicate a failure of basic values, like those associated with the work ethic, and the institutions that had traditionally sustained them? And, if this were true, was there anything that could be done to reinvigorate them?[13]

Thinking like this led both idleness and vagrancy to become associated with the rise of criminal and other forms of deviant behavior. For many Americans, idleness and crime had the same causes. They were both the result of the breakdown of an individual's moral machinery to a lesser (in the case of the idler) or greater (in that of the criminal) degree. One reason that the debate over convict labor became so prominent in this period was related to the recognition that a special effort to return individuals to work-oriented values was necessary. The nature of work had changed, and its psychological rewards had declined. Public institutions, as surrogates for private ones that were apparently malfunctioning, would have to take on a larger share of the work.[14]

As the problem began to manifest itself in discussions of rising crime rates and labor unrest, the criminal justice system attracted more serious attention. And just as reformers recommended additional manual training schools, kindergarten classes, and social welfare programs as ways of reviving the values of work, they also focused on the value of work programs in reformatories, asylums, and penal institutions for many of the same reasons. Given the feared rise in deviance, much of it attributed to the strains and stresses being placed on a belief in the efficacy of work, these programs could pay valuable dividends in the battle for social order. If it was desirable in the interest of preserving values of deference and stability for indus-

---

self-supporting." ("Industrial and Technological Training," *Proceedings* of the National Conference of Charities and Correction [1884], pp. 210-211.)

[13] See James B. Gilbert, *Work Without Salvation: America's Intellectuals and Industrial Alienation, 1880-1910* (Baltimore, Md., 1977); and Daniel T. Rodgers, *The Work Ethic in Industrial America, 1850-1920* (Chicago, 1978), on the general problem.

[14] See [U.S. Bureau of Labor], *Second Annual Report of the Commissioner of Labor, 1886. Convict Labor.* (Washington, D.C., 1887), pp. 316-318. See also Gilbert, p. 29.

trial slowdown to be accepted, it was also desirable that the slowdown should be accompanied by as little social turbulence as possible. Accordingly, the question of the suitability of convict labor received the interest and comment of social reformers throughout the nation. Convict labor might be an important way to renew a lost ethic of work and might thereby remove the mental imbalance that led to criminal deviance. It might also be suitable as a source of cheap labor.

But as reformers soon discovered, the issue had implications that extended far beyond prison walls. The decline in the work ethic seemed to be occurring precipitously throughout the society; the question of convict labor, therefore, also involved facing its effects on that part of the population that had not been forcibly deprived of its freedom. Now faced with competition from convicts, would not workers, with only a tenuous grasp on the will to work themselves, further question its value? What would they think of exercising good work habits when they saw employers turn to labor of lesser skill and more doubtful morals, and available at lower pay?

In 1886 Butler was not yet much of a reformer. But with apparently unlimited access to the pages of *Science*, he entered the discussion. He started by wondering what the fuss was all about. As far as he could tell, the only reason the subject was receiving any attention at all was because of the noise being made by "labor agitators." "Perhaps not more than one out of every ten thousand laboring men," he wrote, "gives the question of convict labor competition a thought, but this odd one has during the last decade managed to stir up a great deal of discussion." No sane man, Butler said, doubted that convicts should be employed, and employed profitably if possible, by the state. But now agitators were insisting that the "contract" system, the employment that produced the most revenue for the state, injured the "honest laborer by compelling him to submit to an unfair competition."

How this was possible Butler could not imagine. How, he asked, could the insignificant number of 60,000 convicts, the total given in the last census, "working as they do under peculiarly disadvantageous circumstances, and consisting of the lowest and most ignorant classes of the population," have any appreciable competitive effect on millions of "honest and free workingmen"? It was clear to him that "those who join in this outcry are to a great extent communists, and leaders of labor organizations, whose sustenance depends upon the amount of agitation they can create, together with such political aspirants as aid them for purely selfish purposes." Yet somehow in a few cases these forces had managed to get the old laws changed, "abolishing the system of contracting for the labor of prisoners at so much per day." They had now passed legislation that increased competition, not reduced it.[15] Contractors now paid the state less, earned more, and sold more cheaply. The obvious conclusion, said Butler, was that although "the labor agitators are many...the mass of political scientists and humanitarians were right in supporting the old system."[16]

Two weeks later Butler wrote again, offering a more refined analysis to refute those who suggested that contract labor led to unfair competition with free labor. If all 60,000 were employed in a single industry it "might" be that prices and wages would fall. (As Butler would be instructed shortly, employment in a single industry was precisely the issue; and it was one that had been well-debated among prison reformers as far back as 1871.) But despite the fact that reformers had agreed that this was a very real problem, Butler denied that the employment of convicts was concentrated in that way. Drawing on Carrol D. Wright's figures in the 1879 annual report of the Massachusetts Bureau of Labor Statistics, he showed how 23,000 convict laborers spread out in over one hundred skilled industries and nearly 12,000 in one quarter the number of unskilled industries amounted to only 1.83 percent of the total workforce. This figure represented an even smaller competitive force, Butler argued, because the productive power of a convict was only three-fifths that of a free laborer. To be exact, he said, "competitive productive power" was only 1.1 percent of that of the free laborer.[17] Then, drawing on statistics compiled by another Bay State free trader, businessman Edward Atkinson (perhaps best remembered for inventing the pressure cooker to help the poor prepare inexpensive foods), he noted further that the total product of state prisons throughout the nation was a mere two-fifths of one percent of the total output of manufactured goods. Adjusting for the actual wage of convict laborers—forty cents a day versus two dollars a day for free labor—brought the percentage down even lower. The evidence apparently spoke for itself, and those, said Butler, who

---

[15] The legislation was called the "piece-price" plan. According to the Commissioner of Labor, Carroll Wright, it worked in the following way: "The contractor furnishes to the prison the materials in a proper shape for working, and receives from the prison the manufactured articles at an agreed piece price, the supervision of the work being wholly in the hands of the prison officials." (*Second Annual Report of the Commissioner of Labor*, p. 4.)

[16] *Science* VII (January 8, 1886):28-29. In fact, as Butler probably knew, they didn't support it. See the second annual report of the U.S. Commissioner of Labor (1886), pp. 318 and 379. Most reformers seemed to have supported the public account system in which "the penal institution involved carried on the work of manufacturing just as a private firm would—from buying raw materials to producing and selling the finished product."

[17] Interestingly, Carroll Wright in his second annual report as U.S. Commissioner of Labor (1886)—a report devoted wholly to the convict labor question—noted that the overall ratio was four-fifths and that in the shoe industry, soon to become the focus of debate between Butler and a correspondent to the magazine (see below), productivity between convict and free labor was virtually identical. See pp. 291, 294 of the report.

participated in the anti-convict labor crusade were obviously "innocent of any acquaintance with the facts that bear on the question."[18]

The matter did not end here, however. In its February 5 issue, the magazine printed the first of what would amount to three letters by an E. Langerfeld that had Butler, by the end of their exchange, running for cover. Perhaps because the author challenged Butler's moral stature—in addition to his arithmetic—the latter felt compelled to respond. At any rate, the two were about to engage in a debate that would carry them through the month. Langerfeld charged Butler with being captivated by "that system or school of political economy which is taught in the colleges, and which rules in business." The kind of political economy he had in mind was science "'for revenue only,' and it ignores morality or humanity. It judges all human activity by the standard of profitableness." To this group, anything humane was sentimental nonsense and anything unbusinesslike such as charity, was insane. Fortunately, Langerfeld pointed out, "this form of 'insanity' is increasing rapidly in the world, and developing a new school of political economy, whose central principle is to further the welfare of all men." Possibly thinking of the parallel between Butler's argument and that of another anti-free labor contingent before the Civil War, the correspondent noted that a prison was not a "slave-pen for grinding out 'profit' to the state." Instead, it should be either a refuge for the morally infirm, or a school that would provide the moral education necessary for full citizenship.

Langerfeld also disputed Butler's characterization of the forces opposing contract labor. They were hardly comprised of a few isolated individuals and agitators in search of a meal ticket. "The facts are, that whole groups, trades, have directly been affected wherever prison labor has entered the market." The so-called agitator was in a losing business—only the ignorant or those whose interests were threatened by him thought differently. In fact, the "agitator" was "persecuted, blacklisted, hunted, and misunderstood and denounced; and that he still remains true to what he deems his duty is a trait that should be honored by all who can appreciate an unselfish action." This said, Langerfeld returned to his main point. The charge made by supporters of the system, that "convict labor at fifty cents a day is not cheaper than free labor," was incredible, "for the prisoners are driven and tortured to daily perform a set task." Agitation would not stop until production by convicts for the general market was stopped.

Butler answered with all the feigned innocence he could muster. The correspondent had entirely missed "the tenor" of his articles. "They were not written from the stand-point of any school of political economy whatsoever, but from the stand-point of practical ethics." His articles took the

---

[18] *Science* VII (January 22, 1886): 68-69.

"ennobling" purposes of prisons for granted. His aim was to focus, as many others were beginning to, on a more troubling moral issue. He hoped to establish "that idleness is [not] an ennobling influence, that [therefore] productive labor on the part of convicts is of no injury to the community." The facts, based on the statistics he offered earlier, refuted clearly any contention that the competition of convicts posed a threat to free labor. And if it were granted—as all reformers had—that convicts were best employed in productive industries, it was necessary only to determine which system served this purpose best. In conclusion, Butler added that the subject was a large one "and, in the article criticized by your correspondent, but a small portion of it was touched upon."

Langerfeld's second letter appeared the following week. Butler's figures, he claimed, stood up to scrutiny no better than his argument from "the standpoint of practical ethics." His reasoning was faulty from the start. The only reason contractors hired convicts in trades where free labor was plentiful was cheapness; any other suggestion "involves just such an infraction in the order of nature as is expressed in the commonplace reference to water running up hill." Butler's way of dealing with figures was no less peculiar, wrote Langerfeld. Saying that the total proportion of convict labor to free is only 1.1 percent was completely misleading. The place to see the pressure of convict labor competition was in specific areas and trades, such as the shoe and hat making industries of New York State. "There the percentage has been large enough to injure both employers and employed, and if Mr. Butler wishes to show the causelessness of the 'hue and cry' he ought to show the percentage in special trades and localities. A shoemaker does not compete with a tinsmith." Of course, even unaffected trades had taken up the fight, strictly on the grounds of morality: "their ethics differ from the 'ruling school,' where the principle 'every one for himself,' is held, and instead of that their ethical doctrine is 'an injury to one is the concern of all.'"

To this Butler offered only a lame reply. The writer's point about the hat and shoe trades in New York was admittedly hard to dismiss (even though it did not have any bearing "on the question of the general merits of the contract system"). "Perhaps," Butler conceded, "a restriction as to the number of convicts to be employed in any one industry would be desirable." But Butler would not quit until this case was examined also. Again citing "official figures," Butler concluded that even in this particular instance (the shoe and hat industries of New York), "the competitive force" of convict labor was only about four percent, larger perhaps than the 1.1 percent he had cited nationally, but "surely it is not so formidable." He refrained from offering other figures "for fear they may be summarily rejected as useless, because they do not fit in with some person's ideas as to how the 'course of nature' ought to go."

Langerfeld was still not satisfied however, and wrote to answer Butler again. It was no wonder that Butler was hesitant to offer other figures he feared might be rejected as useless. The ones he had already presented were simply incorrect: when you calculate the percentage of "competitive force" using the figures Butler himself supplied, the answer was not 4 percent but 6.45 percent in the case of hats and 7.88 for shoes. The reason his figures would be "summarily rejected" had nothing to do with whether or not they "fit into some person's idea of how the 'course of nature' ought to go." Butler simply did not know how to divide. ("One who thus figures may well have, as he says, 'some hesitation in adducing fresh figures...for fear they may be summarily rejected as useless.' True, Mr. Butler, but not for the reason you give,—'because they do not fit some person's idea of how the "course of nature" ought to go.'")

The writer then went on to give Butler an education in the facts of trade union work and the free labor ideology that much of it was based on:

> Those who are organizing the working-classes into a political party, to obtain what they deem justice, are in earnest. Only one who has not felt the dreadful sensation of being unable to sell his labor, when that is necessary to sustain life, can realize the bitterness and pain of such a situation. For every convict whose labor product is sold in the market, a free laborer becomes superfluous, and therefore fewer work, or all are laid off temporarily, in that branch into which the convict is introduced. Here the "political economist" of the prevailing order says, "Find something else to do." In most cases it is impossible.

There was a further evil effect on free labor, Langerfeld continued. Competition with prison labor lowered the rate of wages in whatever area it entered. Talking like an antebellum Republican, he explained: "It [prison labor] must gain its market by underselling free-labor products; and however small the percentage, both as to its amount and of the decrease of its price it lowers the standard of prices, including wages, in that entire branch."[19]

This was exactly what workers and their allies who believed in industrial growth had been arguing against the "new" doctrines associated with academic political economy and scientific philanthropy. According to these doctrines, relations between capital and labor were regulated by an impersonal market responding to fixed laws of the universe. Those who could not find work were lazy and intemperate and those who agreed to contracts that

---

[19] The exchanges between Langerfeld and Butler to this point appear in *Science* VII, February 5, 1886, p. 117; February 12, 1886, pp. 143-144; February 19, 1886, p. 168 (Langerfeld). For a recent discussion of the strains informing Langerfeld's arguments, see James L. Huston, "A Political Response to Industrialism: The Republican Embrace of Protectionist Labor Doctrines," *Journal of American History* 70, no.1 (June 1983): 35-57.

unjustly paid too little, "have nobody to blame but themselves."[20] Langerfeld lumped Butler among adherents to the latter notions. They were a group that he felt had little understanding of or respect for the older traditions that had been responsible for the nation's economic gains. A broad alliance of workingmen and other industrially-minded Republicans had been fighting since the antebellum period to establish this outlook, but apparently Butler, more a Mugwump in outlook than the nominal Republican he always remained, was not among those stirred by their message.[21]

For a man with Butler's emerging political and social commitments, the prison labor issue was a kind of tune-up for the more important political battle soon to involve him. Like the school reorganization fight of the 1890s, the issue not far beneath the surface was the power of locally-based constituent political groups. School reorganization would threaten this power by removing control of the largesse available in the form of school appropriations from their hands. Salaries for teachers, funds for textbooks and other supplies, allocations for new buildings and maintenance of old ones offered great possibilities to reward friends and punish enemies. Though not as directly, and not on as large a scale, the prison labor dispute concerned the same issue. The contract plan, the one that Butler favored, though fraught with the most moral danger for the incarcerated,[22] had the least moral danger for the members of the community at large. Viewing morality through the same political lens as his friend and colleague James B. Reynolds,[23] the young educator supported the plan that, as was widely believed, offered the fewest patronage opportunities—in the form of gov-

---

[20] Sidney Fine, *Laissez Faire and the General Welfare State: A Study of Conflict in American Thought, 1865-1901* (Ann Arbor, Mich., 1956), pp. 59, 62. The quotation is from Arthur Latham Perry, *Elements of Political Economy* (New York, 1872), pp. 140-141. The laissez faire doctrines to which Langerfeld referred were not, Fine makes clear, as new as Langerfeld thought. But they did dominate orthodox economic circles. As the first president of the American Economic Association, Francis Amasa Walker, asserted in 1889: "Here it [laissez faire] was not made the test of economic orthodoxy, merely. It was used to decide whether a man was an economist at all." (Fine, p. 48.)

[21] For accounts of the new political economy and scientific philanthropy, see Mary O. Furner, *Advocacy and Objectivity: A Crisis in the Professionalization of American Social Science, 1865-1905* (Lexington, Ky., 1975); Thomas L. Haskell, *The Emergence of Professional Social Science: The American Social Science Association and the Nineteenth Century Crisis of Authority* (Urbana, Ill., 1977); Robert Bremner, *American Philanthropy* (Chicago, 1960). On the alliance between labor and industry, see Alan Dawley, *Class and Community: The Industrial Revolution in Lynn* (Cambridge, Mass., 1976); and David Montgomery, *Beyond Equality: Labor and the Radical Republicans, 1862-1872* (New York, 1967).

[22] At least in the opinion of the New York State Commissioner of Labor, who, in an 1884 report, feared the effects of contact between outside contractors and prisoners on the latter's discipline and morals. See Wright's 1886 *Report*, p. 312.

[23] Both worked together on the Seth Low mayoral campaign and at the University Settlement in which Butler also took an interest.

ernment jobs—to local machines, and hence the fewest additional levers of
partisan influence and advantage.

In addition, and of equal importance in understanding Butler's position,
was that contract labor was the plan most opposed by organized labor. It
was the one that appeared to threaten most the gains they had made by providing workers to employers that would otherwise have to deal with them.
Butler held to an antagonism to trade unions that bordered on the pathological throughout his life. In 1919, for example, talking to Columbia's Institute
of Arts and Sciences about the steel strike of that year, he sounded remarkably like the young writer for *Science* who, over thirty years earlier, had
denounced working class organizers as self-seeking agitators. Like the
latter, the 1919 strike leaders were "all bent upon destruction in the wild
hope that after their joy in tearing down has had full satisfaction, somewhere and somehow personal advantage may accrue to them. In the process
they would not hesitate to destroy America."[24]

To a large extent, this opposition to trade unions was due to the same
thinking that shaped his opposition to political machines. Both institutions
represented an alternate locus of political power and social fealty. Both
institutions defended their constituents against reductions in their living
standards—the trade union by protecting wages and on-the-job working
conditions, the political machine by protecting and extending municipal
services, even if at times it did so under duress. In acting this way, the two
institutions, in the eyes of an elitist like Butler, were exercising power that
was not properly theirs. The ability to determine wages or service levels
was the prerogative of the ruing elite, an elite that saw the questions not so
much in terms of economic profit as in terms of social discipline and status
reinforcement. The issue of prison labor presented the same opportunity as
did the issue of school reorganization. Both represented attempts (the latter
far more active than the former) to reestablish a loss of control increasingly
intolerable to patricians unaccustomed to sharing power graciously.

It took Butler more time than usual to compose an answer to
Langerfeld's last, remarkable letter. He let a week pass, and on March 5,
noted only that his arithmetic was not mistaken. He had said earlier that the
competing power of convicts was only about 60 percent of their numerical
strength; this was the percentage he had assumed in making his later com-
putations. About the other issues Langerfeld raised he said nothing.[25]

The evidence that Butler had pondered closely the parts of Langerfeld's
letter he did not then comment upon appeared a month and a half later in a
review of a recent pamphlet that called for the settlement of labor difficul-

---

[24] Butler, "The Real Labor Problem," in *Is America Worth Saving?* (New York, 1920), p.
94.
[25] *Science* VII (March 5, 1886): 220.

ties through the establishment of permanent arbitration boards. Butler noted that the "present crisis" had made arbitration attractive. "No thoughtful man," he said, "can have watched the development of labor troubles during the last few years with any feeling short of anxiety. The increase in the number and frequency of strikes, the growing percentage of them that are successful, the hostility and ill feeling too often shown by employers and employed have all forced themselves upon our notice, but society seems helpless before them." Part of the problem could be attributed to employer attitudes toward workers that had not kept pace with the increasing rate of social change. Feudal relations between masters and servants did not exist any more, and the continued treatment of employees as inferiors not surprisingly resulted in "ill feeling, desire for retaliation, [and] perhaps criminal recklessness." This was not to say that the two groups were equals, however. "We need not blind ourselves to the ethical fact that there is a superiority of possessions as well as a superiority of physical force and of intellect." His point was simply that in economic matters this kind of superiority could no longer "safely be pushed very far." Employers would have to climb off their "feudal pedestals" and meet their workers half way. They had to stop assuming that since they paid the wages they could "settle them as they see fit." Butler had not forsaken his elitism; he just had another point to make at the moment. This point grew out of a dominating fear of social dislocation that motivated the interventions of so many patricians in this period. It was because he shared their point of view that he could advise them so well.

Both employers and workers had to understand that in many ways neither had much control over determining wages unilaterally. The amounts workers received, and the product sale itself, were apparently determined by forces beyond the employers' control. Strikes, boycotts, and lockouts could have little effect on the outcome, something permanent boards of arbitration could make clear to both parties. Regular meetings between capitalist and worker would nurture the sympathy for each other's problems that could result in a true *entente cordiale*. If meetings to talk over common problems could be institutionalized, they "would have a magic effect in ascertaining the facts and suggesting concessions, as well as in removing that false pride and foolish obstinacy that aggravate so much every dispute about labor. The present appeal to brute force is as absurd and worthless as it is antiquated. It is economically and ethically a crime. Knowledge, moderation, and Christian charity will permanently re-organize industry on a plane where the strikes and boycotts of medieval inheritance will be unknown."[26]

Butler's optimism and tone of conciliation did not last long, however. The first half of 1886 shattered it quickly enough. In quick succession, the

---

[26] *Science* VII (April 16, 1886): 339-341.

nation witnessed a wave of strikes in support of the eight hour day, the Haymarket Riot, major railroad strikes, and the brush fire growth of the politically-minded Knights of Labor. In an October review of Richard T. Ely's *The Labor Movement in America*, Butler now could mock only derisively the sentiments for cooperative social organization and an end to "warfare of all kinds" between worker and boss that he had been close to endorsing a few months earlier. Butler was unhappy about Ely's apparent approval of the growth of organized labor. What was needed was the "general elevation of 'men at large' and not either the regeneration or the extinction of a class." Still clinging to the "individualism" he had called outworn and feudal when it appeared in employers he had hoped to interest in arbitration in the spring, he reprimanded Ely for failing to recognize

> the fact, so clearly and so frequently proven during the past year, that their [trade union] demands are not for the laboring class at large, but for themselves, the small fraction of the whole that is banded together. Furthermore, they have not infrequently trampled under foot men quite as competent and quite as deserving as themselves, simply because they did not belong to the "union." It is this selfish feature in the labor organizations that has drawn down upon them opposition and contempt where often they would have had aid and sympathy.

Once again he noted how easily workers could be stirred up by "mischievous agitators," and criticized Ely for denying it. For one thing, Ely did not distance himself far enough from the program of the Knights of Labor. To Butler, the program was a disaster ("their denunciation of convict labor," for example, returning to his old hobby horse, "is either pure ignorance or else an invitation to the tax-paying population to support criminals in idleness"). Ely's book would have been much better if the author was less of an "idealist and *doctrinaire*," and did not allow "the demands of his theory to blind him to the true nature and tendency of the facts of which he treats." His call for the forging of ethical as well as industrial bonds of social cohesion, for the definition of "an ethical end toward which all true progress must move," and his sharp condemnation of violence and force in effecting social and industrial changes" had, however, Butler's complete approval.[27]

Butler did not continue to comment in as sustained a way on the concerns of labor and trade unions in his long career. That he did so at this time, however, is important in understanding the educational work he was beginning to embark upon. As noted at the beginning of the chapter, Butler's thinking was rooted in the rapid economic change and social instability of his society. Far from being an impractical, ivory tower academic, he was a hard-headed realist and problem solver, responding to specific

---

[27] *Science* VII (October 15, 1886): 353-355.

developments around him. The most significant of these developments raised profound questions about a secure and work-oriented labor force.[28] Many social leaders too often assumed a fealty and commitment to common purpose that no longer existed among workers.[29] Men like Butler were needed to anticipate the consequences that resulted from such negligence. At least some of the damage of oversight could be avoided by offering soon-to-be workers a set of values that would begin to inhibit their aspirations early in life. Schools, the social agencies to which potential laborers would have long and early exposure, presented themselves as ideal mediums for this purpose.[30]

No better opportunity to begin work in this direction could have presented itself to Butler than the chance to become president of the Industrial Education Association. The job was offered to him in 1887, and by his own account, he planned at the earliest moment of his new affiliation to turn the IEA toward teacher training. The focus of this training was always meant, as it had been for his friend Adler as well, to be preparation in manual training techniques for use in *all* aspects of the curriculum. The IEA, though not founded with this goal firmly in mind, had been moving steadily toward it before Butler was asked to lead the organization. When Butler more aggressively pushed it in this direction, he encountered little active resistance. The women who brought the IEA to life from its forerunner, the Kitchen Garden Association, had seen for some time that an expansion of their brainchild along the path Butler and others counseled was the most likely way to achieve their own more limited goals.

III

The Kitchen Garden Association grew out of the work of Emily Huntington with slum children in lower Manhattan. In the late 1870s at the Wilson Mission Industrial School on St. Marks Place, she began giving classes in

---

[28] On this issue in post-Civil War America, see Eric Foner, *Nothing But Freedom: Emancipation and its Legacy* (Baton Rouge, La., 1983). The concerns of northerners on this aspect of the labor question were addressed adroitly by Atlanta *Constitution* editor Henry W. Grady in his 1886 speech, "The New South," delivered to the New England Society of New York City. See Henry Woodfin Grady, *The New South and Other Addresses* (New York, 1969; orig. 1904).

[29] The earlier set of values and their erosion are discussed in Nick Salvatore, *Eugene V. Debs: Citizen and Socialist* (Urbana, Ill., 1982), chapter three. For a recent assessment of the Knights' importance, see Leon Fink, "The New Labor History and the Powers of Historical Pessimism: Consensus, Hegemony, and the Case of the Knights of Labor," *Journal of American History* 75, no. 1 (June 1988): 115-136.

[30] The concern of educators with the problem of worker intractability first became prominent after the railroad strikes of 1877. See, for example, the discussion in Edward Chase Kirkland, *Dream and Thought in the Business Community, 1860-1900* (Ithaca, N.Y., 1956), p. 55.

housework to the young girls of the area. Her plan was to use Froebel's notion that play was the proper work of children to teach them, in a better, more self-important and efficient way, to do the work of their own homes or that of others' (in the event they decided to take up domestic service). "All accustomed to dealing with children," she wrote in the introduction to the 1884 edition of her book explaining kitchen garden methods, "recognize the fact that the hour of labor must be varied, brightened and cheered, to make it endurable to the little workers."

There was nothing wrong with work. Indeed, she said, the words "by the sweat of thy brow," pronounced in the Garden of Eden were doubtless "intended by a loving and merciful heavenly Father to be a blessing to the race." The remedy for the misery of the poor was to get them to exchange their ignorance of this blessing for "intelligence, and so unto joy." "How to teach the masses," she wrote, "how to put courage into the drudgery, that was the problem." Then one day she visited a kindergarten and watched the "children of the wealthy" building with blocks in a sunny room surrounded by birds and flowers. "In a moment my fancy painted my poor children in the same pretty framing, setting little tables, washing little dishes, all the time listening to corrections and suggestions from kind teachers. What happy little faces! Work had become play, and the instruments of toil were playthings.—The same broom, only a little smaller, with a bright ribbon tied on the handle—the same cups to wash, only these were toys and so cunning!"[31]

Mrs. Harriet Mann Miller, writing in a national children's magazine in 1879 about Huntington's work, noted that the poor were sure to benefit from the good times coming. She was pleased at the opening of a school where children could play and learn at the same time. "While they are playing, and having delightful times," she wrote, it would be possible to teach them "what will really open to them a better life when too old to play." It brought tears to her eyes to see "these little ones, gathered from the streets and alleys of the great city, hands and faces washed, and all at happy play, while learning to be neat little housemaids, ready when big enough, to become busy with honest work instead of mischief."[32]

---

[31] Emily Huntington, *The Kitchen Garden; Or Object Lessons in Household Work* (New York, 1884; orig. 1878), p. 10. Interestingly, much of this early hopefulness, even though repeated unchanged in later editions of the book, did not, apparently, last. In her 1901 edition, Huntington added a new section to the introduction admitting that "it is doubtful if Kitchen Garden will ever, in this country or any other, so elevate the honorable duties of house-maid and house-keeper that the position will be in demand. All we can hope for Kitchen Garden for years to come is to make house-keeping easier, home more comfortable and cheerful, manners more self-respecting and gentle, and if Cooking Garden is added to the Kitchen Garden, living more economical and healthful." (1901 edition, p. 11.)

[32] "Little Housemaids," in *St. Nicholas: Scribner's Illustrated Magazine for Boys and Girls* (April, 1879): 403.

Soon after classes were begun, Huntington approached a number of
local philanthropists for help. One of them, Grace Hoadley Dodge, the
eldest daughter of the powerful merchant William E. Dodge, had already
been involved in a number of charitable projects. The latest was the
Working Girl's Club movement which, she said during a promotional trip to
London, had been started to attract young women "who are too conservative
to take an active part in labour movements." Classes were given in dressmaking, cooking, singing, and foreign languages; discussions of "deep"
subjects were also offered. But after a decade of this work, a decade that
would see the emergence of a national Association of Working Girls'
Societies, Grace Dodge felt compelled to move on. The organization she
had started, the one for "conservative" young women had, despite her
intentions, begun to consider wider social and economic issues, finally going so far as to ally with the labor movement she had hoped to steer it away
from. The Kitchen Garden movement—so much like the philanthropic
activity she knew—was more to her taste; in the years ahead she would be
its primary backer and promoter.[33]

Between 1880 and 1884 the KGA grew impressively. It employed both
voluntary and salaried teachers, and gave classes in a number of cities (and
by 1884 in a number of countries as well). It also began a publishing program for books on household economy and songs, the latter represented by
such fare as the following: "...Each morning so early I open the windows/To
let in the sunlight so fair;/For tenement houses, if crowded with
people,/Must always have plenty of air./So let every good house-
keeper,/Learn from my song here today,/That tenement houses need never
be dirty./Whatever the landlord may say."[34]

In addition, and almost from the beginning, the KGA recognized that
broader educational work was open to it. Huntington had hopes of introducing the system widely among Indians and blacks, and had visited Hampton
Institute to train its teachers in the work. The Association also hoped to see
it spread throughout the public schools. "The necessity of such an education," said Grace Dodge in the Association's first annual report, "is
becoming more and more apparent as [the managers] become better acquainted with the ways of living among the poor." Girls of today, she went
on, were not interested in household work. In fact, many of them, having
been through the public and normal schools, thought housework debasing,
as people like Godkin had recognized. Almost without exception, they preferred positions in stores as clerks, saleswomen, bookkeepers, and cashiers.

---

[33] Grace Dodge Notebooks, pp. 122-123, Teachers College Archives; Lawrence A. Cremin,
David A. Shannon, Mary E. Townsend, *A History of Teachers College, Columbia University*
(New York, 1954), p. 12; and Whittemore, p. 34.
[34] Kitchen Garden Association, *Lessons and Songs* (New York, 1880), p. 8.

The dangers that this environment posed—the risk of overexcitement, the strain of bad weather, the constant standing and bad food, in addition to the awful pay—were compounded by a more general worry, that "this avenue of employment is rapidly becoming overcrowded with applicants." Domestic service offered a far better future, and the KGA pledged itself to making it attractive.[35] An important side benefit was also promising. Like settlement workers, Kitchen Garden workers understood that the skills they were teaching the poor would be carried back to their dwelling places. "Through the promise of jobs," one writer noted, "the poor would clean up their own homes."[36]

The prominence of worry about the "great problem of the much vexed 'servant girl' question," as an early KGA document put it, may have had another source as well. During a period of increased immigration, economic uncertainty, and a need for more servants to manage households growing in size and affluence, adequate tests for reliability, punctuality, and competence may have been difficult to devise. The home was beginning to face employment problems much like those that had troubled the business world a generation earlier. Indeed, the statement that the IEA (soon to absorb the KGA) would provide certificates of recommendation for girls who had satisfactorily completed its course, indicated the extent of this recapitulation. Grace Dodge would appropriate for her own purposes an idea first used by her father and the founders of the YMCA to find young clerks "of character" thirty years before.[37]

But the most important reason for the preoccupation with the problem is suggested by a writer with no formal tie to the movement. An essay by E. L. Godkin, the political godfather of so many of the reformers, provides a valuable clue. In the "Morals and Manners of the Kitchen," what started as an attack on the incompetence of Irish domestics became an attack on something very different. Godkin began by noting that "Bridget" was a complete failure. She could not cook, she had no respect for a contract with her employer, and she had no conception of proper household deportment. In short, it appeared, she did not act servile enough. Godkin had a tendency to attribute her failings to heredity, but their cause ultimately turned out to be the company she kept. She had simply assimilated the attitudes of the American women who had hired her. These women were themselves too busy to care about food and too independent to care about ministering to men's tastes; themselves too interested in self-betterment to be faithful to an

---

[35] Kitchen Garden Association, *First Annual Report* (New York, 1880), pp. 7-8.

[36] George M. Simonson, "An Experimental Course in Philanthropy," in *Leslie's Weekly* (October 24, 1895).

[37] See "The Kitchen Garden Association," May 1, 1880, in Teachers College Archives; and my *Country Boys and Merchant Princes: The Social Control of Young Men in New York* (Lewisburg, Pa., 1975), chapters three and nine.

employer ("the only restraint on laborers of any class among us nowadays is the difficulty of finding another place"); and themselves too contemptuous of service. Bridget was given little reason to do better. "The things," Godkin concluded, "which American life and manners preach to her are not patience, sober-mindedness, faithfulness, diligence, and honesty, and eagerness for physical enjoyment." If Americans wanted their servants to be competent, it was necessary to sound a "gospel which is to win the natives [meaning old stock Americans] back to the ancient and noble ways" first.

Americans just seemed incapable of conveying an idea of the values servants had to acquire to do their job properly. The egalitarianism in their own attitudes toward one another made it impossible for Bridget to know how to act responsibly. Americans themselves were too impatient and restless in their drive to "better themselves" to offer a decent model for their help. And those in a position to lead had no understanding of, or interest in, the importance of taste and manners in defining their position and status.[38]

To remedy this deficiency was one of the most important functions of the university that Butler, who constantly talked of the need to fashion a leadership class, was soon to lead. This, at any rate, was the perception of one young man who spent his undergraduate years there in the 1940s. Columbia, he came to recognize, was in the business of altering sensibilities no less so in his time than in the period before the first World War when it "was the college of Old New York society—a kind of finishing school for young gentlemen who would soon enter the governing elite of the nation." The education he received at Columbia worked a radical change in his tastes, "and in changing my tastes it was ensuring that I would no longer be comfortable in the world from which I had come. For taste is an overwhelmingly important sociological force, capable by itself of turning strangers into brothers and brothers into strangers."[39]

By 1884 Grace Dodge understood that the Kitchen Garden format was too narrow for the work it was being pressured to do. The KGA's fourth (and last) annual report announced that the Association would be dissolved and reorganized on a broader basis to support industrial education in general. The new organization was to be called the Industrial Education Association to reflect its enlarged purpose to "promote special training of both sexes in any of those industries which affect the house and home...and which will enable those receiving it to become self-supporting"; to "introduce methods and systems of domestic and industrial training into schools"; and to "train teachers."[40]

---

[38] E. L. Godkin, *Reflections and Comments, 1865-1895* (New York, 1895), pp. 65-66.

[39] Norman Podhoretz, *Making It* (New York, 1967), p. 47. See also Wechsler, pp. 72-76.

[40] Whittemore, p. 35.

Although an application for space in the New York City schools was rejected (along with the Association's petition to begin such training under the city's own auspices), the IEA was hopeful "that the results achieved by other cities in the direction of manual training will sooner or later be reached in our own." In addition to the needs of school children, the Association made it clear in its second annual report, the needs "of those for whom changes in the school curriculum will come too late" also had to be considered. Striking the practical note that was in sharp contrast to the denial of interest in such matters that often appeared in more theoretical statements—such as those by Butler and Adler—the Association argued that it sought to respond to the "demand for preparation for the every day duties of life [that] is too urgent to be ignored or denied." Work with both school children and the laboring population had the same end, "the development of character and the cultivation of all the faculties for the *stern uses* of practical life." The two goals could easily be combined. Perhaps the New York school system, with its more than 3,000 teachers and 150,000 children, would soon reverse its current position, and end its resistance to "the tide of strong popular conviction, now sensibly felt, in favor of an education which claims for its pupils the cultivation of every faculty as a factor in the development of well-rounded character." In the meantime, the Association would continue to feel its way. Its work was worth doing, it knew. It pointed, said Secretary Jane Cattell, "toward the solution of some of the social and political problems that agitate our land. It touches the very roots of our civilization."

If it could not immediately gain entry into the public schools, the IEA would demonstrate its effectiveness wherever it could gain entry—in private schools, and, interestingly, in reformatories, asylums, and orphanages. It also ran training sessions in New York, Rochester, Philadelphia, and Toronto, and set up a school for domestics in lower Manhattan. After-school classes for public school children were begun there as well.

Within two years its efforts had created a demand for trained teachers that it could not fill without further reorientation and guidance from a skilled administrator and educator. At this point the needs of the IEA and the hopes of Barnard and Butler converged. On the recommendation of John B. Pine, a Columbia trustee, and no doubt also that of Barnard and Low (both honorary members of the IEA), and of C. R. Agnew, another trustee whose wife was close to Grace Dodge, Butler was chosen to lead the Association in the work of establishing a full-time teacher training facility. Butler, who had been writing on and advocating both manual training for

the public schools and the need for improved teacher training for over a
year, was well prepared.[41]

Butler's first report as president (two years later) made many of the
same points emphasized by earlier executives. He noted the enlarged promotional and publishing work the Association had taken up, and expressed
special pride in the educational leaflets and monographs that would soon
"raise the tone of reading of the teachers of the nation." The first of the
leaflets was an argument for manual training.

Butler then turned to his main focus, the immediate need for a teachers
college to provide teachers well versed in manual training. The need, he
emphasized, "arose from the lack of teachers competent to put into practice
the doctrines taught by the Association, even where such doctrines were
accepted and their immediate application asked for." If this training was to
be of greatest value, it had to be an integral part of general education. "The
teacher of manual training," he wrote, "should be the teacher of the other
subjects and not a special teacher." This was especially necessary in the
primary grades. "At this age," Butler noted, "what the pupils most need is a
constant, firm and consistent influence exerted upon them." This was something the high school plan of department teaching could not provide, and as
a result "character-training is sacrificed for doubtful gain in merely intellectual progress."

Yet the whole thrust of the pedagogy emerging in this period was to do
precisely this, to emphasize "character-training," at the expense of "mere
intellectual progress." With the widespread interest in child study and child
psychology, the skills of the new "character-training" pedagogy could
become an essential possession of every teacher regardless of specialty. As
it did, it would soon have the effect of downgrading both the pursuits of
intellect themselves and the qualities of mind necessary to achieve them. It
would also undermine the pride of accomplishment that teachers had taken
in mastering and transmitting these pursuits. Character traits appropriate to
the monotonous work of what was widely felt to be a stagnating economy
would become far more important to inculcate than the "mere intellectual
progress" that such an economy could not absorb and therefore need not
value.[42]

---

[41] *First Annual Report* of the Industrial Education Association (April, 1885), pp. 10-11, 16,
22; Whittemore, pp. 36-37; *Second Annual Report* of the Industrial Education Association
(April, 1886), pp. 13-15.

[42] On the belief that the economy was stagnating, see Charles A. Conant, "Can New
Openings Be Found for Capital?" *Atlantic Monthly* LXXXIV (November, 1899): 600-608; and
Eugene V. Smalley, "What are Normal Times?" *Forum* 23 (March, 1897): 96-100. Conant
recommended investment in underdeveloped countries as the hope of avoiding what otherwise
appeared to be a grim future: "This duty [of investment], imposed upon the superior races by
the evolution of events...affords the opportunity for the absorption of the surplus of savings not
applied to current consumption which is going on under the existing social system. Those who

There was also another reason "why the regular class teacher should...give the instruction in manual training." Subjects taught by a special teacher never had the same esteem as reading, writing, and arithmetic. They were seen simply as "excrescences" on the regular curriculum. "It would be fatal to manual training," said Butler, "to create the impression that this is true of it. Manual training must be an integral part of the curriculum or it should not be introduced at all."

The problem before the Association, therefore, became not "How to train teachers of manual training?" but "How to train teachers who shall know how to teach manual training?" What was needed was a professional school, not another normal school that was largely a glorified high school with a curriculum, according to one educator Butler quoted, "hampered by academic work." In addition to a new course of study rooted in psychology and methodology, the college would also include a model school. It was here that an actual demonstration that manual training in the school was both "feasible and beneficial" would take place.

For those following the progress of manual training, Butler had good news. "Intelligent" interest was increasing almost daily. In fact, he noted, "the opposition to it is now confined to the sluggish, the stupid and the educationally blind." Manual training was simply one of many reforms "demanded by the spirit of educational progress." Like the kindergarten and object teaching, "it is one of the many protests against that sacrifice of the pupil to rule and to system which is only too common." Schools, especially those in large cities, were to a great extent "educationally unhealthy." Although the teachers were partly to blame for this situation, the problem had other causes as well. According to Butler, the trouble "is principally with the system, with those who organize it and insist on its retention." The advent of manual training, along with a course of study "based on the nature of the child's mind," Butler was certain, "must bring improvement. It will substitute naturalness for unnaturalness and individuality for educational communism."[43]

Butler lost few opportunities to publicize the work of the IEA. In June, 1887, already knowing he was to become its first salaried president, he used his association with *Science* to discuss the organization's work. In the

---

do not welcome the responsibilities and the opportunity which this situation creates are fostering the discontent within the old civilized communities which breeds social and political revolution. The excess of production of finished goods over effective demand, the creation of trust combinations to check production, the resulting reduction of wages and of opportunity for the employment of labor,— all these are the consequences of shutting up capital to feed upon itself by closing the fields for new investments." (Conant, p. 607.) On Conant's importance, see Martin J. Sklar, *The Corporate Reconstruction of American Capitalism, 1890-1916: The Market, the Law, and Politics* (Cambridge, Eng., 1988), pp. 62-68, 72-85.
[43] *Annual Reports of the President and Treasurer of the Industrial Education Association made to the Board of Trustees* (May 4, 1888), pp. 10-11, 14, 17.

course of doing so, he gives us a further insight into his understanding of the IEA's purpose and his own motivations. Reviewing the antecedents of the IEA, Butler emphasized again its early commitment to teacher training and noted that a college for that purpose would be started in the fall. Butler then discussed the tenets that were meant to serve as the school's *raison d'etre*. He focused on the familiar arguments in favor of manual training as a part of general education but, interestingly, tried to clothe them in the rhetoric traditionally reserved for the common school curriculum it was, in fact, designed to replace. Like common school reformers decades ago, he argued that all "children wherever found, possess the same characteristics." It therefore followed that the innovations he and the IEA proposed "should be introduced into all classes and grades of schools, the private as well as the public school, and not alone in the primary public schools, but in all those of more advanced grades." Manual training recommended itself because of its general methodological and pedagogical benefits.

Then, before he finished, he touched the note that made the call for hand work emerging in this period historically distinctive. It had nothing at all to do with pedagogy. Instead, it related to social and economic changes that had made the search for a new pedagogy so important. The Association held, said its new president,

> that there exists in this country a widespread disinclination for manual labor which the present system seems powerless to overcome. There is a wide range of occupations which our boys and girls might with advantage enter were it not that they are prevented from doing so by a false view of the dignity of labor. That one of the results of this system of education will be to destroy a prejudice which in a measure arises from a want of familiarity with hand-work.

Butler, in other words, struck the note that accompanied so many of the arguments for manual training in the initial period of its promotion by patricians. The assumption common to all of them was that the upward mobility of the past was becoming little more than a memory. Butler, like many others, assumed that capital intensive development was no longer possible. Continuing changes in technology and expanded personal and social horizons, especially the expectation that grinding physical toil could be abandoned, was an illusion. Instead, the future would bring economic slowdown; labor intensive jobs would remain widespread—and even increase. Opportunity now lay in abandoning hopes of vertical mobility and instead looking to the possibilities of horizontal mobility that the coming slowdown, with its increased reliance on obsolete industrial methods, would present.

It was simply necessary that an older, unworkable set of beliefs be exchanged for one more in accord with present realities. Existing institutional arrangements did not seem capable of bringing this transformation of belief about; perhaps the new "system of education" would be more successful. This system would be embodied in new institutions specifically defined by their differences from existing normal schools. To make these differences clear was the reason for founding the New York College for the Training of Teachers. Until its program was available, education would continue to be behind the times. "The work of the schools, speaking broadly," he said a year and a half later in a magazine article promoting the new school's work, "has been poorly done and the mass of the school population has not even been properly instructed, much less educated....Popular education has not accomplished all the results hoped for, simply because popular education does not as yet exist. The framework, constitutional and administrative, is generally provided, but the proper supply of the necessary agents, thoroughly trained and equipped teachers, is not yet forthcoming."[44]

Butler hoped to remedy this situation as quickly as possible. A stream of pamphlets to make the arguments for manual training and domestic economy and the campaign for their widespread adoption well-known throughout the country soon issued from the Association's offices. Butler himself spoke on behalf of the cause whenever opportunity presented. In 1888 alone he addressed the New York State Teachers Association, the Convocation of the University of the State of New York, the American Institute for Instruction, and many less important groups about the need to make manual training an integral part of the entire curriculum. The College was determined to turn itself into a mecca for students of the new techniques and programs. According to the official history of Teachers College, "Visitors, boards of education, principals and teachers were all welcomed and their inquiries answered."[45] Its announcements and bulletins throughout the nineties virtually headlined the school's commitment to its hand work program.

When this focus on hand work began to change in the early years of the twentieth century, the school's orientation was firmly set. Teachers College would offer the practical advice that would help accommodate those exposed to it to the vicissitudes of American experience. With time that advice would be less dominated by the manual training offerings that it was at first. But the cast of mind that had originally permitted, and even encouraged, manual training to acquire so prominent a place in the curriculum would always remain. Teachers College, and the other schools of education that were modeled on it, would always retain the trade school mentality with which it began and with which it would hunker after whatever school-

---

[44] "The Industrial Education Association," *Science* IX (June 10, 1887): 558; *The Century* (October 16, 1889): 915.

[45] Cremin *et al.*, p. 24.

linked constituency it could attract. Sometimes these constituencies would be large (as in the 1940s and 1950s), at other times small (as today). But given the assumptions that shaped the College's direction from the beginning, it could never do much more than pursue the ephemeral and ultimately barren in education.

Teachers College would make its way as the fountainhead of pragmatic educational know-how and the source of needed credentials for generations of students determined to make academic careers for themselves. Coming from poor and immigrant backgrounds, they had little chance of acceptance at the nation's most prestigious graduate centers. But if they would lower their sights and strive for places in the nation's school systems, the fulfillment of their dreams for intellectually stimulating lives was possible; rewarding positions in primary and secondary teaching were available. And if the proper training was acquired, the proper techniques learned, these men and women might aspire to careers, within their chosen orbit, of responsibility and esteem. This was the opportunity that Teachers College offered its students, and they, grateful for it, flocked to its classrooms. Identifying the institution's chosen clientele, one trustee noted in 1895 that the school hoped "to make good the claim sometimes advanced on its behalf, that this is, indeed, the true type of the people's college."[46]

IV

With his departure in 1891 from the College for Teachers (to become head of Columbia's Department of Philosophy, Ethics, and Psychology), Butler's active promotional work on behalf of manual training seemed to come to a close. But his commitment to the premises and ideas that lay behind it did not. The *Educational Review*, founded in the same year he left the teachers college, was intended as a counterpoint to traditionalist educational journals such as *Education* and the *Journal of Education*, both edited by Thomas Bicknell. In it and his own speeches, the dominant note, for all the expressions of concern for traditional values and standards that he offered, was of the educational relativism that had made the promotion of manual training possible in the first place.

---

[46] Spencer Trask, "The Growth of Teachers College," in *Teachers College Bulletin* (January, 1895), p. 18. John Dewey, much involved in the work of preparing teachers in Chicago at this time, may have been thinking in these terms when he proposed a two-tiered system of teacher training: a higher tier to prepare educational leaders and a lower one to prepare the rank and file. The lower tier would include places, Dewey said, where "it will rarely be advisable to undertake [teachers'] initiation into ideas or methods not having some guarantee of time and experience back of them." (John Dewey, "Pedagogy as a University Discipline," [1896] in *Early Works, Volume 5, 1895-1898* [Carbondale, Ill., 1972], pp. 281-289.)

William James's Harvard philosophy colleague Josiah Royce set the tone for the new journal when in its first issue he asked, "Is There a Science of Education?" Royce's answer was no, a science of education, with uniformly applicable laws, did not exist. No educator, he argued, could define "with abstract universality, either the material upon which he must always work, namely, human nature, nor the end toward which he must always aim, namely the highest moral perfection of his pupil. Both these matters are modified for him by the course of evolution, and by the actual social environment." Local conditions and situations, he told his audience, "will properly interfere with anything like a truly scientific application of your pedagogical principles."

There simply was "no universally valid science of pedagogy that is capable of any complete formulation, and of direct application to individual pupils and teachers." Nor, he told his readers—many of whom might by now have been getting more than a little edgy about the hope of controlling the school children they would be facing—"will there ever be one so long as human nature develops, through cross-breeding in each new generation, individual types that never were there before; so long as history furnishes, in every age, novel social environments, new forms of faith, new ideals, a new industrial organization, and thus new problems for the educator."

In another article, Royce wanted to prepare his readers for the unpleasant reality that the classroom presented. It was, in his view, an area literally dominated by madness and irrationality. "Nearly if not quite all of us," he said, "must sooner or later have to try to teach not a few young people who are quite distinctly mental sufferers, pathological cases, burdened by heredity or by ill-fortune with sensitive, ill-working or constitutionally deficient brains, and yet not sufficiently diseased to find, under present social conditions, any more expert educational care than we can give them."[47] Instead of a stable, predictable environment to impart knowledge and learning, Royce offered a picture of the classroom that was a laboratory to study mental disorder and aberration. Instead of hope, guidance, and reassurance, the reader of Royce's remarks got a dose of despair, chaos, and disorder. To the teacher, whether inexperienced or not, the prospect was sure to be dispiriting; it was hardly the kind of news she needed to avoid the demoralization and sense of helplessness she was already beginning to experience as a result of other attacks on her independence and competence.[48]

---

[47] Royce, "Is There a Science of Education?" in *Educational Review* 1 (January, 1891): 17, 21 and (February, 1891): 127-128; "Mental Defect and Disorder from the Teacher's Point of View," in *Educational Review* 6 (1893): 209.

[48] See, in particular, muckraking tracts like Joseph Rice's *The Public School System in the United States* (1893) which Butler, in a review, especially hailed for its attack on the St. Louis school system. While Butler also noted that Rice was involved in efforts to displace traditional-

A theme that constantly appeared in Butler's speeches and writings in the 1890s also contributed to the erosion of the qualities of independence and competence. Again and again, he returned to the need for more flexibility and practicality in dealing with children. Childhood, he said, was the period of adjustment, the period that served as the point of departure for all educational theory and practice. "It must," he said, overturning everything that people like William T. Harris had argued for a generation, "at the same time provide us with our ideals." Since teachers would become the recognized experts in child management, the acceptance of Butler's ideas may have initially appeared to promise greater professionalism and control. In fact, however, accepting Butler's ideas would be one more accommodation to plans to replace the command of traditional knowledge the teacher did have with a shallow and vague method that could be acquired by anyone (at least in form), including superintendents and substitutes. When this happened, teachers would feel more insecure, vulnerable, and expendable, not less.

Like others of his day who came to embrace the non-traditional doctrines that were offered in the early issues of *Educational Review,* Butler also seemed to have lost faith in man's ability to set the goals toward which his society should advance. The development of science and modern life had not made him more certain of the path to the future. "Man has come to doubt not only his supremacy in the universe," he said in his 1895 NEA presidential address, but even his importance. He finds that "far from dwelling at the center of things, he is but 'the denizen of an obscure and tiny speck of cosmic matter quite invisible amid the innumerable throng of flaming suns that make up our galaxy.'" New scientific discoveries in biology, chemistry, physics, and geology may have initially been welcomed with enthusiasm and excitement. Too soon, however, these feelings had been

> succeeded by one [*sic*] of perplexity and doubt in the presence of the wholly new problems that they raise. The old self-assurance is lost. Men first stumble, blinded by the new and unaccustomed light, and then despair....Standards of truth are more definite than ever before; but standards of worth are strangely confused and at times even their existence is denied.

Butler demonstrated this no better than in the remainder of his speech, an equivocating mixture acknowledging the claims of utility in a democracy, and warning (with a note of resignation) of "a new series of dangers" against which the schools must guard. Later that same year he endorsed the doctrine that based teaching methods on the differences between individual

---

ists in Worcester, Massachusetts, and that this did "not tend to make one lean to the belief that his judgment, in the case of Worcester at least, is an unbiased one," he wanted to reassure readers that his recommendations for other cities—like New York—were sound. (*Educational Review* 6 [1893]: 500-502.)

students. Butler quoted Francis Parker, already being called the father of Progressive education, in support: "We dwell on those who have been saved by our older methods, but who has counted the lost?" A few minutes later he quoted Parker's enemy, William T. Harris, in the process of defending the opposite position, using Harris's words to serve his own purposes. Butler quoted Harris to the effect that "the chief consideration to which all others are to be subordinated is the 'requirement of the civilization into which the child is born, as determining not only what he shall study in school, but what habits and customs he shall be taught in the family before the school age arrives.'" Then he glossed this by saying, "Instead of forcing the course of study to suit the necessities of some preconceived system of educational organization, it [based, on the doctrine of interest developed above, the context suggested] should determine and control that organization absolutely."[49]

This kind of two-faced language may have enhanced Butler's position as a skilled mediator and broker. His abilities in this area were no doubt one of the sources of the great political power that Butler was in the process of amassing, both inside and outside purely educational circles. But the language should not obscure the underlying consistency of his views. When the National Society for the Promotion of Industrial Education met in 1907 to determine the best way to promote national legislation for vocational training, Butler, along with people like Jane Addams, welcomed the new organization with words that he could have spoken twenty years earlier. In his address opening the meeting, Butler assumed that the only question to be settled was the particular uses to which a vocational education movement eschewing any commitment to advance scientific training would be put. His remarks were meant to establish the framework within which the new organization would operate. Talking about "everyday" labor he made this framework plain. "Are we," he asked,

> depending too largely, perhaps, upon the vast natural resources which may some day begin to diminish, and are we depending too largely, perhaps, upon the widespread inventive faculty which has accomplished literally stupendous results in the past 100 years but which cannot be expected in the long run to win in the industrial race...?[50]

Although the immediate focus had changed—manual training, according to Dean James Russell of Teachers College, was no longer taken very

---

[49] Both speeches are reprinted in Butler's *The Meaning of Education and Other Essays and Addresses* (New York, 1898). For the first, "What Knowledge is Most Worth?" see pp. 38-40, 59; for the second, "Is There a New Education?" (also reprinted in *Educational Review* 11 [1896]), see pp. 84, 87-88.

[50] Butler, address to National Society for the Promotion of Industrial Education, in *Bulletin Number 1*, 1907, p. 18.

seriously[51]—the premises necessary to justify it and vocationalism were identical. Without first establishing the doctrine that technological progress based on vast resources and innovative talent (the twin assumptions of Mann and Harris) was past history, the new social purposes of either manual or vocational training could never have been realized.

Speaking on vocational education to the Commercial Club of Chicago a few years later, Butler emphasized the point again. "The select few," might still survive the struggle for advancement, "but," he pointed out, "to the great mass of human beings this opportunity is not open." Although the masses could take advantage of the elementary schools up to the age of thirteen or fourteen, "for well known economic reasons they cannot take advantage of what society has to offer beyond that." Instead, "they are compelled to go out and take hold of life as best they can at that tender age, unadapted, unfitted, with no specific tentacle ready to grip any particular hanging rope on which to climb to economic independence or security."

This lack of preparation was regrettable to Butler, but he easily resigned himself to the situation. Like Godkin before him, causality was a hard thing to pin down. The outcome, however unfortunate, was "the result of conditions for which no one in particular is responsible." Twenty five or thirty years ago when life was simple, when the home was more central to the family's livelihood, "much that was practically helpful was done for the boy." Today things were different. "Under our modern conditions, of huge city communities, of congested population, and the highly specialized character of all industrial work," he said, "unless one knows some particular thing, he knows nothing." The dilemma facing the thirteen or fourteen year old, forced to leave school and begin making a living, was "sad in the extreme." He or she, Butler noted in the Darwinian language that accorded well with his ideas of upward struggle in a hostile, unfavorable environment, was simply not adapted to do well. The problem this deficiency created was little different from that which first led him and others to consider the plight of convict labor a quarter century earlier: the "lack of adaptation leads directly to the problem of unemployment." Vocational education was meant to address this problem, "the problem of how to take this great mass of young people and to see to it that while they are beginning to learn life they shall learn it in some effective fashion, by making use of some talent, of some predisposition, taste, desire or need." If vocational education was successful, when the years of schooling were over, the young might be self-supporting and "do something...that is economically worth while."

---

[51] James E. Russell, "The School and Industrial Life," *Educational Review 38* (December, 1909), p. 3 of reprint in Teachers College Archives.

Changes in the schools would be necessary for such a program to work. Most important was the need to get rid of both old, formal pedagogic notions and "the apparatus and point of view of the old-fashioned school." The required point of view was that "of a special industry, of a particular vocation." In a sharp departure from his arguments for manual training during the 1880s, Butler now maintained that the successful approach to vocational education required intense practicality. No longer did the notion have to be sugar-coated with the patina of liberal studies as it did when he first introduced it. "We must get away," he said, "from those general aspects of training that are sometimes called by the ugly word 'cultural,' and take hold rather of that side of training which has to do with the mastery of some definite calling, career or activity."[52]

The common education of the elementary school years had its place; but now realism counseled pragmatism. For the masses, vocationalism would be just the way to help them find the places they would occupy in their adult years. Certainly they could not be accommodated by institutions like his own Columbia that would turn out the nation's leaders. Because of limited opportunities, dwindling resources, and the consequent decline in the value of innovation, most people had very limited prospects indeed. It was well to get them used to the idea that there was little point in expecting anything better. In the hope that this could be accomplished, Butler remained wedded to the faith and commitments of his earlier years.

---

[52] Nicholas Murray Butler, "Vocational Education: An Address," (Chicago, 1913), p. 11.

CHAPTER SIX

ACADEMIC CAREERS AND THE REFORM IMPULSE:
THE EXAMPLE OF JOHN DEWEY

I

The culminating expression of the educational thinking that arose as a reaction to the work of the common school system-builders was that of John Dewey. In contrast to people like Butler and Adler, Dewey was able to make his ideas acceptable to a much greater number of Americans. Although he had the preparatory efforts of his predecessors in the work of school reform to thank for some of his success, the largest part of it was due to a singular blend of elements that he alone was able to devise. Where their philosophy too often seemed elitist, Dewey's appeared democratic. Where theirs conjured up fear and distaste in confronting the discordant activity of cities, factories, and the immigrants that filled both, Dewey's, by comparison, appeared to accept the new environment and to encourage the hopes of its denizens. Instead of rebuking the new urban masses for their strivings, Dewey appeared to offer an approving and benevolent hand to help them on their way. Less worried about the tempering experiences of individual struggle that reformers like Butler at some level still believed were a necessary part of social survival, Dewey would lead the way into a world that emphasized association and community, accommodation of weakness, assimilation of differences, and toleration of limitation.

To a younger generation seeking to justify the institutional proliferation it believed necessary to cushion the blows of urban life—in the form, for example, of settlements, vocational guidance bureaus, correctional facilities, and juvenile courts— Dewey was a godsend. Conservative reformers who still clung to Darwinian ideas, were never able to fully shake off their fear that the social fabric Progressives sought to create could have dangerously enfeebling effects. Like Dewey they may have rejected the unrealistic optimism and selfishness of materialistic Americans. But they also were attracted to the toughness that propelled the acquisitive, and unlike Dewey, could never be consistently approving of the work of building the network of support apparently needed by all too many city dwellers.

Dewey's educational thinking was free of these doubts. It posed a vision of harmony and shared experience that promised both order and sta-

ble, if not spectacular, improvement. Many of the other educational reformers whose views we have examined offered only struggle, sacrifice,
resignation, and the acceptance of ineradicable inequalities for those who
lost out. For Dewey, the common man, as a valuable member of a growing
democracy, deserved charity and sympathy. The common man may not
have been going as far as he hoped in late nineteenth century America, but
he deserved encouragement and appreciation for the contribution, however
limited, he would be able to make. The interests of neighborhood integrity
and occupational pride, no small matters to Dewey, would at least be well
served. This outlook may have contrasted sharply with the Lincolnian
vision offered two generations earlier, but it was still more easily assimilated to the nation's democratic creed than the attitude of the gentry and its
spokesmen who saw the common man as either an unpleasant problem to be
faced only when it could not be ignored or a junior partner in an alliance
against more fearful enemies in business and industry. Compared to gentry
reformers, Dewey seemed compassionate and humane.

As it turned out, many of the differences between Dewey and others
who preceded him in educational work were more superficial than they appeared, and the application of Dewey's views only moved the schools more
quickly into channels already charted by disaffected reformers years before.
His views enabled the schools to more easily disavow an earlier commitment to disciplinary mastery, and to succumb to the cost efficient thinking
that would soon infect them. As the widespread adoption of the Gary pla-
toon system in the 1920s suggests,[1] in education the roots of the scientific
management notions associated with Frederick W. Taylor go back to pedagogical innovations introduced in the 1890s under Dewey's aegis. The reason the views of a cost accountant like Newton, Massachusetts school
superintendent Frank Spaulding (who asserted that questions about subject
matter were to be decided by determining how much each subject cost to
offer)[2] got any hearing at all was because Dewey, twenty years earlier, had
divorced the notion of purpose, defined by social need, from the determination of school curriculum.[3]

---

[1] See the accounts in Raymond E. Callahan, *Education and the Cult of Efficiency* (Chicago,
1962); and Ronald D. Cohen and Raymond A. Mohl, *The Paradox of Progressive Education:
The Gary Plan and Urban Schooling* (Port Washington, N.Y., 1979), chapter 6. For Dewey's
view of the system he inspired, see John and Evelyn Dewey, *Schools of Tomorrow* (New York,
1915).

[2] See the discussion of Frank Spaulding's address in the 1913 *Proceedings* of the National
Education Association, pp. 249-279, in Callahan, pp. 67-79.

[3] For a contrasting view of Dewey's significance—one, as noted in the introduction, that I
believe is not supported by the evidence—see Robert B. Westbrook, *John Dewey and
American Democracy* (Ithaca, N. Y., 1991).

II

Dewey was well-prepared for the educational work he undertook. Throughout his early career he had associated—sometimes casually, at other times more closely—with the institutions and individuals at the center of efforts to shape the new world of educational reform. Dewey had a unique background that fused two elements invaluable in making his views appealing. He had both populist associations and a careful tutoring in the rules for successfully managing a career in the academy, the setting that more and more would be the home of reform activity. Almost alone among his contemporaries, he understood the preoccupations of the general public and of the genteel reformers who had so much influence in the new universities where he spent most of his working life.

The learning experience that may have been most decisive for him is the one we know least about. This was his relation to the social and political life at Johns Hopkins University, where Dewey was a graduate student in the early 1880s. Born in 1859, and educated in the public schools and college of his hometown, Burlington, Vermont, Dewey came to Hopkins during years of freshness and excitement, years when a special closeness and atmosphere was said to be widespread among those who taught and studied there. Dewey was unlikely to have escaped contact with other soon-to-be famous students and faculty, a group that included Woodrow Wilson, Frederick Jackson Turner, Albert Shaw, H. C. Adams, J. Franklin Jameson, Josiah Royce, Richard T. Ely, and G. Stanley Hall (from whom Dewey would receive his doctoral degree). Moving to universities around the nation, these were the men who would alter the nature of the academy, bringing to it, especially, a new concern with public service and the formulation of social policies popular with a variety of Progressive politicians and their patrons.[4]

The sense of illumination that Frederic C. Howe, a small-town Pennsylvanian who became a leading urban reformer, experienced at Hopkins a few years later may have been akin to Dewey's own feelings. Because of the revelation he received, so strong that he talked about it as a "rebirth," Howe maintained that his life really began in the 1890s when he came to Hopkins after graduating from his hometown Alleghany College. "Under the influence of Richard T. Ely, Woodrow Wilson, Albert Shaw, James Bryce," he wrote in his autobiography years later, "I came alive."

---

[4] Hugh Hawkins, *Pioneer: A History of the Johns Hopkins University, 1874-1889* (Ithaca, 1960), pp. 272-84 and 308. On progressive policies the best place to start is still Richard Hofstadter, *The Age of Reform: From Bryan to F.D.R.* (New York, 1955). See also Robert Wiebe, *The Search for Order, 1877-1920* (New York, 1967); and Daniel T. Rodgers, "In Search of Progressivism," in Stanley I. Kutler and Stanley N. Katz, eds., *The Promise of American History: Progress and Prospects* (Baltimore, Md., 1982), pp. 113-132.

From Ely he learned that employers were capitalists who exploited their workers; from Bryce and Wilson, that the evils of party politics, the "struggle of vulgar interests, of ignoble motives, of untrained men," demanded the participation of the scholar as an antidote; and from Shaw, that corrupt cities could be cleansed by the detergent of objective business methods. These men seemed to be a "new kind of people," and with them he would form a "brotherhood of service" to assist a population "hungry for guidance...guidance which we, the scholars, alone could provide."[5]

In addition to the excitement generated by the new possibilities of university careers, Dewey learned other lessons also. The new academic professionals who first came to prominence in the United States during the 1880s and 1890s learned that the opportunity to engage in public service, either through direct action or more purely advisory work, was hedged in by a set of conditions that placed definite limits on the exercise of reform activity. The commitment to service, social change, and academic freedom was regulated both by a number of external, administrative barriers not always well-identified (and more inhibiting for that very reason), and by cautions self-imposed in the pursuit of personal advancement. Partly because of the newness of the confrontations that took place between administrators and faculty, and partly because of the untested strength of the antagonists, there was much over-reaction by administrators and much feeble or non-existent defense by faculty. In a series of academic freedom episodes, institutional muscle-flexing caused recantations, disavowals, and wholesale changes of scholarly direction and orientation.[6]

As ambitious as any of the men whose careers had been jeopardized by the open support of causes unpopular with powerful university patrons, Dewey passed through four of the institutions prominently involved in these confrontations (and was probably acquainted with the faculty involved). In the course of this passage it is doubtful that he failed to absorb the obvious lessons about the relationship between academic success and political circumspection. He probably learned early what kind of reform work could help and what kind could hurt his academic progress; by the time he got to the University of Chicago in 1894 he began to channel his reform efforts

---

[5] Frederic C. Howe, *The Confessions of a Reformer* (New York, 1925), pp. 1-8.

[6] These episodes are recounted in Mary O. Furner, *Advocacy and Objectivity: A Crisis in the Professionalization of American Social Science, 1865-1905* (Lexington, Ky., 1975). Other studies that discuss the constraints new academic careerists worked under are Dorothy Ross, *The Origins of American Social Science* (Cambridge, Eng., 1991); Stephen J. Diner, *Chicago and Its Universities: Public Policy in Chicago, 1892-1919* (Chapel Hill, N.C., 1980); Thomas L. Haskell, *The Emergence of Professional Social Science: The American Social Science Association and the Nineteenth Century Crisis of Authority* (Urbana, Ill., 1977); Burton J. Bledstein, *The Culture of Professionalism: The Middle Class and the Development of Higher Education in America* (New York, 1976); Laurence R. Veysey, *The Emergence of the American University* (Chicago, 1965); and Hawkins, *Pioneer*, pp. 312-314.

into paths that were likely to stir little controversy when scrutinized by the University's strong-willed president, William R. Harper and his supporters.

Dewey had already been well-exposed to the brand of reform that, when properly disciplined, was acceptable for a University of Chicago academic. In the years he spent at the University of Michigan in the eighties and early nineties he had been introduced by his wife to midwestern populism; he had established ties to teachers' organizations working to better themselves; and he had come under the influence of a syndicalist socialist with whom he almost collaborated on a radical newspaper and of whom he told William James (in 1891) that he owed "whatever freedom of sight and treatment there is in my ethics." It is probably not accidental that it was at this time that he stopped publishing in theological journals and began placing his writings in publications connected to Felix Adler's Ethical Culture movement. He had no doubt guessed that there was a better way than left-wing journalism to break into print on social questions.[7]

With this preoccupation, Dewey was ready for the association with the Chicago settlement movement he took up. He began working with Jane Addams's Hull-House, soon joining with her, and the members of other civic organizations, in support of an educational effort directed toward many of the same clientele as the settlement. Together, they hoped to keep alive the normal school run by Francis W. Parker. Parker had been in Chicago since being forced out of Boston in 1883,[8] and, as head of the Cook County Normal School, engaged in yearly skirmishing with the Board of Education over his budget. His educational policies, similar to the ones advocated by his old patron Charles Francis Adams, Jr. and Felix Adler, were at the bottom of these fights, and Dewey, Addams, and others who admired Parker's work did what they could to help him get the money he needed to continue. The fights finally ended when the private teachers' institute set up for Parker by Cyrus McCormick's daughter was absorbed, at President Harper's urging, by the University of Chicago.[9]

---

[7] Material about these years can be found in Arthur G. Wirth, *John Dewey as Educator: His Design for Work in Education* (New York, 1966), p. 15; Lewis Feuer, "John Dewey and the Back to the People Movement," *Journal of the History of Ideas* 20 (1959): 548; and Neil Coughlan, *Young John Dewey* (Chicago, 1975), pp. 69, 74, 93-106. Dewey's letter to William James is quoted in Ralph Barton Perry, *The Thought and Character of William James* 2 vols. (Boston, 1935), 2: 518. See also George Dykhuizen, "John Dewey at Johns Hopkins (1882-1884)," in *Journal of the History of Ideas* 22 (1961): 103-04.

[8] Michael B. Katz discusses the circumstances of Parker's departure from Boston in "The Emergence of Bureaucracy in Urban Education: The Boston Case, 1850-1884, Part II," *History of Education Quarterly* 8 (Fall, 1968): 319-358.

[9] Darnell Rucker, *The Chicago Pragmatists* (Minneapolis, 1969), pp. 83-85. This consolidation meant that in 1901 the university had a department of pedagogy and a laboratory school, run by Dewey, a School of Education (as the institute was called) and an elementary school run by Parker, and the Chicago Manual Training School, and the South Side Academy. After Parker's death the next year, the units under his control passed to Dewey.

Harper, a dominating personality, usually got what he wanted. His sympathies and allegiances set the tone for most of what his faculty considered permissible political activity, and his actions were no doubt, as he intended they should be, carefully monitored by them for clues to what he considered appropriate. Although the university community shared the emerging consensus about the importance of influencing social policy, there were also, as at other institutions of higher learning, correspondingly sharp limits to faculty activism, dictated by academic ties to and dependence on a host of civic elites for funding, approval, and advancement. As the embodiment of patron predilections and prejudices, Harper was not always tolerant of professors who exceeded the limits of the permissible that he and his constituency had set. Espousing ideas and causes that were unpopular with university benefactors got extremely short shrift from him and them both.[10]

On the other hand, ideas and causes that were in favor with them and the patrician reform movement were a different matter. Harper himself pointed the way toward the acceptable, with an involvement in a wide range of reform efforts. Especially important, in light of the direction Dewey's own work took, was the leadership Harper gave to the forces seeking to reform public education in Chicago. Like other efforts being led by Nicholas Murray Butler in New York,[11] Harper was fighting to reduce the size and centralize the control of the city board of education as a way of eliminating "corrupt," "inferior," and "special interest" members with local, and hence independent, political bases.

Through a city commission he chaired in the late 1890s, Harper proposed legislation designed to have this effect. The commission's report

---

[10] See Diner, pp. 6-8, and 47-48. The most well-known example of Harper's intolerance was the firing of Edward Bemis, an economist and student of Richard T. Ely who attacked railroad owners during the Pullman strike of 1894. Diner notes that "colleagues around the country who shared Bemis's views did not rally, publicly, to his defense....In part they too feared for their positions, but the manner of Bemis's advocacy also proved embarrassing." See also Furner for an account of Harper's role and the lack of support Bemis received (Chapter 8, "The Perils of Radicalism"); and George Dykhuizen, *The Life and Mind of John Dewey* (Carbondale, Ill., 1973), p. 102. Dykhuizen details the constant stream of political advice that John D. Rockefeller's secretary, F. T. Gates, sent to Harper. Apparently, Dewey was not any more attentive to the matter than the rest of his colleagues. In 1902 he could write that there was little threat to academic freedom in nonsectarian universities (like his own University of Chicago). Regarding university benefactors, Dewey wrote that "the man with money hardly dare [*sic*] directly interfere with freedom of inquiry, even if he wished to, and no respectable university administration would have the courage, even if it were willing to defy the combined condemnation of other universities and of the general public." When a faculty member did come under attack, Dewey argued that it was style, not content, that was the issue: "Lack of reverence for the things that mean much to humanity, joined with a craving for public notoriety, may induce a man to pose as a martyr to truth when in reality he is a victim of his own lack of mental and moral poise." (Dykhuizen, pp. 101-102, quoting Dewey on "Academic Freedom," *Educational Review* 13 [1902]: 1-14.)

[11] Interestingly, when Dewey left Chicago in 1904 it was to Butler's Columbia University that he went.

made clear how sweeping were the changes he sought. Most important was
to give legal recognition and expanded duties to the superintendent.
According to Harper, the superintendent's duties should include "direct responsibility for hiring and promoting teachers, determining curriculum,
choosing textbooks and apparatus." Harper also argued for upgrading the
preparation of teachers. To him, this meant increasing university influence
in preparing and certifying them (graduates of "approved colleges" would
be chosen by examination), a process that would bypass training in the system's own normal schools. In addition, Harper urged independent testing
for promotions, and "wider latitude" for principals and teachers to choose
textbooks and modify the curriculum. Teachers, in particular, could now be
given these opportunities as more and more of them would be coming out of
the university's own education programs (programs that Dewey headed).
The report also called for the introduction of kindergartens, the expansion of
evening and vacation schools, citizenship training, and the organization of
advisory teachers' councils. The councils, an alternative to the growing
strength of the teachers' union, would be yet another way to undercut the
influence of local political groupings. Merit pay, which Chicago teachers
had long believed to encourage favoritism and reduce payrolls, was another
commission recommendation that would weaken the position of the existing
teaching staff.[12]

The point of reviewing these activities is not to suggest that Dewey's
own educational and reform ideas ran parallel to Harper's at every point.
Indeed, the reason he is well-known and Harper forgotten (except by students of higher education) is that they did not. It is, instead, to suggest the
context in which Dewey's ideas and activities took form. Neither in public
nor while he was establishing his reputation (and forging his own channels
of approach to the Chicago elite whose good opinion and largesse he needed
to fund his educational projects) did Dewey embark on a path that, for political reasons, would displease Harper or the men at whose pleasure he
served. Like other academics feeling their way into new and unfamiliar
roles, Dewey understood the value, as Diner has noted, "of forg[ing] a style
of activism and advocacy consistent with one's professional aspirations."[13]

---

[12] See Diner, p. 83; Mary J. Herrick, *The Chicago Schools: A Social and Political History*
(Beverly Hills, Cal., 1971), p. 83; and Julia Wrigley, *Class Politics and Public Schools:
Chicago, 1900-1950* (New Brunswick, N.J., 1982), pp. 92-97.

[13] Diner, p. 7. Given the strains and anxieties incident to the emergence of academic careers
in which, according to another historian, "promising young men wore themselves down
through worry and overwork as they exhausted themselves in the classroom, anxiously curried
the favor of their mentors and patrons, neglected their health, postponed marriages, moon-
lighted and borrowed money to make ends meet," circumspection was to be expected. "The
victims of such a system, their emotions paralyzed," Burton Bledstein continues about the
people who went through the institutions that had Dewey as one of their earliest products,
"proceeded cautiously and conservatively in all their movements." (Bledstein, p. 103.) See also

Dewey was not likely to take any foolhardy or adventurous position far in advance of the public opinion shared by his peers or the people on whom they were dependent (in a way, for those with a desire to do "useful," public-spirited work requiring outside funding, more than before). That opinion led him to a reform posture that, for all its populist rhetorical trappings, committed him only to a program already being pressed, in most of its particulars, by Chicago political forces and university patrons who appeared to talk a very different game. Dewey had a close relationship to these forces, and the reform climate they fostered must be seen as a decisive influence on the thinking for which he is best remembered. Lewis Feuer, who has studied the origins of this thinking closely, is therefore only partly correct when he writes, "It is a mistake to see the source of Dewey's philosophy in its manifest content. It is wrong to define its central generating problem as the statement of the philosophical significance of evolution, or the elimination of formalism and dualism....What was distinctive in Dewey's thought was the perspective of the back to the people movement [Feuer's name for Dewey's brand of democratic reform]."[14] What in fact was distinctive in Dewey's thought was the perspective of the back to the people movement wedded to the career aspirations of the new professoriat of which Dewey was an early and leading member.

III

As we have seen, those aspirations demanded orthodoxy in opinion and demeanor. Orthodoxy made opinion (and those who offered it) authoritative, and many of the newer universities in this period saw themselves above all as the agencies that housed and nurtured both. To the most aggressive gentry-connected university builders of the late nineteenth century—men like Charles William Eliot, Andrew D. White, Daniel Coit Gilman, and Harper—the production, certification, and appropriate presentation of indisputable opinion was one of the most important ingredients of the claims to position and deference made by the elites they served. For generations much of the work of certifying opinion had resided in institutions monopolized or controlled by the patrician elite itself. But by the 1880s, a rapidly industrializing and urbanizing society, requiring a more sophisticated and knowledgeable public and more precise and reliable information about a host of technical and social matters, had undermined the credibility of the elite's custodial claims. To the university presidents who were among the most class conscious members of this elite and its retainers,

---

Bledstein, p. 113. There is a wealth of material relating to this point in Veysey as well; some of it is quoted in the discussion that follows.
[14] Feuer: 568.

a new source of sound opinion, one that would still leave secure the elite's prerogatives, had to be found.[15]

Electoral politics did not seem to be easily applied to the purpose of securing these prerogatives. Tammany boss Richard Croker thought the problem, as he told British journalist (and Mugwump supporter) W. T. Stead, was that Mugwumps had no staying power when it came to the job of winning office. Unlike some Mugwumps, such as Cornell's White (who feared the problem may have been purely one of physical strength),[16] Croker attributed their lack of political endurance to cultural inhibitors. After the heat of the campaign had passed, reform organizations broke up, this kind of politics apparently too dirty a business for men of breeding to consider as full-time work.[17] But Croker was only partly right. There are many examples of fierce and protracted patrician political activity. The issue was not just the uncongeniality of electoral politics, but of its ineffectiveness as well. It was becoming clear that frontal political defense of one's interests could not be counted on to work in the face of popular opposition and poor elite preparation. Both locally and nationally, as in the Liberal Republican movement of 1872, it proved notably unsuccessful as a way to hold power and command deference.[18]

---

[15] For an understanding of the "crisis of authority" and the search for a new way to make opinion authoritative, I am indebted to Thomas Haskell's excellent book cited above. A brief exposition of his argument appears in his review of Bledstein's *Culture of Professionalism* in the *New York Review of Books*, October 13, 1977. It is there, against Bledstein's view (p.32), that he says, "The struggle to modernize higher education and extend the orbit of institutionalized expertise in American culture did not pit the middle class against the rest of the population: it pitted a small, cultivated forward-looking gentry elite against the inert middle class and nearly everyone else. The university presidents Bledstein discusses were important spokesmen for this elite." See also pp. 64 and 120-121 of Haskell's book. Although she puts the case somewhat differently, Dorothy Ross writing about the rise of academic social science, follows Haskell's account. See her *Origins of American Social Science*, pp. xvi, 53-54, 62-64, 158-161. For a view that stresses the more liberal, humanitarian middle class origins of the social sciences, see William Leach, *True Love and Perfect Union: The Feminist Reform of Sex and Society* (New York, 1980).

[16] White, at one point, for example, posed the problem this way: "There is perhaps nothing so wretched in our country today as the frequently servile acquiescence of many excellent men in the rule of 'bosses.' With the proper system of physical education, I believe the tyranny of unworthy leaders would be more and more difficult, and finally impossible. There is something in the possession of a sound physical frame in good training of great value to any man in resisting encroachments, whether physical or political." (Bledstein, p. 152.)

[17] Bernard Crick, *The American Science of Politics: Its Origins and Conditions* (Berkeley, Cal., 1959), p. 33.

[18] On the questions of political commitment and effectiveness, see David C. Hammack, *Power and Society: Greater New York at the Turn of the Century* (New York, 1982); Geoffrey Blodgett, *The Gentle Reformers: Massachusetts Democrats in the Cleveland Era* (Cambridge, Mass., 1966); John G. Sproat, *"The Best Men": Liberal Reformers in the Gilded Age* (New York, 1968); and Peter Dobkin Hall, *The Organization of American Culture, 1700-1900: Private Institutions, Elites, and the Origins of American Nationality* (New York, 1982).

Not that the attempt was to be given up; but a more effective institutional launching pad had to be secured. For some of the patrician elite, the university was the best candidate possible. As Bernard Crick has suggested, electoral defeat "only increased the faith...of 'the better elements' in the *long-run* [his italics] remedial effects of Higher Education." E. L. Godkin, Crick writes, "spoke for the new College Presidents like Gilman, White, and Eliot as well as for his fellow-editors of the high-toned journals" when he noted:

> In the popular mind there is what may be called a disposition to believe not only that one man is as good as another, but that he knows as much on any matter of general interest. In any particular business the superiority of the man who has long followed it is freely acknowledged, but in public affairs this is not so much denied as disregarded.

Godkin's reference to the "superiority of the man who has long followed it," as Crick says the context of his argument makes clear, is "meant to be an argument for the greater participation of the *student* [his italics] of politics, not for a greater trust of the political regular."[19] Those students, it was felt by people like Godkin, should be supplied by the colleges and universities that leading Mugwumps were proceeding to modernize.

More farsighted men, like Daniel Coit Gilman of Johns Hopkins, realized that Godkin only saw part of the problem. They agreed that the universities were to serve what were, in the end, political goals, but not that electoral work had much place in reaching them. Ultimately, the gentry elite was seeking a style and posture that would insure continued influence and regard; this purpose dictated retreat from, not involvement in, party politics. Certainly a role in the front lines was increasingly untenable. The ability to command deference and authority came from an association with the production of creditable opinion, opinion that was dispassionate and objective. Activities such as electoral campaigning, party maneuvering, and dealmaking would taint its practitioners with the qualities from which they wanted to appear free.[20] Emotionalism, partisanship, and compromise were not the best advertisements for scientific detachment. As paradoxical as it may have seemed, it was the apparent distance from politics that could assure political success.

---

[19] Crick, *The American Science of Politics* p. 33. On the supply of students (by colleges, in particular) for the Mugwump cause, see also James McLachlan, "American Colleges and the Transmission of Culture: The Case of the Mugwumps," in Stanley Elkins and Eric McKitrick, eds., *The Hofstadter Aegis: A Memorial* (New York, 1974).

[20] Haskell has a good discussion of this recognition in his *Emergence of Professional Social Science*, pp. 162-168. He also talks about the effects of the failure of Liberal Republicanism, pp. 126-130.

Properly limited in expansion to prevent the culturally unworthy from gaining entry,[21] the university, with its separate departments, specialized disciplines and methods, would provide a new foundation for the consolidation of elite influence. Employing new tools (the methods of "objective science") and a new custodial staff (the experts with advanced university degrees), they could continue to control the opinion on which their social role rested. Opinion would serve the same end that it always had; only its point of origin would be different. The task of explaining the workings of a complex society would be entrusted to men and women who were specially trained to uncover its secrets and who possessed the special credentials to present those secrets to the public. Their work, tested against commonly accepted criteria that, as Haskell puts it, "were not in any obvious way personal, partisan, or particular," would receive approbation from a public viewed as increasingly reluctant to extend it. The organized skills and expertise of professors enabled them to pose as "communities of practitioners who police each other's opinions and thereby create something approaching a consensus of the competent."[22] Perhaps they could now win for the opinions they reclothed in the linguistic dress of their special disciplines the respect in danger of being withdrawn from them.

To many of its proponents, therefore, the encouragement of professionalism offered an unexcelled opportunity. They would welcome the professionals and give them permanent institutional homes in the reorganized universities over which they presided. They would offer them security (after a period of chastening uncertainty during which it could be made clear how the university could determine which individuals within the new professions would receive protection and preferment), promote their accomplishments, and help assure the longevity of the beliefs they deemed most valuable.

At one time, the men that university executives represented may have feared that the control of opinion and the authority it conferred was permanently slipping away. But by the 1890s they would grow more confident; by then they had begun to see that this hardly needed to be the case. The choice of aggressive chief executives and the judicious application of the influence and power the latter came to wield would see to that. The communities of experts given sanctuary behind university walls would in time come to understand that the independence they thought they were gaining was bought

---

[21] On this point, see the chapter on E. L. Godkin above; and the remarks of G. Stanley Hall, in his *Adolescence: Its Psychology and Its Relations to Physiology, Anthropology, Sociology, Sex, Crime, Religion and Education* 2 vols. (New York, 1904), II: 558-560. Hall, after teaching at Johns Hopkins during the 1880s, went on to a prominent career as an educator and university builder. See Dorothy Ross, *G. Stanley Hall: The Psychologist as Prophet* (Chicago, 1972). Gilman also worried about "the dangers of an overexpansion of the colleges and universities." (Crick, p. 34.)

[22] The first Haskell quotation is in his *Emergence of Professional Social Science*, p. 89; the second, in his *New York Review of Books* article (cited above), p. 33.

at a price that ruled out any ventures into the realm of the controversial or unseemly. By then, however, the patterns of the future would be well set; career aspirations, including Dewey's, would proceed within this framework or not at all.

Whatever academics may have thought, many of the assumptions and opinions they would end up sanctifying would differ little from those cherished by the early gentry belief custodians of the American Social Science Association and the traditional professions of the law, medicine, and clergy. Beneath the change in emphasis from competition to community, from laissez faire to government interference, and from voluntaristic to environmental theories of social causation lay the same attempt to deny the relevance of popular intellectual and educational growth to continued economic expansion. This attitude in part explains why the research ideal promoted by university leaders was early identified with pure scientific investigation.[23] Pure science was not yet felt to involve the controversy that could overwhelm explorations in other academic areas more obviously related to questions of public policy and debate. In addition, its pursuit was believed to promote values of selfless dedication, sacrifice, and persistence. These values, so opposed to thoughts of immediate reward, might help divert attention from the crass materialism of American industrial expansion that so many patricians deplored. In time, it was no doubt hoped, the associations developed between pure science, an ideal of personal conduct, and a dedication to truth and accuracy might spill over to social science disciplines as well.

Whether or not academics themselves were aware of the imperatives restructuring the academy, they profited immensely from them, as long, that is, as they tailored their inquiries to correspond to the assumptions and conclusions of the gentry elite that provided their funds. It was not that the gentry could not accommodate disagreement. It was just that in this early period when universities were first establishing their social claims, authoritative opinion—opinion produced by scientific methods and subject to scientific tests—should be as uniform as possible. Uniformity suggested infallibility, infallibility justified orthodoxy, and orthodoxy conferred authority. If accepted members of the academic community proffered opinions of too much variety, the idea that any of them had a special authority, or that the university, the place where the opinions were produced, had any special relation to authority, would be difficult to establish.

The problem was not really in determining where the consensus of opinion should rest. Through the control of funding, hiring, and promotion, this posed no insuperable difficulty. Rather, the problem was to bring the population to think of the university, and its sequestered scholars, as alone

---

[23] See Veysey, p. 139.

the source of opinion confidently embraceable as sound. The problem was
to connect authority and the university as if they were tied by the logic of an
Aristotelian syllogism. Here was where authoritative opinion came from.
And opinion open to challenge, dispute, or question (within, of course, the
limits set by the keepers of disciplinary purity) simply could not carry the
kind of assertive weight its purveyors were seeking. This notion of indis-
putability, not the plausibility or integrity of any one opinion, was the issue
at stake in the demands for orthodoxy and the acute intolerance of deviance
that appeared in the period of university direction setting. To its patrons, the
university had to speak with one voice or its function would be seriously
compromised. Not that there was any reason to fear that it would not. As
long as those providing the opinions upon which the university's reputation
would rest understood its goals there should not be any problem. By a process combining heavy-handed education and subtle cajolery, the terms of
survival and even prosperity within the university were soon to be well understood by those who struggled to make their way within it.

Dewey's colleague at the University of Chicago, I. W. Howerth, was
one of those who made this understanding plain. Speaking in 1900 about
academic freedom, he noted that "thought is free so long as it is sound, and
the authorities have their own convictions in regard to what constitutes
sound thinking.... [T]here is not a college or university in the country that
would long tolerate an active and formidable advocate of serious changes in
the present social order." When Harvard's Eliot said that academics "ought
to be leaders of opinion in a civilized commonwealth, ought to have more
influence and power than the less educated classes," it was, no doubt, with
the expectation that they had well-internalized Howerth's perceptions.[24]
Called the "single most important figure in the professionalization of the
academic world," Gilman for example, claimed that the university should
promote "intellectual freedom in the pursuit of truth" and "the broadest
charity toward those from whom we differ in opinion." But he was also certain, as he wrote to a Hopkins trustee, that the university's spirit could not
tolerate the existence of "ecclesiastical differences" or "political strife"
within it. As Laurence Veysey has understated the case, views like
Gilman's "might mean that in controversial fields professors were to be
favored who promoted calm reconciliation rather than antagonisms."[25]

Social behavior was no less important than belief; here too orthodoxy
was required. University leaders, about to hire a new faculty member, said
Daniel Coit Gilman, must take into account "certain moral and social considerations" to guarantee that he will "be cultivated in manner & at his ease

[24] Howerth and Eliot are quoted in Veysey, pp. 417 and 94, respectively.
[25] The opinion of Gilman's importance is Haskell's (*Emergence of Professional Social Science*, p. 145); Gilman is quoted by Veysey, p. 163.

in the social relations which we are called upon to maintain." As Columbia's Butler wrote without choosing which was more important, the college professor "owes something to ordinary standards of sanity and good breeding as well as to the truth"; and Berkeley's Benjamin Ide Wheeler made it clear that the "ascetic, teetotal radical, reformer [or] agitator" had no place in a teaching post. In bargaining for a higher salary to come to the University of Chicago in 1894, Dewey was probably not just throwing administration arguments like those of Gilman, Butler, and Wheeler the way they had come when he said he could not consider President Harper's $4000 offer (Dewey wanted $5000) because it was not "an adequate basis for living as we should want to live (and as the University would want us to live) in Chicago." For all his professed egalitarianism, he too, may have felt the desire, as a contributor to the *Educational Review* put it a few years later, to "share without effort in the life of the best society—the aristocracy, in the literal sense" that was expected to characterize the social style of university faculty.[26]

That attitudes like these would lead to an intellectual sterility and predictability on college and university campuses is not surprising. Given the aggressive and dominating posture taken in this period by administrators trying to please their patrons, the pressures toward consensus in attitude and conformity in outward behavior would prove almost irresistible. Both aspects of university life, the consensus and the conformity, were important. The university should speak with one voice and, as it did so, reflect a well-established, well-agreed upon set of beliefs.

When David Starr Jordan explained to E. A. Ross why Mrs. Leland Stanford wanted Ross fired, he was touching on the conformity educators expected their schools to advance. Where Mrs. Stanford told Jordan that Ross had to go because he held political opinions (opposing Asian immigration and favoring municipal ownership of utilities) contrary to her own, he told Ross that Mrs. Stanford felt "that the reputation of the University for serious conservatism is impared [*sic*], and that "the University should be a source of unprejudiced, sound, and conservative opinion." "The matter of immigration," he noted significantly, "she takes most seriously, but it is rather that she is jealous of the good name of the University, than that she supports any particular ideas."[27] Translating Mrs. Stanford's personal, political, and locally defined objections into general terms of institutional stature, Jordan was saying that tolerance of Ross and his views would damage the credibility of a school one of whose most important reasons to exist was the drive to establish itself as a source of wisdom above question.

---

[26] Veysey, pp. 163, (Gilman); 363-364 (Butler and Wheeler); 391 (Dewey and *The Educational Review*).

[27] Veysey, p. 403.

If opinion was to be sanctified and enshrined as estimable by its very institutional origins and associations, it had to divorce itself from any hint of controversy.

IV

As we have seen, central to what was proper in presupposition and conclusion was an emphasis on the way scarce opportunity and resources would make continued reliance on an integrating, cosmopolitan minority necessary. And while a host of changes took place in overseeing the process by which opinion was produced, none challenged this bedrock notion. People like Dewey, Robert Park, Frederic C. Howe, Charles H. Cooley, and Frederick Jackson Turner may have adopted a new, impersonal language and mode of "causal attribution," as Haskell puts it,[28] to talk about social phenomena. All of them, however, drew from this language the same inferences about the ultimate possibilities for social freedom as the gentry elite from which they had supposedly broken. The modern university's academic minions, though they clothed their views in the paraphernalia of method and objectivity, had appropriated the same anti-science, anti-expansion attitudes that had propelled its original spokesmen into action in the decades after the Civil War.

Many of those who would become leaders in their particular disciplines found the appropriation of restrictive attitudes especially hard to resist. These men had more fully internalized the university's role as the source of authoritative opinion, and they worked tirelessly to establish its reputation for "standardized" credibility. Not that they always succeeded. Countervailing economic and social tendencies set into motion at the same time—such as the state university movement and the industrial thrust it was tied to, in both manufacturing and, especially in the Midwest, agricultural areas[29]—would make success elusive. But this should not obscure the effort these academics made. Instead of showing how the university could assist the economic growth that the majority of Americans were committed to, they were determined to show how the university could act as a counterweight to it.

---

[28] See Haskell, p. 14, and his conclusion, for a discussion of the changes in "causal attribution" occurring in this period.

[29] On the state university movement and its differences from gentry-led institutions of higher education, see Frederick Rudolph, *The American College and University: A History* (New York, 1962), pp. 254-65; Earle D. Ross, *Democracy's College: The Land-Grant Movement in the Formative Stage* (Ames, Iowa, 1942); and Edward D. Eddy, Jr., *Colleges for Our Land and Time: The Land-Grant Idea in American Education* (New York, 1957). See also Veysey, pp. 77, 88, 95-96.

Frederick Jackson Turner is a good example of a new academic leader who tried to describe the university's mission in this way.[30] On a number of occasions he expressed the hope that the university could point to goals other than the materialistic ones that appeared to dominate the lives of so many Americans. Ambition, the mainspring of American development, could not, he knew, be denied. Even in a period when, as he thought, economic progress was not likely to come easily, Americans would strive to get ahead. But perhaps the way they thought about getting ahead could itself be changed. Perhaps ambition could be redirected into more neglected, and ethereal, channels.

The fact that the doors were closing for American opportunity and opportunists, Turner argued in a famous address delivered four years after he moved to Harvard University, should be seen not as a cause for despair but as a challenge:

> What is needed [he said] is the multiplication of motives for ambition and the opening of new lines of achievement for the strongest. As we turn from the task of the first rough conquest of the continent there lies before us a whole wealth of unexploited resources in the realm of the spirit. Arts and letters, science and better social creation, loyalty and political service to the commonweal,—these and a thousand other directions of activity are open to the men, who formerly under the incentive of attaining distinction by amassing extraordinary wealth, saw success only in material display. Newer and finer careers will open to the ambitious when once public opinion shall award the laurels to those who rise above their fellows in these new fields of labor....A new era will come if schools and universities can only widen the intellectual horizon of the people, help lay the foundations of a better industrial life, show them new goals for endeavor, inspire them with more varied and higher ideals.[31]

---

[30] Although a native of Wisconsin and a long-time member of the University of Wisconsin's history department, a good argument can be made that much of Turner's intellectual framework was indebted more to British Malthusian assumptions about life and economy than to the republican ones that informed the orientation of his university. On the way Turner assimilated these assumptions—transmitted in particular through the work of Italian economist Achille Loria and made available to Turner by his colleague Richard Ely—see Lee Benson, *Turner and Beard: American Historical Writing Reconsidered* (Glencoe, Ill., 1960), pp. 5-9, 17-19, 28-29; Ray Allen Billington, *The Genesis of the Frontier Thesis: A Study in Historical Creativity* (San Marino, Cal., 1971), pp. 134-135; Luigi Einaudi, obituary for Loria in the *Economic Journal* (London) 56 (March, 1946): 146-147. Loria's most important work was his *Analisi della Proprieta Capitalista* 2 vols. (Turin, 1889); significant sections are reprinted in Benson, *Turner and Beard*, pp. 34-40. See also Achille Loria, *The Economic Foundations of Society* (London, 1902), p. 7; Ugo Rabbeno, "Loria's Landed System," *Political Science Quarterly* 7 (June, 1892): 276; and James C. Malin, "Space and History: Reflections on the Closed-Space Doctrines of Turner and Mackinder," *Agricultural History* 18 (April, 1944). On the University of Wisconsin's republican traditions and its development during the period when Turner came to prominence, see Merle Curti and Vernon Carstensen, *The University of Wisconsin: A History, 1848-1925*, 2 vols. (Madison, Wis., 1949), 1: chapters 1, 3, 11, and 18 in particular.

[31] "The West and American Ideals," reprinted in Ray A. Billington, ed., *Frontier and Section: Selected Essays of Frederick Jackson Turner* (Englewood Cliffs, N. J., 1961), p. 113.

In this passage, Turner combined a number of themes that would define
the work of the universities created with large infusions of gentry support.
Like academics of an older style, different social class, and more openly elitist sympathies, he understood that the "strongest" had to be targeted: where
they led others would follow. The message that had to be taken to the public
was that growth occurred through the depletion of resources external to
man, and that when these resources were exhausted growth could proceed
only in a spiritual realm where they were alone infinite. As he put it in
another commencement address on the same theme four years earlier, the
very survival of the American experiment might be at stake. "An inharmo-
nious group of reformers," he wrote in approval, "are sounding the warning
that American democratic ideals and society are menaced and already invaded by the very conditions that make this apparent prosperity [of the
United States]; that the economic resources are no longer limitless and free;
that the aggregate national wealth is increasing at the cost of present social
justice and moral health, and the future well-being of the American
people....As land values rise, as meat and bread grow dearer, as the process
of industrial consolidation goes on, and as Eastern industrial conditions
spread across the land, the problems of traditional American democracy will
become increasingly grave."[32]

Careers that would make the connections between democratic survival
and a redirection of national purpose well understood, careers more closely
identified with university training that, presumably, lacked direct material

---

The address was delivered at the commencement exercises of the University of Washington,
June 17, 1914.

[32] "Pioneer Ideals and the State University," in Frederick Jackson Turner, *The Frontier in
American History* (New York, 1920), p. 281. Elsewhere in the speech he made a related point:
"The pressure of population upon the food supply is already felt and we are at the beginning
only of this transformation. It is profoundly significant that at the very time when American
democracy is becoming conscious that its pioneer basis of free land and sparse population is
giving way, it is also brought face to face with the startling outcome of its old ideas of
individualism and exploration under competition uncontrolled by governments" (p. 279).

An editorial note in *The New York Times* of October 1, 1980 suggests that the teaching of
Turner's own specialty could heighten Americans' understanding of crises of resource scarcity.
The *Times* writer was ruminating about the match that might be made between certain college
courses and the time of day they were offered. As an example, he noted the appropriateness of
a course about the New England Puritans to the early morning hours. He then commented:
"But there's a theme in Western American history that fits the hour even better: the frontier. A
few weeks hence, we reckon, students of 'Cowboys and Indians' will be studying Frederick
Jackson Turner on how the American frontier and its disappearance changed things spiritually
as well as socially. Living with less energy in a formerly energy-prodigal nation is a frontier of
sorts, and has its wild and woolen satisfactions. It can be a challenge conquering the morning:
to rise, shrug off the cold, read the latest news of war in the Persian Gulf—and walk briskly off
to hear how Americans faced reality in the past."

application, should become the focus of the ambitions of society's future leaders. The creation of public opinion and the work of the new university would be the same: to "widen the intellectual horizon of the people," to help it encompass the new goals that reflected modern realities.[33]

---

[33] "The West and American Ideals," p. 113. See also, "Pioneer Ideals and the State University," p. 288.

CHAPTER SEVEN

THE USES OF PEDAGOGY:
CHILDREN'S NEEDS AND THE MEANING OF WORK

I

This look at the context in which Dewey's ideas took shape provides the background necessary to explain the pedagogy—the decisive weapon against traditionalist power and influence—that he fashioned. Dewey's pedagogy became such a weapon because it both incorporated the uncertainties and fears of the period from which it emerged and reinforced the political leanings popular among Dewey's patrons in higher education and reform circles.

There was very little that was new in Dewey's pedagogy. It did not express a new understanding of the mind or the way learning took place. In general, Dewey accepted the picture of the mind becoming popular in leading academic centers at the time. Behavioristic in nature, this picture stressed the response of an organism to specific, immediate, and largely external environmental stimuli. Instead, Dewey's success lay in the way his theories reflected his times. Dewey's pedagogy embodied the despair of a population struggling to survive a series of concentrated economic and social shocks.[1] It recognized that the shocks would forever change the

---

[1] For an indication of the profoundly unsettling effects of the worst of these shocks, the Depression of 1893, see Gerald T. White, *The United States and the Problem of Recovery After 1893* (University, Ala., 1982); Samuel Rezneck, "Unemployment, Unrest, and Relief in the United States during the Depression of 1893-97," *Journal of Political Economy* LXI (August, 1953): 324-340; Harold U. Faulkner, *Politics, Reform and Expansion* (New York, 1959), pp. 141-145, 164; and Nell Irvin Painter, *Standing at Armageddon: The United States, 1877-1919* (New York, 1987), chapter 4, "The Depression of the 1890s," pp. 110-141. Many observers had the sense, confirmed by historians, that economic growth had slowed to levels that justified the nervous introspection that the period produced. See Peter George, *The Emergence of Industrial America: Strategic Factors in American Economic Growth Since 1870* (Albany, N.Y., 1982), pp. 14-15. "The rate of change in total factor productivity," writes George, "was substantial in the decades before 1899, and then decreased to quite low levels in both agriculture and manufacturing between 1899 and 1919, increasing rapidly again after 1919." See also James Livingston, "The Social Analysis of Economic History and Theory: Conjectures on Late Nineteenth-Century American Development," *American Historical Review* 92, no. 1 (February, 1987): 69-95; Gabriel Kolko, *The Triumph of Conservatism: A Reinterpretation of American History, 1900-1916* (Chicago, paperback edition, 1967), chapter one; and Thomas C. Cochran and William Miller, *The Age of Enterprise: A Social History of Industrial America* (revised edition, New York, 1961), pp. 188-189. Talking about the late 1890s, the authors note:

expectations of Americans about their future, and emphasized adjustment to the disturbances by concentrating on the close-at-hand, day-to-day activity that would minimize their impact.

To Americans facing the overpowering disorganization of the late nineteenth century, Dewey's emphasis made sense. It corresponded with visceral clarity to their own perceptions about the world they inhabited and the safest way to make one's way in it. Reluctantly, many Americans were reaching the conclusion that the responses most likely to see them through the uprooting and disorienting times they confronted centered on the local, narrow, and protected areas of their lives. Little, it seemed, could be counted upon that could not be personally confirmed; little could be trusted that was untested by one's own experience, or that did not have quick, practical, life-sustaining results. Americans felt helpless and victimized; they turned inward toward the familiar and predictable in a search for secure and fixed guideposts. An earlier buoyancy and willingness to take risks seemed likely only to expose one to the forces of social disconnection and marginality. Gaining a tighter hold on local social space, however narrow and parochial, became far more attractive than looking outward toward the unknown and uncharted. Movement toward the unknown increased the chance of losing one's already tenuous grip on the local ties that social attachment seemed most reliably based on. Becoming too adventuresome could lead to the loss of one's way, and even a temporary unmooring could result in a return to space that was occupied by someone else. The community provided protection and stability for its members, but its ability to satisfy the demands made upon it had distinct limits. To move away from the reliable and familiar might make re-connection to secure ground impossible. It would be better to concentrate on "personal" needs than to explore possibilities that increased one's vulnerability to enemies too distant or powerful to combat.[2]

"Despite the return of prosperity, however, the *rate* of growth in American capital-goods industries had perceptibly begun to fall; the demand for capital for *productive* purposes had at last begun to slow down....The new consumers' goods industries also failed to absorb [the funds that were accumulating in trust and insurance companies], and the government itself could find no use for them. They were left available, therefore, for speculative purposes. And since mergers proved the simplest way to create speculative opportunities, these funds began to find their way into the securities of new combinations instead of into their plants."

[2] One study of the kind of turning inward that occurred in the period is H. Roger Grant, *Self-Help in the 1890s Depression* (Ames, Iowa, 1983). In many ways, the 1893 Depression only intensified tendencies that were developing earlier. According to Richard Sennett in *Families Against the City: Middle Class Homes of Industrial Chicago, 1872-1890* (Cambridge, Mass., 1970), in the two decades before the depression, the middle class Chicago family became noticeably insular. Sennett speculates that the head of the household, in "an era of rapid social change," "might have lost his acquisitive energy, and thereby part of his manhood in this culture, out of fearful withdrawal into the shelter of his family" (p. 187).

Unfortunately, politics presented few avenues of escape from the pressures to withdrawal. Political alternatives that might have led beyond the insularity and search for shelter hardly existed. To a growing, unsettled urban population, the Populist and socialist movements were too rural, alien, and isolated to offer easy identification or wide appeal.[3] Progressivism, in either the variations of Theodore Roosevelt or Woodrow Wilson, accepted the individual's eclipse and retirement from public affairs. For both men, public action now would be through large, impersonal organizations and the leadership collectives that ran them.[4] Only private life, tied to home and neighborhood, seemed open to individual control and direction. Looking beyond private life to express concerns of broad public interest invited overreaching, further demoralization, and the dissipation of energies better applied to more pressing needs. Evidence supporting an older belief in progress and the possibilities of continuing social transformation through individual effort no longer seemed to be forthcoming; optimism seemed only the possession of fools who would not recognize their own limits or the natural forces that established them.

In such a world Dewey's ideas commanded a wide public, no more so than in the liberal political circles active in urban and national reform. For in the process of providing the withdrawal and pessimism of the period with a foundation in "objective science," Dewey also helped create the justification for an outlook that was locally focused, resigned to slowed growth, and willing to accept the sacrifices—so long as they were equally shared—that were likely to be necessary. The language of experimental psychology constantly promoted by Dewey (in association with none too veiled disparagement of William T. Harris's work in particular)[5] gained wide acceptance in the period, in other words, not because of its scientific richness, but because the view of the mind it represented became a major philosophical prop for the political and social policies of the liberal reformers to whom he was tied.

---

[3] Lawrence Goodwyn, *The Populist Moment: A Short History of the Agrarian Revolt in America* (New York, 1978), pp. 290-298; and Robert C. McMath, *Populist Vanguard: A History of the Southern Farmers' Alliance* (New York, 1977), p. 154.

[4] See R. Jeffrey Lustig, *Corporate Liberalism: The Origins of Modern American Political Theory, 1890-1920* (Berkeley, Cal., 1982), pp. 30, 97, 104, 110.

[5] See Dewey's review of Harris's *Psychologic Foundations of Education* (1898), reprinted in *John Dewey: The Early Works, Volume 5, 1895-1898* (Carbondale, Ill., 1972), p. 272 ff.; and also Dewey's "The Psychological Aspects of the School Curriculum," in ibid., pp. 165-167.

II

As he elaborated it in the 1890s—the critical decade for the development
and dissemination of his views—Dewey based his psychology, and the
pedagogy that flowed from it, on a biological model, the outlines of which
were drawn from William James.[6] Living things fell out of adjustment with
their environment and then struggled to restore equilibrium. "In thinking,"
as one student of Dewey has put it, "the counterpart was the encounter with
troublesome, problematic situations that needed resolution before advances
could be made."[7] Dewey was concerned with the functioning of an
organism within its environment and with the "drive to reconstitute
adaptive, continuous and habitual behavior" in the face of external changes.
Habit dominated the model; problematic situations arose when environmental changes caused habits to break down. When this happened—because, it
is important to emphasize, of some external impulse—the organism
attempted to maintain itself in its particular environment by responding as
much as necessary to restore its earlier stability.[8]

In this view, thinking was distinguished by no special preparation,
development, or human quality. It was simply an activity, performed when
the need for readjustment arose, "just as at other needs," Dewey said, "we
engage in other sorts of activity, as converse with a friend, draw a plan for a
house, take a walk."[9] Not only was there no place in such a model for the
creative innovations designed to change the environment itself. There was
also no way such a model could anticipate when the creation of "new
habits," determined from a perception of mankind's future needs, should be
initiated. According to Dewey's model there was no way these needs could
ever be known.

Dewey's emphasis, for all his attempt to modify crude stimulus-
response psychology, was thoroughly behaviorist. "Only through what the

---

[6] In "From Absolutism to Experimentation," Dewey, talking about the influences on him,
wrote, "the great exception to what was said about no fundamental vital influence issuing from
books; it concerns the influence of William James. As far as I can discover, one specifiable
philosophic factor which entered into my thinking so as to give it a new direction and quality,
it is this one. To say that it proceeded from his *Psychology* rather than from the essays in the
volume called *Will to Believe*, his *Pluralistic Universe*, or *Pragmatism*, is to say something
that needs explanation." Quoted in C. Wright Mills, *Sociology and Pragmatism: The Higher
Learning in America* (New York, 1964), p. 376. Mills makes a similar point about the
biological nature of Dewey's ideas on pp. 375-376. James's *Talks to Teachers on Psychology
and to Students on Some of Life's Ideals*, first published in 1899 but including ideas that he had
worked out much earlier, is full of examples of ideas that Dewey found congenial. See, especially (in the 1958 paperback edition published by W. W. Norton & Co.), pp. 25, 27, 34-36, 40,
42, 47, 64, 74-75, 104.
[7] Arthur G. Wirth, *John Dewey as Educator: His Design for Work in Education* (New York,
1966), pp. 25-26.
[8] See ibid., and pp. 38, 81.
[9] Ibid., p. 86.

child does," he declared, "can we know what he is."[10] Talking about the
formulation of habits and interests, the main categories of personality for
Dewey, he noted the kinds of questions that needed to be asked:

> What stimuli shall be presented to the sense-organs and how? What stable
> complexes of associations shall be organized? What motor impulses shall be
> evoked?...How shall they be induced in such a way as to bring favorable stim-
> uli under greater control and to lessen the danger of excitation from undesir-
> able stimuli?

Teachers, especially, faced these questions daily, he continued. "The
instruments and materials with which [they deal] must be considered as
psychical stimuli," and the psychology they employed would determine
how well they instructed the "mechanisms," that is, the children, in their
charge. By this reasoning, ethical and social questions could only profit by
being translated into questions of psychological method. We then would be
able "to see the pupil as a mechanism," and "define his own relations and
that of the study taught in terms of causal influence acting upon this
mechanism."[11]

Dewey's conclusion played directly into the social philosophy he
worked out in the following decades. Defending the value of his psychology, he denied "the logic which says that because mechanism is
mechanism, and because acts, aims, values are vital, therefore a statement in
terms of one [his own behaviorist psychology] is alien to the comprehension
and proper management of the other." In fact, he admitted, he had come "to
suspect any ideal which exists purely at large, out of relation to machinery
of execution, and equally a machinery that operates in no particular direction." And since the "ideals" that Dewey had in mind could operate only in
the "particular direction" defined by the existing political and social environment (the "machinery of execution"), universal ideals and natural moral
law would have little relevance for him. As Dewey said in another place,
referring to one educational application of this view, "It was certainly a gain
for educational theory and practice when appeal to personal and immediate
sense-perception displaced reliance upon symbols and abstract ideas."[12]
Given this view of things, it is no surprise to find that Dewey in his more
strictly philosophical writings was shedding his earlier Hegelianism at just
this time.

The "instrumental logic" he developed is so accurately expressed by
Dewey's biographer that it is worth quoting. Dewey, says George

---

[10] "The Psychological Aspects of the School Curriculum," (1897) in *John Dewey: The
Early Works, Volume 5, 1895-1898*, p. 173.
[11] "Psychology and Social Practice," (1899) in *John Dewey, The Middle Works, Volume 1,
1899-1901* (Carbondale, Ill., 1976), pp. 139-140, 141-144.
[12] "The Place of Manual Training in the Elementary Course of Study," (1901) in ibid., p.
235.

Dykhuizen, defined moral goals and ideals "not by reference to some abso-lute, transcendent Self or Personality but in terms of individual needs, wants, capacities, and the conditions under which these must be fulfilled." Self-realization became the concrete undertaking of "the performance by a person of his specific function, this function consisting in an activity which realizes wants and powers with reference to their peculiar surroundings." The act of thinking for Dewey was therefore "always a specific affair aimed at overcoming a specific problem arising in experience." An idea was "simply a plan of action designed to solve a specific problem; its truth depends not upon its correspondence to some prior reality but upon its 'functional or instrumental use in effecting the transition from a relatively conflicting experience to a relatively integrated one.'"[13]

In educational terms, these psychological and epistemological views taken together meant that the needs of the child were established by looking at his immediate setting instead of starting, as an older generation of educa-tors did, from the achievements of civilization and its future requirements to determine what the child can, or ought to, learn. As we will see below, using the child's immediate setting as a starting point would change radi-cally the conception of life possibility open to the child. It would also sug-gest major curricular revisions that would completely reorient his learning and career experience.

When looked at from the standpoint Dewey advanced, opportunity would appear increasingly hemmed in by very specific and ever-narrowing boundaries. When the president of Muncie, Indiana's Board of Education told the authors of *Middletown*, "For a long time all boys were trained to be President. Then for a while we trained them all to be professional men. Now we are training boys to get jobs,"[14] he might just as well have been speaking of the first decade of the twentieth century as of the second or third. The curriculum that Dewey built around occupations, and the school that he designed to reproduce the experiences of the child's community, could never, under the conditions of slowed industrial growth of the turn of the century, provide a way to integrate the aspects of the child's learning supposedly fragmented by older teaching methods. It could not, at any rate, if that learning was as stimulating and suggestive of possibility as theory proposed. But if it was not, it could only reinforce the sense that education was meant to fit the child for a future that could not be much different from that of his parents. Dominated by doubts about the society's ability to gen-erate new opportunities and the higher scientific and intellectual levels these

---

[13] George Dykhuizen, *The Life and Mind of John Dewey* (Carbondale, Ill., 1973), pp. 70 and 84.
[14] Robert S. and Helen M. Lynd, *Middletown: A Study in American Culture* (New York, 1929), p. 194.

opportunities would call forth, this state of mind encouraged children, no less than their parents, to deny the value of a traditional education and to repudiate the need to submit to the "unpleasant" discipline or mental rigor demanded by the traditional school system.

This atmosphere was the ideal environment for the specific conception of "interest"—the notion central to the pedagogical debates of the period—that Dewey developed. Like others before him, Dewey related interest to particular stages of a child's development; subject matter had to be based on a reading of the child's psyche. And like them, Dewey also made little room in his thinking for questions about the rate of intellectual growth children must undergo, the educational investment required, and the kind of facilities and teachers necessary if the entire society was to produce the innovations required for its ongoing improvement.

Even so, Dewey's special focus and area of concern differed from the newer reformers in important ways. Dewey pondered the significance of social experience and worked to connect it to the daily life of the child in school in a way others never bothered to do. Along with the sensitivity he showed for the urban culture that defined the lives of his students and the modern idiom in which he phrased his message, Dewey found himself enormously popular. Alone among education writers who sought sweeping changes in policy, Dewey concentrated on classroom operations and on the details of learning and teaching. Because he did, his social conclusions seemed to emerge more directly from the pedagogical relationship between teacher and pupil alone—not tacked onto it by previous commitments and assumptions. Dewey believed that a child had to be specifically, and if possible individually, motivated to learn. Contrary to everything that people like Harris maintained, this assumed that the child would not ordinarily be inclined to do so, and given what the child could expect to achieve in the industrial environment of the turn of the century, he was right. As Dewey said in one of his essays of this period commenting on the traditionalist position, "when a child feels that his work is a task, it is only under compulsion that he gives himself to it. At the least let-up of external pressure we find his attention at once directed to what interests him."[15] Once this premise was granted, the way was open for the introduction, in the guise of child-centered education, of whatever short-sighted, parochial schemes cost-conscious administrators were becoming enamored of. Unless a child could be shown how what he was being taught had immediate value for him (especially as a young adult about to leave school for a job in the local neighborhood beyond which he was given little reason to hope he might

---

[15] "Interest in Relation to Training of the Will," (1896) in *John Dewey: The Early Works, Volume 5, 1895-1898*, p. 115. See also Dewey's 1897 article, "The Psychology of Effort," in ibid., especially pp. 158 and 162.

reach) he would have no reason to learn the subject matter or submit to the discipline of the schools, no matter how diluted they had become under Progressive rule.

Explicitly attacking Harris's formulation of the same problem in an early paper about curriculum planning, Dewey maintained that the curriculum had to be "determined" and "selected" by considering what the "motive or stimulus for study is." The first pedagogical question was, "How experience grows; not what experience the adult has succeeded in getting together during his development from childhood to maturity." Dewey early argued, and continued to elaborate in his later writings, that "the child will never realize a fact or possess an idea which does not grow out of this equipment of experiences and interest which he already has." Subject matter would be determined by being, as Dewey put it, "psychologized," by being examined to see what some "concrete individual may experience in virtue of his own impulses, interests, and powers." "Subject matter," he said, "is the present experience of the child taken in light of what it may lead to."[16]

Here was a major change in educational direction. The departure from the views of traditionalists who believed that the needs of an expanding economy with an upwardly mobile workforce required everyone to receive the same rigorous education to prepare them for increasingly complex scientific tasks was unmistakable. Drastic revisions in the curriculum would be necessary. The course of study would now have to be developed "not only with reference to the child in general, but with reference to the specific child—the child of a certain age, of a certain degree of attainment, and of specific home and neighborhood contacts."[17]

III

This point of view never changed in Dewey's writings; with varying degrees of emphasis it appeared over and over again, acting as the organizing principle of all of his educational work. This is particularly true in his most well-known books, *The Child and the Curriculum, The School and Society, Schools of Tomorrow,* and *Democracy and Education.* These writings have had a dominating influence throughout the twentieth century, and it is important to look at them closely with the foregoing introduction to Dewey's thought in mind. The earliest full statements, *The Child and the Curriculum* (1902) and *The School and Society* (1899), did as much as anything Dewey ever wrote to make his outlook well-known.

---

[16] "Psychological Aspects of the School Curriculum," pp. 170, 175.
[17] Ibid., p. 170.

No small reason for this may have been the position Dewey took vis-a-vis the feuding pedagogical groups of his day. In the 1902 essay, in particular, Dewey assumed the role of mediator and synthesizer that was responsible for much of his popularity in the years ahead. Dewey always remained a behaviorist committed to reorganizing the curriculum so that it corresponded to the observed stages of child development. But here he offered an argument meant to appear as a compromise between the two poles that he maintained were, to the detriment of all, dominating educational debate at the time. Without identifying them by name, Dewey began by noting how the orientations associated with G. Stanley Hall, the leader of the child study movement, on the one hand, and with Mann and Harris on the other, exaggerated different elements of a single problem that simply required "adjustment" to one another. The educative process had two components, one corresponding to the native capacities of the child, and the other to the goals and aims of adults. A focus on one to the exclusion of the other distorted the process as a whole, and created seemingly insoluble conflicts among partisans of the claims of each. "We get," said Dewey, "the case of the child vs. the curriculum; of the individual nature vs. social nature. Below all other divisions in pedagogic opinion lies this opposition."[18]

By itself neither side of this dispute provided an answer to the new problems society faced in confronting the education of its young. The contending sides had formed themselves into "educational sects" that, Dewey suggested, made each blind to its own deficiencies. One group, clearly meant to represent the common school tradition of Mann and Harris, believed that subject matter took precedence over "the contents of the child's own experience" (p. 7). Viewing the child as self-centered, confused, and impulsive, this group would arrange the child's school life on the basis of an unchanging, objective world of truth and order, a world, said Dewey, "where all is measured and defined." Their message, he explained, was to "ignore and minimize the child's individual peculiarities, whims and experiences." For this group, individual differences had to be completely "obscured or eliminated," pushed as far from consideration as possible. "As educators," he wrote, paraphrasing what he took to be the group's arguments, "our work is precisely to substitute for these superficial and casual affairs stable and well-ordered realities; and these are found in studies and lessons. The child is simply the immature being who is to be matured; he is the superficial being who is to be deepened; his is narrow experience which is to be widened. It is his to receive, to accept. His part is fulfilled when he is ductile and docile" (p. 8). For Dewey, this position paralleled that of the old-line philosophers bent on maintaining the separation between

---

[18] *The Child and the Curriculum* in *The Child and the Curriculum and The School and Society* (Chicago, 1956), p. 5.

knowledge (conceived as an abstraction from the real world of human affairs) and action (requiring day-to-day problem-solving and decision-making). This was the group on which Dewey set his sights throughout his long career; it is not surprising that he does did not treat it gently.

But the opposing group, growing up around his old teacher G. Stanley Hall and the child study movement he led, did not fare any better. To Dewey, it too was a "sect," a characterization that denoted the kind of dogmatic rigidity and unreasoning close-mindedness that imperiled the possibility of compromise and meliorism at the heart of Dewey's hopes for peaceful social change. Dewey wanted it clear that he intended to be no more closely identified with it than he did with the first group—even though he could barely define its views in language very different from his own.[19] To chart a position that could override the antagonism of each group toward the other and thereby begin to build a new consensus for educational policy, Dewey had to establish a position that obscured the broader issues dividing them. He denied, therefore, that there was anything much worth fighting over; it was only a "gap in kind (as distinct from degree)" that separated the two extremes. "The child and the curriculum are simply two limits which define a single process." To set one against the other was "to hold that the nature and destiny of the child war with each other" (pp. 11-12).

More was at stake here than an abstract pedagogical point, however. The division that Dewey tried to smooth over represented two sharply opposed factional positions within educational circles. Tied to each pedagogical conception were related notions about the kind of system necessary for the success of each. Discussions of pedagogy inevitably led to discussions of teacher training, curriculum planning, building expansion, and teacher salaries. These issues, in the midst of rising pressures for "fiscal responsibility" and "budgetary restraint," fears of teacher unionization, and calls for administrative reorganization and governmental centralization,[20] were the focus of bitter struggles inside the education profession. Few people concerned with public affairs failed to understand which pedagogical position was associated with which factional position. Dewey's reputation

---

[19] See ibid., p. 9. Though Dewey may have had personal motives to distance himself from Hall's approach to education (as Hall's biographer Dorothy Ross suggests in her *G. Stanley Hall: The Psychologist as Prophet* [Chicago, 1972], pp. 145-146), he may have learned more from his one-time teacher than he wanted to admit. See, in particular, Hall's early essay, "New Departures in Education," *North American Review* CXL (February, 1885).

[20] Background for an understanding of these questions can be found in Samuel P. Hays, "The Politics of Reform in Municipal Government in the Progressive Era," *Pacific Northwest Quarterly* LV (October, 1964): 157-169; Mary J. Herrick, *The Chicago Schools: A Social and Political History* (Beverly Hills, Cal., 1971); Robert Wiebe, *Businessmen and Reform: A Study of the Progressive Movement* (Cambridge, Mass., 1962); David B. Tyack, *The One Best System: A History of American Urban Education* (Cambridge, Mass., 1974); and David W. Swift, *Ideology and Change in the Public Schools: Latent Functions of Progressive Education* (Columbus, Ohio, 1971).

was due to his ability to appear independent of both groups, an ability exemplified by *The Child and the Curriculum* where he denied that anything more than a discussion of teaching method was involved.

But the issues were hardly as narrow as Dewey wanted to make it appear. Dewey said that the contending sides foolishly made it seem as if "the nature of and destiny of the child war with each other." This contrast was, however, exactly what the partisans of each of the opposing sides wanted to insist on. They understood that the vantage point chosen—nature or environmentally determined destiny—made all the difference, and should make all the difference, for policy. In denying that the distinction was one of substance, Dewey was denying that there was much at stake worth fighting about so passionately. To minimize the conflict in this way was also to minimize the solution. The latter might then be agreed on without heated argument, and turned over to professional managers for implementation.

The issue, for Dewey, was one of science—of experience and expertise. It could be settled without raising issues of political belief, and the possibility of irresolvable dispute. If the child's nature and destiny were examined as they developed in the real world, it was apparent that both were part of a single continuum, all parts of which were closely tied. If this were true, nature and destiny could not then point in different directions. Looking at actual cases, the experimental way to proceed, would make it clear that the child's destiny could not be much different from that decreed by his nature: his youthful instincts and interest were not likely to be modified by any experience that would deflect him from a course set by circumstances very early in life. For this deflection to occur "infancy and maturity of the same growing life" would have to be "opposed" in a way Dewey did not believe possible. The subject matter of the schools "as we have agreed," said Dewey in tones reaching for consensus, had to be an indication of "the possibilities of development inherent in the child's immediate crude experience" (p. 12).

But how were these possibilities to be used in framing curricular goals? People like Hall, placing all their attention on the static elements of the child's nature, never seemed to take them into account. Dewey believed that the question suggested its own answer: "To see the outcome is to know in what direction the present experience is moving, provided it move normally and soundly." Once we knew what this normal and sound direction was we had "a guiding method" for dealing with the individual child. "The systematized and defined experience of the adult mind, in other words, is of value to us in interpreting the child's life as it immediately shows itself" (p. 13).

This was not William T. Harris talking, however. The "defined experience of the adult mind" (the outcome toward which present experience, when it moved "normally and soundly" was trending) did not get its meaning from anything so abstract as the needs or regenerative requirements of the population as a whole. Dewey may have criticized the crude and anarchic formulations of people like Hall—who, he felt, confined their "gaze to what the child here and now puts forth," fixated on the survivals instead of the potentialities of his nature, and idealized him sentimentally (p. 14). Even so, it is not clear that he entertained an effectively different standpoint. The "normal" development of experience had to be defined contextually— as did everything for Dewey—and the guidance this provided for *"freeing the life-process for its own most adequate fulfillment"* (p. 17, Dewey's italics) would vary depending on the situation each child found himself in— or, more accurately, was found to be in by those charged with setting the course of study for him.

Dewey felt that proponents of the "new education" took "the idea of development in altogether too formal and empty a way." Arguing (he thought against this), he wanted development to be seen as "a definite process, having its own law which can be fulfilled only when adequate and normal conditions are provided" (p. 18). In stipulating the latter—that normal and adequate conditions had to be provided to allow the process of development to work (and thereby acknowledging that their influence could not be escaped, as people like Hall persistently refused to recognize)[21]— Dewey differed from the "new educators." In the end, however, as Hall's curricular proposals suggested (he promoted vocational education and a curriculum that generally reduced intellectual demands on students),[22] the results would not be far different. That it seemed as if they might be was part of Dewey's appeal. But when the "adequate and normal conditions" Dewey talked about regularly turned out be the depressed working class and immigrant wards of the nation's cities, wards filled with already disconsolate residents who could entertain little hope of assured advancement for themselves and their children, it began to appear to some community groups

---

[21] Hall's distaste for modern industrial society and its implications for life and work continued throughout his life. See the early *Aspects of German Culture* (Boston, 1881), especially pp. 298-320; and his later *Adolescence: Its Psychology and Its Relations to Physiology, Anthropology, Sociology, Sex, Crime, Religion and Education* 2 vols. (New York, 1904), I: xv, 111-113, 166-167; II: 145-148, 150-153, 157, 174, 229, 231; and his *Educational Problems* 2 vols. (New York, 1911), I: 550, 558-559, 617; "The Fall of Atlantis," in *Recreations of a Psychologist* (New York, 1920), 52-53, 62-69; and *Life and Confessions of a Psychologist* (New York, 1923), pp. 146, 177.

[22] In addition to the pages cited in note 21, also see Hall's *Adolescence*, I: 49-50, 142, 171, 173, 196, 321-324, 376-377; II: 71, 303, 513; *Educational Problems*, I: 541, 545, 581, 632, 638-639; and his 1902 address to the National Education Association, "The High School as the People's College," reprinted in Charles E. Strickland and Charles Burgess eds., *Health, Growth and Heredity: G. Stanley Hall on Natural Education* (New York, 1965).

that "development" could prove as restrictive as other educators' appeal to heredity and evolutionary determinism.[23]

The passage in which Dewey went on to explain further his ideas of development is worth examining with this in mind. Again taking issue with the static views held by the "new educators," Dewey wrote:

> Development does not mean just getting something out of [generating something from] the mind. It is a development of experience and into experience that is really wanted. And this is impossible save as just that educative medium is provided which will enable the powers and interests that have been selected as valuable to function. They must operate, and how they operate will depend almost entirely upon the stimuli themselves. The problem of direction is thus the problem of selecting appropriate stimuli for instincts and impulses which it is desired to employ in the gaining of new experience. What new experiences are desirable, and thus what stimuli are needed, it is impossible to tell except as there is some comprehension of the development which is aimed at; except, in a word, as the adult knowledge is drawn upon as revealing the possible career open to the child. (p. 19)

A passage that begins in generalities about development and experience, that then traverses a middle ground concerning the judgments that need to be made about the "selection" of "valuable powers and interests" and the "stimuli" needed to activate them, ends in a depressingly specific reference that comes upon the reader more suddenly than he expects. In the last sentence Dewey quickly moved from abstract "stimuli" to concrete "possible" career choices, those based on a child's background and expectations. In doing so he gave the reader an indication of the social assumptions that lay behind his pedagogical thinking. Modifying "career" with "possible" could only mean that Dewey assumed that specific limits to the opportunities available to each child existed. What these limits were an examination of each child's social background would reveal.

IV

In *The School and Society* Dewey provided specific examples of the general curricular orientation he would later suggest in *The Child and the Curriculum*. He also tried to come to grips with the way a standard by which to judge the worth of particular curricular proposals could be defined. In the process he made even more clear how his approach to curriculum

---

[23] In this regard, see the resistance by New York City residents to reform mayor John P. Mitchel's attempt to introduce the highly-touted Gary Plan there just before the First World War. Accounts of the fight can be found in Diane Ravitch, *The Great School Wars: New York City, 1805-1973* (New York, 1974); Edwin Lewinson, *John Purroy Mitchel, The Boy Mayor of New York* (New York, 1965); Ronald D. Cohen and Raymond A. Mohl, *The Paradox of Progressive Education: The Gary Plan and Urban Schooling* (Port Washington, N. Y., 1979).

planning was tied to assumptions of limited opportunity and the social rigidity of modern industrial society.

Dewey's ideas about the benefits of the teaching of occupations were at the center of his approach. As he conceived it, a curriculum organized around occupations would not primarily teach trades or distinct studies but would instead train children "in relation to the physical realities of life."[24] It would engage their interest and attention. It would encourage their active involvement in school and to some extent, even though he disavowed such a purpose a few sentences before, would prepare them "for the practical duties of later life." Girls would learn to be better homemakers, perhaps even to be cooks and seamstresses. Boys, if "our educational system [were] only adequately rounded out into trade schools," would learn their future vocations (p. 13). This was a secondary goal, of course. More important were the broader social functions of the program, especially its service as an agency "for bringing home to the child some of the primal necessities of community life." This could occur in school because the school, emphasizing the values of social cooperation and productive activity that Dewey favored, would be turned into a community—"instead of a place set apart in which to learn lessons."

In such an atmosphere, selfishness and individual competitiveness would wither. Schools dominated by traditional methods may have encouraged "the mere absorbing of facts and truths," and may have considered helping one another "a school crime." His would be different. His school would become in effect "an embryonic society," (p. 18) where students interacted as all of mankind apparently had at some primeval moment when the pressures of community—when the need to work "along common lines, in a common spirit, and with reference to common aims"—predominated (p. 14). This was hardly the principle on which society was organized at present, but youngsters passing through the "miniature community" of the school would, he hoped, gain the "social power and insight" required to change this.[25] Children, as Dewey wrote elsewhere, would show adults the path to right living. Sharing an infatuation with the revivifying and associational powers of uncorrupted youth that infected many educational reformers of his day, Dewey was convinced that "for certain moral and intellectual purposes adults must become as little children." Somehow, in the process of growing up, adults had lost some of the positive qualities he had observed in children. In his view there were now "few grown-up persons [who] retain all of the flexible and sensitive ability of children to

---

[24] *The School and Society* in *The Child and the Curriculum and The School and Society*, p. 12.

[25] Ibid., p. 18. In the next sentence Dewey wrote, "It is this liberation from narrow utilities, this openness to the possibilities of the human spirit that makes these practical activities in the school allies of art and centers of science and history."

vibrate sympathetically with the attitudes and doings of those about them."
To help adults recapture the child-like ability "to vibrate sympathetically"
would be another important role Dewey hoped the schools could perform.[26]

How this would actually occur was a question much on Dewey's mind
but his approach to the issue was not generally straightforward. The slipper-
iness of his approach was not because, as some have argued, he saw any
conflict between his advocacy of more freedom for the child and the imperatives of adult society.[27] Since he never imagined that this freedom,
manifested in the "needs and interests" of the young, would go undirected
by adults, the question for him was only how, as a matter of practical
method, to harness the interests of the young to the adult imperatives he
considered most inescapable. The boundary conditions defining these "adult
imperatives" were set by his fear of conflict and his related commitment to
order and stability.

In this light, Dewey's assertion that "until the instincts of construction
and production are systematically laid hold of in years of childhood and
youth, until they are trained in social directions...we certainly are in no
position even to locate the source of our economic evils, much less to deal
with them effectively,"[28] made perfect sense. Social adjustment and social
change were two sides of the same coin, as the elements fused in the
passage were meant to underscore. Dewey was not especially hopeful that
the worker could escape his subservience to either those in positions above
him or to the machine he operated. But he did hope that an exposure to the
educational program he advocated would lead the worker to an appreciation
and more cheerful acceptance of his job.[29] The worker was a "mere
appendage" to his machine because, in large part, he "has had no opportunity to develop his imagination and his sympathetic insights as to the social
and scientific values found in his work" (p. 24). Training youth in "social
directions" was a step toward locating and dealing with economic evils just
as infusing a society with the spirit of cooperating, unselfish youth was a
step toward social reform and the removal of conflict—and hence
disorder—from social relations. Both processes (the training of youth and
the infusion of society with their spirit) reduced hostility among worker and
employer; both helped replace resentment and anger with rational discourse.

---

[26] See Dewey's *Democracy and Education* (New York, 1966; orig. 1916), pp. 42-43; the
discussion in Christopher Lasch, *The New Radicalism in America, 1889-1963: The Intellectual
as Social Type* (New York, 1965), p. 88; and the works of G. Stanley Hall referred to in note
21 above. Also see Richard Hofstadter, *Anti-Intellectualism in America* (New York, 1962), p.
363.

[27] For example, see the discussion in Hofstadter, pp. 379-383.

[28] *The School and Society*, p. 24.

[29] See *The School and Society*, pp. 23-24. For a contrasting interpretation of this material,
see Robert L. Church and Michael W. Sedlak, *Education in the United States: An Interpretive
History* (New York, 1976), p. 268. Note also the discussion in the following chapter.

To critics, it might appear that this was nothing but an attempt to cool out dissent. But to Dewey, this was the way to achieve the social peace required for social progress.

Dewey's orientation to the problem is further illuminated by the shift in discussion that took place at the point at which he raised the question of dealing with "our economic evils." Instead of taking up the question directly, Dewey began to talk about the way the monopoly of learning that had dominated the premodern era had been broken with the coming of industrial culture. Learning and knowledge in the modern age were no longer restricted to an upper class as they had been. They were no longer dominated by an elite bent on perpetuating artificial distinctions of class and status: learning was now accessible to all. Unfortunately, a "specialized aim," limited to the liberal studies favored by the "cultured" elite, still continued to crowd out the more utilitarian knowledge most valuable to the "workers," "those whose dominant interest is to do and to make" (pp. 17-18). The conception of learning held by the elite was a throwback to medieval times, said Dewey, and the labels they tried to apply to the practical studies they opposed—calling them "highly specialized, one-sided and narrow"—really applied to their own candidates for curricular dominance. Those subjects were the ones that appealed only to "the intellectual aspect of our natures, our desire to learn, to accumulate information and to get control of the symbols of learning; not to our impulses and tendencies to make, to do, to create, to produce, whether in the form of utility or art."

Not only did this kind of language set up the very dualism that would maintain the class-biased education Dewey supposedly wanted to eliminate. It also set up two fateful associations. On the one hand, intellectuality was tied to accumulation and control, qualities central to the acquisitive, aggressive, competitive creatures of the marketplace he abhorred. On the other hand, handwork was tied to creativity and productivity. Setting up these associations opened the door for the pedestrian demands of others, in areas like vocational education, and later, life adjustment, who argued that truly democratic education meant pandering to the lowest common denominator of performance that schoolmen could identify.[30]

Having created the division between intellectual work and handwork forced on him by an underlying pessimism, Dewey now had to choose half of it as a foundation for the modern school. The choice was not too hard to make given the statistics of school-leaving he offered. Barely one percent of the school population got beyond high school; only five percent got that far. More than half left before beginning the sixth grade. "The simple facts of the case," said Dewey, "are that in the great majority of human beings the

---

[30] See Hofstadter's excellent discussion of the life adjustment movement in his *Anti-Intellectualism*, pp. 341-354.

distinctively intellectual interest is not dominant. They have the so-called practical impulse and disposition. In many of those in whom by nature intellectual interest is strong, social conditions prevent its adequate realization."[31]

Because of this, most students, presumably even those of superior aptitude, left school as soon as they decided that they had learned enough to earn a living. Educational leaders might talk of schooling as a way to develop culture and personality, but most of those enrolled saw it only as a "narrowly practical tool with which to get bread and butter enough to eke out a restricted life." Dewey's advice for restructuring school work flowed from this assessment. If we conceived educational aims less exclusively, he said, if we introduced into educational processes the kinds of activities that had an appeal to those who were interested in the practical and the applied—as most seemed destined to be—"we should find the hold of the school upon its members to be more vital, more prolonged, containing more of culture" (p. 28).

The kind of culture Dewey had in mind was not that of the elite. Instead, it was the kind relevant to the life of the working man. Industrial society had thrust the worker into the center of educational discussion; whether schoolmen wanted to admit it or not the schools had to reflect this reality. What Dewey called his "labored presentation" was intended to press the point home. "The obvious fact," he wrote, speaking about the new (and, it now seemed, permanent) working class, "is that our social life has undergone a thorough and radical change. If our education is to have any meaning for life, it must pass through an equally complete transformation" (p. 28).

This transformation would bring the schools into correspondence with "present social needs" (p. 30), and point the way toward an answer to the question Dewey had posed earlier about the source and cure of "our economic evils." For the problem, it turned out, was not economic at all. That is, it had nothing to do with the production of wealth and its use to raise the intellectual and material level of the population. Like many other liberal reformers of his day, these questions never entered Dewey's mind. Instead, it was a question of social relations that occupied him. The problem of "dealing" with our economic evils was a problem of perceived differences in status and position. Given the scarcity of resources that Dewey always assumed, the reality of class differences was likely to remain troublesome for some time. But the disruptive potential that it embodied could not be ignored; some approach to the problem of class was required.

This seemed to be what Dewey was trying to do when he connected the source and cure of economic evil to the "systematic laying hold" and "training in social directions" of the instincts of children. It also helps

---

[31] *The School and Society*, p. 27.

explain why the school was so important to him and his followers. The school, especially through a revision of its teaching method and curriculum, could be used to impart the knowledge (of practical utility) and values (of social cooperation) that would enable the majority of school-goers to overcome the distance they felt developing between themselves and those above them. The changes in the school, Dewey wrote, "which often appear to be mere changes of detail, mere improvements within the school mechanism, are in reality signs and evidences of evolution. The introduction of active occupations, of nature-study, of elementary science, of art, of history; the relegation of the merely symbolic and formal to a secondary position; the change in the moral school atmosphere, in the relation of pupils and teachers—of discipline; the introduction of more active, expressive, and self-directing factors—all these are not mere accidents, they are necessities of the larger social evolution" (pp. 28-29).

It may have been true that existing social conditions prevented most people from acquiring very broad intellectual interests, and that without them their social and economic horizons would always be narrow. It may have been true that the boundaries between classes and the limits to opportunity were more firmly fixed than ever. Existing social conditions had indeed forced the majority to be "practical" and to confine its goals to the acquisition of the tools "to get bread and butter enough to eke out a restricted life." But this majority fate did not mean that a social concert, productive of cooperative and useful work on behalf of others, could not be established. When the school, defined by the attitudes and activities that Dewey noted above, became "an embryonic community life, active with types of occupations that reflect the life of the larger society," "when the school introduces and trains each child of society into membership within such a little community, saturating him with the spirit of service and [he added, adopting the language of the earlier generation he often criticized] providing him with the instruments of effective self-direction," at that point "we shall have the deepest and best guaranty of a larger society which is worthy, lovely and harmonious" (p. 29). Here was the heart of Dewey's message—not economic expansion or increased mobility, but harmony and the social peace it reflected.[32]

---

[32] For another important attempt that Dewey made at this time to explore the conflict between worker needs and social needs, see "Ethical Principles Underlying Education," in *Third Yearbook of the National Herbart Society* (Chicago, 1897), pp. 11-26. The contribution of Dewey's University of Chicago colleague I. W. Howerth to a later Herbart Society yearbook suggests something of the solution toward which many educators were more openly moving. "For his own good, as well as for the good of others," wrote Howerth, the individual's "interests must be secondary, he must yield himself to discipline, he must recognize that his rational relation to society is that of subordination." ("The Social Aim in Education," in *Fifth Yearbook of the National Herbart Society* [Chicago, 1899], pp. 71-107.)

V

In many ways this preoccupation with social amity and concord also lay at the heart of Dewey's central pedagogical preoccupation, the interests of the child. Interest was not only the best way to motivate the child, it was also the best way to create the miniature community he sought. A focus on interest allowed educators to avoid the tension and contest of wills that accompanied the discipline and authoritarianism of traditional classrooms.

Yet a persistent theme of his critics followed him throughout the book, and near its end he faced it. "One of the objections regularly brought against giving in school work any large or positive place to the child's interest," he wrote, "is the impossibility on such a basis of proper selection" (p. 135). It was true that interest-based teaching might keep the child's attention and make him amenable to instruction, no small achievement in the heterogeneous classrooms of immigrant-filled cities. But how, it was asked, would such teaching advance the absorption of what adults considered important? How would it be possible to decide between interests that were significant and those that were not, interests that were helpful and those that were not, interests that were ephemeral and those that were "permanently influential"? Realizing the extent to which the moral legitimacy of his system was at stake, Dewey acknowledged, not altogether comfortably, that "it would seem as if we had to go beyond interest to get to any basis for interest." The question obviously required some kind of answer, and once raised Dewey did not ignore it. But his response, in the way if shifted ground between two very different educational ideals, could not have been as reassuring as some of his more troubled readers may have hoped.

Dewey's first approach to an answer seemed to be that interest was a justifiable starting point for curricular innovation because so much of it was tied to "occupation work." "There are certain reasons," he said, "for believing that the type of interest which springs up along with these occupations is of a thoroughly healthy, permanent, and really educative sort." Basing school work on these occupations offered the guarantee that the "spontaneous interest" they generated will go beyond "what is merely pleasure-giving, exciting or transient" (p. 136). But what was so "healthy," "permanent," or "really educative" about occupationally-tied interests? Here Dewey introduced an important standard of evaluation. Partly no doubt because of his continuing faith in the primitive residue within youth, and partly because of his continuing biologism, Dewey believed that the interests that children developed were always the outgrowth "of some instinct or some habit that in turn is finally based upon an original instinct." Many instincts inherited by mankind were not particularly useful, he admitted, but those expressed in occupational terms were; these were the ones "bound to be of an exceedingly fundamental and permanent type."

> The activities of life [Dewey explained] are of necessity directed to bringing the materials and forces of nature under the control of our purposes; of making them tributary to ends of life. Men have had to work in order to live. In and through their work they have mastered nature, they have protected and enriched the conditions of their own life, they have been awakened to the sense of their own powers—have been led to invent, to plan, and to rejoice in the acquisition of skill. (p. 137)

Interests based on instincts like these had to be worthy ones; a curriculum based on them would be too. "All occupations," Dewey noted, "may be classified as gathering about man's fundamental relations to the world in which he lives through getting food to maintain life, securing clothing and shelter to protect and ornament it, and thus, finally, to provide a permanent home in which all of the higher and more spiritual interests may center." But here Dewey's contextualism posed serious problems for him. Since, as he went on to admit, occupationally-based interests made up so much of the child's world—"and this not only on the material side, but as regards intellectual, aesthetic, and moral activities, for these are largely and necessarily bound up with occupations" as well—how could Dewey be so sure that the progression from "getting food to maintain life" to providing a home for the "higher and more spiritual interests" would occur? What would happen if the child's "present social life" denied him access to interests that were elevating or inspiring? How worthy would they be then?

Dewey assumed that interests growing out of the instincts that had brought "the materials and forces of nature under the control of our purposes," that had led to the work whereby men had "been awakened to the sense of their own powers—have been led to invent, to plan, and to rejoice in the acquisition of skill" would be of this kind. It was Dewey's fundamental point in defense of his curricular proposals "that interests which have such a history behind them must be of the worthy sort" (p. 137). But these interests, generated by the work of invention and planning, by taking responsibility for building one's society, were located by Dewey in the past. They had been part of mankind's history, not necessarily its present or future, the temporal condition he was speaking about now. Under present circumstances, under conditions of life where many feared productivity was falling, where the introduction of new technology and the proliferation of new industry was slowing, where science was becoming progressively more distant from the working population, his ideal of worth was forced to undergo a significant change.

Dewey expected all occupations to provide men with access to "higher and more spiritual interests" in addition to the tools of simple survival. Yet

what was the route—he seemed to suggest there was one—from the latter to
the former? In the historical work of building a society where literally
nothing had existed before, the route was easy to see and take pride in. But
how did the process work in Dewey's own day? His idea of "worth"—the
idea he introduced to justify his proposals—implicitly rested not only on the
relationship between industriousness and its perceived results, but also on
the object of one's industry. The kind of work engaged in was as essential
as the effort put into it. What Dewey considered "worthy" was labor that
embodied a sense of control, invention, and planning; labor, in other words,
that engaged the qualities of "directive power" that so concerned an earlier
generation of educators.

But what work embodied those qualities today? As he surveyed the
industrial landscape, Dewey was apparently hard pressed to find any that
did, and in the paragraph following the one where the justification of interest was initially presented he introduced a very different notion of worth
that acknowledged this. For here he began talking about the *frequency of
contact* with occupational work, not its nature. The occupational interests
that developed in the contemporary child, he wrote

> not only recapitulate past important activities of the race, but reproduce those
> of the child's present environment. He continually sees his elders engaged in
> such pursuits. He daily has to do things which are the results of just such
> occupations. He comes in contact with facts that have no meaning, except in
> reference to them. Take these things out of the present social life and see how
> little would remain....The child's instinctive interests in this direction are,
> therefore, constantly reinforced by what he sees, feels, and hears going on
> around him. Suggestions along this line are continually coming to him;
> motives are awakened; his energies are stirred to action. Again, it is not unrea-
> sonable to suppose that *interests which are touched so constantly, and on so
> many sides, belong to the worthy and enduring type* [italics mine]. (pp. 137-
> 138)

Dewey here was saying something very different from what he had at
first. Instead of "worth" being defined by the kind and importance of work
to be performed by the child, it was now being defined by its proximity to
him. The two formulations had vastly different implications, each reflecting,
in a sense, the changes that had taken place in American thinking during the
years Dewey was writing. The first tied individual work to social development, with the contributions of human intelligence the link between them.
The second tied individual work to social location, with the limitations of
inherited condition the link between them. When Dewey considered the past
he could connect work to growth. But when he considered the present there
was no longer room for it. He now could connect work only to the hand-me-
down activity of a child's locale, to what was "going on around him." The
change was a profound measure of how the vision of a new generation of

educators had contracted. No longer did they think of the communities of mind that linked Americans wherever they lived and whatever their background. Now they thought of fixed geographical communities increasingly seen as posing barriers not easily scaled. It was a shift from values connecting the individual to the purposes of the whole society to values connecting him to a narrow preoccupation with the purposes of his immediate environment of neighborhood or town. In terms of its practical consequences, this shift would be among the most important achievements of Dewey's "revolution" in educational philosophy.

CHAPTER EIGHT

EDUCATION AND UTOPIA: THE COMMUNITY
OF THE SELF-FULFILLED

I

When Dewey considered educational questions in an extended way again, it was a decade and a half later. Dewey had given up none of his earlier views, but he now seemed more aware of the need to demonstrate their implications for social policy. The overriding concern for him was to make clear the value of his ideas for quieting the possibility of a social conflict that seemed even more likely than before. Although the commitment to harmony and the need to adjust the various elements of the social community to one another had always been prominent in his thinking, they now took on an almost compulsive quality. By the mid-teens his uncertainty about the ability to create a truly democratic society had increased considerably. Such a society for Dewey was, above all, one purged of deep social divisions and the hatreds that accompanied them. It was one that included, and was responsive to the needs of, both rich and poor. It was a society where barriers of race and nationality had been broken down, one where the recognition of shared and mutual interests brought people together into patterns of common interaction and "associated living."[1]

Dewey's belief in the value of this society was strong. But despite his many pronouncements on its behalf, the formulations that appeared in his writings of this period revealed less than complete confidence that it was close to realization. On more than one occasion it seemed that his reservations were so deep that he was able to overcome them only in the most fanciful, and ultimately unrealistic, way. At these times, Dewey could imagine democracy only by calling into being the kind of class cooperation and common feeling that, he made clear elsewhere, did not appear to be very widespread. A democratic society could exist when conflicts between its members were not great, when the distance that social groups had to travel to satisfy each other's desires was not far. Shared values and interests meant that disagreement never extended to fundamentals; compromise, the essence

---

[1] John Dewey, *Democracy and Education: An Introduction to the Philosophy of Education* (New York, 1966; orig. 1916), pp. 86-88.

of a society's ability to reach agreement politically and to carry on its affairs peaceably, thereby became possible.

By the years after 1910, however, Dewey found it more difficult than he wanted to admit to believe that nothing fundamental separated social classes. At the same time that he promoted schools that advanced harmony, egalitarian social relations, and diffused decision-making, he also noted how class lines were sharpening, how indeed his own plans for educational reform, took the sharpening for granted.

But to have recognized the disparity between what he hoped for and what he actually saw when he looked at his society would have been difficult for Dewey. Admitting that unpleasant confrontation and hard bargaining instead of easy agreement and friendly accommodation were in the nation's future did not come easily to a thinker who was committed to the idea that democracy could be achieved without serious social and political discord. Instead, he looked to the schools and their curriculum. Achieving the ideal society, he was convinced, "depends more upon the adoption of educational methods calculated to effect the change than upon anything else."[2]

Effecting a democratic society through education was attractive to Dewey for good reasons. Experts trained in the arrangement of its various elements could devise the environment in which the values necessary to community peace and individual growth could be kept in balance, plan and action could be based on impartial assessment and evaluation, and "flexible readjustment"[3] could be introduced as needed. Politics, in effect, could be replaced by administrative science. Consent and agreement could be created not by argument and discussion, but by skillful management.

In the real world something would have to give. Dewey wanted "social change without disorder," but he was not eager to face the issue of how eliminating the latter would affect the quality of the former. He spoke about liberating "the diversity of personal capacities," but did not notice how this conflicted with talk of placing "greater reliance upon the recognition of mutual interests as a factor in social control."[4]

Dewey's unwillingness to face this issue helps explain why the attempts that he did make to deal with the tension between managed order and a society of free individuals assumed an almost utopian tone. The solution he seemed most comfortable posing led him to look less to the real world and more to an imaginary one in which members were united by common desires cut loose from the practical necessities of daily survival. These necessities could prove extremely divisive, especially in a society

---

[2] Ibid., p. 316.
[3] Ibid., p. 99.
[4] Ibid., pp. 86, 87.

where competitive pressures were increasing. Real economic growth, Dewey long believed, had been sharply curtailed; society was becoming a more dangerous place.

In earlier writings at the turn of the century, Dewey had urged Americans to focus on practical necessities. Successfully finding and making a living that kept family and community intact then seemed a high achievement.[5] But now the rewards of such an accomplishment appeared to be less attractive to him. Dewey now seemed to believe that he had to offer additional incentives to convince the population to remain loyal and tolerant members of his envisioned consensus. It was, after all, going to be a community so harmonious and tranquil that even the rich—their selfish and isolating opposition to the needs and desires of the masses having dissipated voluntarily—would seek entry.

Unfortunately, others looking at the same world did not find Dewey's ideal an easy one to embrace. Increasingly, they became compelled to speak out against it. Piecemeal tinkering and rearrangement by expert social mechanics no longer seemed adequate to the scale of social problems they saw. Insistently and in growing numbers they made their case. But Dewey could hardly be expected to hear the critics. Admitting the force of their arguments would make it impossible to keep central to his ideal of social change the values of closely monitored adjustment, cooperative agreement, and measured social improvement. His reputation had been based on the projection of these values, and even as contrary evidence mounted—especially as revealed by the passions of war—he held fast to them.

II

Dewey's thinking about social divisiveness played a prominent role in his most extended work of educational theory. In *Democracy and Education* (1916), curriculum planning, as before, grew out of a specific context, defined by the needs and aspirations of the population to be served. That population was again distinguished from a handful of aristocrats who, he said, still refused to acknowledge the need to apply scientific knowledge to daily life, and persisted in basing its educational schemes on the specialized interests of its own members. The intervening years had done nothing to make him think that the distinctions between classes had diminished. In fact, the development of industrial culture had in certain ways only intensified the "cleavage of society into a learned and an unlearned class, a leisure and a laboring class," and it was deplorable if schoolmen were "content that an unintelligent, unfree state persists in those who engage directly in turning

---

[5] See the previous chapter.

nature to use, and leave the intelligence which controls to be the exclusive possession of remote scientists and captains of industry."[6]

Educators, Dewey felt, were in a position to criticize this division, but only if they were "free from responsibility for perpetuating the educational practices which train the many for pursuits involving mere skill in production, and the few for a knowledge that is an ornament and a cultural embellishment" (p. 256). This kind of division, as he had insisted earlier,[7] was a residue of the past, and it had to be cast off from educational practice. Only then could a course of study that was "useful and liberal at the same time" be developed.[8]

This thinking led Dewey to a problem he had raised in his earlier books. How, he asked, could an education that led to social adjustment be reconciled with one that led to social change? The problem bothered him considerably but he had not made any further progress in solving it. Earlier the problem did not seem difficult to deal with: adjustment promoted social change.[9] Now, however, he was more concerned. He still answered that there was no conflict between the two ideas, but he put the point more assertively, perhaps to quiet new uncertainty. Successfully giving workers an "insight into the social aims of their pursuits," and therefore a "direct personal interest in them" (both the result of an injection of the right kind of liberal studies) was the same as helping to change the situation for the better. An education, Dewey wrote, that reconciled "liberal nurture" with an "ability to share efficiently and happily in occupations which are productive...*will of itself* [my italics] tend to do away with the evils of the existing economic situation." Sounding like an advocate of the co-participation and worker democracy plans advanced by many critics of industrial culture in recent decades (to whom Dewey is a particular hero), he explained what he meant:

> In the degree to which men have an active concern in the ends that control their activity, their activity becomes free or voluntary and loses its externally enforced and servile quality, *even though the physical aspect of behavior remains the same* [my italics]. In what is termed politics, democratic social organization makes provision for this direct participation in control: in the economic region, control remains external and autocratic. (p. 260)

Because Dewey doubted that a change in the latter situation would soon occur, and apparently because he doubted that action in the political arena was likely to affect the economic, an improvement in the worker's internal state would have to suffice. This was all the more reason why the curricu-

---

[6] *Democracy and Education*, p. 256.
[7] In his *The School and Society* in *The Child and the Curriculum and the School and Society* (Chicago, 1956), p. 27.
[8] *Democracy and Education*, p. 258.
[9] See the discussion of Dewey's *The School and Society* in chapter seven above.

lum he proposed was an indispensable element of public policy. The split between "inner mental action and outer physical action," mirrored in the distinction between liberal and utilitarian studies, could be closed. The two realms of action, connected through an educational program that applied the methods of the first to the work of the second, would then be able to unify the "disposition of the members of society," and "do much to unify society itself" (p. 260).

Undertaking the task of unification that Dewey had in mind was long overdue. The new science, he wrote, had wrought major changes in the productive and commercial methods of society centuries ago; it was time a new moral consciousness accompanied it. The exploitation of one human being by another, common in medieval times, was as firmly entrenched as ever. Instead of providing mankind with new ethical ends, the new science "put at the disposal of a class the means to secure their old ends of aggrandizement at the expense of another class." Industrialism transferred power from the landed nobility to the manufacturing centers but, Dewey noted, "capitalism rather than a social humanism"—which grew up as a minority cry against the materialism, the urge for the "making, saving, and spending money" that characterized capitalism—had taken its place. (p. 283)

Dewey again turned to the proper teaching of occupations for a solution. He was still convinced such teaching would remedy the disjunction between materialism and humanism. It would create a unity of purpose and understanding within the population that was now unknown. Here also was the "key to happiness"—"to find out what one is fitted to do and to secure an opportunity to do it." Dewey elaborated, showing no awareness that his words might have more of a dispiriting than an uplifting effect on an audience that could no longer imagine how to apply his ideal to its own inchoate and unsettled perception of the future.[10] "Nothing is more tragic," he wrote, "than failure to discover one's true business in life, or to find that one has drifted or been forced by circumstances into an uncongenial calling."[11] To men already pushed into degrading jobs in an economy shifting from manufacturing employment to less productive white collar positions, his words may have seemed only to bring the disheartening reality of their lives closer to the surface. Divorced as his words were from a political program to expand satisfying economic opportunities, they may only have seemed to advise his audience to get used to lives it was powerless to alter, except in an inner realm of "consciousness."[12]

---

[10] Some idea of these perceptions can be found in Walter Lippmann, *Drift and Mastery* (Englewood Cliffs, N.J., 1961; orig. 1914), esp. pp. 109, 111, 117, 118, 148, 151, 152; and Jane Addams, *The Spirit of Youth and the City Streets* (Urbana, Ill., 1972; orig. 1909), passim.

[11] *Democracy and Education*, p. 308.

[12] See the discussion below, section III.

Occupations, he maintained in *Democracy and Education*, should form the core of the student's curriculum because of the way they organized information and ideas, and because of the way they provided a "constant, working stimulus to note and relate whatever had to do with his concern." What Dewey meant, as he went on to explain, was that the pressure of making a living encouraged one to pay attention. "No classification, no selection and arrangement of facts," he said, "which is consciously worked out for purely abstract ends, can ever compare in solidity or effectiveness with that knit under the stress of an occupation; in comparison the former sort is formal, superficial, and cold."[13]

But this association only furthered the outcome Dewey said he wanted to avoid—making it more difficult for the worker to discover his true business in life. As Dewey presented the issue, occupational choice and personal needs were wedded in an alliance against broad social needs and arrangements, dismissed with the terms "abstract," or "formal, superficial, and cold." These needs became distant and removed, not so much unworthy of consideration as irrelevant to any "real" problem that could be effectively dealt with and managed.

They were also irrelevant for another reason. Dewey believed that most workers could not expect to have any experience in these "abstract" lines of work. On the occasions when he did suggest that the worker was closer to science now than before, he quickly made clear that he excluded any real appreciation of, or introduction to, its workings or generative principles. In one place in *Democracy and Education*, for example, he wrote that "the subject matter of industrial occupation presents not only more of the content of science than it used to, but greater opportunity for familiarity with the method by which knowledge is made." But in immediately adding, "The ordinary worker in the factory is of course under too immediate economic pressure to have a chance to produce a knowledge like that of the worker in the laboratory," he indicated the limitations he had in mind. Even in school, where the situation should be more favorable to learning, the worker's exposure to scientific principles would remain restricted, defined by his expected occupational status. "In schools," Dewey wrote, after the discussion of vocational education that we have followed above,

> association with machines and industrial processes may be had under conditions where the chief conscious concern of the students is insight. The separation of shop and laboratory, where these conditions are fulfilled, is largely conventional, the laboratory having the advantage of permitting the following up of any intellectual interest a problem may suggest; the shop the advantage

---

[13] *Democracy and Education*, p. 310.

of emphasizing the social bearings of the scientific principle, as well as, with many pupils, of stimulating a livelier interest.[14]

The student destined for industry, Dewey assumed, would want his insight to come from "association with machines and industrial processes," the tools of his trade, "the objects of his experience." This learning would take place in the shop where the "social bearings of the scientific principle" could be explained, and where a "livelier interest" could be engaged. In a division of work Dewey called purely conventional, the laboratory would be reserved for those students with an "intellectual interest," the kind most workers did not have. Limited to the few, interest could be given the wide-ranging freedom that the imperatives of economic pressure denied to the many. For this group Dewey offered a version of scientific enterprise that was much more constraining. It held out little hope that the mass of school children might enter the conceptual universe that characterized true scientific investigation.

Once the masses were excluded in this way, the need to upgrade intellectual standards and the living standards that had to attend them would be of receding importance to Dewey. Students who were denied the scientific literacy to assimilate the revolutionary developments of the period would not require them.[15] For things to have turned out differently, a human investment Dewey's political and economic assumptions ruled out from the start would have been necessary. But because Dewey could not imagine that such an investment was possible, he could never suggest the educational program that could make it a reality. An appeal to science, for Dewey, was never an appeal for creative innovation and widespread intellectual development. Instead, it was an appeal to the practical, to the use of the science of experience by the technician laboring quietly, diligently and expertly, to fine-tune a mechanism the overall characteristics of which were largely fixed.[16] In this area, it seemed, Dewey's desire to abolish the division between aristocratic and democratic education did not apply.

---

[14] *Democracy and Education*, p. 315.

[15] For some of the curricular changes that in part resulted from thinking like Dewey's, see Raymond Callahan, *Education and the Cult of Efficiency* (Chicago, 1962); Selwyn K. Troen, *The Public and the Schools: Shaping the St. Louis School System, 1838-1920* (Columbia, Mo., 1975), chapter 9, esp. pp. 184-187; and Richard Hofstadter, *Anti-intellectualism in American Life* (New York, 1963), part V: "Education in a Democracy."

[16] On this theme, see Robert H. Wiebe, *The Search for Order, 1877-1920* (New York, 1967), pp. 145, 152-154. See also Randolph Bourne's essay, "Twilight of Idols," to be considered at the end of this chapter. It has been reprinted in Randolph S. Bourne, *War and the Intellectuals: Collected Essays, 1915-1919*, ed. Carl Resek (New York, 1964). Dewey's more formal thinking about the scientific issues related to this discussion can be found in *The Quest for Certainty: A Study of the Relation of Knowledge and Action* (New York, 1960; orig. 1929), pp. 37, 45.

III

Dewey was discovering how difficult it was to conceive of a truly egalitarian society. But the belief was one he could hardly abandon. Equality and the shared interests it fostered was the basis of community, and without community democratic society would fall apart. "Since democracies forbid, by their very nature," Dewey wrote at the same time he was preparing *Democracy and Education*, "highly centralized governments working by coercion, they depend upon shared interests and experiences for their unity and upon personal appreciation of the value of institutions for stability and defense." Unless society created a "lively and ardent sense of common life, it is hopeless to secure in individuals that loyalty to the organized group which needs to be an animating motive of conduct."[17] Given its importance, Dewey would continue to search for space to locate it, even though the space might be increasingly marginal to the actual life and work in his society.

In his writings at the turn of the century, Dewey seemed to want to escape the emphasis many educators placed on the immediate needs of the child. Unfortunately, his own devotion to the politics of harmony and conciliation complicated the task for him. The child for Dewey as well as other educators became the guide to the future for the very reason that the child did not concern himself with the future. In a world where concern for the future might imply a plan for bending refractory experience to one's will, and where an assumed scarcity suggested disappointment and conflict, the adult, bent on success, might forge ahead, heedless of the social disruption to which he was contributing. To these disorganizing tendencies, the example of the child's response to his environment was viewed as a valuable counterpoint. His natural impulses toward self-expression, instant gratification, cooperation, and affection had much to recommend them. When Dewey wrote, "To predetermine some future occupation for which education is to be a strict preparation is to injure the possibilities of present development and thereby reduce the adequacy of preparation for a future right employment,"[18] he may easily have had the ambition and aggressive planning of adults in mind. It is possible to view the warning against "predetermination" as simply a caution against early tracking. But given the assumptions with which Dewey wrote, it was more likely an expression of his fear that unrealistic self-willed activity could have disruptive consequences. In choosing phrasing that set up an opposition between "the possi-

---

[17] "The Need of an Industrial Education in an Industrial Democracy," *Manual Training and Vocational Education* XVII (February, 1916): 414.
[18] *Democracy and Education*, p. 310.

bilities of present development" and "predetermination," he made it necessary to embrace one to avoid the other.

The important thing was that the emphasis on the child's background
and capacities be maintained as primary. This was the one element Dewey's
particular version of vocational education never compromised. Opposed as
he was to narrow trade training, he nevertheless argued that preparation for
one's life-work should proceed by "engaging in those active occupations
which are indicated by the needs and interests of the pupil at the time." In so
doing, both teachers and pupils could come to "a genuine discovery of personal aptitudes so that the proper choice of a specialized pursuit in later life
may be indicated" (p. 311). In practice the job choice eventually made
would not be altered very much by this interactive process. But the social
dividends—the result of a change in values and attitudes—might be, and
this was the area that always concerned Dewey most. It was not the work
itself, but the attitude toward work and one's life chances that deserved
attention. Because Dewey's moral commitments made it impossible for him
to comment on which kinds of work were more worthwhile than others, this
was all that could be expected.

Trade training for most people of his day was supported by the same
assumptions about growth and development that underlay Dewey's own
views. One of the most important exceptions, judging by the amount of discussion it generated, was represented by the Cooley bill, a piece of Illinois
legislation designed to reserve part of the state's education budget for trade
training to be provided in schools set aside for that purpose alone. The hope
of the bill's backers, a group that included many leading Chicago industrialists, was that separate trade schools would be easier to protect against interference from progressive reformers. To Chicago industrialists, these
reformers were insensitive to the claim that directed trade training was the
best way to increase the supply of skilled workers needed to remain competitive in international markets. Though arguments for the scheme were
attacked as socially and economically divisive, narrowly self-interested, and
anti-union,[19] people like Dewey had other objections as well. An emphasis

---

[19] Mary J. Herrick, *The Chicago Schools: A Social and Political History* (Beverly Hills,
Cal., 1971), pp. 117-120. Herrick notes that the high-handedness of the business community in
pushing the plan, and the traditions of bitter labor conflict in Chicago led to a prolonged fight
over the bill (lasting from 1912 to 1917). The Chicago Federation of Labor, which in 1908 had
offered to cooperate with business in developing a plan for industrial education, now said that
business only wanted cheap, submissive labor lacking the educational background that all
Americans should have. To the CFL the campaign for the bill was "one of the most direct of all
open-shop, anti-union drives ever made." Business, pointing to the success of similar legislation in Wisconsin, could not, in three tries (1913, 1915, and 1917), get the bill passed. See also
Julia Wrigley, *Class Politics and Public Schools: Chicago, 1900-1950* (New Brunswick, N.J.,
1982), chapter three, "Conflicts Over the Content of Schooling"; and Edwin G. Cooley,
"Professor Dewey's Criticism of the Chicago Commercial Club and its Vocational Education
Bill," *Vocational Education* 3 (September, 1913): 27.

on trade training, though it ultimately played into assumptions of economic stagnation, could also, at least in specific applications, be integrated into plans for expansion and development.

In this sense, the significance of the vocational educational movement was more far-reaching than the social engineering and tracking it performed, or the narrow trade training it offered. Although an economy growing at a far slower rate than before the 1893 depression did require a reorganization of the educational plant to fulfill its restricted economic and productive tasks, and although dwindling real opportunities in industry would impose greater social channeling responsibilities on the schools, the movement served other purposes as well. What the language of people as different as Dewey, Jane Addams, Nicholas Murray Butler, and Harvard's Charles William Eliot[20] makes clear is that vocational education was the ideal vehicle to raise questions about traditional notions of progress, and the value of investment to expand the intellectual powers of the whole population. From the start it was tied to ideas particularly well-suited to carry what Lewis Feuer has called the "back to the people" mentality[21] that was to become powerfully influential among protesters against American materialism in the years ahead.

The promotion of the ideas that lay behind this mentality—such as the absorption with local community and the egalitarian benefits of sharing the limited resources available for economic and social revitalization—was the real "hidden curriculum" of the schools. Vocational education was the ideal vehicle for these ideas, and any version of it detached from this focus (like the Cooley Plan), was certain to become the object of intense critical scrutiny. To reformers, vocational education without a rejection of economic growth made no sense. Yet Cooleyites could often speak as if one were possible without the other. In their discussions they tied vocational education to innovation and industrial expansion, a combination difficult for Progressives like Dewey to imagine.

---

[20] The views of Addams, Butler, and Eliot are available in the early bulletins of the National Society for the Promotion of Industrial Education, an organization founded to promote the vocational ideal, and federal legislation embodying it, in 1906. Some of the most open social engineering language came from Eliot in his 1907 address to the Society. For him, schools now could do little else but direct children to the vocational programs appropriate to their talents. "It must," Eliot said, "be a choice or a selection." Teachers in the elementary schools would have to "sort the pupils and sort them by their evident or probable destinies....The doctrine that a Yankee can turn his hand to anything does not fit this new [industrial] world." (Charles W. Eliot, "Industrial Education as an Essential Factor in Our National Prosperity," National Society for the Promotion of Industrial Education, *Bulletin Number 5* [1908], pp. 12-13.)

[21] Lewis S. Feuer, "John Dewey and the Back to the People Movement in American Thought," *Journal of the History of Ideas* 20 (October-December, 1959): 545. See also T. J. Jackson Lears, *No Place of Grace: Antimodernism and the Transformation of American Culture, 1880-1920* (New York, 1981), chapter 2, part 2, "Revitalization and Transformation in Arts and Crafts Ideology: The Simple Life, Aestheticism, Educational Reform."

Progressives wanted to put the educational system to other uses. This was especially true if using the schools to promote innovation and industrial expansion involved a part of the system whose control was located outside the supervisory apparatus establishing itself throughout the nation's schools. It might set a bad example. If any group demonstrated that vocational education could be tied to expressions of economic growth, as the representatives of many business groups were trying to do, it would show that alternatives existed, and make it impossible easily to justify reformers' own system with notions of restricted growth. Allowing discussions of vocational education to be tied to notions of development would raise questions that could undermine the associations upon which all their work depended.

The reformers were saying that new, and worsening, industrial conditions required new approaches to education. But if it could be assumed that the economy was not fixed forever, or for the foreseeable future, on a declining course, why need one assume that the radical changes that Progressives advocated for education were necessary either? Thinking that cast doubt on future growth led to vocational programs emphasizing narrow trade training (though not necessarily in separate schools, as Cooleyites proposed). Talk of an expanding economy, however, led to calls for training in versatility and the development of highly articulated cognitive skills. That kind of vocational education was very different from what reform-minded schoolmen had in mind. Instead of leading to the compromises of the widely promoted Gary system,[22] it could mean an increased investment

---

[22] First developed for use in Gary, Indiana but soon introduced in many other cities, the plan, which enabled existing schools to accommodate twice their usual number of students, purported to embody Progressive hopes for providing a well-rounded education based on each child's particular interests. More often the plan attracted school officials and politicians because it promised to cut costs and weaken teachers' organizations. When a financially strapped New York City tried to introduce the plan in 1914, an alliance of teachers, parents, and students defeated it. See Diane Ravitch, *The Great School Wars: New York City, 1805-1973* (New York, 1974); Ronald D. Cohen and Raymond A. Mohl, *The Paradox of Progressive Education: The Gary Plan and Urban Schooling* (Port Washington, N. Y. 1979), pp. 23, 29, 42, 47; Callahan, *Education and the Cult of Efficiency*; Edwin Lewinson, *John Purroy Mitchel, The Boy Mayor of New York* (New York, 1976), pp. 125-126; and Thomas M. Henderson, *Tammany Hall and the New Immigrants: The Progressive Years* (New York, 1976), pp. 201-215. For an example of the attacks on teachers that accompanied the introduction of Gary reforms in New York, see Mary G. Bonner, "School Riots and the Gary System: A Pitiful Incident of the New York Mayoral Contest," *The Outlook* 117 (October 31, 1917): 334-335. On the way Progressive educational innovations were used in other cities to counter the awakening of teacher militancy, see (for Chicago) the books by Mary J. Herrick and Julia Wrigley, note 19 above; and (for Atlanta) H. Wayne Urban, "Progressive Education in the Urban South: The Reform of the Atlanta Schools, 1914-1918," in Michael H. Ebner and Eugene M. Tobin, eds., *The Age of Urban Reform: New Perspectives on the Progressive Era* (Port Washington, N.Y., 1977), pp. 131-142.

in scientific facilities, smaller classes, and an expanded emphasis on academic disciplines.[23]

There were also other reasons that reformers found the Cooley Plan troubling. Undermining restricted growth ideas endangered the conception of democratic community with which reformers felt most at home. Dewey's own case for industrial education was intimately bound to such a conception, and the bill engaged his attention early. In a number of journal and magazine pieces occasioned by the fight, Dewey made the case against Cooley's plan. Cooley backers were out to appropriate the already meager educational resources of the state for their selfish interests, dividing schools and students—first economically and socially; later ethnically and religiously—in the process. They were men who wanted docile workers in the "subordinate ranks of the industrial army," who made "the pecuniary factors in industry supreme," and who sought the "exploitation of others for private ends."[24]

So much it was easy to assert with confidence. What, however, did Dewey want? On the one hand, the answer seemed obvious. In one important article written in response to the Cooley bill, Dewey spoke of initiative, self-command, and resistance to the "forces which are always at work to restore, in however changed a form, feudal oligarchy." This seemed clear enough except for the frustrating ambiguity that was evident throughout the article. For almost as soon as Dewey stated the first set of values, he attached them to others with a competing meaning, one that effectively qualified his endorsement of the first. Dewey talked about factory laborers taking control of their work from "the soulless monotony of machine industry," but he also talked about how they could adjust to it by storing their imagination so "that in the inevitable monotonous stretches of work, it may have worthy material of art and literature and science upon which to feed, instead of being frittered away upon undisciplined dreamings and sensual fancies." He spoke of the new inventions and technical innovations that were remaking industry, but he also said that "the desire for immediate results and immediate efficiency must be held in check by the need of securing powers which will enable individuals to adapt themselves to inevitable change." He talked about doing battle against "those who most profit by the perpetuation of existing conditions," but then seemed to rule out employing political channels ("we have already a political machinery

---

[23] The possibility that discussions like this might occur was no abstract worry. Even within the relatively controlled environment of the NSPIE, assumptions different from those of Dewey, Butler, Eliot, and Addams could at times emerge. See the speech of American Telephone and Telegraph President Frederick Fish who addressed the NSPIE in 1907. (National Society for the Promotion of Industrial Education, *Bulletin Number 5* [1908], p. 25.)

[24] "The Need of an Industrial Education in an Industrial Democracy," *Manual Training and Vocational Education* XVII (February, 1916): 409-414.

adapted for securing control of the masses") to do it. In the same discussions, Dewey could propose both an active and positive approach to change and a wary and hesitating one. Conceivably the two approaches were not mutually exclusive. Adjustment did not make initiative impossible, adaptation did not rule out innovation, and forswearing political action did not prohibit resistance to backward industrial methods by other means (such as the educational ones Dewey recommended in the article). But the close intermingling of concerns that most readers would consider distinct suggested that Dewey did not expect much in the life of the worker to improve. No matter how much Dewey may have wanted to better the worker's lot, the qualified messages he offered in his case for industrial education conveyed the idea that he was pulling back from the more assertive position his prose at first suggested. At the very least, Dewey seemed less certain about the basis for integrating workers into the new industrial order than he appeared to be at first glance.[25]

Dewey provided no satisfactory answer to—or even recognition of— the dilemma in the article; the tension may have been too great to resolve in articles written on short notice. But it was clearly on his mind. In *Democracy and Education*, written at the same time, he gave the subject more thought. Again he examined the issues of the Cooley fight, and again related its educational implications to questions that went to the heart of his and others' fears about democracy's ability to survive. Strict trade training was wrong not on pedagogical grounds, but because it strengthened the forces of autocracy and class repression:

> In an autocratically managed society, it is often a conscious object to prevent the development of freedom and responsibility; a few do the planning and ordering, the others follow directions and are deliberately confined to narrow and prescribed channels of endeavor. Howevermuch such a scheme may inure to the prestige and profit of a class it is evident that it limits the development of the subject class; hardens and confines the opportunities for learning through experience of the master class, and in both ways hampers the life of the society as a whole.[26]

As usual in his writings, Dewey raised no questions about economic growth. He discussed neither the way economic growth distinguished American society from less successful ones of the past, nor the way it was relevant to understanding the issues of class and opposition that occupied him here. Instead, he repeated the liberal fears of narrow vocational training that were legitimate only when the results of a malfunctioning economic generator were taken into account. As Dewey demonstrated when he tried

---

[25] "Learning to Earn: The Place of Vocational Education in a Comprehensive Scheme of Public Education," *School and Society* 5 (March 24, 1917): 331-334. See also "Splitting Up the School System," *The New Republic*, April 17, 1915, p. 283.

[26] *Democracy and Education*, pp. 310-311.

it, considering invidious social relations alone would not prove very satisfying. Much like more recent writers who also fear the consequences of rapid
economic growth,[27] he made a plea for an alternative community of the
mutually self-fulfilled.

With a starting point that denied the expansion that alone could ensure
truly equitable and cooperative social relations, Dewey at times found himself conjuring up a vision that was as other-worldly as that of social commentators from whom he generally wanted to keep his distance. Dewey had
no political views that committed him to fight for the urban and industrial
development that could create new material wealth. His focus was on the
redistribution of wealth that already existed. This would not be a simple
matter to arrange politically, however, and despite his best intentions, he
was ineluctably led to tie the hope of a better life to the embrace of a vision
of spiritual or inner richness nurtured among like-minded seekers. For all
his professed realism, his thinking, ultimately, led in a romantic direction.
According to Dewey, locked-in trade training represented a serious danger
to American society; an educational system based on it could easily
"perpetuate the older traditions for a select few, and effect its [education's]
adjustment to the newer economic conditions more or less on the basis of
acquiescence in the untransformed, unrationalized, and unsocialized phases
of our defective industrial regime." Education, in other words, could all too
easily become the agent for extending "the existing industrial order of society" unchanged, "instead of operating as a means of its transformation."

But what kind of "transformation" did Dewey have in mind? Although
he was reluctant to provide details, he was willing to sketch its general features. "The desired transformation," he said, "is not difficult to define in a
formal way."

> It signifies [he wrote] a society in which every person shall be occupied in
> something which makes the lives of others better worth living, and which
> accordingly makes the ties which bind persons together more perceptible—
> which breaks down the barriers of distance between them. It denotes a state of
> affairs in which the interest of each in his work is uncoerced and intelligent:
> based upon its congeniality to his own aptitudes.[28]

What is important about this passage is not its vagueness—to be
expected from Dewey—but the way it made work tributary to self-gratifica-
tion and equitable social relations, instead of the reverse. Work here had
little to do with the indispensable physical or intellectual labor that powers
society and guarantees its continuation. Instead, it was linked to an ability to
throw off these necessities, to live in a world of the "uncoerced" and

---

[27] See, in particular, Samuel Bowles and Herbert Gintis, *Schooling in Capitalist America*
(New York, 1976); and my review in *The Review of Education* 3 (May-June, 1977): 168-181.
[28] *Democracy and Education*, p. 316.

"congenial," a world that was cut loose from the activities that insure the future existence of mankind. Dewey's vision was, for this reason, another example of the way his thinking helped to uncouple the ideas of work, education, and cognition—the connection of which was the central achievement of an earlier generation of educators.

It is therefore no wonder that radical critics like Bowles and Gintis have said they "could not be in closer agreement with John Dewey's philosophy."[29] When they defined "personal development" in terms of the "creative energies unleashed by liberated education and unalienated work," when they located such work in a separate, "vital craft and artistic sector in production as a voluntary supplement to socially necessary work" (p. 269), they were echoing sentiments Dewey gave voice to sixty years before they wrote. Dewey's views lacked the same appreciation as theirs did of the forces that guarantee ongoing human life, and were based in the same limited perception of social possibility. Like them, Dewey sought harmony and the absence of conflict. Unable to locate such relations, either through empirical or imaginative means, in the real world, he devised one of scaled-down purpose and reduced expectation (and one that tolerated "uncoerced" and even socially irrelevant work) where they could flourish. "Congeniality" to an inner voice of "aptitude" was sufficient reason for membership in the communal bonding he envisioned. Worried, like others of his day, about the erosion of traditional work values, he was willing to forestall their disappearance by permitting them to retreat to an area where, paradoxically, the original impetus for retaining them—their relation to a real world of social re-creation—would no longer operate. In this sense, despite his avowed intention to give the world of work new meaning, he could do so only by drawing more firmly a distinction that he supposedly wanted to erase. He had to distinguish between work that was personally unrewarding but social necessary and work that was personally fulfilling but socially vacuous.[30] Like those who in recent decades have relied on and advocated consciousness raising, personal awareness, and sensitivity training as ways to effect change,[31] Dewey could also fall into language

---

[29] Bowles and Gintis, p. 266.

[30] For the way Bowles and Gintis fall into similar thinking, see my review of their *Schooling in Capitalist America* (cited above), pp. 178-179.

[31] An example appears in Marilyn Ferguson's *The Aquarian Conspiracy: Personal and Social Transformation in the 1980s* (Los Angeles, 1980). Ferguson includes Dewey (p. 45) as one of the progenitors of the "transformational" revolution she discusses and, interestingly, one of her statements about the nature of the problems that concern her has a familiar ring: "Our crises show us the ways in which our institutions have betrayed nature. We have equated the good life with material consumption, we have dehumanized work and made it needlessly competitive, we are uneasy about our capacities for learning and teaching" (p. 29). Expanding individual consciousness is the remedy for the group she speaks for, a group that in response to the question, "What major ideas did you have to give up?" typically answered, "Scientific proof as the only way to understand," "Belief in the purely rational," and "Causality." "After

about changing one's "mental disposition"—a change he called fundamentally "educative."

Not that mind and character would be altered by "direct instruction and exhortation," however. This could never occur "apart from a change in industrial and political conditions," and, as we have seen above, Dewey had deep reservations that such changes on the scale necessary would be forthcoming. The widespread popular political activity on which the changes depended was unlikely to appear. And since it was, Dewey had little choice but to argue that the ability to alter mental dispositions directly "contradicts our basic idea that character and mind are attitudes of participative response in social affairs." The populations he was talking about educating did not seem to be capable of such a response. The schools would therefore have to do the job by becoming "a projection in type of the society we should like to realize, and by forming minds in accord with it gradually modify the larger and more recalcitrant features of adult society."[32]

The problem was that having ruled out popular intervention, Dewey was narrowing his options for achieving his ideal. Even if not in a "literal and quantitative sense," he seemed to believe that the direction of social change was moving toward the "social state" he envisioned. Somehow the "recalcitrant" features of adult society would be made more amenable to humane direction. Once again, he defined these features in a way that focused attention on the opposing ideal of an egalitarian community of congenial members. The greatest evil of the present regime was not poverty or the "suffering which it entails" (p. 317). Instead, he said, disregarding the fact that many had more primary needs, it was "the fact that so many persons have callings which make no appeal to them, which are pursued simply for the money reward that accrues." The ever-present danger of social division and the lack of adjustment and contentment it led to was again the problem. Unappealing callings, Dewey stressed, "constantly provoke one to aversion, ill will, and a desire to slight and evade." They led, in other words, to the impulses that made "congenial" social life impossible. They prodded individuals to separate from their fellows, to sever the human bond that was based on trust and confidence.

The problem extended to all levels of society—the rich suffered along with everyone else. Their "excessive, if not monopolistic, control of the activities of the many" had shut them off "from equality and generality of social intercourse" (p. 317). To compensate they engaged in further alienating acts of display and self-indulgence that only increased their isolation, and a further resort to "the impression of force and superior possession and

---

many years of intellectual, left-brain pursuit of reality," she writes, "an LSD experience taught me that there were alternate realities" (p. 106).

[32] *Democracy and Education*, pp. 316-317.

enjoyment which they can make upon others." By Dewey's reckoning, there was nothing preordained about this behavior. Social separation, the result of an alienated position and the work that went with it, had cut the rich off from the community of men that the best side of their nature would have them join. Because of this separation, the reforms Dewey urged would come as a blessing to the worker's employer as much as to the worker himself; both could enter the community life of the congenial together. The impulse to separate from one's fellows, the most disorganizing feature of adult society, could be overcome by the rich and powerful as much as by those positioned lower on the social ladder. Even the existence of a class like the rich posed no unalterable obstacle to the vision of community he held. And if that were true, the rich might also be won over to his vision of educational reform, the program that would bring his vision of community to life.

But it was the very trade training schemes promoted by the rich that prevented the realization of this dream. Schemes like trade training only sharpened the division Dewey wanted to dissolve because they assumed "that some are to continue to be wage earners under economic conditions like the present" (p. 317). Not that the technical proficiency this training provided was bad. But it was an insufficient bridge to the social ideal Dewey harbored. Competence had to be extended "to insight into [the work's] social bearings." The rich employer needed to understand this facet of work as much as the worker. For without this understanding of work, profit or power would continue to be the dominating concerns, with the rich, especially, losing from a fixation on them. "Social sympathy and humane disposition," said Dewey, were found not among them but among "the economically unfortunate, who have not experienced the hardening effects of a one-sided control of the affairs of others" (p. 319).

This was not to say that the rich, even with the obstacles they would have to overcome, too could not develop these virtues. At least Dewey hoped so; those who "controlled the affairs of others" were the people who ran the schools, and Dewey feared that without a change of heart the scheme of vocational education that they backed would "assume and perpetuate" the divisions and weaknesses of "the industrial regime that now exists" (p. 318). Yet having ruled out popular agitation to secure his goal, he had no place but to these same forces to turn. He therefore urged them—his reference to "those who are in a position to make their wishes good" could, in this context, apply to no other social grouping—to "demand a liberal, a cultural occupation, and one which fits for directive power the youth in whom they are directly interested." With the Cooley battle firmly in mind, he urged them not "to split the system." Doing so would doom his goal of using the school as an agent of integration, equality, and community. It would treat it "as an agency for transferring the older division of labor and leisure, culture and service, mind and body, directed and directive class, into a society nominally democratic" (p. 318).

The issue, as always for Dewey, was not presented in terms of the debate over industrial growth that lay at its heart, but as a fight over social status and prerogative. Dewey had anticipated the arguments of latter day deschoolers and cultural radicals: the school, through its structure of preferment and selection, would reproduce the unequal, unjust social relations of the wider society.[33] That is, unless its anti-egalitarian tendencies were carefully monitored and blocked, and unless alternative curricular designs were provided. The attack on the Cooley bill was an example of the former; his own plan was an example of the latter.

Dewey had such high hopes for success that he calmly disregarded the realities of political control. Perhaps he understood, despite what appeared to be the case, that control was already changing hands. Certainly this was the case ideologically, where it counted the most. Dewey might talk about the opposition of a "controlling class" that recognized how educational plans like his could be "dangerous to [its] interests," how [it] might arouse "discontent or ambitions 'beyond the station' of those working under the direction of others," and how [it] might "threaten [its] ability to use others for [its] own ends." But, with an optimism that pointed to an understanding of how surely his ideas were gaining ground, he then noted how "this very fact [of "opposition of those who are intrenched in command of the industrial machinery"] is the presage of a more equitable and enlightened social order, for it gives evidence of the dependence of social reorganization upon educational reconstruction."[34]

The Cooleyite industrialists, he was saying, understood the game perfectly—the battleground of politics was the school. They knew that it was there that questions of social policy would be decided, and had taken the fight to that terrain. Dewey also knew, but did not bother to add, that they were not doing very well. "Educational reconstruction," in the form of curriculum revision, structural alteration, and methodological change, was winning supporters and leading the way toward a social order "more equitable and enlightened" than what had gone before. Industrialists might as well save the energy they put into opposition and change sides now. Once the plan was implemented, its remarkable powers would transform their

---

[33] Besides Bowles and Gintis's effort, noted above, there are many other examples of this viewpoint. See, for example, the most well-known, Ivan Illich, *Deschooling Society* (New York, 1971); and Randall Collins, *The Credential Society: An Historical Sociology of Education and Stratification* (New York, 1979). R. W. Apple discusses the literature in "What Correspondence Theories of the Hidden Curriculum Miss," *The Review of Education* 5 (Spring, 1979): 101-112.

[34] *Democracy and Education*, pp. 318-319.

thinking anyway. The plan, he said, "would turn the increasing fund of social sympathy to constructive account, instead of leaving it a somewhat blind philanthropic sentiment....It would increase sympathy for labor, create a disposition of mind which can discover the culturing elements in useful activity, and increase a sense [on the part of the rich] of social responsibility" (p. 320).

Dewey did not elaborate further here. He had already explained why "the more privileged portion of the community" would be pleased with his plans in the book he had published the year before.[35]

IV

Schools of Tomorrow (1915) is the closest thing we have to an explicitly programmatic statement of Dewey's educational ideas. Focusing, in particular, on the experience of industrial cities like Chicago, Gary, Indianapolis and Cincinnati, it offered specific examples of schools that seemed to embody the pedagogical approaches that Dewey felt were most valuable. In a way, the book was the laboratory manual to accompany more abstract statements like *Democracy and Education*; through it we have a way to see more clearly the kind of experimental results Dewey sought.

As we might expect, education for the possible dominated his outlook. Acceptance of one's circumstances, acceptance of the limitations on opportunity and the strictures this placed on possible achievement were required in a world where scarcity ruled, and where conflict threatened to disrupt the flow of social life. Narrowing one's sights, in terms of both geography and aspiration, to a focus on the delimited, local environment appropriate to a realistic assessment of one's future prospects, provided the most workable basis for stable community relations. Frustration would be minimized, minor achievements would be magnified, and one's sense of worth would be inflated. In the process, social goals would also be reformulated: they too would become more tangible and instantly gratifying.

With the help of his daughter Evelyn, who gathered the material on each school, Dewey offered accounts of civics clubs, vocational education programs, home visiting work, work-study plans and more. The civics clubs undertook neighborhood surveys and local self-help projects, each club deciding "what [it] wanted to do for [its] own district and setting out to accomplish it, whether it was the cleaning up of a bad alley or the better

---

[35] Dewey was not unaccustomed to trying to influence the powerful. See, in particular, his writing on America's role in World War I, and Christopher Lasch's discussion of it in his *New Radicalism in America, 1889-1963: The Intellectual as Social Type* (New York, 1965), chapter 6, "*The New Republic* and the War: 'An Unanalyzable Feeling,'" especially pp. 202-204, 210-216.

lighting of a street." To achieve its ends, said Dewey, it would use "all the methods that an adult citizen's club would employ, writing letters to the city departments, calling at the City Hall, and besides actually went into the alleys and cleaned them up [*sic*]."[36] He reported on citizenship classes whose content consisted of taking care of the school building and grounds. "Pupils who have made the furniture and cement walks with their own hands, and who know how much it cost," said Dewey pointing up the social value of the work, "are slow to destroy walks or furniture, nor are they going to be very easily fooled as to the value they get in service and improvements when they themselves become taxpayers" (p. 146). Nature study, conducted through cultivation of urban gardens, served as civics instruction also. As Dewey explained, "the value of gardens to the child and to the neighborhood is demonstrated: to the child as a means of making money or helping his family by supplying them with vegetables, to the community in showing how gardens are a means of cleaning up and beautifying the neighborhood" (p. 70). Especially in poor districts, Dewey noted, "the gardens have been a real economic help to the people" (p. 70). Cooking classes were used to teach children and parents "about cheap and nutritious bills of fare" (p. 144).

Students of stenography and bookkeeping did "real work" in the school office or storeroom, drawing small salaries that helped offset falling school budgets; students of domestic science and cooking learned their subjects in tenements converted for "laboratory" use. In this setting they received lessons "in buying, the comparative costs and values of food,...and large quantity cooking...done in connection with the soup kitchen." Here the children bought, cooked, and served the soup at a charge of three cents to the pupils and neighborhood residents. "They keep all the accounts and not only have to make all their expenses, but are expected to make some profit for the use of the school as well" (p. 156). Other students learned carpentry by "making things that are needed in the school building...and by doing some of the repairing on the building." Girls learned millinery and crocheting "from the commercial point of view, to teach the girls to do something that will enable them to earn some money" (p. 154). In dressmaking classes they learned "to sew from the point of view of the worker who has to produce her own things" (p. 187). Boys learned shoe-repairing and tailoring "to teach habits of personal neatness and of industry," and in the latter case could soon "patch and mend their own clothes, as well as to sponge and press them." This outlook, Dewey concluded, "has resulted in a very marked improvement in the appearance and habits of the boys in the class,

---

[36] John Dewey and Evelyn Dewey, *Schools of Tomorrow* (New York, 1962; orig. 1915), p. 61.

and has had an influence not only on the whole school, but on the neighborhood as well" (p. 155).

The influence worked in the reverse direction also—the neighborhood
assisted the school. Dewey noted that a spirit of cooperation and interest
among parents and students was replacing the older one of "distrust and
antagonism." In response to a call by a school principal for community help
in building a boys' clubhouse and manual training shops, time and materials
were contributed by skilled workers. The latter also contributed $350 in
cash, "no small sum for people as poor as they are" (p. 158). The teachers of
the school constantly made the link between school and neighborhood
community, frankly discussing the poverty of the area, and urging the pupils
"to earn money to help their parents by becoming as nearly self-supporting
as possible. Each grade keeps track of what its members earn and how they
earn it" (p. 160).

For Dewey, this interaction with the neighborhood was the ideal relationship between school and community. The emphasis in the school
accounts was constantly on the needs of the individual determined from the
standpoint of the local neighborhood, the immediate area in which the student could be expected to move once out of school. Here was the theory of
Democracy and Education and of *The School and Society* made concrete.
Here was the meaning of a program where emphasis fell "on the larger
freedom of using and testing senses and judgment in situations typical of
life." Liberal culture by itself might be appropriate to an earlier time when
the country offered "unlimited and unexplored opportunities," when "the
pioneer was dependent upon his own ability in seizing these opportunities"
(p. 122). Not, said Dewey, because this kind of learning was at that time of
immediate value in the work of getting on, but precisely because it was not.
To recent European immigrants especially, its acquisition would be a mark
of refinement setting one man off from his fellows, and offer some respite
from the day-to-day struggle against nature. Dewey ignored the practical
value that European culture had for early Americans, in terms of the cognitive powers it nurtured and the sense of purpose and mission it provided.
Instead, he set up the division we have seen him introduce before. On the
one hand was the irrelevant learning of past generations. "Learning," he
said, "did not mean finding out about the things around them or about what
was going on in other parts of the world; it meant reviewing the achievements of the past, learning to read dead languages, the deader the language
the greater the reputation for 'learning'" (p. 122). On the other was what
should be "obviously the first business of the public school[,]...to teach the
child to live in the world in which he finds himself, to understand his share
in it, and to get a good start in adjusting himself to it" (p. 123).[37]

---

[37] See also p. 168.

This goal, more explicit in *Schools of Tomorrow* but no different from the views that he expressed elsewhere, played directly into Dewey's thinking about the relationship between education and social meliorism. An important example of the connection he made was his account of the school for black children in Indianapolis. The nature of school and neighborhood there well-exhibited the laboratory conditions that interested him. It was a "poor, crowded, colored district of the city," he wrote, "and once had a bad reputation for lawlessness and disorder as well." The students were hostile and attendance irregular. Yet out of these conditions a settlement-like school, as Dewey saw it, was able to make the children "healthy, happy, and competent both economically and socially." The key to the school's success was that "there is nothing in the school not entirely practical in any district where the children come from homes with limited resources and meager surroundings." The school, armed with this knowledge, recognized that arousing the people to a sense of their needs (practically speaking, the same as contributing to "the best interests of the community") meant especially that "they must be taught how to earn a living, and how to use their resources for themselves and their neighbors" (pp. 151-153).

In this regard, the school was a school for colored children, said Dewey, "only in the sense that the work has been arranged in relation to the conditions in the neighborhood; these modify the needs of the particular children who are the pupils." This was how all the work in the schools he admired was arranged. The ease with which he invoked the bromide as explanation of the specific shape that the Indianapolis school's program was taking demonstrated how well-accepted the idea was becoming as a general working principle among educators. What Dewey made sound obvious and above question had been, in fact, the heart of the most hotly argued issue among educators just a few years before.

To Dewey, significant social dividends would accrue if his approach were adopted. "The success of the experiment," he wrote, "would mean a real step forward in solving the 'race question' and peculiar problems of any immigrant district as well" (pp. 151-152). School would mirror community in ideal Deweyan correspondence. Starting with an acceptance of squalid local conditions, the school would set the curriculum accordingly. Children of blacks or of immigrants would be taught the practical skills valuable not in transcending the community or transforming it but in adapting to it. Doing so would make them "happy, healthy, and competent," and, by, presumably, giving them a trade, solve the race (or ethnic) question as well. Dewey seemed to assume that the expectations of black children were so low that providing them with cooking or shoemaking skills would elicit gratitude and satisfaction; animus reflecting an earlier denial of opportunity would dissolve. While "the more remote end of teaching the child processes which will be useful to him later is not lost sight of," Dewey remarked, "material is always used which has some immediate value to the child or to the school" (p. 154). The photographs in the book, reinforced this message. With no trace of irony, white suburban children were pictured performing Greek tragedy in flowing robes early in the book (p. 96), while black slum children were pictured in cooks' hats and aprons, and "mending their own shoes, to learn cobbling" later on (p. 159).

This orientation gave new meaning to the kind of equality of opportunity the schools fostered. No longer did equality of opportunity consist in offering the same training to all students regardless of background. Now it meant an equal chance in the competition in which one had already been pre-assigned to run, according to the local circumstances that seemed to exert a compelling hold on whomever came within their sphere. When Dewey, speaking of the child of a recent immigrant to Gary from rural Europe, noted that he had "as much chance to prepare for a vocation, that is really to learn his own capabilities for the environment in which he finds himself, as the child of the educated American" (pp. 185-186), he was registering this change.[38] For Dewey, it was clear that the immigrant child and the "educated American" had an equal chance to prepare for a vocation only if one assumed that each was headed for a very different place in the social hierarchy. In understanding that this point needed no further elaboration or defense, Dewey was again marking how far he had moved from schoolmen of an earlier generation. His attention was fixed on the social problem that the immigrant child's presence created, and simply continued his lesson in realistic adjustment, his lesson in making the immigrant "see things as they are, and in teaching him how to do things." This kind of practicality did not mean that students should be discouraged from following an academic track; it only meant that in the nature of things it was doubtful if they would. Family needs and restricted personal aspirations would most likely keep them close to home, both literally and figuratively. The schools had to be ready by "linking their curriculum more closely to the lives of their pupils."[39]

This perspective must be kept in mind when considering Dewey's statement that, for instance, to achieve the linkage above required "furnishing the children with the general training and outlook on life which will fit them for their place in the world as adults" (p. 193). The examples

---

[38] In 1908 the Boston School Committee had defined educational democracy the same way. Until very recently, it said, the schools "have offered equal opportunity for all to receive one kind of education. But," it continued, "what will make them democratic is to provide opportunity for all to receive such education as will fit them equally well for their particular life work." (Quoted in Marvin Lazerson and David Cohen, "Education and the Corporate Order," *Socialist Revolution* [March-April, 1972]: 69.)

[39] *Schools of Tomorrow*, p. 122.

of vocational educational developments in Chicago and Gary that immediately followed provided the clarifying amplification. Courses in metalwork, woodwork, printing for boys, and sewing, cooking, laundry and general homemaking for girls were growing in importance, differing from school to school only "to meet the needs of the neighborhood or because of the resources of the [school] building" (p. 195). Generally, all pupils in a school, he went on, did the same work, and on graduation (from the eighth grade) had a good beginner's knowledge of "the principles and processes underlying two or three trades." The purpose of the training, for which specialization often began quite early, was "to enable the child to pick up the thread of life in his own community." The appended disclaimer, "it is not to confine him to the industries of his neighborhood by teaching him some one skilled trade," could only be taken, given the context, to anticipate and deflect the force of objections he knew would be forthcoming.

Dewey took conflicting positions on this issue—the heart of his argument—on other occasions as well. One extended passage, in a chapter-end summing up, is particularly revealing. Here, an effort to explain the meaning of the "educational readjustment" at the core of his philosophy became so filled with qualifying phrases that it had the effect of drawing attention to what he was trying to play down. Instead of confusing his meaning, the consistency and regularity of the disclaimers had the paradoxical effect of clarifying it. By the end of the passage, one becomes convinced that Dewey was almost consciously trying to blunt the force of a conclusion that had a growing inexorability about it. Try as he would to avoid it, the unpalatable conclusion kept presenting itself to him.

Dewey was talking about the teaching of mathematics in "a way that each step which the [student] takes in advance of his knowledge of number shall be connected with some situation of human need and activity, so that he shall see the bearing and application of what is learned." In particular, he had in mind the time when the student will join "the mass of workers" in industry who would otherwise become "blind cogs and pinions in the apparatus they employ" (p. 178). To clarify the connection between the student's instruction in arithmetic and his understanding of the industrial and social activities he would likely be engaged in, he continued:

> The industrial phase of the situation comes in, of course, in the fact that these social experiences have their industrial aspect. This does not mean that his number work shall be crassly utilitarian, or that all the problems shall be in terms of money and pecuniary gain or loss. On the contrary, it means that the pecuniary side shall be relegated to its proportionate place, and emphasis put upon the place occupied by knowledge of weight, form, size, measure, numerical quantity, as well as money, in the carrying on of the activities of life. The purpose of the readjustment of education to existing social conditions is not to substitute the acquiring of money or of bread and butter for the acquiring of

information as an educational aim. It is to supply men and women who as they go forth from school shall be intelligent in the pursuit of the activities in which they engage. That a part of that intelligence will, however, have to do with the place which bread and butter actually occupy in the lives of people today, is a necessity. Those who fail to recognize this fact are still imbued, consciously or unconsciously, with the intellectual prejudices of an aristocratic state. But the primary and fundamental problem is not to prepare individuals to work at particular callings, but to be vitally and sincerely interested in the calling upon which they must enter if they are not to be social parasites, and to be informed as to the social and scientific bearings of that calling. The aim is not to prepare breadwinners. But since men and women are normally engaged in bread-winning vocations, they need to be intelligent in the conduct of households, the care of children, the management of farms and shops, and in the political conduct of a democracy where industry is the prime factor. (pp. 179-180)

Here, compressed into one paragraph, was the outpouring of qualification that Dewey was led to when he tried to abstract a single message from the wealth of examples provided in the book. The thrust of the examples strongly pushed him in a practical direction. Yet any "crassly utilitarian" orientation could not be reconciled with the democratic, equality of opportunity posture that he wished to project. Rhetorically at least, Dewey was not yet willing to admit how far he had strayed from an earlier meaning of these terms. It was on an optimistic note about equal opportunity that he planned to end the book,[40] yet he knew that any such note, tarnished by references to "readjustment" to one's work, warding off "social parasitism," and "breadwinning vocations" might fail in its intended effect. At the end of the passage quoted above he therefore settled on a compromise formulation. He called for training that would "steer between the extremes of an inherited bookish education and a narrow, so-called practical education" (p. 180). Even then, in a sentence ending the chapter (to be followed by another on the vocational programs in midwestern cities), he wrote, "But since the real question is one of reorganization of all education to meet the changed conditions of life—scientific, social, political—accompanying the revolution in industry, the experiments which have been made with this wider end in view [meaning those of vocationalism that were to follow] are especially deserving of sympathetic recognition and intelligent examination" (p. 180).

It was through this kind of recognition and examination that Dewey hoped the danger of fixed classes might be avoided. Differences of wealth, the existence of large masses of unskilled workers, the contempt for hand work, and the inability to secure the training that offered mobility were not impossible to overcome. "Equality of opportunity" could be secured as well. Both the avoidance of fixed classes and equality of opportunity were

---

[40] See *Schools of Tomorrow*, p. 226.

essential to the survival of democracy. In this work, Dewey placed his faith in the public school; for him it was "the only fundamental agency for good." Among a heterogeneous population, he hoped the schools could foster unity, brotherhood, and a sense of common interest. They would thereby eliminate the divisions and neutralize the complexities of modern life that made "the task of democracy constantly more difficult" (pp. 225-226).

Unfortunately, the book he wrote provided little encouragement that the goals he sought could be reached. The examples and endorsements that abounded in it enforced, rather than undercut, the idea that what Dewey saw as fatal to democracy was inevitable. Indeed, in the pages immediately preceding his final exhortation for social peace and equal opportunity, he admitted again to the apparently fixed existence of "the great majority whose interests are not abstract, and who have had to pass their lives in some practical occupation, usually in actually working with their hands." Adding, as he did in the next sentence, that in a democracy "everyone, regardless of the class to which he happens to belong, has the right to demand an education which shall meet his own needs," only had the effect of intensifying this impression. Since by this point, most readers would have been conditioned to associate an appeal to "needs" with the limited opportunities available in crowded immigrant neighborhoods, or with the locally determined interests of a child only minimally directed by the promptings of a teacher[41] or the vision of his importance to the whole society, little else could be expected. Supplying the definition of meeting one's needs by focusing on areas where the majority, having no time for "abstract" interests, labored "with their hands" had in effect been the subject of the entire book. The cumulative impact of the examples that Dewey offered was that the gulf between rich and poor and the "complexities" that this caused were more permanent than he generally wanted to admit. Despite its expressions of hope, the book left the reader with the feeling that the nation's political system, or the philosophy that Dewey offered as the system's proper method, might not be strong enough to bear up under the increasing strains it was being forced to undergo.

V

That this might be the case was brought home to a number of former disciples of Dewey by the American entry into the First World War. Randolph Bourne was one of the leaders of this group, and had been as closely identified with Dewey's ideas as anyone. But when Dewey endorsed America's decision to fight, Bourne broke with his former teacher and

---

[41] See ibid., pp. 104, 113, 126.

wrote an indictment that with minor alterations could have been applied to educational, as well as to foreign, policy. Bourne criticized Dewey's use of the term "democracy" because it was "an unanalyzed term, useful as a call to battle, but not an intellectual tool, turning up fresh sod for the changing future."[42] He said that "the emphasis [by liberal supporters of the war] was on technical organization, rather than organization of ideas," and that the liberals burrowed "into war-technique" to hide "the void where a democratic philosophy should be." He castigated defenders of the war effort who said their support was due "to the fact that the war is not only saving the cause of democracy, but is immensely accelerating its progress."

Bourne had war making policy in mind in saying what he did, but he could just as easily have been talking of curriculum making policy. His attack on Dewey's followers who had gone into war management was equally applicable to his followers who had gone into school management:

> His disciples [Bourne wrote] have learned all too literally the instrumental attitude toward life, and being immensely intelligent and energetic, they are making themselves efficient instruments of the war technique, accepting with little question the ends as announced from above. That those ends are largely negative does not concern them, because they have never learned not to subordinate idea to technique. Their education has not given them a coherent system of large ideas, or a feeling for democratic goals. They have, in short, no clear philosophy of life, except that of intelligent service, the admirable adaptation of means to ends. They are vague as to what kind of society America needs, but are equipped with all the administrative attitudes and talents necessary to attain it. (p. 60)

The substitution of "educational reform" and "educational technique" for "war" and "war-technique" in the passage quoted above would provide the kind of trenchant criticism that might have helped redirect the practices of professional educators in the decades following the war.

Unfortunately, it seemed to be easier for Bourne to analyze the thinking of the supporters and managers of the war machine than to analyze the thinking of the supporters and managers of the educational machine. It was not just that the men who would man the machinery of war were the same as those who, as efficiency-minded government bureau heads, would also man the machinery of education. More significant for understanding the reform efforts of the twentieth century was the fact that the critics, "the malcontents," as Bourne called them, who remained aloof from the mechanics of government and policy implementation, who so vigorously challenged the morality of American war-making put forward by the liberals, had nothing to say about the morality of American school-making when it was put forward by the same people. They denounced the premises of a

---

[42] Randolph Bourne, "Twilight of Idols" (originally published in *The Seven Arts*, October, 1917), in *War and the Intellectuals*, p. 57.

philosophy that so easily led to active participation in war, yet could see nothing wrong with them during peacetime.

For all the invective he loosed against Dewey's support for the war, Bourne continued to defend the appropriateness of Dewey's philosophical outlook to education. Dewey's philosophy, said Bourne in the same essay attacking its use by pro-war liberals, was "inspiring enough for a society at peace, prosperous and with a fund of progressive good will." "Where institutions are at all malleable"—and, he pointed out, it was the school, where Dewey's philosophy was first applied, that was the most malleable of our institutions—"it is the only clue for improvement" (pp. 55-55). For Bourne, "it was education, and almost education alone, that seemed susceptible to the steady pressure of an 'instrumental' philosophy....For both our revolutionary conceptions of what education means, and for the intellectual strategy of its approach, this country is immeasurably indebted to the influence of Professor Dewey's philosophy" (p. 56). It was not just that Bourne was interested in war philosophy but not in educational philosophy. The point is that he specifically exempted education, near the start of the essay, from an analysis that would otherwise have been taken to apply to it. He was not just uninterested in applying this analysis; he did not want the analysis to be applied.

Bourne criticized the technocrats for their reliance on Dewey's philosophy in justifying their participation in the war effort, but he had little objection to their application of the same doctrines to education. He argued that a philosophy that relied on "'adaptation' or 'adjustment,' even when it means adjustment to changing, living experience," was defective. It made "no provision for thought or experience getting beyond itself" (p. 61), and therefore could not possibly provide guidance about the war. But why could it provide any more guidance about education? If Bourne could characterize Dewey's philosophy as one motivated by the ideal of "adjustment to one's situation, in radiant cooperation with reality," one where "success is likely to be that and no more" (p. 61), what made it any more applicable to education than it was to war?

Bourne gave the answer but it has been ignored by many historians and critics of our educational plight. Including himself among those who had been attracted to Dewey, he wrote of the dangers of the pragmatic point of view:

> To those who have taken Dewey's philosophy almost as our American religion, it never occurred that values could be subordinated to technique. We were instrumentalists, but we had our private utopias so clearly before our minds that the means always fell into its place as contributory. And Dewey, of course, always meant his philosophy, when taken as a philosophy of life, to start with values. But there was always an unhappy ambiguity in his doctrine as to just how values were created, and it became easier to assume that just any

growth was justified and almost any activity valuable as long as it achieved ends. The American, in living out this philosophy, has habitually confused results with product and has been content with getting somewhere without asking too closely whether it was the desirable place to get. (p. 61)

But what kind of "private utopia" motivated Bourne and gave *him* a conception of "the desirable place to get"? Bourne saw himself as part of a band of "malcontents," a "tribe of talent," that would become the nucleus of critical reaction to traditional American values in the post-war period. It was a group that would, said Bourne, be contemptuous and irreverent and "take institutions very lightly" (p. 63). In place of these empty forms, the "malcontents" would establish the claims of "the happiness of the individual, the vivifying of the personality, the comprehension of social forces, the flair of art,—in other words, the quality of life" (p.63).

In this account, the only one we get from him, Bourne's utopia, seemed like nothing so much as a paradise for graduates of sensitivity training and self-awareness, a retreat for advocates of communal living and personal expression. He sounded, in other words, much as Dewey did when he gave expression to his own utopia, or the way current advocates of school dismantling sound when they talk of institutionalized school systems as agencies that repress, coerce, and restrain children's instincts and feelings. The "utopian" views of Dewey and Bourne translated easily into a design for schooling very different from schooling that repressed, coerced, and restrained. Bourne accepted the outlines of this design no less than Dewey did. At bottom, he too had deep reservations about the capacity of America to generate the forms of opportunity and mobility that had once sustained the nation-building process. These goals may no longer have been attainable through the schools but a new kind of "personal" freedom and "private" release was.

To disaffected malcontents with no place to go—they were, said Bourne, "too much entangled emotionally in the possibilities of American life to leave it, and they have no desire whatever to starve" (p. 64)— Dewey's philosophy, in the hands of educators, meant liberation from teacher tyranny and bureaucratic regimentation; in the hands of the managers of a society at war, it meant being bound by fetters from which they sought deliverance. Neil Coughlan is right to notice that there were two kinds of students in Dewey's classrooms—the cultural radicals (like Bourne) and future public servants[43] (like the park and road builder Robert Moses). It is important to note only that each type, under a different banner, could be mobilized to march in the same parade. Bourne and his friends might seem to occupy no common ground with the managers he accused of

---

[43] Neil Coughlan, *Young John Dewey: An Essay in American Intellectual History* (Chicago, 1975), p. 161.

submitting so quickly to the imperatives of war. But in the area of education, where calls for efficiency and economy were complemented by calls for individual freedom and spontaneity, they could wage separate but mutually reinforcing attacks on the schools, and justify them both by an appeal to the man at whose feet the two groups had studied.

Bourne's radicalism had always made a virtue of the values of self-expression that Dewey in many ways first voiced. But those values took life as it existed and did not raise questions about how best to ensure its further development. The values were rooted in the here and now, in the adjustments that had to be made so that the individual whose place in the larger society had been disturbed could continue to go about his business with as little trauma as possible. Applied to education, this view led to a confidence in the easy manipulation of the child's immediate interests and needs; applied to international politics, it led to a similar confidence in manipulation, just on a wider scale.[44] Bourne, like Dewey, looked to the child to show adult society how a true community of cooperating individuals might be built. To explain, he adopted Dewey's instrumentalism without pausing to worry about its broader political implications. Nothing he saw in prewar society gave him any cause to worry that it might not be adequate. (Pre-war America, he had said, was "a society at peace, prosperous, and with a fund of progressive good-will.") But even when, in confronting the war issue in 1917, he did begin worrying about the political implications of Dewey's philosophy, he still made no move to apply his insights to the educational reforms in which so much of his own hopes for cultural change and his own focus of radical energy had been invested.[45]

Bourne wrote that Dewey's philosophy, "this experimental working out of control over brute forces and dead matter in the interests of communal

---

[44] To see how easily he extrapolated to the international arena thinking that had evolved from addressing problems of urban areas, see Dewey's war essays in *The New Republic*. A good example is in "What America Will Fight For," (August 18, 1917), where he spoke of the need to appeal to "the American desire for stable peace and an established amity of peoples through comity of democratic nations. A task has to be accomplished to abate an international nuisance, but in the accomplishing there is the prospect of a world organization and the beginnings of a public control which crosses nationalistic boundaries and interests." With a few substitutions, the passage could as easily be about the neighborhoods to which he brought his educational reforms as about the nations he hoped to influence through participation in the war.

[45] Along with another self-proclaimed Dewey disciple, Alice Barrows, Bourne had been one of the main publicists for the Gary Plan. Bourne himself, in language very similar to his teacher's, wrote that the school using Gary methods "carries out a belief in educating the whole child, physically, artistically, manually, scientifically, as well as intellectually. Mr. Wirt [the plan's originator] believes that by putting in the child's way all the opportunities for varied development, the child will be able to select those activities for which he is best suited." As mentioned above (note 22), the plan often received the attentions of public officials for very different reasons. See Bourne's *The Gary Schools* (Boston, 1916), an expansion of articles he originally wrote for *The New Republic* in 1915. The quotation from Bourne is in Ravitch, p. 199.

life, depends on a store of rationality."[46] That rationality, while disappearing from discussions of war policy, still characterized educational discourse because what was considered rational in educational discourse, by Bourne's time, no longer included the sense that the advancement of intellectual ability and its application to social and economic development was primary to education. So well had Dewey done his work that the tradition preceding him had been almost irrecoverably lost to his successors.

---

[46] "Twilight of Idols," p. 55.

BIBLIOGRAPHY

Primary Sources

Adams, Brooks. "Abuse of Taxation." *Atlantic Monthly* 42 (October, 1878).
_____. "The New Departure in the Public Schools." *Atlantic Monthly* 45 (March, 1880).
Adams, Charles Francis, Jr. *An Autobiography, 1835-1915.* Boston, 1916.
_____. "The Development of the Superintendency." National Education Association. *Proceedings* (1880).
_____. *The New Departure in the Common Schools of Quincy.* Boston, 1879.
_____. "Protection of the Ballot in National Elections." *Journal of Social Science* I (June, 1869).
Addams, Jane. *The Spirit of Youth and the City Streets.* Urbana, Ill., 1972; orig. 1909.
_____. *Twenty Years at Hull-House.* New York 1910.
Adler, Felix. "Address of May 15, 1876." *Ethical Addresses*, Series III, no. 5.
_____. "The Aims of the Ethical Society." *The Ethical Record* (October, 1889).
_____. "The Distinctive Aims of the Ethical Culture Schools: Four Addresses Delivered Before the Teachers of the Schools." New York, 1902. New York Society for Ethical Culture Archives.
_____. *An Ethical Philosophy of Life: Presented in its Main Outlines.* New York, 1918.
_____. "Ethical Problems: Inaugural Discourse." New York, 1876. New York Society for Ethical Culture Archives.
_____. "The Ethics of Neighborhood." University Settlement Society Papers. Manuscript Division, State Historical Society of Wisconsin, Madison, Wis.
_____. "The Ethics of the Political Situation." New York, 1884. New York Society for Ethical Culture Archives.
_____. "The Ethics of the Social Question" (1878). In *The Radical Pulpit.* By O. B. Frothingham and Felix Adler. New York, 1878.
_____. "Great Accumulations: The Present and Future Relations of Labor and Capital." Unidentified newspaper clipping dated January 3, 1881. New York Society for Ethical Culture Archives.
_____. "The Influence of Manual Training on Character" (1888). In *The Moral Instruction of Children.* New York, 1895.
_____. "Is There Danger of Conflict Between Classes?" Clipping from *The New York Times*, November 1, 1887. New York Society for Ethical Culture Archives.
_____. "The Just Measures of Social Reform." Felix Adler Papers. Manuscript Division, Columbia University, New York.
_____. "The Need of a New Moral Movement in Religion." *North American Review* 134 (February 11, 1883).
_____. "The Redemption of New York." *The Ethical Record* (December, 1900).

_____. "When Are We Justified in Leaving Our Religious Fellowship?" New York, 1886. New York Society for Ethical Culture Archives.

_____. "The Workingman's School, A Discourse Delivered Before the Society for Ethical Culture....October 24, 1880."

Baldwin, Joseph. "The Culture Most Valuable for Educating Law-Abiding and Law Respecting Citizens." National Education Association. *Proceedings* (1888).

Barnard, F. A. P. [Letter to the Editor.] *The Critic*, May 29, 1886.

Bjork, Robert M. and Fraser, Stewart E. "Alternatives to Growth: Education for a Stable Society." Phi Delta Kappa Educational Foundation "Fastback" Series. Bloomington, Indiana, 1976.

Blair, Henry W. *Address Delivered at the American Federation of Labor Convention at Philadelphia, Pa., 1892.* New York, 1892.

_____. "The Common School Bill." American Institute of Instruction. *Lectures, Discussions, and Proceedings* (1889).

_____. "Conditions and Prospects of Temporary National Aid to Common Schools." In *Christian Educators in Council. Sixty Addresses by American Educators with Historical Notes Upon the National Education Assembly...1883.* Edited by J. C. Hartzell. New York, 1884.

_____. [Speeches on the Blair Bill, 1884.] *Congressional Record.* 48 Cong., 1 sess., pp. 1999-2030, 2063-2070, 2100, 2147.

_____. [Speeches on the Blair Bill, 1886.] *Congressional Record.* 49 Cong., 1 sess., pp. 1482, 1725-1726, 2104.

Bonner, Mary G. "School Riots and the Gary System: A Pitiful Incident of the New York Mayoral Contest." *The Outlook* 117 (October 31, 1917).

Bourne, Randolph. *The Gary Schools.* Boston, 1916.

_____. "Twilight of Idols" (1917). In *War and the Intellectuals: Collected Essays, 1915-1919.* Edited by Carl Resek. New York, 1964.

Bowles, Samuel and Gintis, Herbert. *Democracy and Capitalism: Property, Community, and the Contradictions of Modern Social Thought.* New York, 1987.

_____. *Schooling in Capitalist America.* New York, 1976.

Brown, Duncan. "The Discipline Most Valuable to the End." National Education Association. *Proceedings* (1888).

Butler, Nicholas Murray. Address to National Society for the Promotion of Industrial Education. *Bulletin Number 1,* 1907.

_____. "The Industrial Education Association." *Science* IX (June 10, 1887).

_____. [Letters to the Editor.] *Science* VII (February 5, 12; March 5, 1886).

_____. *The Meaning of Education and Other Essays and Addresses.* New York, 1898.

_____. "The Real Labor Problem." In *Is America Worth Saving?* New York, 1920.

_____. Review of *The Labor Movement in America,* by Richard T. Ely. *Science* VII (October 15, 1886).

_____. "The Scientific Treatment of Education." *New Princeton Review* II (September, 1886).

_____. "Settlement of Labor Differences." *Science* VII (April 16, 1886).

_____. "The Training of the Teacher." *The Century* 16 (October, 1889).

_____. "Vocational Education: An Address." Chicago, 1913.

Carnegie, Andrew. "The Gospel of Wealth." In *Words that Made American History.* 3rd ed. Vol. 2. Edited by Richard N. Current; John A. Garraty; and Julius Weinberg. Boston, 1978.

Chubb, John E. and Moe, Terry M. *Politics, Markets, and America's Schools.*
Washington, D. C., 1990.

[Clark, E.P.] *A Bill to Promote Mendicancy: Facts and Figures Showing that the
South Does Not Need Federal Aid for Her Schools.* New York, 1888.

Conant, Charles A. "Can New Openings Be Found for Capital?" *Atlantic Monthly*
LXXXIV (November, 1899).

Cook, John W. "The Schools Fail to Teach Morality or to Cultivate the Religious
Sentiment." National Education Association. *Proceedings* (1888).

Cooley, Edwin G. "Professor Dewey's Criticism of the Chicago Commercial Club
and its Vocational Education Bill." *Vocational Education* 3 (September,
1913).

Current, Richard, ed. *The Political Thought of Abraham Lincoln.* Indianapolis, Ind.,
1967.

Davis, Rebecca Harding. "The Curse in Education." *North American Review* 168
(May, 1899).

Dewey, John and Evelyn. *Schools of Tomorrow.* New York, 1915.

Dewey, John. "Academic Freedom." *Educational Review* 13 (1902).

_____. *The Child and the Curriculum and The School and Society.* Chicago,
paperback ed., 1956; orig. 1902 and 1899, respectively.

_____. *Democracy and Education: An Introduction to the Philosophy of Education.*
New York, 1966; orig. 1916.

_____. "Ethical Principles Underlying Education." *Third Yearbook of the National
Herbart Society.* Chicago, 1897.

_____. "Interest in Relation to Training of the Will" (1896). In *John Dewey: The
Early Works, Volume 5, 895-1898.* Carbondale, Ill., 1972.

_____. "Learning to Earn: The Place of Vocational Education in a Comprehensive
Scheme of Public Education." *School and Society* 5 (March 24, 1917).

_____. "The Need of an Industrial Education in an Industrial Democracy." *Manual
Training and Vocational Education* XVII (February, 1916).

_____. "Pedagogy as a University Discipline" (1896). In *ohn Dewey: The Early
Works, Volume 5, 1895-1898.* Carbondale, Ill., 1972.

_____. "The Place of Manual Training in the Elementary Course of Study" (1901).
In *John Dewey: The Middle orks, Volume 1, 1899-1901.* Carbondale, Ill.,
1976.

_____. "The Psychological Aspects of the School Curriculum" (1897). In *John
Dewey: The Early Works, olume 5, 1895-1898.* Carbondale, Ill., 1972.

_____. "Psychology and Social Practice" (1899). In *John ewey: The Middle Works,
Volume 1, 1899-1901.* Carbondale, Ill., 1976.

_____. "The Psychology of Effort" (1897). In *John ewey: The Early Works,
Volume 5, 1895-1898.* Carbondale, Ill., 1972.

_____. *The Quest for Certainty: A Study of the Relation of Knowledge and Action.*
New York, 1960; orig. 1929.

_____. Review of William T. Harris, *Psychologic Foundations of Education*
(1898). In *John Dewey: The arly Works, Volume 5, 1895-1898.* Carbondale,
Ill., 1972.

_____. "Splitting Up the School System." *The New Republic*, April 17, 1915.

_____. "What America Will Fight For." *The New Republic*, (August 18, 1917).

Dix, Morgan. Columbia College Commencement, 1888 Baccalaureate Sermon.
Columbiana Collection, Low Library, Columbia University, New York.

_____. "The Relation of Dr. Morgan Dix to Columbia University: Data taken from the Diary of Dr. Dix, 1878-1907." Columbiana Collection, Low Library, Columbia University, New York.

Dodge, Grace. Notebooks. Teachers College Archives, Columbia University, New York.

Dutton, Samuel T. "Education as a Preventive and Cure for Crime." American Institute of Instruction. *Lectures, Discussions, Proceedings* (1886).

_____. *Social Phases of Education in the School and the Home.* New York, 1903; orig. 1899.

"The Duty of the Hour." *New England Journal of Education* XI (February 26, 1880).

Eliot, Charles W. "Industrial Education as an Essential Factor in Our National Prosperity." National Society for the Promotion of Industrial Education. *Bulletin Number 5* (1908).

Ethical Culture School. *General Outline of Course of Study, 1904.* New York Society for Ethical Culture Archives.

Everett, Edward. *Importance of Practical Education and Useful Knowledge: Being a Selection from his Orations and Other Discourses.* New York, 1854.

Ferguson, Marilyn. *The Aquarian Conspiracy: Personal and Social Transformation in the 1980s.* Los Angeles, 1980.

Fish, Frederick. Address to the National Society for the Promotion of Industrial Education. *Bulletin Number 5* (1908).

Godkin, E. L. *Problems of Modern Democracy: Political and Economic Essays.* Edited by Morton Keller. Cambridge, Mass., 1966; orig. 1896.

_____. *Reflections and Comments, 1865-1895.* New York, 1895.

_____. *The Triumph of Reform: A History of the Great Political Revolution, November 6, 1894.* New York, 1895.

_____. *Unforeseen Tendencies of Democracy.* Boston, 1898.

"The Gospel According to Gail." *New England Journal of Education* XI (March 4, 1880).

Grady, Henry W. "The New South. In *The New South and Other Addresses.* New York, 1969; orig. 1904.

Hall, G. Stanley. *Adolescence: Its Psychology and Its Relations to Physiology, Anthropology, Sociology, Sex, Crime, Religion and Education.* 2 vols. New York, 1904.

_____. *Aspects of German Culture.* Boston, 1881.

_____. *Educational Problems.* 2 vols. New York, 1911.

_____. "The High School as the People's College" (1902). In *Health, Growth and Heredity: G. Stanley Hall on Natural Education.* Edited by Charles E. Strickland and Charles Burgess. New York, 1965.

_____. *Life and Confessions of a Psychologist.* New York, 1923.

_____. "New Departures in Education." *North American Review* CXL (February, 1885).

_____. *Recreations of a Psychologist.* New York, 1920.

Harris, William T. *Annual Reports to St. Louis Board of Education.* St. Louis, 1868-1875.

_____. "Does the Common School Educate Children Above the Station They are Expected to Occupy in Life?" *Education III* (May, 1883).

_____. "Educational Needs of Urban Civilization." *Education V* (May, 1885).

_____. "Excessive Helps in Education." *Education IX* (December, 1888).

_____. "Industrial Education in the Common Schools," *Education VI* (June, 1886).

_____. "The Intellectual Value of Tool Work." National Education Association. *Proceedings* (1889).

_____. "Is There Work Enough for All?" *Forum* XXV (April, 1898).

_____. "The Mutual Relation of Property and Education." *New England Journal of Education* XI (February 5, 1880).

_____. "Professor John Dewey's Doctrine of Interest as Related to Will." *Educational Review XI* (May, 1896).

_____. *Psychologic Foundations of Education.* New York, 1912; orig. 1898.

_____. "The Psychology of Manual Training," *Education* IX (May, 1889).

_____. "The Study of Arrested Development in Children as Produced by Injudicious School Methods." *Education* XX (April, 1900).

_____. "Vocation Versus Culture; Or the Two Aspects of Education." *Education* XII (December, 1891).

_____. "What Shall the Public Schools Teach?" *Forum* IV (February, 1888).

Howe, Frederic C. *The Confessions of a Reformer.* New York, 1925.

Howerth, I. W. "The Social Aim in Education." *Fifth Yearbook of the National Herbart Society.* Chicago, 1899.

Huntington, Emily. *The Kitchen Garden; Or Object Lessons in Household Work.* New York, 1884; orig. 1878.

Illich, Ivan. *Deschooling Society.* New York, paperback ed., 1970.

Industrial Education Association. *Annual Reports.* New York, 1885-1888.

Ivins, William. "Municipal Finance." *Harper's* 69 (1884).

Jackson, Andrew. "Bank Veto Message." In *Great Issues in American History.* Vol. 1. Edited by Richard Hofstadter. New York, 1958.

James, William. *Talks to Teachers on Psychology and to Students on Some of Life's Ideals.* New York, paperback ed., 1958; orig. 1899.

Katz, Michael, ed. *School Reform: Past and Present.* Boston, 1971.

Kitchen Garden Association. *First Annual Report.* New York, 1880.

_____. *Lessons and Songs.* New York, 1880.

Langerfeld, E. [Letters to the Editor.] *Science* VII (February 5, 12, 19, 1886).

Lannie, Vincent P., ed., *Henry Barnard: American Educator.* New York, 1974.

Lazerson, Marvin and Grubb, W. Norton, eds., *American Education and Vocationalism: A Documentary History, 1870-1970.* New York, 1974.

Lippmann, Walter. *Drift and Mastery.* Englewood Cliffs, N. J., 1961; orig. 1914.

Littlefield, George A. "Chief Needs of the Schools." American Institute of Instruction. *Lectures, Discussions, Proceedings* (1886).

Loria, Achille. *The Economic Foundations of Society.* London, 1902.

Mann, Horace. "Argument for a Western Rail Road." Horace Mann Papers. Massachusetts Historical Society, Boston, Mass.

_____. "A Few Thoughts for a Young Man." Boston, 1850.

_____. *Lectures on Education.* Boston, 1855.

Mann, Mary P. *Life and Works of Horace Mann.* 5 vols. Boston, 1891.

Mayo, A. D. "The Assault on the Normal Schools." American Institute of Instruction. *Lectures* (1877).

_____. "Demands of the Coming Century on the American Common School." National Education Association. *Proceedings* (1876).

_____. "The South at School." American Institute of Instruction. *Lectures and Journal of Proceedings* (1882).

McMurry, Charles A. *Course of Study in the Eight Grades.* New York, 1906.

Miller, Mrs. Harriet Mann. "Little Housemaids." *St. Nicholas: Scribner's Illustrated Magazine for Boys and Girls* (April, 1879).

National Commission on Excellence in Education. *A Nation at Risk: The Imperative for Educational Reform.* Washington, D. C., 1983.

Nevins, Allan, ed. *The Diary of Philip Hone, 1828-1851.* New York, 1936.

New York Evening Post. 1884-1888.

Paddock, Sarah Sands. "Industrial and Technological Training." National Conference of Charities and Correction. *Proceedings* (1884).

"The People and the Schools." *New England Journal of Education* XI (February 19, 1880).

Perry, Arthur Latham. *Elements of Political Economy.* New York, 1872.

Phelps, W. F. "Inaugural Address." National Education Association. *Proceedings* (1876).

Philbrick, John D. "Course of Study for Grammar Schools; Special Report to the Committee on Textbooks by the Superintendent of Public Schools...." Boston, 1868.

_____. "The New Departure." *New England Journal of Education* V (January, 1877).

_____. "The New Departure in Boston: The Annual Report of the School Board, 1879." *New England Journal of Education* XI (February 12, 1880).

_____. "The New Departure in Boston: The Annual Report of the School Board, 1879." *New England Journal of Education* XI (February 19, 1880).

_____. "Organize the Machine." *New England Journal of Education* XI (January 29, 1880).

_____. "Second Semi-Annual Report of the Superintendent of Public Schools, for the Year 1861." *Annual Report of the School Committee of the City of Boston, 1861.* Boston, 1861.

_____. "The Situation." *New England Journal of Education* XI (January 22, 1880).

_____. "The Success of the Free-School System." *North American Review* 132 (March, 1881).

_____. *Thirtieth Semi-Annual Report of the Superintendent of the Public Schools.* Boston, 1876.

_____. "Which is the True Ideal of the Public School?" *Education* I (January, 1881).

Plaut, W. Gunther. *The Growth of Reform Judaism: American and European Sources Until 1948.* New York, 1965.

Plumb, Preston. [Speech on the Blair Bill, 1886.] *Congressional Record.* 49 Cong., 1 sess., pp. 1699, 2104.

Podhoretz, Norman. *Making It.* New York, 1967.

Rabbeno, Ugo. "Loria's Landed System." *Political Science Quarterly* 7 (June, 1892).

Reynolds, James B. Letters to A.L. Kalman (October 23, 1895) and Adolph M. Radin (September 14, 1895). University Settlement Society Papers. Manuscript Division, State Historical Society of Wisconsin, Madison, Wis.

Rice, Joseph M. *The Public School System of the United States.* New York, 1893.

Rossington, W. H. [Welcome to Topeka.] National Education Association. *Proceedings* (1886).

Royce, Josiah. "Is There a Science of Education?" *Educational Review* 1 (January and February, 1891).

_____. "Mental Defect and Disorder from the Teacher's Point of View." *Educational Review* 6 (1893).

Russell, James E. "The School and Industrial Life." *Educational Review 38* (December, 1909).

Sears, Barnas. "Fifty Years of Educational Progress." American Institute of
    Instruction. *Lectures* (1880).
Simonson, George M. "An Experimental Course in Philanthropy." *Leslie's Weekly*,
    October 24, 1895.
Smalley, Eugene V. "What are Normal Times?" *Forum* 23 (March, 1897).
Smith, Wilson, ed. *Theories of Education in Early America, 1655-1819*.
    Indianapolis, Ind., 1973.
Stone, A. P. "The Educational Outlook, and its Lessons." American Institute of
    Instruction. *Lectures* (1877).
Trask, Spencer. "The Growth of Teachers College." *Teachers College Bulletin*
    (January, 1895).
Turner, Frederick Jackson. "Pioneer Ideals and the State University." In *The
    Frontier in American History*. New York, 1920.
_____. "The West and American Ideals." In *Frontier and Section: Selected Essays
    of Frederick Jackson Turner*. Edited by Ray A. Billington. Englewood Cliffs,
    N. J., 1961.
[U. S. Bureau of Education.] *Report of the Commissioner of Education, for the Year
    1897-98*. Volume 1. Washington, D. C., 1899.
[U. S. Bureau of Labor.] *Second Annual Report of the Commissioner of Labor,
    1886. Convict Labor*. Washington, D. C., 1887.
Van Rensselaer, Mrs. Schuyler. "Our Public Schools: A Reply." *North American
    Review* 169 (July, 1899).
Vorhees, Daniel W. [Speech on the Blair Bill, 1884.] *Congressional Record*. 48
    Cong., 1 sess., p. 2688.
Warren, H. P. "The Spiritual Side of the High School Question." American Institute
    of Instruction. *Lectures* (1877).
Webster, Daniel. [Speech to the Society for the Diffusion of Useful Knowledge,
    Boston, 1836.] In *Ideology and Power in the Age of Jackson*. Edited by Edwin
    C. Rozwenc. Garden City, N. Y., 1964.
Welter, Rush, ed. *American Writings on Popular Education: The Nineteenth
    Century*. Indianapolis, Ind., 1971.
White, E. E. "The Relation of Education to Industry and Technical Training in
    American Schools." *Circulars of Information, No. 2*. U.S. Bureau of
    Education. Washington, D.C., 1881.
White, Richard Grant. "The Public-School Failure." *North American Review* 131
    (December, 1880).
Woodward, Calvin. "The Function of the American Manual Training School."
    Education III (May, 1883).
_____. "Manual Training." National Education Association. *Proceedings* (1889).
Workingman's School. *Catalogue*. New York, 1895. New York Society for
    Ethical Culture Archives.

Secondary Sources

Ahlstrom, Sidney E. *A Religious History of the American People*. New Haven,
    1972.
Apple, R. W. "What Correspondence Theories of the Hidden Curriculum Miss."
    The Review of Education 5 (Spring, 1979).
Armstrong, William M. *E. L. Godkin: A Biography*. Albany, N. Y., 1978.
_____. *E. L. Godkin and American Foreign Policy*. New York, 1957.

_____. *The Gilded Age Letters of E. L. Godkin.* Albany, N. Y., 1974.

Arnstein, Walter L. "The Survival of the Victorian Aristocracy." In *The Rich, the Wellborn, and the Powerful: Elites and Upper Classes in History.* Edited by Frederic Cople Jaher. Champaign, Ill., 1973.

Bailyn, Bernard. *Education in the Forming of American Society: Needs and Opportunities for Study.* Chapel Hill, N.C., 1960.

Baritz, Loren. *Servants of Power: A History of the Use of Social Science in American Industry.* Middletown, Conn., 1960.

Beisner, Robert L. *Twelve Against Empire: The Anti-Imperialists, 1898-1900.* New York, 1968.

Benson, Lee. *Turner and Beard: American Historical Writing Reconsidered.* Glencoe, Ill., 1960.

Best, Geoffrey. *Mid-Victorian Britain, 1851-1875.* New York, 1972.

Birmingham, Stephen. *Our Crowd: The Great Jewish Families of New York.* New York, paperback ed., 1968.

Bledstein, Burton J. *The Culture of Professionalism: The Middle Class and the Development of Higher Education in America.* New York, 1976.

Blodgett, Geoffrey. *The Gentle Reformers: Massachusetts Democrats in the Cleveland Era.* Cambridge, Mass., 1966.

_____. "Reform Thought and the Genteel Tradition." In *The Gilded Age: Revised and Enlarged Edition.* Edited by H. Wayne Morgan. Syracuse, N. Y., 1970.

Brecher, Jeremy. *Strike!* New York, 1972.

Bremner, Robert. *American Philanthropy.* Chicago, 1960.

Brock, William R. *An American Crisis: Congress and Reconstruction, 1865-1867.* New York, 1963.

_____. *Conflict and Transformation: The United States, 1844-1877.* Baltimore, 1973.

Calhoun, Daniel. *The Intelligence of a People.* Princeton University Press, 1973.

Callahan, Raymond E. *Education and the Cult of Efficiency.* Chicago, 1962.

Church, Robert and Sedlak, Michael W. *Education in the United States: An Interpretive History.* New York, 1976.

Cochran, Thomas C. and Miller, William. *The Age of Enterprise: A Social History of Industrial America.* Revised edition, New York, 1961.

Cohen, Ronald D. and Mohl, Raymond A. *The Paradox of Progressive Education: The Gary Plan and Urban Schooling.* Port Washington, N. Y., 1979.

Cohen, Sol. *Progressives and Urban School Reform.* New York, 1964.

Cohen, Stephen S. and Zysman, John. *Manufacturing Matters: The Myth of the Post-Industrial Economy.* New York, 1987.

Collins, Randall. *The Credential Society: An Historical Sociology of Education and Stratification.* New York, 1979.

Commager, Henry Steele. *The American Mind: An Interpretation of American Thought and Character Since the 1880s.* New Haven, 1950.

Conway, Jill. "Jane Addams: An American Heroine." *Daedalus* 93 (1964).

Coughlan, Neil. *Young John Dewey.* Chicago, 1975.

Cremin, Lawrence A.; Shannon, David A.; and Townsend, Mary E. *A History of Teachers College, Columbia University.* New York, 1954.

Cremin, Lawrence. *The Transformation of the School: Progressivism in American Education, 1876-1957.* New York, 1961.

Crick, Bernard. *The American Science of Politics: Its Origins and Conditions.* Berkeley, Cal., 1959.

Crofts, Daniel W. "The Black Response to the Blair Education Bill." *Journal of Southern History* 37 (February, 1971).

Curti, Merle and Carstensen, Vernon. *The University of Wisconsin: A History, 1848-1925.* 2 vols. Madison, Wis., 1949.

Curti, Merle. *Social Ideas of American Educators.* New York, 1935.

Cyert, Richard M. and Mowery, David C. "Technology, Employment, and U. S. Competitiveness." *Scientific American* 260, number 5 (May, 1989).

Dalzell, Robert F., Jr. *Enterprising Elite: The Boston Associates and the World They Made.* Cambridge, Mass., 1987.

Davis, Allen. *American Heroine: The Life and Legend of Jane Addams.* New York, 1973.

_____. *Spearheads for Reform: The Social Settlements and the Progressive Movement, 1890-1914.* New York, 1967.

Dawley, Alan. *Class and Community: The Industrial Revolution in Lynn.* Cambridge, Mass., 1976.

Diner, Stephen J. *Chicago and Its Universities: Public Policy in Chicago, 1892-1919.* Chapel Hill, N. C., 1980.

Dorfman, Joseph. *The Economic Mind in American Civilization, 1606-1933.* 5 vols. New York, 1946-1959.

Dunkel, Harold B. *Herbart and Education.* New York, 1969.

_____. *Herbart and Herbartianism.* Chicago, 1970.

Dye, Charles M. *Calvin Milton Woodward and American Urban Education.* Ann Arbor, Mich., 1976.

Dykhuizen, George. "John Dewey at Johns Hopkins (1882-1884)." *Journal of the History of Ideas* 22 (1961).

_____. *The Life and Mind of John Dewey.* Carbondale, Ill., 1973.

Eddy, Edward D., Jr., *Colleges for Our Land and Time: The Land-Grant Idea in American Education.* New York, 1957.

Edwards, Richard. *Contested Terrain: The Transformation of the Workplace in the Twentieth Century.* New York, 1979.

Evans, John Whitney. "Catholics and the Blair Educational Bill." *Catholic Historical Review* 46 (October, 1960).

Faulkner, Harold U. *Politics, Reform and Expansion.* New York, 1959.

Feuer, Lewis. "John Dewey and the Back to the People Movement." *Journal of the History of Ideas* 20 (1959).

Fine, Sidney. *Laissez Faire and the General Welfare State: A Study of Conflict in American Thought, 1865-1901.* Ann Arbor, Mich., 1956.

Fink, Leon. "The New Labor History and the Powers of Historical Pessimism: Consensus, Hegemony, and the Case of the Knights of Labor." *Journal of American History* 75, no. 1 (June, 1988).

Fishlow, Albert. "The American Common School Revival: Fact or Fancy?" In *Industrialization in Two Systems.* Edited by Henry Rosovsky. New York, 1966.

Foner, Eric. *Free Soil, Free Labor, Free Men: The Ideology of the Republican Party before the Civil War.* New York, 1970.

_____. *Nothing But Freedom: Emancipation and its Legacy.* Baton Rouge, La., 1983.

_____. *Reconstruction: America's Unfinished Revolution, 1863-1877.* New York, 1988.

Foner, Philip S. *History of the Labor Movement in the United States, Volume II: From the Founding of the American Federation of Labor to the Emergence of American Imperialism.* New York, 1955.

Ford, Worthington Chauncey. "Adams, Charles Francis [Jr.]." *Dictionary of American Biography.* Vol. 1. Edited by Allen Johnson. New York, 1928.

Forgie, George B. *Patricide in the House Divided: A Psychological Interpretation of Lincoln and His Age.* New York, 1979.

Furner, Mary O. *Advocacy and Objectivity: A Crisis in the Professionalization of American Social Science, 1865-1905.* Lexington, Ky., 1975.

Genovese, Eugene. *The Political Economy of Slavery: Studies in the Economy and Society of the Slave South.* New York, 1965.

George, Peter. *The Emergence of Industrial America: Strategic Factors in American Economic Growth Since 1870.* Albany, N. Y., 1982.

Gilbert, James B. *Work Without Salvation: America's Intellectuals and Industrial Alienation, 1880-1910.* Baltimore, Md., 1977.

Gillette, William. *Retreat from Reconstruction, 1869-1879.* Baton Rouge, La., 1979.

Glazer, Nathan. *American Judaism.* Chicago, 1972.

Going, Allen J. "The South and the Blair Educational Bill." *Mississippi Valley Historical Review* 44 (September, 1957).

Goodwyn, Lawrence. *The Populist Moment: A Short History of the Agrarian Revolt in America.* New York, 1978.

Gottheil, Richard. *The Life of Gustav Gottheil.* Williamsport, Pa., 1936.

Grant, H. Roger. *Self-Help in the 1890s Depression.* Ames, Iowa, 1983.

Greer, Colin. *The Great School Legend: A Revisionist Interpretation of American Public Education.* New York, 1972.

Grimsted, David. "Rioting in its Jacksonian Setting." *American Historical Review* 77 (April, 1972).

Hacker, Andrew. "The Schools Flunk Out." *New York Review of Books* , April 12, 1984.

Hall, Peter Dobkin. *The Organization of American Culture, 1700-1900: Private Institutions, Elites, and the Origins of American Nationality.* New York, 1982.

Hammack, David C. *Power and Society: Greater New York at the Turn of the Century.* New York, 1982.

Haskell, Thomas L. *The Emergence of American Social Science: The American Social Science Association and the Nineteenth Century Crisis of Authority.* Urbana, Ill., 1977.

_____. Review of *The Culture of Professionalism*, by Burton Bledstein. *New York Review of Books*, October 13, 1977.

Hawkins, Hugh. *Pioneer: A History of the Johns Hopkins University, 1874-1889.* Ithaca, 1960.

Hays, Samuel P. "The Politics of Reform in Municipal Government in the Progressive Era." *Pacific Northwest Quarterly* LV (October, 1964).

Henderson, Thomas M. *Tammany Hall and the New Immigrants: The Progressive Years.* New York, 1976.

Herrick, Mary J. *The Chicago Schools: A Social and Political History.* Beverly Hills, Cal., 1971.

Hershkowitz, Leo. *Tweed's New York: Another Look.* Garden City, N. Y., 1977.

Higham, John. *Strangers in the Land: Patterns of American Nativism, 1860-1925.* New Brunswick, N. J., 1955.

Hirshson, Stanley P. *Farewell to the Bloody Shirt: Northern Republicans and the Southern Negro, 1877-1893*. Bloomington, Ind., 1962.

Hofstadter, Richard. *The Age of Reform: From Bryan to F. D. R.* New York, paperback ed., 1955.

_____. *Anti-intellectualism in American Life*. New York, 1963.

Horlick, Allan S. "Comprehensiveness Versus Comprehension in American Educational History." *The Review of Education* 7 (Summer, 1981).

_____. *Country Boys and Merchant Princes: The Social Control of Young Men in New York*. Lewisburg, Pa., 1975.

_____. "Phrenology and the Social Education of Young Men." *History of Education Quarterly* XI (Spring, 1971).

_____. Review of *Schooling in Capitalist America*, by Samuel Bowles and Herbert Gintis. *The Review of Education* 3 (May-June, 1977).

_____. Review of *The Great School Legend*, by Colin Greer. *History of Education Quarterly* XIV (Summer, 1974).

Horowitz, Helen L. *Culture and the City: Cultural Philanthropy in Chicago from the 1880s to 1917*. Lexington, Ky., 1976.

Howe, Daniel Walker. *The Political Culture of the American Whigs*. Chicago, 1979.

Huse, Charles Phillips. *The Financial History of Boston, 1822-1909*. Cambridge, Mass., 1916.

Huston, James L. "A Political Response to Industrialism: The Republican Embrace of Protectionist Labor Doctrines." *Journal of American History* 70, no. 1 (June, 1983).

Kaestle, Carl F. and Vinovskis, Maris A. *Education and Social Change in Nineteenth Century Massachusetts*. New York, 1980.

Kaestle, Carl F. *Pillars of the Republic: Common Schools and American Society, 1780-1860*. New York, 1983.

Karier, Clarence J; Violas, Paul C; and Spring, Joel H. *Roots of Crisis: American Education in the Twentieth Century*. Chicago, 1973.

Katz, Michael B. *Class, Bureaucracy, and the Schools*. New York, 1971.

_____. "The Emergence of Bureaucracy in Urban ducation: The Boston Case, 1850-1884, Parts I and II." *History of Education Quarterly* 8 (Summer and Fall, 1968).

_____. *The Irony of Early School Reform: Educational Innovation in Mid-Nineteenth Century Massachusetts*. Cambridge, Mass., 1968.

_____. "The 'New Departure' in Quincy, 1873-1881: The Nature of Nineteenth Century Educational Reform." *New England Quarterly* 40 (1967).

Keller, Morton. *Affairs of State: Public Life in Late Nineteenth Century America*. Cambridge, Mass., 1977.

Kelley, Robert. *The Transatlantic Persuasion: The Liberal-Democratic Mind in the Age of Gladstone*. New York, 1969.

Kirkland, Edward Chase. *Charles Francis Adams, Jr., 835-1915: The Patrician at Bay*. Cambridge, Mass., 1965.

_____. *Dream and Thought in the Business Community, 860-1900*. Ithaca, N. Y., 1956.

_____. *Industry Comes of Age: Business, Labor and ublic Policy, 1860-1897*. New York, 1961.

Klebanow, Diana. "Edwin L. Godkin and the American City." Ph.D. dissertation, New York University, 1965.

Kliebard, Herbert M. *The Struggle for the American Curriculum, 1893-1958*. London, 1986.

Kohl, Lawrence. *The Politics of Individualism: Parties and the American Character in the Jacksonian Era.* New York, 1989.

Kolko, Gabriel. *The Triumph of Conservatism: A Reinterpretation of American History, 1900-1916.* Chicago, paperback ed., 1967.

Kraut, Benny. *From Reform Judaism to Ethical Culture: The Religious Evolution of Felix Adler.* Cincinnati, Ohio, 1979.

Kuttner, Robert. *The Economic Illusion: False Choices Between Prosperity and Social Justice.* Boston, 1984.

———. *The Life of the Party: Democratic Prospects in 1988 and Beyond.* New York, 1987.

Langworthy, Margaret Wyman. "Dodge, Mary Abigail." In *Notable American Women, 1607-1950: A Biographical Dictionary.* Vol. 1. Edited by E. T. James. Cambridge, Mass., 1971.

Lasch, Christopher. *The New Radicalism in America, 1889-1963: The Intellectual as Social Type.* New York, 1965.

Lazerson, Marvin. *Origins of the Urban School: Public Education in Massachusetts, 1870-1915.* Cambridge, Mass., 1971.

Leach, William. *True Love and Perfect Union: The Feminist Reform of Sex and Society.* New York, 1980.

Lears, T. J. Jackson. *No Place of Grace: Antimodernism and the Transformation of American Culture, 1880-1920.* New York, 1981.

Lebowitz, Michael A. "The Jacksonians: Paradox Lost?" In *Towards a New Past: Dissenting Essays in American History.* Edited by Barton J. Bernstein. New York, 1968.

Lee, Gordon C. *The Struggle for Federal Aid, First Phase: A History of the Attempts to Obtain Federal Aid for the Common Schools, 1870-1890.* New York, 1949.

Leidecker, Kurt. *Yankee Teacher: The Life of William Torrey Harris.* New York, 1946.

Lewinson, Edwin. *John Purroy Mitchel, The Boy Mayor of New York.* New York, 1976.

Livingston, James. "The Social Analysis of Economic History and Theory: Conjectures on Late Nineteenth-Century American Development." *American Historical Review* 92, no. 1 (February, 1987).

Lowry, H. Graham. "The Social Settlement and the Search for Community: The Neighborhood Guild in New York." M.A. thesis, University of Wisconsin, 1968.

Lustig, R. Jeffrey. *Corporate Liberalism: The Origins of Modern American Political Theory, 1890-1920.* Berkeley, Cal., 1982.

Lynd, Robert S. and Helen M. *Middletown: A Study in American Culture.* New York, 1929.

Madsen, David. *The National University: Enduring Dream of the USA.* Detroit, 1966.

Malin, James C. "Space and History: Reflections on the Closed-Space Doctrines of Turner and Mackinder." *Agricultural History* 18 (April, 1944).

Mann, Arthur. *Yankee Reformers in an Urban Age: Social Reform in Boston, 1880-1900.* Chicago, 1974; orig. 1954.

Marrin, Albert. *Nicholas Murray Butler.* Boston, 1976.

Martin, Albro. *Enterprise Denied: Origins of the Decline of American Railroads, 1897-1917.* New York, 1971.

Mattingly, Paul H. *The Classless Profession: American Schoolmen in the Nineteenth Century.* New York, 1975.

McLachlan, James. "American Colleges and the Transmission of Culture: The Case of the Mugwumps." In *The Hofstadter Aegis: A Memorial.* Edited by Stanley Elkins and Eric McKitrick. New York, 1974.

McMath, Robert C. *Populist Vanguard: A History of the Southern Farmers' Alliance.* New York, 1977.

Messerli, Jonathan. *Horace Mann: A Biography.* New York, 1972.

Mills, C. Wright. *Sociology and Pragmatism: The Higher Learning in America.* New York, 1964.

Montgomery, David. *Beyond Equality: Labor and the Radical Republicans, 1862-1872.* New York, 1967.

_____. *The Fall of the House of Labor: The Workplace, the State, and American Labor Activism, 1865-1925.* New York, 1987.

Morgan, H. Wayne. *From Hayes to McKinley: National Party Politics, 1877-1896.* Syracuse, N. Y. 1969.

Murray, James G. "Edwin Lawrence Godkin in the *Nation*: A Study in Political, Economic and Social Morality." Ph.D. dissertation, New York University, 1954.

Myers, Marvin. *The Jacksonian Persuasion: Politics and Belief.* Stanford, Cal., 1957.

Nasaw, David. *Schooled to Order: A Social History of Public Schooling in the United States.* New York, 1979.

Ogden, Rollo. "Godkin, Edwin Lawrence." In *Dictionary of American Biography.* Vol. 7. Edited by Allen Johnson and Dumas Malone. New York, 1931.

Painter, Nell Irvin. *Standing at Armageddon: The United States, 1877-1919.* New York, 1987.

Perry, Ralph Barton. *The Thought and Character of William James.* 2 vols. Boston, 1935.

Radest, Howard B. *Toward Common Ground: The Story of the Ethical Culture Societies in the United States.* New York, 1969.

Ravitch, Diane. *The Great School Wars: New York City, 1805-1973.* New York, 1974.

_____. *The Troubled Crusade: American Education, 1945-1980.* New York, 1983.

Reich, Robert. *The Next American Frontier.* New York, 1983.

Rezneck, Samuel. "Unemployment, Unrest, and Relief in the United States during the Depression of 1893-97." *Journal of Political Economy* LXI (August, 1953).

Ringenbach, Paul T. *Tramps and Reformers, 1873-1916: The Discovery of Unemployment in New York.* Westport, Ct., 1973.

Rodgers, Daniel T. "In Search of Progressivism." In *The Promise of American History: Progress and Prospects.* Edited by Stanley I. Kutler and Stanley N. Katz. Baltimore, Md., 1982.

_____. *The Work Ethic in Industrial America, 1850-1920.* Chicago, 1978.

Rogin, Michael Paul. *The Intellectuals and McCarthy: The Radical Specter.* Cambridge, Mass., 1967.

Ross, Dorothy G. *Stanley Hall: The Psychologist as Prophet.* Chicago, 1972.

_____. *The Origins of American Social Science.* Cambridge, Eng., 1991.

Ross, Earle D. *Democracy's College: The Land-Grant Movement in the Formative Stage.* Ames, Iowa, 1942.

Rothman, David J. *The Discovery of the Asylum: Social Order and Disorder in the New Republic.* Boston, 1971.

Rucker, Darnell. *The Chicago Pragmatists.* Minneapolis, 1969.

Rudolph, Frederick. *The American College and University: A History.* New York, 1962.

Salvatore, Nick. *Eugene V. Debs: Citizen and Socialist.* Urbana, Ill., 1982.

Schlesinger, Arthur M., Jr. *The Age of Jackson.* Boston, 1945.

Schultz, Stanley. *The Culture Factory: Boston Public Schools, 1789-1860.* New York, 1973.

Sennett, Richard. *Families Against the City: Middle Class Homes of Industrial Chicago, 1872-1890.* Cambridge, Mass., 1970.

Sklar, Martin J. *The Corporate Reconstruction of American Capitalism, 1890-1916: The Market, the Law, and Politics.* Cambridge, Eng., 1988.

Solomon, Barbara Miller. *Ancestors and Immigrants: A Changing New England Tradition.* Cambridge, Mass., 1956.

Spring, Joel H. *Education and the Rise of the Corporate State.* Boston, 1972.

_____. *The Sorting Machine: National Education Policy Since 1945.* New York, 1976.

Sproat, John G. *"The Best Men": Liberal Reformers in the Gilded Age.* New York, 1968.

Story, Ronald. *The Forging of an Aristocracy: Harvard and the Boston Upper Class, 1800-1870.* Middletown, Conn., 1980.

Swift, David W. *Ideology and Change in the Public Schools: Latent Functions of Progressive Education.* Columbus, Ohio, 1971.

Taylor, William R. "Toward a Definition of Orthodoxy: The Patrician South and the Common Schools." *Harvard Educational Review* 36 (Fall, 1966).

Thelen, David P. "Social Tensions and the Origins of Progressivism." *Journal of American History* 56 (September, 1969).

Thurow, Lester. *The Zero-Sum Solution: Building a World-Class American Economy.* New York, 1985.

Tomsich, John. *A Genteel Endeavor: American Culture and Politics in the Gilded Age.* Stanford, Cal., 1971.

Trachtenberg, Alan. *The Incorporation of America: Culture and Society in the Gilded Age.* New York, 1982.

Troen, Selwyn. *The Public and the Schools: Shaping the St. Louis System, 1838-1920.* Columbia, Mo., 1975.

Tuchman, Barbara W. *The Proud Tower: A Portrait of the World Before the War, 1890-1914.* New York, 1966.

Tyack, David B. "Education and Social Unrest, 1873-1878." *Harvard Educational Review* 31 (1961).

_____. *The One Best System: A History of American Urban Education.* Cambridge, Mass., 1974.

Urban, H. Wayne. "Progressive Education in the Urban South: The Reform of the Atlanta Schools, 1914-1918." In *The Age of Urban Reform: New Perspectives on the Progressive Era.* Edited by Michael H. Ebner and Eugene M. Tobin. Port Washington, N. Y., 1977.

Veysey, Laurence R. *The Emergence of the American University.* Chicago, 1965.

Ward, John William. *Andrew Jackson: Symbol for an Age.* New York, 1955.

Wechsler, Harold S. *The Qualified Student: A History of Selective College Admission in America.* New York, 1977.

Welter, Rush. *The Mind of America, 1820-1860.* New York, 1975.

Westbrook, Robert B. *John Dewey and American Democracy*. Ithaca, N. Y., 1991.

White, G. Edward. *The Eastern Establishment and the Western Experience: The West of Frederic Remington, Theodore Roosevelt, and Owen Wister*. New Haven, Conn., 1968.

White, Gerald T. *The United States and the Problem of Recovery After 1893*. University, Ala., 1982.

Whittemore, Richard. *Nicholas Murray Butler and Public Education, 1862-1911*. New York, 1970.

Wiebe, Robert. *Businessmen and Reform: A Study of the Progressive Movement*. Cambridge, Mass., 1962.

_____. *The Search for Order, 1877-1920*. New York, 1967.

Wiener, Jonathan. *Social Origins of the New South: Alabama, 1860-1885*. Baton Rouge, La., 1978.

Wiener, Martin J. *English Culture and the Decline of the Industrial Spirit, 1850-1980*. Cambridge, Eng., 1981.

Wirth, Arthur G. *John Dewey as Educator: His Design for Work in Education*. New York, 1966.

Woodward, C. Vann. *Origins of the New South, 1877-1913*. Baton Rouge, La., 1951.

_____. *Reunion and Reaction*. Boston, 1951.

Wrigley, Julia. *Class Politics and Public Schools: Chicago, 1900-1950*. New Brunswick, N. J., 1982.

Yearley, C. K. *The Money Machines: The Breakdown and Reform of Governmental and Party Finance in the North, 1860-1920*. Albany, N. Y., 1970.

INDEX

academic profession, 11; basic assumptions of, 186-189; beginnings of, 175, 178n.13, 179-183; and educational reform, 12; research ideal of, 183-184; social behavior expected of, 183-186

Adams, Brooks, 79, 95n.41; as educational reformer, 86-87, 96-97, 95n.41; on tax reform, 80-81

Adams, Charles Francis, Jr., 5, 101, 141, 176; Anglo-Saxonism of, 77; on cost reduction, need for, 82, 83-84; and educational reform in Quincy, Mass., 76; on educational utility, 83; and immigration, 77-78; on Irish, 78; library reform, 80; limitations of normal schools, 84; questions "material progress," 77; as Mugwump, 75; pedagogical ideas of, 79, 85; on role of superintendent, 81-82, 84

Adams, H. C., 6n.17, 174

Adams, Henry: on national elite, value of, 76n.2

Adams, John Quincy, 27

Adams, John Quincy II, 78

Addams, Jane, 108, 126, 176

Adler, Felix, 5, 139, 183, 176; on character and curriculum, 108n.10; cultural relativism of, 123; on equality, 107; and Ethical Culture School, 128-129; ethical ideas of, 123-125; on "great monopolists," 119-120; on industrial education, 105n.5; on Judaism and reform, 104; on liberal education, 107-108; on manual training, 108n.10; on Pittsburgh riot, 105; political evolution of, 129; on Reform Judaism, 122n.33; religious ideas of, 121-123; on settlements, role of, 130-131; on social activism, 112-115, 118-121; on social crisis, 104-106, 106n.8, 110-111; on suburbs and urban reform, 130-131; on worker discontent, 103; and Workingman's School, 100-103, 109, 116-118, 128

Adolescence (Hall), 123n.34

Agnew, C. R., 161

Age of Reform, The (Hofstadter), 8n.24

"Agrarianism," 23

Atlanta Constitution, 156n.28

American Journal of Education, 142

American Commonwealth, The (Bryce), 55

American Federation of Labor, 49

American revolutionaries: attitude toward education, 18

American Social Science Association, 85, 85n.23, 184

Association of Working Girls' Societies, 158

Arthur, Timothy Shay, 67

Atkinson, Edward, 148

Atlantic Monthly, 81, 95

Bamberger, G. (Workingman's School), 109-110

Barnard, F. A. P., 139, 142

Barnard, Henry, 19, 142

Barnett, Rev. Samuel, 125

Barrows, Alice, 241n.45

Bemis, Edward, 6n.17, 177n.10

Bicknell, Thomas, 88, 166

Bill to Promote Mendicancy, A (Clark), 48, 50n.11

Blaine, James G., 52, 91, 91n.36; opposed by Mugwumps, 124

Blair bill, 29, 46; opposition to, 47n.6; 48n.8, 48-51; and Republican Party ideals, 46-48

Blair, Henry W., 46; on opposition to the Blair bill, 49; Republicanism of, 47

Board of Education (Mass.), 19, 21

BRILL'S STUDIES
IN
INTELLECTUAL HISTORY

28. BOUCHER, W.I. *Spinoza in English*. A Bibliography from the Seventeenth-Century to the Present. 1991. ISBN 90 04 09499 7
29. McINTOSH, C. *The Rose Cross and the Age of Reason*. Eighteenth-Century Rosicrucianism in Central Europe and its Relationship to the Enlightenment. 1992. ISBN 90 04 09502 0
30. CRAVEN, K. *Jonathan Swift and the Millennium of Madness*. The Information Age in Swift's *A Tale of a Tub*. 1992. ISBN 90 04 09524 1
31. BERKVENS-STEVELINCK, C., H. BOTS, P.G. HOFTIJZER & O.S. LANKHORST (eds.). *Le Magasin de l'Univers*. *The Dutch Republic as the Centre of the European Book Trade*. Papers Presented at the International Colloquium, held at Wassenaar, 5-7 July 1990. 1992. ISBN 90 04 09493 8
32. GRIFFIN, JR., M.I.J. *Latitudinarianism in the Seventeenth-Century Church of England*. Annoted by R.H. Popkin. Edited by L. Freedman. 1992. ISBN 90 04 09653 1
33. WES, M.A. *Classics in Russia 1700-1855*. Between two Bronze Horsemen. 1992. ISBN 90 04 09664 7
34. BULHOF, I.N. *The Language of Science*. A Study in the Relationship between Literature and Science in the Perspective of a Hermeneutical Ontology. With a Case Study in Darwin's *The Origin of Species*. 1992. ISBN 90 04 09644 2
35. LAURSEN, J.C. *The Politics of Skepticism in the Ancients, Montaigne, Hume and Kant*. 1992. ISBN 90 04 09459 8
36. COHEN, E. *The Crossroads of Justice*. Law and Culture in Late Medieval France. 1993. ISBN 90 04 09569 1
37. POPKIN, R.H. & A.J. VANDERJAGT (eds.). *Scepticism and Irreligion in the Seventeenth and Eighteenth Centuries*. 1993. ISBN 90 04 09596 9
38. MAZZOCCO, A. *Linguistic Theories in Dante and the Humanists*. Studies of Language and Intellectual History in Late Medieval and Early Renaissance Italy. 1993. ISBN 90 04 09702 3
39. KROOK, D. *John Sergeant and His Circle*. A Study of Three Seventeenth-Century English Aristotelians. Edited with an Introduction by B.C. Southgate. 1993. ISBN 90 04 09756 2
40. AKKERMAN, F., G.C. HUISMAN & A.J. VANDERJAGT (eds.). *Wessel Gansfort (1419-1489) and Northern Humanism*. 1993. ISBN 90 04 09857 7
41. COLISH, M.L. *Peter Lombard*. 2 volumes. 1994. ISBN 90 04 09859 3 (Vol. 1), ISBN 90 04 09860 7 (Vol. 2), ISBN 90 04 09861 5 (Set)
42. VAN STRIEN, C.D. *British Travellers in Holland During the Stuart Period*. Edward Browne and John Locke as Tourists in the United Provinces. 1993. ISBN 90 04 09482 2
43. MACK, P. *Renaissance Argument*. Valla and Agricola in the Traditions of Rhetoric and Dialectic. 1993. ISBN 90 04 09879 8
44. DA COSTA, U. *Examination of Pharisaic Traditions*. Supplemented by SEMUEL DA SILVA's *Treatise on the Immortality of the Soul*. Tratado da immortalidade da alma. Translation, Notes and Introduction by H.P. Salomon & I.S.D. Sassoon. 1993. ISBN 90 04 09923 9
45. MANNS, J.W. *Reid and His French Disciples*. Aesthetics and Metaphysics. 1994. ISBN 90 04 09942 5
46. SPRUNGER, K.L. *Trumpets from the Tower*. English Puritan Printing in the Netherlands, 1600-1640. 1994. ISBN 90 04 09935 2
47. RUSSELL, G.A. (ed.). *The 'Arabick' Interest of the Natural Philosophers in Seventeenth-Century England*. 1994. ISBN 90 04 09888 7
48. SPRUIT, L. Species intelligibilis: *From Perception to Knowledge*. Volume I: Classical Roots and Medieval Discussions. 1994. ISBN 90 04 09883 6
49. SPRUIT, L. Species intelligibilis: *From Perception to Knowledge*. Volume II. (in preparation)
50. HYATTE, R. *The Arts of Friendship*. The Literary Idealization of Friendship in Medieval and Early Renaissance Literature. 1994. ISBN 90 04 10018 0
51. CARRÉ, J. (ed.). *The Crisis of Courtesy*. Studies in the Conduct-Book in Britain, 1600-1900. 1994. ISBN 90 04 10005 9
52. BURMAN, T. *Spain's Arab-Christians and Islam, 1050-1200*. 1994. ISBN 90 04 09910 7
53. HORLICK, A.S. *Patricians, Professors, and Public Schools*. The Origins of Modern Educational Thought in America. 1994. ISBN 90 04 10054 7